The Epic of Humanity, Or, the Quest of the Ideal

Apologist

4

THE

EPIC OF HUMANITY

OR

THE QUEST OF THE IDEAL

EDITED BY

AN APOLOGIST

LONDON

KEGAN PAUL, TRENCH, TRÜBNER & CO., Ltᴅ

PATERNOSTER HOUSE, CHARING CROSS ROAD

1898

PREFACE.

———◆———

THE alternative title of this book might have
been "Law, Love, and Life," had not the Editor
reflected, that some might read no further than the
back, or title page, and humorsome say, "The
Epic of Humanity is a rhyme about the three Ls,"
which too they might purposely pronounce with
a flagrant aspirate; for, to the diseased apprehension of many, Law, Love, and Life are verily
Hells.

The evident object, however, of the poet has
been to show, that Law and Love, in their highest
and deepest sense, are unmixed good, and in every
sense tend to good; also that Life may be and is
worth living.

That the poet owes much to others, goes without saying; and he has occasionally named the
sources from which he has drawn, whether by
translation, or otherwise. But the Editor has
refrained from further indications, fearing to burden the book with manifold references,

a

Headed the roll of gods all drunk with love.
Neptune, Pan, Mercury, Mars beside himself,
Venus with Dian plained the bad boy-elf.
Archer Apollo found in herbs no cure
For love-sped arrows, than his own more sure,
Conquering the all-conqueror with so potent dart;
Laurel of Daphne soothed the grievous smart.
Bacchus, all gods abased to Cupid fell;
Some say they clipped his wings on earth to dwell.
Him, Dœmon Magnus, all resist in vain;
This god of gods is governor of men.
Achilles for Briséis shunned the spear,
And for Polyxena called Hector dear.
Samson to wife his riddle told, and strength
Gave to Delilah shears in locks of length.
Double was David, and his wise son daft.
To harlot Vivienne Merlin taught his craft,
And was himself walked round and lost that day;
And Faust for love had eke the devil to pay.
Thus love prevails; thus wisdom, force, all power
Divine and human, have their fated hour.
Tiger, bear, bull, each jealous of its kind,
Oft kill their fellows, him alone to find.
Ramping on lions, by their manes he hales,
The while they fawn upon him with their tails.
And him the nightingale, the Dolphin hymn,
Swimming or flying, everlasting him.
To him the very palms confess undone,
And breathe on all the winds their love to one.
Hard-hearted metals, rocks have soft desires;
The elements are fused in kindred fires.
He, rare contriver fond of seasons round,
Fire, air, earth, water hath together bound;
All nature to its glowing centre yearns;
In every atom love a friend discerns;
Then, as he lists to make thee, sane or sotte,
Sore, sick, or sound, for God's sake curse him not."

And with this imprecation full of fire,

Love vanished, with his dissipated choir,
Having some arrows dropped, while verses making.
I looked alive now, all his arrows breaking,
And from that Love had suffered ; but I knew
Another higher God, of love more true,
Who could that imp control and eke his bow,
And tip his arrow with a heavenly woe.
How this to right converts that other's wrong
Is the prime motive strain of Edward's song.

Spirit of Love, abroad as air
   Through space unutterable, longing
Thine infinite free grace to share
   With universes more still thronging
To melt in thee like burning sighs :
Lightnings of hate may thee surprise,
Blinding ; but, touched by thy despite,
They melt in rocket tears brief, bright,
Repentant, ravished like sunned dew
Into thy fervours ever new
Equally eager to caress
Whether a joy, or a distress.
Yet mortal seeking truest love,
Which found below is from above,
Beware of rhododendron flower
Of honey suck but rueful hour,
Or that you grow of hunger old,
Famished and poor 'mid dreams more bright than gold.
Ears wax and close like those of crew,
Which past concerting syrens flew ;
Eyes downcast with lids drooping veil—
Confucius so bade Nan Tsee hail ;
Still mind its fantasies will dress
In instant seeming steadfastness ;
Faith shipwrecked saving from despair,
Make land of water, form of air.
So Edward lone his spirit lent
Prompt to unconscious ravishment ;
Could Rishyasringa-anchorites,

Islands of hermitage delights,
Each lovely surface pleased believe,
Since God made nothing to deceive ;
Having no sister, took for good
Mary-Mother's whole sisterhood.

His soul with ardency of passion
  In sacrifice round woman flamed,
Until she in transfigured fashion
  Own pupil of Aurora shamed,
Like sacred bush, that brighter bloomed
In fires of glory unconsumed.
And by so shining loveliness
  Of vision, less or more than human,
He, mothlike dazed, not spiritless
  The while conceiving it still woman,
Dreaded to blow a kiss, which might
Too lusty on her cheek alight.
Seemed she an 'twere lone roe in dell,
That upon chanceful way befell,
Or loner disincorporate thing
To which even worship dared not sing ;
Stray spirit resting but to fly,
Which ardent song, or passion sigh,
On breath too wild, might sweep afar
To bosom of more distant star.

Not Petrarch glowed at Laura's name
With half so bright and pure a flame ;
Not Paradise with holier bliss,
When shone on Dante Beatrice.
Yet no Rousseau mere self-fermental,
Least when most seeming transcendental ;
No fair Narcissus imaged fine,
O'er self reflection pleased to pine,
He love of venture well might boast
  Of blood and being first emotion,
Both born and cradled on wild coast
  Nursed by and native unto ocean,

Child of bold sire, who could not sleep
Dreamless or calm save upon deep.

That sword, which, drawn, a Dyrnwyn flame
From handle unto point became,
And never could from foe retire,
   Though idling now on student wall,
England had given to his sire
   Wont gleesomely to answer call
Of battle, as when fearless sea,
   At shriek of winds and roar
Of thunders, which the lightnings free,
Leaps rising into jubilee,
While marshalled by the Furies Three,
Rank upon rank, its chevachie
   Bound, foaming on the shore.
Brave father, gallant and true blue,
Skilled to contend with and subdue
Of man and element commotion,
From fury of ensanguined ocean
Aloft when his bold spirit went,
'Twas on wide sails of smoke distent
By whirlwinds from huge cannon-lips,
   To their music roaring high,
Lit by grim holocaust of ships
   Flaming to upper sky :
Nor Drake nor Blake in battle died,
Although at sea each Britain's pride,
More favored he, and not inglorious,
Like Nelson fell in death victorious.

Of widowed mother now sole joy,
   The student on to rival fame
Such memories both chide and buoy,
   Law and its heights his choice and aim :
To Mansfields Murrays may attain,
And Hardwickes spring from Yorkes again.
Purposing high, with leaden freight
   Of added tomes most slow advancing,

On hillside steep of trackless fate
   Foot by foot, resolute, upward chancing ;
Horse spurring not 'gainst steep unkind,
Presumptuous with mounting mind ;
Nor as St. David trusting dim
While hill grew heaving under him—
For genius bold is nothing rash
As ignorant or insolent dash—
   He laboured more than other seven,
And liker to Chaldean host
With brick on brick, no moment lost,
   Exalting Babel into heaven.
Yet deemed he Drake's converted ship
   Bettered all other Oxford chairs,
And loved brave sport with manly slip
   Out of the leash of college cares ;
Nor run, nor leap, nor bat, nor ball,
Nor oar neglected, honouring all,
Though of few persons rather was
Than friend of every hour and cause.

Thus narrowing not to one refrain
The energetic play of brain,
This great wide world before him, few
   With energies unwrecked so wrought,
As he to know of useful, true,
   Good, beautiful, whate'er was taught—
Physical, mental, moral lore ;
Then, wont though legal to explore,
Were more Baconian ventures driven
To depths of earth, and heights of heaven,
'Less gentler Kirke White's simpler bliss
Prolonged recruiting energies.
For he could, taking lute as wand
   While round him danced each idle care,
Roam at a breath enchanted land,
   With flashing eyes and floating hair
Returning, not as one who grieves
O'er fancy's lovely make-believes,

But ardent more to entertain
And toil for mother earth again.
Preluding tragedy with jest,
Turning mad sport to serious quest,
Knowing of future, careful while
Preventing sigh with present smile,
His heart ne'er crimsoned Hebrus tide,
Yet lyre Pangoean strung and dyed.
Such was the man, whose love is told.
   This artist draws with justice blind,
Arranging from epistles old
   And records of another mind
Dim story of an honest heart,
Which bled, but from most generous smart ;
As balsam pierced and grape pressed bleed,
Crushed fragrant leaf, bruised milky reed,
By suffering taught each mood of pain
   And tenderness for woe and mirth ;
That riches are not always gain,
   And charity is heaven on earth ;
And wise as worthy, meek as can
True manhood show in gentleman,
Singing
First birdlike with mere tuneful rote,
Singing
At last with meaning in each note,

EDWARD'S SONG.

" Time is a bitter draught, unless
   Its sweetness love impart ;
Eternity will fail to bless
   The breast without a heart.
No other bliss hath earth below,
   Or paradise above
Save ever more of God to know :
   For God Himself is love."

Hushed he and absent, yet his lyre
In other hand may God inspire,

And the rhyme-clusters prove more vinous
In song of Edward, than of Scribble Linus,
No mere Arabian jingles, Kabel
Supplanting Cain to rhyme with Abel,
But royal grapes to all men's view
Sun-drinking, tempered by no dew,
Not livid in eternal shades
Oppressing Fronto colonnades.
For nods Jovine it courts, yet rates
Brains bulky less than shaggy pates,
And, reader, fain thy heart would win :
Open, and pass the stranger in.

One sought, engraving line by line,
Mary of Dresde in ink to shrine,
While Raphael's conception grand
Awed to suspense the daring hand.
Defeat still bold to dare, yet sad,
Then melancholy, after mad,
Inspired to finish it, he died:
But lives his labour glorified.
Not vain eight long-drawn years of sighs,
Which graved Our Lady for all eyes.
Trembling another looks to trace
Young heaven flushing earth's shamed face—
Love, supra-entity sublime,
Transfiguring last phase of time,
And even now in prospect grand
Dawning a higher law for every land.

No gilded masts and fifty oars
E'er wafted him to Attic shores ;
Anacreon has in him small part—
If some stage whispers for the heart,
Fool deem him not, or in such guise
Receive him as one folly-wise.
Whom meat inflames, conserves will cool ;
So after business loose the fool,
Canzo—sirventes—tenza—pastoreta—

Alba—serena—balada—poeta.
In lucid moments of most barely sane
Shine pearls of truth of an oracular strain ;
'Neath peasant cap lie counsels hard as quince,
Austere, but sugared, syrup for a prince.

If rhymes to you of sense seem bald,
   Meaning and measure oft to halt,
As said to Richelieu Gomhauld,
   He thinks that may not be his fault.
But since he seeks true love to praise,
Spirit of God, attune his lays ;
From modes of an immodest time,
From taint of earth and serpent slime,
Wash all his flowers in thine own dews,
Descend, and sanctify The Muse ;
Reproving share, and grace with oil,
And crown his consecrated toil
With golden truth pearl-gemmed and star
Frontal, by Magi known afar.

Stratonicus, to fame unknown though sage,
When asked how many sought his pupilage,
Having but two disciples and his lyre,
And on it graved the Muses Nine and Sire
Apollo 'mid them luting, wise replied,
" Twelve with the gods ; " and, not by God denied,
This artist would not with Apelles use
To answer critic cobbler, " Mend your shoes,"
But, thinking now to profit unto some,
Trust the large issues of the time to come.
Homer may celebrate Tiresias dead
As alone sage 'mid shadows round his shade ;
In library of Althorpe Wordsworth find,
Save his own poems, nothing to his mind ;
Sick Rogers have a Kemble sound his verse
Sole worthy—poets plumed show vain as scarce ;
Still when as Canterbury, Primate famed,
Bartholemew Priory to visit claimed,

Received with pomp processional, he thus—
" We visit you, ye do not honour us : "
So may some singer for earth's honour care
To dock its weeds, more than its laurels wear ;
Less to live wise than well, may fixedly aim
At virtuous nature, more than rival fame ;
Not of all England trumpet-major great,
May Minor Prophet be—no laureate.

BOOK I.

CANTO I.

HER cups for Gods bright Hebe can
Surcharge with overflow for man ;
Makes Love not only still a boy,
But source eterne and Spring of joy,
Cherishing May-flowers under snows,
For aged Jeans, and Johns, their Joes.
Friendship too, love with wisdom tooth,
Conserving an untainted youth,
Enchanteth often mutual hearts
To know not as a year departs,
Nor mark time's nether oval fill,
Each young unto the other still ;
Damon and Pythias the choice
Manlike to die dispute, like boys.
Friendship and love, through years prolonged,
Wrinkles forget ; forgive, when wronged ;
Brave draughts of subtle pleasaunce share,
Drink with the gods, and drown dull care.

Lucy a babe, a small boy I,
    She was from nursling hours my pet.
Fast friends ; too soon our fathers die,
    Our mothers barely visit ; but " Good-bye "
        I have not said to Lucy yet ;
    Once sung of her, now years ago,
    My first fond rhyme, she pleased me so.

EDWARD'S FIRST RHYME.

" Sure you look with countenance glad and bright
And a sparkle in eye, causing love at sight,
    Under raven tresses sheeny with light,
        Brave child, a bright little star.

For bright is its face, and, though afar,
Shines sometimes by day and often by night ;
And I've made up my mind, you nothing are
    But a bright little star.
How the stars all revel by night, ah me ;
How they sparkle in it, and dance with glee
Ever round and through it to lighten and see
    The darkness.   Bright little star,
Much warmer thy heart is.   Aglow they are
With nothing but light, thou with love for me ;
And love than light is warmer far,
    Mine own dear little star."

Though charming she, the flight of time
From me had borne her no more flighty rhyme.
From school, from college, oft returned,
Welcomed, though not when absent mourned,
As Sir Amys never sought for sign,
If Belisante for him might pine,
I surely looked not once to see,
If she had special eyes for me ;
But came to know a songful thing,
Honest though wild and fresh as spring,
Nought heeding, while defying not,
Misprizing word of envious thought ;
In every guileless ply of heart
Patent as clouds, which quick depart.

Like Angelo, modelling snow so svelt
In infant breath of Spring to melt,
Or Gibson, marble tinting true
Till Venus in it seems to woo,
Doubtless each skilful-handed year,
Sculptor and painter both, draws near
With wondering pleasure and address
To heighten virgin loveliness.
But silent with no beat of drum
Steal colours into peach and plum ;
Bud, too, which gentle nature blows

With promise of more florid rose,
Startles not by each lesser change
Than which less only would be strange.
And as the little insects skilled
Frail surface-seeking corals build
　To swell the reef, which still shall be,
Rising in ocean's broadening smile,
Ever an unapparent isle
　Until it breaks the startled sea;
So, growing in love's widening eyes,
Unconscious of a world's surprise,
Woman lies hidden in the child,
Till, as with coral reef new-isled,
Some agitating moment wild,
Sudden reveals her, fixed as fate,
Crowned Sovereign of Love's new-formed state.

Pursuit of knowledge year by year
Absorbing me, and growing dear,
As to Euphemion, whom his Sire
Thus sought to raise from low desire,
Surely so wrought, that other charms
Seemed foreign to my folded arms.
But lark unfledged with puffy breast
Stirs not more rousantly in nest
With hope to mount the Empyrean
And rival the paternal pæan,
Than callow youth is longing-ful
An apple with some eve to pull.
In silent anguish of unquiet,
He chews a too ambrosial diet—
Ideal manna from above,
The code, not yet the cud of love,
His soul, the while of want aware,
Has flashes, but no steady glare,
Inklings, that are mere darklings, given
With prospect of a vacant heaven,
Where surely shall arise a sun
To be his all adorable one.

Not yet a chanticleer to crow,
The bantling tries, and utters woe.
Yet has he memory of dreams,
  Faint twitterings under hanging eaves,
Memnonic stones in gurgling streams,
  Prelusive airs in rustling leaves,
Floating to him all whispers tender
Of morning coming fresh with splendour ;
Nor ever ocean humbler fell,
When first rose Luna its pride to quell,
Than he shall kneel, when love shall sunlike rise,
Fulfil his dreams, though it should blind his eyes.

Thus, as when Wycherley, plain-dealing, spells
Duchess of Drogheda at Tunbridge Wells ;
Prompt as electric sparks unfold
In dross of mines still latent gold ;
Like Jesu flashing on the two,
Who loved him so before they knew ;
On me this very day there shone
Swift revelation, come, not gone,
The present sudden firing, bright
Informing all the past with light.
So various the ways of love,
  Each beautiful when chaste,
Now wooful circling like a dove,
  Now hot with eagle haste.
For now, a barrister without a brief
I came to everlasting grief :
Invited by some chance unkind,
Her garden-party joined to find,
Though lost as when Odysseus strayed
Ææan, or Ogygian shade,
Rapture with pain, and hope with fear,
Myself lost, found my Lucy here.

A modest mansion, quaint and old,
Gabled and chimneyed, manifold
Faces towards far-glancing sea

A vined and jasmined Arcadie,
   Whence steps drop every way
To many fair terraces lovingly nursed,
Oh, surely by an Eve uncursed.
    There pranksome, diverse, play
Cool fountains wastefully, and please
Choice flowering shrubs attracting humming bees.
Blackbird sings, linnet chants, or thrush,
Or bullfinch. All again is hush ;
Only the water leaps, falls, flows ;
The bees are busy in repose ;
The frolic zephyr no more blows,
But hovers as with sails unbent
Yet oversteeped in syrupped scent
By variegated parterres lent,
While scattered statues, curious vases,
Stay wanderer who idling passes
From one to other terrace on,
Until he gains pied slope of lawn,
Which, bare but for some sweet-toothed sheep
   And shady, stray, occasional tree,
Runs down to topple on quick deep,
   Or gather pebbles by beached sea,
Whose barks admiring breathless sit,
   Or drift this silver strand too near ;
Perhaps they know my bliss in it,
   Or fancy, Avalon is here.

It surely is, at least to me,
Here, or wherever she may be.
Praxidicé her robe combined
Of tissue, Dyseris designed ;
And the curious may detect
Order in the fine neglect
Of folds and falls, whose chaste array
Unwantonly a form display
Taught by Urania to glide
In elegance of blameless pride ;
While, true delight of eye and heart,

C

She, over and above all art,
Would be unequalled fair, though less
Illustrious for loveliness.
For beautiful and not afraid,
Beautified more by decorous shade
Of woman's finest armoury,
The haviour of true modesty—
Itself an artless simple trust
Beyond the venomed canker of lust—
Like sunshine she, dispelling fear,
And free as light, is pure as clear ;
Not like black desert well-pit deep
Where lurking dragon dreads to sleep,
But as Wakulla spring so pure,
A hundred feet down coins allure,
Or as lagoon round South-Sea Isle,
   Where finny schools gay-coloured play,
Like bright thoughts in her bosom, while
   No clouds obscure the live-long day.

Poppœa, washed in asses' milk,
Looked never of such lily ilk ;
Though prickly stem a rose may wear,
Yet not Sir Lambewell's wondrous Fair
Had worthy been her train to bear.
Oh ! curves and tints were ne'er before
   So sinlessly related :
Can she have missed some blessed shore
Her demiurge had meant her for,
   Adorable created?
More glowing bright than Iris even,
Or loves of angels by Moore all shriven,
No Undine she, nor stray of heaven,
But, destined for earth-humble duty,
I swear upon the soul of beauty,
Yea, by herself—the very best
Of all conjurements, not unblest—
'Twas in most transcendental mood,
   And finest of fine weather,

Moved by exuberance of good,
Nature put her sweet flesh and blood
  In eucrasy together,
And made her so exceeding fair,
That passing angels may in air
Spell-bound, with pinions furled near,
  And mingled thoughts bewildering,
Gaze, yet not wonder that a sphere,
Which bore our Lord—to it so dear—
  Should mother beauteous children.

Sources of light and glow, her eyes
  Dissolved me with a modest glance :
And beauties, which I canonize,
  Her graceful movements more enhance,
Each added grace all making me
Quiver like noon on shimmering sea.
I, vanquished, but in happy way
  A subject, seemed to be desired ;
And, unconfused, due homage pay
  With hope of conquering her inspired.
I thrill with sense of growing might,
To see the bliss of young love light
Her face suffuse with warmer glow
Than fronts of Gods to nectar owe.
Not light yet of her eyes indeed,
Dust rather neath her feet at need
Attending to sustain her pride,
I, not by it to be denied,
Am hers, but so to make her mine,
And our futurity divine.
I sing, and though she is my song,
Her notes of being run along :
Wild harp she, I Hermesian breeze
  Drawing her passionate being forth.
Oh, give me just such maid to please ;
  All other maids are minor worth.

Morgana Ogier loving bound,

When him with gold she proudly crowned,
Youth fadeless gave, but glory took ;
All memory his soul forsook
Of Denmark, England, Acre won,
Jerusalem, and Babylon,
France too, and greater Charlemain :
But my young love of higher strain,
With longing infinite to please,
Fond as was clerkly Degore's,
Would glory conquer, and not ease.
To me from solitary bliss,
Of books and bookish honours, this,
As summer unto late Spring ice,
Seemed noontide high in Paradise.
Though captive only of to-day,
All felt so natural, her sway,
As Blanchefleur's to Florice endeared,
Born to old sovereignty appeared.
My past remembered only showed,
With love for her I always glowed.

And now, by rivals circled, I,
Prepared to combat, not to fly,
No feeling have, nor thought of terror,
More than in heaven saints have of error :
Insurgent love, attaining power,
Has cast fear out of all the hour,
Hearing no envious voice of hell
Mockingly chant " Le Chaitivel,"
While echo makes both heaven and earth
Companions of our guileless mirth ;
And in a transcendental way
Thus round the theme of love we play

EDWARD.

" Courteous and kind with neither halting foot,
Nor mincing step, nor a restrained salute,
Love lives in a perpetual jubilee,
Or quiet heaven of excellent majesty.

Nightingale tongues, not peacock brains are cates
Of which love, festive, never satiates."

LUCY.

" Unnatural natural, and less than brother,
More fool is he, who gecks and jibes another."

EDWARD.

" Not like a ball which dances on a jet,
And with the spray of many tears is wet,
Rising and falling with remittent force,
But circling round one sun love holds its course,
A star in orbit fixed, decay the while
Having no finger powerful to exile
From night its blessedness, from day its smile."

LUCY.

" Thou would'st thy feminine Teutonic Sun
Should, warm to thee, be fair to every one ;
Earliest and latest ardours special sped
Over inferior heights to crown thy head,
From Nabathœan realms her first of rays,
Her last from where her steeds unharnessed graze."

EDWARD.

" I would all gentle virtues should unite
In her containing soul, and love excite
Into a constant fervour of desire,
Emboldened by my love's impetuous fire,
To form her destiny, allied with fates
Not as presiding geniuses, but mates.
I wish her to be noble, therefore free,
No mere blind worshipper of even me ; "

LUCY.

" But, not forgetting mortal virtue halts,
To see our kindred in our very faults ;
And, ever sunning to relent
The winter of all discontent,

Through spring's brave carnival of flowers
Revel to bloom of summer hours.
This you desire?"

EDWARD.

"Yes."

LUCY.

"To be true

You promise?"

EDWARD.

"Faithfully I do."

She laughed.   Her laugh had bliss in it,
A throb of heart, a sense of grit.
I also laughed ; for she was gay.
I can be serious some other day.
And now her parting breath and tendered hand,
Soft sweet as only love has at command,
With gentle stress and dear "Good-bye,"
Consummated my destiny.
We part.   Once more I am abroad
On lonely stretch of leafy road.
Ah, God, we take no thought of time
   Till past beyond recall, and then
Soon to have sped it seems a crime.
   I think to live it o'er again
In draughts of memory sweetly spiced,
Not watered, only lively iced—
Tempered like that pure Thespian Spring,
Of which swans drink before they sing
Tumbling the dungeon of despair
Upon the future of all care.
I laugh low in my heart, the while
I see in allegoric style
On weanling lamb love mounted come
With happy hours attendant, drum,
Cymbal, and lute, and pipe, and dance ;

And hell upon him look askance,
But quiver fly of ambushed dart,
Which soon had quenched the hateful heart ;
And heaven accompanies with song,
As love in triumph moves along.

HEAVEN'S ACCOMPANIMENT.

" From triumph unto triumph, lo,
All heaven accompanies thee; go,
Triumph over every foe."

Off turning then into the wood, I found
That I was wandering enchanted ground ;
And after graving " Lucy " on a tree,
Each cut held a remembered joy for me,
Each letter there was continent of thought ;
Whether the spirit of that tree so wrought,
Or other common unto all the wood,
I only knew it was a spirit good,
Not hurt, nor angry, that I graved the name,
But pleased to hold it up to lasting fame.
Desire appeared, a fresh young form of fire,
In starry stole and alb ; and with a lyre,
Harping before the potent name it saw,
Counselled of love as sacred full of awe.

DESIRE.

" Thy love, pure woman,
    I hold to be much higher prize
Than Mahomet's seventh heaven, though human
    With more than Eves of Paradise,
    And starry with bright houris' eyes.
Thine eyes are open doors of heaven ;
    Thyself art more.   For one embrace
The wisdom of The Sages Seven
I'd give away, and be forgiven,
    To feel and see love's rapture in thy face."

CANTO II.

TRAVELLING the sacred grove anew
My wood-engraving to review,
And visit Lucy, whose dear name
The woods through me uphold to fame,
I deemed the future, due to bless,
Waiting on tip-toe my caress,
But found the hours untimely born
To purse its lips at me in scorn.
No more it roseate appears :
One breezy whirl of rushing spheres
Has shed the roses on the winds.
Like lion-roar dispersing hinds,
She speaks, and hope in instant gloom
With torch extinct seeks desert doom.

LUCY.

" Charmed thus so soon to see you : books,
    I fancied, would detain their lover.'
And having said she coldly looks,
Like western sun on eastern brooks ;
    To others turning, turns me over,
From noonday to antipodal night,
Ah, blessed, if only there I might
In distant but illumined space,
Though dumb, yet fixed, find some remains of grace.
Doth she my studious habit scorn ?
It never hath been over-worn.
Though she of old the book-worm mocked,
It was in sport ; I was not shocked ;
I could be gay as other men ;
For I was not a lover then.
Fears she I have in garden been
Too highly favoured by my queen,
And therefore am I now disgraced,

A scape-goat turned into the waste?
Taking brief leave I sadly fare
To find no pity anywhere.
Boon Nature even plays her sorry part,
And seems to scorn me from its happy heart,
As, like leaf wind-tossed fallen from lofty bough,
On highway rude I mourn her, lost I know not how.

Sport, in sunset-glories fading,
   Homeward turns with game and glee :
Frolics brown with laughters aiding
   Nut from filbert tree to tree :
In dim lanes and purple gloaming
   Happy youths and dear hearts meet,
I alone am cheerless roaming,
   Though earth's very dust scents sweet.
Pure and placid hazeless ocean,
   Sprinkled sails, and rowers seem,
Idly or with ripple of motion,
   In a wakeful songful dream,
Fondly zephyrs kisses blowing,
   And in her own ardent sea
Smiling Venus imaged glowing ;
   Everything is glad but me.

Yet one bird keeps throbful singing,
   Robin-mavis—merle in one,
Anguish intermittent flinging
   From its bosom swelling lone.
To that melancholy, gushing
   From the fountain-head of sigh,
Listen I for final hushing
   Sure of sorrow, that must die ;
While stray bursts of sound, that cheerily
   Rise from hollow-hearted earth,
Mockful fall and wearily, drearily,
   Over me with shock of mirth,
Like wild mimicry of pleasure
   Shrouding over-misery.

Sighing I for my heart's treasure,
   Everything is sad with me.

Hopes bright as Spring-romances, grand
As Legends of Enchanted Land,
Unutterable all, too dear,
Too sweet for tongue, too lush for ear ;
Affections passionate as ocean,
   Strong as eternity or death,
Deep and yet timid as devotion,
   May dwindle in strife's first faint breath.
As light winds scatter grains of pollen,
So little and our gods are fallen.
But scattered grains soon vegetate :
Shall grains of love dispersed prove seeds of hate ?
'Twere maddening to think.   Nay, let her be
Whate'er she will—even lofty to me,
Though never may again that first
Full sunshine rapture on me burst,
If it may only glint to die,
On a fond tear of memory,
Still can I lose her not.   Ah ! no,
Still must I to her footstool go ;
   And yet I scorn the mumping art
However fond, not quite so vile
As wear a soul of servile pile,
   I would not beg but win her heart :
And, calling now on holiday,
Find her in undress act of play.
Sun-bonnet dangling from her hand,
I see her in her garden stand ;
While children round choose freshest dyes,
And sweetest scents, and bear as prize
To velvet lawn, and snowy tent
Already decked with ornament
Of hot-house flowers, autumn fruits,
And golden grain, and generous roots.
Her table we a poet's pleasaunce make,
And, wide for fresh spoils ranging, fresh ground break.

Trumpet and passion flower, sun-flower, they
Holly-hock pluck, tiger-lily gay,
Pond-lily also, white and blue,
And from the beach the poppy's yellow hue.
At moment due, again we meet
And show of flowers with these complete ;
Then finely fête the little elves
Only less happy than ourselves.
Opening a window of her mind,
Lucy to me is gently kind,
" I love those little ones," she says ;
   I love her so for so sweet saying
With such bright smile for me, as plays
   On face of Morn with zephyr maying.
Then as the sun aglow descends
   To realms beyond all sail, or oar,
And dear fond glances sinking sends
   Over the waters to the shore,
They crown her with parting wreath woven of roses
White as Seraph, on guard at heaven's entrance, disposes
On the brows of immortals admitted to dwell
In the Edens, that blossom around life's well.
Two then alone, we sought her drawing-room.
   A change came over Lucy, when she found
An Earl in waiting, who could quick assume
   The coronet on less considered ground.
A gallant Captain too of Horse, the heir
And nephew of an aged Duke, was there
With Lucy's mother eager in discourse.
Short time I staid.   I felt, like some spent force,
No longer profitable, worthless quite,
And out of mind while not yet out of sight.
I feared not rivals much : that Lucy cared
For none of us was what I greatly feared.
She, lofty-minded and strong-willed,
To mother only known to yield,
In queenly form a soul of pride,
Not haughty, nor to be denied,
With fond, and yet imperious play

Wins gracefully her own sweet way.
In sport, or earnest, none oppose ;
She charms her friends, enchains her foes :
Though few there are to disapprove
One, whom to see and know is love.
And in a fresh sore lapse of faith,
   Which mystified with doubt my muse,
It was a kind of heavenly breath,
   Such as cherubic winds diffuse
Without a touch of chill or drought,
That o'er my spirit, tossed by doubt,
Blew kindly, with fond thought to roll
The gathering darkness from my soul,
A wondrous legend, quaint and old,
Of Queen Virginal and Dietrich told.

BREEZY CHERUB.

" Higher than Himalaya snows,
In Elf-land high, whence Boreas blows,
In azure grot, on icy mound,
   Unmoved a Sovran Lady sate
With diadem carbuncle crowned,
And silver stole about her wound,
All with her trembling Graces round—
   A sight to see and marvel at.
Howling and monster passions raged
To storm Queen Virginal, but, staged,
In the heaven of her loveliness
   Than bellicose more beautiful,
Beyond a fosse all bottomless
   She shamed the wild misrule.
With pride of heart, which nothing quells,
From iron tablet conning spells,
A horseman black had sunk the fosse,
That nothing fond to her might cross,
And clouds brewed, thunders, lightnings, snows,
With rock and avalanche Dietrich to oppose ;
But, in fair knightly honour skilled,
The crowd he routed, horseman killed,

His tablet shattered and fosse filled,
Whence silence round Queen Virginal grew
Deep, as round sun the boundless blue,
And labouring her breast unfreighted,
Till the very soul of Counsel prated,
When, Dietrich passing to her feet,
She raised him to her royal seat,
Praising his love confessed her own,
And, straight descending from her throne,
Elf-land forsook to be his queen
Far from the horrid glory that had been."

Thus does black pride disdainful Lucy moat,
   And hold at distance in cold shows of state.
Love may the necromancer counterplot,
   And captive lead her, me to captivate.
She drags against the wish ; ah ! not the less
I bless her in her utmost cursedness.
Yet can I feign me dead to scorn,
Who live unto its lightest thorn ?
Of Berthau, feigning death, one said,
" Alas ! poor Berthau then is dead : "
Not " Maitre," mark you.   Agonized
Even in the death, he symptomized,
Loud called he, quick as born debater,
" Liar, I live to be your Maitre."
So wounded Desmond borne from field
Captive upon Ormondian shield,
Hearing—" Where now is Desmond ? "—shrilled,
" Where but in proper place of fear,
Still on the necks of Butlers, here."
I too would conquer by my wound ;
Be strongest when most feeble found ;
Her love, solicited by mine.
Win with a desperation fine ;
Even in fear there is a timely dare,
A stolid virtue in supreme despair.
And love's sun still hath breadths of smile
   With cloudy days and spots to cope ;

Its very storms with ardours thrill ;
  Even her perversity feeds hope.

Both at one eve's reception bright,
Forth Lucy stepped to splendid night ;
I joined on terrace pacing long.
No Philomel made pants of song,
But Luna glowed with thoughts as fond,
And palpitating stars respond ;
Even heaving ocean seems distressed
With moonlight warm upon its breast,
And earth and heaven in embrace :
Peace ardent then lit Lucy's face.
To Romeo too much endeared
Juliet upon such night appeared,
And high her holy balcony
Secret they met : though public we
And love unspoken, she could feel,
Without it, all had been unreal,
So soul to soul was open spread,
As spirits meet when life is sped,
So calm and clear, so pure and true,
So happy, dear, and human too.
We talked of how the scorn-crazed knight
Taught Genevieve to love outright.

EDWARD.

" Lotus and daisy, widest at high noon,
Only in myths are open to the moon.
Cold moonshine never ripened grape ;
Sun giveth it Silenian shape.
Yet many a heart hath glowed awhile
In moonshine of a fair false smile,
Beneath it then to find and know
A tinted Florimel of snow."

LUCY.

" Have you so suffered ?   Do you fear,
That one, you love, is false as dear ? "

EDWARD.

" A breeze may bend a branch, which, now
    Resilient, may backward smite ;
So maid may bend, yet, quick as bough,
    Spring up again to prouder height."

LUCY.

" But, toss her head as heaven high,
All you need give her is a sigh :
Not, should she be of Teucrian line,
Premeditate to hang, or whine :
Sigh may from Araby, the Blest
Melt Himala's far frozen crest."

EDWARD.

" My sighs by her or heard, or felt,
Might readier freeze, than she would melt."

LUCY.

" Yet never frosts of Lebanon
Have whitened Cedars of the Sun.
Scant he of spirit who, by maid disdained,
Is broken-hearted, or crack-brained.
Shall a man go puling, failing
    In the work of life sublime,
All in sackcloth nature veiling
    And his manhood's stately prime,
Since a woman seems to shiver
    In the heats, which make him burn ?
Cupid empty may his quiver
    In her bosom, fired in turn."

EDWARD.

" Woman in wedding looks to rise,
Man only into loving eyes.
Brave Sobieski's true disdain
Without their Marys half to reign ; "

LUCY.

" And over snows, they do not soil,

With Eginhards still Immas toil ;
Though Emperors' sons for them may sigh,
Still perish Audes, when Rolands die.
In Abbey of St. Farron grand
Olivier, Turpin, Roland stand
With Charlemain all marble now,
  And Aude is there by Roland's side ;
Her love so glorious I vow,
  It is the very marble's pride."

EDWARD.

" A modern princess, stooping down
To wed physician, dropped her crown ;
Throne rank for self and heirs resigned,
To heartless honours only blind.
Would Eros might some muse inspire
A pen to dip in molten fire,
Or ichor, blood of gods, that flowed
From Venus' wound to Diomed owed :
But pagan muse and shrine are dumb.
Might then some graver Angel come,
With plume undipped in fascination,
By God and heavenly occasion
Inspired, and write ; for bliss divine
Was in the love of dear Pauline :
Whate'er her charms, they had the beauty
Of glow of heart in light of duty."

LUCY.

" The lady Orgeuilleuse despited
The love of Gawain sore incited,
While, championing her wrongs, he woos
The love, he seems the more to lose ;
Yet ravished heart at last and charms
She rendered to his circling arms."

When I with Lucy think to venture more,
She quick has turned, and through the windowed door
Entered the thronged and brilliant hall.

There with an equal smile for all,
But no more look for me, nor smile,
She shows like glittering berg, the while
Ready in future dark to be
The coolest of all treachery.
Was all then a deceitful dream
  Of starry vapours born and sighs,
Plague breeding with contagious steam?
  May no illuminated skies
Vault thee, base night ; may cruel spheres
Roll down thy cheeks, like wasted tears —
Their influence has been unkind.
May they be miserably blind,
God wreck them out of hopeless sight,
In formless chaos shorn of light
Never again to lustre night.
But sudden missing Lucy, I too leave.
Can love dissemble so and not deceive?

Soon I in wood, now leafed with golden shade,
Revisiting the tree, on which my maid
Is fondly, deeply, memorably graved,
Of its propitious Sprite fresh counsel craved.
From trees to trees deciduous handed down,
Of the long past and passing much is known.
Haunts, homes, and temples of primeval men,
Woods tragedy have nursed to empire vain,
Egypts, Assyrias, Persias, Greece, Rome ; lo,
May still be nursing more to come, and go
Encumbering earth with wide magnificence.
What trees survive have a mute eloquence,
While time is storied on their growing rings,
Attesting acts which wilder legend sings.
The passer reads, or hears what they recall,
Now fitted to delight and now appal.
Ha ! many a hang-dog gallows-tree is here,
And woodsmen many a trysting one revere.
And now the Sprite, of this most sacred tree
In all the hallowed grove, appears to me.

D

Aglaia, Thalia, Euphrosyné,
And Goethe's fair all-healing nymphs attend,
  That haunt streamed shade and float in Oread dance ;
And now in rising song their voices blend
  And kindly counsel of the Sprite enhance.
Passion along the pipes of Pan,
With glowing lips too breathing ran,
Oft the thumbed tambour shook o'erhead,
While Sprite, Nymphs, Graces sang in the dance, it led.

SPRITE, NYMPHS, *and* GRACES *sing in Dance of Passion.*

" Despair not, lest thy reason fail
  Beyond Mnemosyné avail,
Love turn to dread, and fiends combine
To chase from thee the Muses nine.
In moments of most mortal weakness,
When you are love-smit unto sickness,
And Lucy too seems deeply moved,
And you can feel yourself beloved,
To stay the tremour of the time
  She strange reserve of power can bring,
And banish from your heart the crime,
  Of hoping anything.
But Adéle, loved by Eriland,
 Could self restrain, not all command ;
Like inefficiency may prove
In her the spring of summer-love.
Why smile on him she lately scorned,
Scorn him she smiled on, if unwarned
By throes of heart of something there,
Which to be happy needs but dare ?
Ah ! could her words but, issuing, dip
In glow of lush love-purpled lip,
Expression catch from dreamy eyes
Not always looking coldly wise,
They would not only breathe, but burn ;
For thee, they might no longer spurn,
Drop in Anacreontic measure
Formed upon tongue and lips of pleasure."

Sleeking grave gloom of moody thought,
I likewise argue, up to courage wrought.
And now will neither fret nor scold,
While still her beauty makes me bold,
Thus reasoning, " If grand her pride,
It has been happy by my side ;
I could not break but rather bend
   What makes my heart so soft to see :
Love yet may conquer, pride befriend
   And make her proud of me,
As Desdemona of the Moor
When he was most a gibing boor.
Still must I longing feed by chase,
   Hold heaven in view, not idly gaze ;
Has sinner ever yet known grace,
And looking heaven in the face,
   Not with his prayer mingled praise."

CANTO III.

BEHIND her on a loving day,
   Like fan appendant unto kite,
Seemed I in heaven fluttering gay,
   While following on earth her flight,
To her attached, and ever true,
Constant as shadow, not in view :
Till gone, like butterfly on breeze
Over a wall where no one sees,
Home vanished she 'mid nestling trees,
And ravished space still dwelling seemed
On charms, which it had more than dreamed,
As echo when it sings again
A past and unreturning strain ;
While vaguely into shade of wood,
   I knew not where I roved,

I knew not if I walked or stood,
    Knew only that I loved.

Like Psyché, who in tearful dearth
And search of Cupid wandered earth,
 I, opening sudden heaven, roam
On slope observant of her home :
There neighboured by retiring trees,
And dreamy as Elysian breeze,
Not sighlessly pluck flowers wild,
On which she may have sometime smiled ;
And from tuned lips love-numbers spill
    Folily, not for any ear,
As birds, when they with passion thrill,
    Singing their wanton selves to hear,
Or gondolier upon Lagune,
    Careless of blame or praise,
Unburdening his soul to moon,
    And stars, and silent seas.

EDWARD.

"She proud, but neither sly, nor slant,
Could ne'er with Libyan Psapho vaunt,
Birds training close to bruit abroad,
That mine she is not, but my god ;
Elsewise I other bird might train
Round her to fly and wooful plain,
' My love and labour all are lost,'
Which she might buy at any cost,
And I would ask for it the love, which, though concealed,
Is by mine own for her, to me revealed.
In Oreithyia quest no Boreas I,
But a zephyr, all a sigh,
Fain would on gentle zephyr wing,
Find Iris and round Lucy fling
Hope's colours bright ; with ravished airs
    From open heart of every flower,
To captivate her unawares,
    Surround her in her garden bower ;

Then fill her ears with whispering blisses ;
Then sow and reap her lips with kisses ;
And fold, with self-revealing art,
Her longing to my leaping heart,
As from flower-covert once to bliss
In Blanchefleur's bosom sprang Florice."

Soon further roam I vacant shore
Extending near.   Love-fever sore,
Restless as earthquake, strays the will,
And lovers wander dreamers, still
Most gentle madmen, roaming where
Unstartled cony sits, or hare,
Which knows at sight and thanks kind fates
For love's unheedful advocates,
Who scare nor hum, nor bite of fly,
Save with all unconscious sigh,
And tend to utter lonely places,
Crusoe-like from human faces
Flying ; for the dastard tribes
Fret true love with poisoned gibes.

Up the cliff arborous a path and steep
I followed, slow ascending o'er the deep
To where a ruined castle towering stood,
Itself supreme, commanding land and flood.
Lucy and I each stone knew, through had chased
Down to the sea the deer from upland waste ;
And as I higher rose above the brine,
That haunted castle gave me faintest sign.
Amid its ruins gaunt methought that she,
Not for the first time, might be waiting me ;
Might now my coming footstep hail with joy,
As ship unanchored, while near breeze is coy,
Not yet arrived though nigh, sways to and fro,
And stirs through all aloft and all below,
Then to persuasive quest of kissing gales
Yields full blown pleasure of un-numbered sails.

Spurring in glades, a Bruce one day
Chanced on and charmed a Countess gay,
Who, by her Dian maidens aided,
Wooed him to join the chase invaded.
He, coy resisting, was surrounded ;
To castle led ; and bold impounded,
Till, chains relenting to her charms,
Hymen released him to her arms.
These times no Marjory produce
To mother an heroic Bruce :
Yet sudden 'ware was I of feeling
Like heaven quiet o'er me stealing,
And looking up saw Lucy nigh,
Wreathed in bright smiles to greet mine eye :
And could I doubt of bliss to be,
When she was all the world to me ?

We airy thoughts, with nothing in,
Happy exchange in words akin.
As ripple on a roll they trip
Light o'er her soul, but nowhere dip.
Would I its depths might analyse ;
   As solar now and stellar ray
Confess what metals they disguise,
   With spectroscope of soul betray,
And make her inner spirit speak
In many an outer ribald streak
Of passions, which united prove
The incandescent glow of love ;
And thus her heart know, as mine own,
Which open is for her alone,
Not vacant, but with love full filled
Taking her image now unchilled.

Expanding brows 'neath raven braids
   Parted and smoothed with care,
Gathered behind, and thence falling
   Jet cataracts of hair,
Than pale moons breaking through black clouds
   A fairer contrast show.

Her cheeks like Hyperion-flushed, pure
　Drifts of Olympian snow,
Stately as Pallas, from dark eyes
　Brave fires of intellect beam ;
A bow of Cupid curved and stringed
　Her lips imperial seem.
No Grecian she, but Hephæstous ne'er
　Achieved a diviner art ;
Her neck by the Gods upborne, her
　Mere footfall storms the heart.

Oft have we met, but rivals none
Now ice and intercept my sun.
Her subtle charms had made less stern
Past weary hours of winter dern ;
But, nothing now Hyperborean,
Autumn itself shows Hymenean.
Each shout, now parting stray from earth,
Heaven welcomes with responsive mirth,
While birds, late woeful as they sang,
Trill joy-bells with recurring clang.
Ships, here and there, and steamers float,
And many a craft, and rowing-boat,
And mortals gay, and Neptune mighty,
Seem triumphing with Aphrodité.
Had I enough of Crœsus' gold,
Two golden statues would I mould :
Lucy a rose or lyre should bear,
Or fruit to Venus once so dear ;
I purple mantled, then advance
Talarian—ankled round to dance,
Welcoming with religious duty
Avatar fresh of heavenly beauty.
Had providence to me now sent
Some gracious Heemskerk testament,
I in Pradakshina had brave
Revolved around testator's grave.
Yet has our joy a perverse taste of brine,
And hectic glow of day in slow decline.

EDWARD.

" Mother of all things, ocean, bosom-heaving
  With speechless flow of grace, and pure as truth
Converting unto God the unbelieving,
  Can hold in rapture glad impassioned youth
Hearing through wide profundity of calm
God's voice still, small, and grander than all psalm :
While ripples infantine with cadenced measure
Retire, return, and laugh with baby pleasure,
As where eternity approached by time
Cherubic faces glow and voices chime."

LUCY.

" With pinions fanning, or extended fair,
Up, down, out, in, like orbs to ear of air,
Songful, in curves harmonious wheel gulls,
Whether with screeches now, or now in lulls,
Now screech, now lull ; dip fishing beaks and rise,
Or, lapsing brine along, from imaged skies
With plash of wing a universe erase,
Created so to drown, alas ! or blaze."

EDWARD.

" This world is beautiful, and yonder strand
A fitting border to a lovely land.
'Twas upon such knelt Magdalen of France
And kissed choice handful, and with suppliant glance,
Lifted to heaven, blessed the husband isle,
That hailed delighted her too short-lived smile.
Was never coral haunt so dear
In Ægæ, unimaginably clear,
Not Ægir's palace hung with gold all round
In circumambient ocean more profound.
'Neath chequered cliffs, on sands or shingle,
And shells, which liberally mingle
  In rich mosaics, at decline of day
I there have roamed and dreamed the moon
To quiet beach would Naiads soon
  And nymphs of ocean gather in play,

While sleekly sleep
On silken satin deep
Soft airs of Æos and Astræos born,
Which stir no flowing lock unshorn
Of sea-nymphs lightly floating laid,
Or Naiads where they silver-footed wade ;
And flutter not one slumberous plant
In grottoes green as was the haunt
Of Nereid Thetis and her Peleus king ;
Nor stir or leaf, or root of trees, that cling
Shaggy to giddiest brinks ; or even
Flecked osprey plume dropped straight from heaven."

LUCY.

" Oft nature in its beauty cruel shows ;
Its smiles insidious covert are for woes.
Ah me, those screams and lulls, those beaks, that dip
The fish to mangle ; brine, that wrecks the ship,
And drowns the sailor to afflict the shore,
Distressing heaven, till time shall be no more,
Compose a poem full of faulty rhymes,
Fantastic jangle make of unblest chimes."

EDWARD.

" On substance shadow still attends,
Death upon life to part best friends."

LUCY.

" Love too, though blind, may feel to range ;
Whatever is must suffer change.
Who then can give me certain news
Of bliss assured, which hope pursues ;
Of smockless, smirchless, smiling light,
And substance without shadow of night ?
Is empty hope fulfilled above,
This void of soul, this need of love,
This endless longing for a bliss,
Which is to be, and never is ? "

EDWARD.

" The sun is sinking : land, isle, flood,
　And round horizon are alow,
While palaces of crimson cloud,
Of Juno flushed the vapours proud,
　In eyes of Neptune mirrored glow.
Ah, could we flash impulsive flight
To far corridors now golden bright,
Dazed into happiness we might,
Than Dante happier, casting not
A shadow upon holiest spot,
Escape from moon and stars, and run
To light low palaced safe in sun
'Neath glows, which roof with deepening shade,
But bliss offend not, nor invade;
By night pursued, but not too late,
　By night pursued, but flying fast
Passing through Vulcan's ivory gate
To where days, months, years, seasons wait,
Ages and hours untouched by fate,
　And gaining constant bliss at last."

LUCY.

" So light is youth, it seeks to fly,
In its excess of energy,
And hopes to find, yet never knows,
Or where, or after what it goes.
If youth is restive, witless age
Returns upon its earlier stage,
Thinking in change to lose its fears,
And drop the burden of its years.
We never know, when we are sold ;
And all are dotards, young as old."

EDWARD.

" Fate's Ganymede in all his cups,
　Holds not one everlasting draught ;
Time, on eternity that sups,
　Has Protean changes to be quaffed ;

The heavens bow to passing nods,
Successive Æons make new gods ;
From bliss to bliss, from pain to pain,
Change, if not interchange, may reign.
Upon a pace of present land,
Mid universal sea we stand
Still forward stepping ever where,
By sea advancing, is left bare
A further pace for us to dare,
Escaping from the waves ; and we
Are travellers everlastingly,
Even when earth shall be no more.
Still would I hopefully adore,
And, subject to decrees unbending,
In God conceive good never ending.
The Christian is sustained by faith,
And walks the crystal sea at death."

LUCY.

" But fortune is a brazen liar,
    They tell me ; can our choice hopes steal
To seat upon her topmost tire,
    And whirl the crushing base to feel ;
Joab-like, with most smiling bliss,
Embrace, and stab us with a kiss ;
Good give, but not enjoyment—woe,
Worst ill, while we like Atlas go,
Staggering beneath our weight of heaven ;
Or may deny what so is given,
Us tantalize, in water dip
That floateth chin, yet flieth lip ;
In orchard seat, whose wind-tossed trees
Snatch fruits from hands outstretched to seize ;
Or cliff, that shades feast tempting spread,
Drop upon duped doomed reveller's head."

EDWARD.

" If sure of love I without fears
Could chance the music of the Spheres.

Home had I in love's bosom true—
Sole sanctuary time e'er knew—
I worst of fortune could support,
Never its prey, although its sport ;
Round too might I full orb of being,
Run with a Daphné no more fleeing ;
In causing joy find happiness,
Blest as the maid I sought to bless ;
Earth would be heaven with love, night curtained day,
Black darkness safe as light and far more gay."

LUCY.

" As Arabella Stuart anchor weighed,
Yet sail in hope of Seymour long delayed,
Yon distant bark with ready sail and prow
Its true though lingering gale awaiteth now.
Will the breeze play that trusty vessel false ? "

EDWARD.

" It lips my cheeks.   The boatswain's whistle calls.
Soon shall the gale with gentle stress
Bark out of danger guide, and press
Illimitable ocean o'er
Along a path unchanced before,
As that in air of birds in throng
Towards their haunts of brooding song,
And fan with breath of many sighs
Now under sun, now starry eyes,
Laughing in heaven in the dark
To see the gale kissing the bark ;
I so with my love would forward go
Twixt earth and heaven, where fairies show,
And only sun or stars may know.
Oh, sun or stars !   To her mine eyes
   Instead of these would be—as true,
Would be her studies and her skies,
   And teach whate'er she wished to do."

LUCY.

" Our proper course we much have overstrayed."

EDWARD.

" All times and courses are with thee well sped.
Which way soever thy gait lies,
I deem the gate of paradise."

We then her homeward way addressed,
While Cardinal Purple day confessed,
Sun wafer-like sinking into ocean,
   Vermilion sky o'er azure hill,
No sighing zephyrs, no commotion,
   But freshness glad with nothing chill,
Only one star as diamond bright,
Fore-signalling advance of night ;
Lanes, woods, each dead and living thing,
All nature pouring came to fling
Pleasures commingling at our feet,
Such joy 'twas Lucy so to meet.
Even her aimless glances, wide,
   Were like that erring dart,
Which struck a tree, and glanced aside
   Into Red William's heart:
While gloaming's dear and farewell light
Lent idle words a tender might
Of love unspoken, madrigal
Unutterably musical.
Babes, deeming colour all creation,
Find dolour in its deprivation,
And, when our twinned ways smiling part,
" Good-bye" falls dead upon my heart.

A nook I seek, where fairies wone,
And out I take my sheaf of flone—
Flowers, with which she my heart hath filled,
Thence had not one of them been spilled.

The core is warm, but so not vile,
　　While florulent, a perfume hoard ;
Each violet glance, carnation smile,
　　I garner with each primrose word ;
And these I know, as now I con,
Her very gestures all are known.
And I remember, she hath named
A coming ball, and I am claimed,
Pleased, to first-foot with her the mazy ply,
Whose distance lends small charm ; would it were nigh !

Parted by arches, currents will
With natural whirls together rill :
But "Art is long," and Sybarite far-sighted ;
I am a year before the hour invited ;
At least a year and day it seems,
Till I shall dance in ought but dreams.
Ah ! when our single fair so dances,
Our rivals also have fair chances.
Hope in the future hangs a sign,
　　Above brief hostel of to-day,
With printed promise of divine
　　" Good ale to-morrow for nothing ; "　Stay—
Good ale to-morrow who shall see ?
To-morrow come, to-day must be.

How small a matter daunts the cheer,
Once dulled by an irrational fear.
Night on my soul fell, but afar
　　Lustred all heaven at whose top,
In bosom of a glorious star
　　That twinkled, saw I blinking Hope.
" Ah ! leave me not thy loss to mourn,
Good Hope," I cry, " to earth return :
Or wouldst thou heavenward point despair,
　　Death only then may comfort give ;
And though that heaven were thrice as fair,
I would be happy here as there ;
　　While she remains I wish to live.

But of my destiny holdest thou,
The very star ?   I know it now.
Canst thou in it show, she and I,
Are to be happy by-and-by ?
Laugh to me, sweet one." Hope, beguiled
By my fond pleading, fondly smiled
Thrilling the planet with assent,
And making sullen night relent
Bright now, as phosphorescent wave,
Or lighted vault of Mammoth Cave ;
While on the crowned supreme decree
I sprinkle " Benedicite,"
Happy as stars consentient, proud
As Catherine de' Medici's vain crowd
Cognoscitive of appetitive chances—
Oneiro—and all other—necro—mancies,
With astro Nostradamus at their head
Causing Babe Henry Fourth unprincely dread.

All meaner passions dimmed expire,
Feed rather love's absorbing fire
Darting through obstacles with flare
The distant flame to win and wear,
Or halo then a beaming grace.
Earth ages cooling, but the race
   For ever young grows never cold ;
Hearts are as warm now, heads as long,
Wills as resolved, hands deft, arms strong,
   As e'er loved, schemed, dared, did of old.
Yea, from love's bow a subtle shaft
   Fixed in most simple of all swains,
To him communicates such craft
   As to out-wit much bigger brains,
And fire an ass benighted, lost, to blind
Apollo's eye and further-seeing mind.

CANTO IV.

RICH moss-rose, storing scents and dyes
  On stem in thorns repellent dressed,
Pricking the hand of covetise,
Salves deeper pain, when now a prize
  Inclining on your sweet-heart's breast :
Such not too late in song y-clad
I Lucy sent, who, guessing glad
That I so harbingered the night,
Bore to the ball my gifts aright—
Rose and song just where I meant,
  This in heart, and that in bosom ;
In her heart the song I sent,
  And, not far off, the blossom.
All the world saw my rose
  Pleased, where Cupid placed it, deep
Twixt twin slopes of drifted snows :
Sun his radiant head so shows
  On clouds glowing, when from sleep
Rising to accord his lyre
To the swelling terrene choir.

SONG OF THE ROSE.

" There are seedlings from Eden all stray over earth : "
  Thus sang my moss-rose in thornfullest pride—
" Had a spirit been given me, in fluttering birth
  A cherub had laughed, though a queen-flower had died.

" In a garden gay bloomed I top-laden with beauty,
  And the worshipping flowers swung their censers abroad ;
They offered me incense from love more than duty,
  And I, as their queen, breathed it all back to God.

" Kind zephyr airs fanned, while hot sunbeams caressed me ;
  Showers, dropping like dews, turned to kisses their tears ;
Youths hailed with wild glances, but dared not molest me ;
  To possess me maids longing, all smiled down my fears.

" But now, cruel maiden, my Queendom is over,
  No more to arrest each invidious eye,
At thy bidding I plucked was by yon wicked rover,
  And in death low I sicken—I sicken to die.

" Ah, to die like a queen with all thronging to see !
  But thy glory so ruffs it, I fall in disgrace:
For the youths, crowding round, have no eyes but for thee,
  And I am unnoticed with ribbon and lace.

" Nay, forgive a brief madness ; I would not be riven
  From thee, not for all earth can show to beguile,
No, not to be Queen-flower : it surely is heaven
  Thus to droop on thy bosom, and die in thy smile."

> With death thus love contends, whose sigh,
> And not itself, shall ever die ;
> Death is transformed in love's idolatry,
> And speech is shallow to confess
> Depths of a first full tenderness.
> Though dimly dawns, like tint of dove
>   Or tinge of rose on marble shed,
> In virgin blush the light of love,
>   Soon billow is of ripple bred
> And rushes all a heart undone,
> As stars into the rising sun.
> But dared I not advantage press
>   By verse and flower in pastime gained.
> Some women take a rhyme's caress,
>   And think their poet well hath feigned ;
> His rosebud lay on shelfy breast,
> And deem it quite a fragrant jest.
> Yet more she gave than one proud dance,
> With after-moments such as France
>   Wont to accord the troubadour,
> Whose songs egayed a death not hard,
> For love endured by Chastelard.
>   Then trod I not on boarded floor ;
> 'Twas laid with love on which I floated,

E

A winged extasy devoted,
Uplift, transported, as in air
The radiant torch which Cupids bear.
And when I of blear morrow spake,
How Home I must for town forsake
  And Frowning sorceries of law—
More dread than arms, or hasty news
Bruited by a Byronic muse—
  Upon her face a shade I saw
Chased by quick smile, and such " Good-bye "
As is not given to hopes too high.

LUCY.

" Thy gift, of flower and verse composed,
Kind-hearted is, and, doubly rosed,
Has sweeter breathed and spoken power
Than ever fabler taught to flower :
No papal rose to any Queen,
Not England's royal, could have been
More grateful unto Catherine."

EDWARD.

" Thanks, Lucy; on my harsher tongue,
Let thy dear name be parting song.
Wish me success : for with thy smile,
I shall the deepest law beguile—
Thy beauty is more full of ruse,
And heaven will grace whom thou dost choose."

LUCY.

" Raguenel of Du Guesclin bold
Success not lyingly foretold :
And never Mary roofless air
With night and watchfires longed to share
More, than with Portia I to learn
  What incense scents a well-won cause.
Doubt not rich victories to earn,
  And lead in triumph all our laws."

EDWARD.

'So may thine augury good prove,
  As I too labour for thy— "

LUCY.

                       " Nay,
Not my esteem.   Thine own self-love,
  The world's approval and its pay,
All these command thee to aspire,
While I at distance may admire."

EDWARD.

" At distance !   Life were void to me,
Though crowned with bays, if far from thee."

LUCY.

" Law now must part us for a while.
I still upon thy flower shall smile.
In water dying, it shall drop
Of thornless petals fragrant crop,
And I in alabaster urn,
Anticipating thy return,
Conserve its sweet, if parting, breath—
Thine own goodwill, unchanged by death."

EDWARD.

" Once nurtured under Zion wall,
Rose-leaves pollute not, though they fall.
Cast not one petal then away,
Else may ill chance our joys affray
As, when in Selim's troubled hour,
Zuleika flung away his flower.
For ancient phyllorodomancy
Is not all craft, and not mere fancy :
Anacreon sang it, credulous,
Crowned with choice roses of Pierius."

LUCY.

"I gladly now another hear,
Singing it in my single ear.
But the hour warns me : I must go."

Descending with her silent, slow,
Prolonging bliss, I, then exiled,
Stood by her carriage. But she smiled,
Took from her bosom, e'er she went,
And kissed the rose which I had sent.
As Venus oft in heaven lingers
Kissing the Morn, whose rosy fingers
Deft thrill along Apollo's lyre
To hasten his ascending fire,
That bud o'erqueened was fitly blest
Kissed by that maid, whose joy repressed
And purity, not holy death
In balmy airs of bliss that breathe
From opening heaven, make her be
More welcome than saint yet to me,
As holy but more earthly, while
  She still may answer love with love,
Now mingling with heaven's very smile
  A glow and light unknown above,
Chaste light and glow of dawning passion,
Most summer thing in God's creation
That hath man's fall survived and glows
Undimmed by time, unquenched by woes,
Since Eve unblushing charms displayed,
And Adam kissed God's primal maid.
To her is nothing like, or second ;
  The thought of her is full of laughter ;
With Jocus round, might next be reckoned
Venus, who, though she smirked and beckoned,
  Should have her second place long after.

A leaping, bubbling, frightened fountain,
Irruptive from Vesuvian mountain,
Through ashen rocks of horrid style

Escaping fearfully awhile,
Now, winning vine-empurpled slopes
And palace shades, 'mid blossoms gropes
With fruits immixed, yet longs to gain
The far most pleasant quiet plain.
From shades ambrosial chancing now
On heights unknown, it thinks, I trow,
The vale beneath, and from sheer brow
A tiny body casts below ;
Downward for ever it may go ;
Sunned showers to vapours radiant melt
Waxing, waning, seen, not felt,
And Iris-woven rise
To mingle with the skies.
So leaps my thought with her to wed.
Despair, by rapture quick enlivenèd,
One whirl of rosy ardours swims, like gay
Clouds where love's children, Cupids, toss in play,
Or that fay reverie of Chaucer, dreamer
Who waked to live in hope of bliss supremer.

Oft I bless that dying blossom :
  She has smiled upon my woes,
Though now, from her glowing bosom,
  Cold in water dies the rose
Dear, as unto Sesto's daughter
Hero swimming Helle's water.
I to town her smile have borne,
  But my rose is with her still.
Leaves, that drop without a thorn,
  Alabaster vase shall fill :
For she stoopeth all to gather.
  Withering with fragrant art,
They now incense breathe, or rather
  All the passion of my heart.
Plucked by me, but not amiss,
Dead, my rose shall be in bliss.
Propitious love to mast chaste garlands binds ;
Hope swells each sail, inducing fair fresh winds ;

Sure Fortune steering, Venture at the prow,
Waters around lapse kissing as they go.
Fly, birds of evil omen !   Unforetold
Coming misfortune blesses virtue.   Bold,
Thus with bright dreams to point the promised land,
On eager verge of action now I stand.

Oh, radiant moment ! when on full-fledged wing
Lark lusty thinks to soar about to sing ;
When, mindful of a past's benignant rule,
Hope present hails a future promiseful ;
As though the soul, by conscious strength embraced,
Power new-born felt to toil, and triumph taste,
Enlivened energy each moment counts,
And pants to run before the rider mounts.
Ha, Buller wedded was at seventeen—
A judge at thirty-two, and life still green.

Not all are Bullers: Scotts may fee-less toil,
While hapless wives feed wicks with borrowed oil ;
Or Kenyons lovingly to mate disdain,
Till five long lustres strike a golden vein.
Such lengthened winters kill May-springs with rime,
Whose blossoms fail to fruit in autumn time.
Elastic hopes may lose all power of stretch,
And grow into a strand themselves to ketch,
An irremediable ill shows less ;
Predestination mitigates distress.
'Tis half law's ill, that you have hope therein ;
And are so fast to run, though slow to win.

I in my chambers entertained a few
As briefless as myself, as youthful too.
Together we in hall had early dined ;
But tasting soon of pleasures, more refined,
We seasoned them, so zested, not alloyed,
Discussing questions for the unemployed.
The chair I filled ; but now alone, as fit,
Upon our secretary's minutes sit,

And illustrations, ruder than his scroll ;
Some we shall publish in the Weekly Droll,
And chief a skit of Bacon dressed and hung :
Our arguments he had, as follows, loosely strung.

CHAIRMAN.

" Two grains of sand, or blades of grass the same,
Two men alike, from God's hand never came,
Nor twin affinities of man with man,
All several parts in heaven's expanding plan.
Natively differing, we different grow
More and more with each bond and break below ;
And cause of quarrel find in all, that may
Join men, soon parted, on life's labile way.
So wrongs and rights are, thus too law is born,
And lawyers rise, its affluence of morn ;
Through dark confusion heights of custom gain,
And principle advance to lawful reign."

FIRST BRIEFLESS.

" And yet one scatters wasted years around,
Seeking to find where law is to be found.
Grassy and dull are Inns of Court, in vain
By years of wisdom hallowed and chicane,
Knights of St. John, and nights of frolic too
Bidding to law and labour wild ' Adieu.'
Since roses here were plucked both white and red,
And for these emblems factious England bled,
Under blear glass, preserved from blasts and showers,
Chrysanthemums have bloomed—Mikado flowers :
There have been wars too of Chrysanthemums,
Contentious beauty haunts these legal slums."

SECOND BRIEFLESS.

" But, against pleasures keeping old men warm,
Who impious dare raise finger of reform,
'Gainst Benchers dignified of portly mien,
Or customs out of date, which they antiquely screen ? "

THIRD BRIEFLESS.

"Yet if law might, by wise though rigorous change,
Simpler become, and calling not so strange
Confined and rusting in some pen-folds here,
'Twere worth the loss of much to Benchers dear :
Better un-inned, un-benchered, and unbarred,
Than a waste howling wilderness ill-starred."

FOURTH BRIEFLESS.

"For what wise purpose lawyers' clubs, called 'Inns,'
And Benchers, Keepers learned in favourite binns,
Not of a royal conscience but good wines,
Sole privilege to bar should now possess,
Or having barred disbar, demands a guess."

FIFTH BRIEFLESS.

"Ha, causes poor in worse effects appear :
Young heads think soon to curl and grizzle here :
For privilege of club and lectures pay ;
Fee men already called, whose books they may
And papers read or not, and little learn,
And called themselves then quite as little earn.
Not all are Cockburns living always fast,
Yet with an eye to business to the last.
Like maidens who wed wealth, Inns, being fee'd,
More men of pleasure than of business breed ;
For safe sure stealth monopoly, like night,
Its most will do to hide its want of right,
And lend its own apprentice little light.
Youth mistified goes plunging through the fog,
Issuing an ignorant if racy dog ;
Thus Inns themselves in affluence maintain,
But for no special good on earth remain."

SIXTH BRIEFLESS.

"If such the school of law, what of law's self
And its interpreters, Ghibelline and Guelph ?
Mansfields to principle, or custom bow,

Or precedent, and rule, that we may now
Colonies tax, now sweethearts cane ; but, lo,
Coghill lost one, we all the U. S. so.
Lawyers so differ, Judges too, and Courts,
Where find law's last in cipherless reports?
Ædipus self, although with eyes of lynx,
Could never have looked through so huge a sphinx,
No thread of reason e'er the maze pursue,
So mixed are wrong and right, so changeable too."

SEVENTH BRIEFLESS.

" Still joy has he and pure, who robes in light
Of law and logic hard contested right,
From case to case tracks devious to draw
With hound-like scent most foxlike truth of law.
A Dryas-dust some deem him.   Something more :
If a machine, one good as wise to bore
For duty, rather than great place, or gain,
Black hearts of quarrels, and white lies of men.
An earnest, reasoning, intellectual weed,
He calmly ponders too, what few can read,
Like Troop, in Engadine recruiting late,
Digesting law for a United State;
Or Smith, renowned for Special Case, whose pride
Was overstudy, reading, while he died
In stream of deepest, clearest, coolest bliss,
With just enough of flow to make it kiss."

EIGHTH BRIEFLESS.

" But, though some now themselves rear, since they must ;
Though, as sprang Adam organised from dust,
Men of accomplished strength, not only flies,
From a mere want, or rot of system rise ;
'Tis strange, dead nature should storm off disease,
And living man prefer to rot at ease.
Superbest Wolsey, though a butcher cur,
One to whom butcher King was common Sir ;
Bacon, whom some improving would have swung,
Primest of thinkers, loftiest unhung ;

Great Cromwell, loosely nicknamed ' Brewer's brat ; '
Clarendon, issue too of generous vat ;
All felt how secret, perverse, manifold
Is law uncodified, by judge controlled.
But practice, tricking ignorance and awe,
Too sordid is to rid of chance the law."

NINTH BRIEFLESS.

" Each knowing Chancellor, Brougham himself, has blown
And stopped all large reform by his small own,
Till of haphazard learning, piled to crush,
Campbell tells blushing, if law-lord can blush.
While law, thus indigest, like nightmare sits
On justice powerless, which with scattered wits
Screameth for Cromwell, or some greater still
To prove and quick administer his will,
Shall we do nothing ?   Roused from night-mared sleep,
Come law's Avatar and ripe ruin reap ;
From wealth of Inns misused let now wise state
True legal universities create—
True schools of law, wherever o'er the land
Intelligence or custom may command,
And proper honours sole have right to bar,
And only such be called who lawyers are,
Attorney too his title thus make good,
The whole profession one grand brotherhood
No more apart taught, and, if still so classed
By one great master, Law, all equal passed :
So shall not law long indigest remain."

TENTH BRIEFLESS.

" By schooled beginning we at least shall gain,
Each known and knowing.   While full student course
Illustrates thus each specialty of force
Crowning each victor some fair city's pride,
As erst Olympic games, and, published wide,
Repute and friendship may propitiate chance,
And practise make or win in wise advance."

ELEVENTH BRIEFLESS.

" Mean is this waiting on a shunt.
Etiquette censures push, which goes,
Treads on another's hinder toes,
    And, as he flinches, steps in front.
But push and speech denied him, can
Barrister noted be in gentleman ?
Power inert is unbelieved ;
Masked, is easy misconceived.
Can other than Almighty ears
Attend mute music of fixed spheres ?
·Science, which may dumb nature question,
Perceives but its own dim suggestion,
And meaning deep is slow to plumb :
So clients, watching long the dumb,
Too late approving, may chance one,
When best of life and chance is gone."

TWELFTH BRIEFLESS.

" Yet while his loss is not to gain
Too quick approval of slow men,
Barrister green and budding bold,
    As spring in evolutive year,
May chills abide and sun behold
    Though dull in cloud, or dim through tear,
As, Goat and Waterbearer passed,
Upon the Sun the Ram buts fast,
And earth is in the balance cast.
For he knows, that hispid earth
Waxeth quick to pangs of birth ;
Taken now by sun to wife,
Out of death is bringing life :
Till what was and seems decaying
Shall up spring all maying.
Mind can raise as from the dead ;
Books can live to study wed ;
Thence rich saps of knowledge spring
Through our powers forth blossoming

Into action, organizing
Lives immortalizing.
So law's wrinkled maze of face,
He, perusing, heart of grace
Never losing, Courts frequents ;
While attorneys, his events,
On his life their shadows pour—
Never on his floor."

SECRETARIAL NOTE.

" We have to-night had quite a lively spurt,
On legal schools and practise casting dirt,
And law itself informing with disease—
Call it 'mere indigestion,' if you please.
So, while brave rivalry anticipates
Uncertain issue of impregnate fates,
' B ' briefless, often impecunious, knows
A studious joy, whose ardour leaping grows
To find a right for every tortuous wrong,
    And, for each ill Eve's taste of fruit may cause—
A generous bliss too little known to song—
    Appropriate good provide, or search in laws'
Black letter, real property, or crown,
Leading by meeting roads to sage renown.
Something for glory, nothing much for pay,
And more for country, many a soldier may
Discipline youthful hours, and peril life,
And throw a whole heart into mortal strife ;
One too a heart may stir, and feel with awe
Under the parchment hide of wrangling law.
And not Beranger, dumb with tears divine,
Aged twenty, failing 'Musa' to decline,
But apt with smiles to overrun dull cares,
And wed to simple words as simple airs,
Starving and dreaming, adding rhyme to rhyme
To be a people's poet for all time,
Ever more joyed in a Bohemian life,
Or was more generous in a world of strife."

Our waggish Secretary here suspends,
And with " Roi d'Yvetot " his minute ends,
Himself a kind of mob-and-legal swell
Amid disaster shouting, " All is well. "
In town I of such mingled pleasures taste,
And happiness of time, if lost, not waste.
Fatigue unknown, no obstacle of force,
Though tortuous the way, to stem the course,
I wide expanse of law would traverse, find
Honour and Lucy in a yielding mind ;
And yet both town and law to fly am fain,
Hope's sweet suspense not destitute of pain ;
Would know proud Lucy's smile meant surer bliss ;
Would hear her say she loves, and ten times kiss,
All Venus rushing into me to sip
Her own quintessenced nectar from that lip,
Which knows so well, no Nisian better knows,
How loving upon amorous to impose.

Fresh scented, bright tinted,
  And tuneful at birth,
Spring loving breathes beauty
  All over lush earth:
But Lucy's last glance made
  Such May, that I feel
With fond memory more than
  Spring over me steal.
Cit-linnet uncaged now
  Would fly to broomed wild;
I too will fly thither
  To Lucy, who smiled.
More longed for is Lucy,
  To me far more dear,
Than to bird, tree, or flower is
  The Spring of the year.

CANTO V.

SPRING rampant upon downy bliss,
Rides in her bursten chrysalis
Flower-yoked to peacock butterflies.
Bees hum ; and zephyr rustling sighs
Through bloomy canopy of grove,
   Where mating birds are known
All gurgleful of poignant love,
   That minds me of mine own,
Which yet is no mere fount, but tide
   Profound as ever tossed,
While hopes upon its heavings ride—
   Float, trembling but not lost :
Never old man by sweet Hymettus hill
Had lips of speech so full its depths of sote to spill.

Noble thorns, donning liveries green,
   Strew snowy blooms o'er fervid Balders ;
Winds wooful hazel-tassels preen ;
   Streams ripple fluttering bashful alders ;
To lambs the white and purple clovers
Are dear, as roses unto lovers ;
Cowslips teach nightingales to sing ;
All nature honours passing spring.
Balls golden glow on willow palms,
   And bees are humming pleased with them,
'Twas on Palm Sunday boys with psalms
   Welcomed Christ to Jerusalem ;
And delicately almonds flush ;
Redbreasts and blackbirds choir ; and thrush
Pecks Daphné berried now in wood
   By modest violet regaled,
Where primroses are rathe, and good
   Hyacinths blue as heaven unveiled,

And wall-flowers in lone forest-chase
Tottering ruin generous grace.

The cushats plain, and swallows twitter;
  Deserting heaven's own charms,
Sol hastes from Hesperidian glitter
  To melt in Ægle' arms.
Tint by diviner sorceress,
  I found my Lucy lonely,
And, opening in wilderness
  A heart that held her only,
Called her not "Lucy"—body she,
And soul, my being is to me.
And when her heart in turn she bared,
And heaven the treasure with me shared,
Not Koil e'er to Lotus trilled,
  Nor river unto ocean rolls
With longing true and full as filled
  Swift currents of our mingling souls.

Simplicity straightforward more wins heart,
Than doth more wily glide of serpent art
Concealing under flowers, or disabused
Innocent lying artfully confused;
And nothing holier in life is done,
Than plain confessing of true love to one.
Speechlessly full in under-grottoes, ocean
Tongues upon open shore effuse emotion.
What says the towering billow turgiose,
Extended now on shore and hugging close?
Surely, "Upon thy breast I happy lie,
And from it lapse, to it again to hie,
Rather than quite relapse would wholly die."
Something of this I said, but last: for first
I spoke, with unpremeditated burst,
My therefore best, simplest, and most sincere,
Winning consent of heart through sense of ear:
While songful boughs made covert chaste
For blisses gathering in haste
To bind and crown pure vows of love,

As angels congregate above
When shriven souls return to God,
Or like Auroras, when abroad
They streaming wave and whirling dance,
Investing space with shafts, that glance,
And tremulous round of radiance flaming—
    All shapes and hues of vivid light,
As though some great event acclaiming,
    Paradise won from a Walpurgis night.

And, piteous parting to delay,
How far we strayed romantic way
All human eyes and ears beyond,
As Henry with Fair Rosamond
Into retreatful solitude,
Nothing I noted, till we stood
In centre lone of craggy dell,
Where, some say, fairy people dwell :
Love, azure wings there tranquil folding,
And not one honest joy withholding,
Boldened her upright soul to sing,
Its aspen joys still quivering,
Singing so, winged faces peer
Crowding out of heaven to hear.

LUCY'S SONG.

" In Eden day was a blushing rose,
As bright it opened still bright to close ;
We Eden find, wherever we rove,
In the rosy glow and light of love.

" He, bearing always a torch rose-flamed,
Can rose just lightnings unerring aimed ;
And not to faults, nor to virtues blind,
With rosy ardours make night most kind.

" Life only glad is in love-light liven,
All showers mating with bows in heaven :
My heart would break could it think to see
A future beat in it false to thee."

Haunting me still with latest breath,
That melody, unhushed by death,
Seemed holier than Canute felt
When, as his oars in water melt,
Monks chant, till he would fain again
Row by the cloistered banks of Nenne.
Reynolds of fear, Wolsey of pride,
But first the souls within them, died :
May divers deaths our loves assail,
Hers die of pride, through fear mine fail?
I tremble for so tender love
Timid as deer, which feeding rove.
As when ripples come and go,
I responsive sing and low.

EDWARD'S PRAYER.

"That neither may the other snare,
Uplift us, God, beyond my prayer
And perfect our imperfect loves
To be as thine own carrier doves,
Loosed from thy cote with heavenly messages,
Of everlasting life fond presages,
So cooing, that we cannot but appear
To one another in Thyself folle dear."

My doubt began her eye to fill.
Was never seen so lovable
Reproach with tear bedewed, till gay
She smiled the tender woe away,
And for all answer, in her arms
Smothering my undefined alarms,
Kissed me, exalted heaven-high :
Oh ! never heaven looked so nigh.
Love opened not alone our ears
To choiring dance of hidden spheres,
And vacancies aerial even
Brimmed to the full of hopeful heaven,
But universal nature scored,
And through our souls the rapture poured ;
While gliding fell from twilight skies

F

The mystic dews of Paradise,
Light as may drop from oars that soon,
  When night hath quite excluded day,
Shall speed the Trireme of the Moon
  Across the Milky Way.

When Lucy I to love began,
  So cold she was and scornful,
Earth flowered not or with rue, and wan
  Waters made music mournful ;
Air dumb was, or birds mocked my pain ;
  Fires shone from dim suns coldly
On one who loved, but loved in vain—
  Who loved, but loved too boldly.
Now all things with her love combine
  To make and give me pleasure ;
The bee knows nothing so divine,
  Mute spoiling flowers of treasure ;
The lark, which heaven's own cherubs move
  To sing, to them all round it :
For neither ever knew the love,
  That broke my heart and bound it.
No net of Vulcan could more take,
  Or hold me unaware ;
I would not through the meshes break,
  I know not they are there.
Hearts, born to love, which freely do,
  Then only truly free,
Compassing space, like Comets true,
Confess their suns : Saints never knew,
When tranced in beatific view,
  More utter liberty ;
Nor he, the plumiped divine,
Winnowing upper hyaline.
To Cupid bearing Psyché, while
Heaven oped with universal smile.

High up now in heaven sate Luna, that loved—
  A queen, loved Endymion,

And, though pallid, not cold looked : for orb, full of love,
  Was burning behind her throne,
As we fitfully wandered by oceans frow marge
  On sands smooth and fair as was sea ;
And frownced ripples bright whispered how gentle they were,
  And stars flocking all smiled to me.

EDWARD sings.

  "Oh ! calm is ocean, Lucy,
    And fair is heaven above,
  Which bending, smiling o'er it,
    Has filled it full of love ;
  Calm too my spirit as ocean,
    Rejoicing inwardly,
  It is full of love to Lucy :
    For Lucy is heaven to me."

But the tide ever higher rose driving us back,
  Like throned Canute, from drowning strand ;
And up the frayèd ripples ran gleeful and kissed
  Our footprints out of the sand.
Full to brim was heart mighty of ocean, its lips
  Lifting heavenward their low sweet moan,
Up adoringly drawn to implacable Lune,
  Who loved only Endymion.

EDWARD sings.

  " Such murmur as of kissing
    Is 'twixt the sea and land,
  Soft ripple-lips of ocean
    And fair smooth cheeks of sand,
  That I, soon finding Lucy,
    Who is not far to seek,
  Now overflow with kisses
    Her happy dimpling cheek."

And though ocean is mighty and gentle far moon,
  Yet by moon so controlled is sea,
It lies like a babe there, and plays at our feet,
  Moon and stars all smiling to me ;
At my side too Lucy is happy, and God

Smiles also on this hour ;
So native is power to gentleness,
  And gentleness to power.
Bright smiles ever new, of each other in chase,
Phosphoresce all dim shadows of night on her face :
Sunrise may be rapture, daylight may be bliss,
Sunset may be glory—but none rival this.
Yet lack lustre Luna with quieter gladness
  Fills the universe near to excess of a sigh ;
And my bliss, strong as Una, knows somewhat of sadness,
  As faint passes shadow of change with " Good-bye."

    Surely from life, and on the spot,
      Mixing bright colours with a tear,
    Truth painted Millais' Huguenot,
      Black Brunswicker, and Cavalier.
    Gay suns and worlds have partings too ;
      Only to change can time be steady :
    But dearest hearts are then most true,
      At call of honour instant ready
    For Gorgonlike Abantiades,
    For Nasebys, Waterloos, or Hades,
    Not sacrificing love to fame,
    But preferable death to shame.

    And only two we parted there,
    But each the other's truth can swear.
    Charity's milk makes love robust ;
    Honesty can to honour trust ;
    And chords, uniting mutual hearts,
    So draw together, whom space parts,
    Most drawing aye the widest parted,
    And, binding still the broken-hearted,
    To Egan's heart-of-Erin knit
    One to the grave drawn after it.
    Thus Lucy in thought is
      Still present to cheer me,
    As the sun still in star shines earth's night to dispel
    With my heart she inwrought is,

Her love is as near me,
As dear voice of old ocean still sounds to far shell.
Yet at my lattice lone I mind,
As wild my harp has caught the wind
   Struggling through its strings with wail,
How I had heard the cuckoo sing,
Auguring ill so ushering spring,
   Before the nightingale.

EDWARD *to his Harp.*

" Harp of Æolus, unholy
   On so sweet an eve thy strain
Full of, full of melancholy,
   Wherefore do thy strings complain?
Hush.   Now hushed, no more deep sighing
   Zephyrs through their mazes fly ;
Still I hear their echoes dying
   Or themselves in fancy sigh.

" Wherefore, when the soul is purely,
   Deeply, truly, sweetly blessed,
Must it also sad be ?   Surely
   'Tis a sorry bitter jest,
Or a melancholy madness ;
   But each sweetest thing will sigh ;
Sweetness hath a sister sadness :
   For the sweetest thing must die—

" Die the soonest though the rarest,
   As in winter hours of May,
Seldom come they brightest, fairest ;
   And they never never stay.
Harp of Æolus, most holy
   On so sweet an eve thy strain
Full of—full of melancholy ;
   Take it up, O ! harp again.
If larklike song to dawning light,
Nenia is due to-night."

I duskily now townward hie,

On wings of steam vehicular fly
To be absorbed in hope and search of spoil
Beyond attainment of perfunctory toil.
Born in fourth lunar quarter was my ease
Under one planet with strong Hercules,
Who, no Achilles, would near Rotten Row
Be labourer out of place : I never go.
Love-labour is so hard if kindly sort,
I have no time to look on idling sport.
Yet vain my labour, though without recess,
Although iced Hecla never slumbered less,
Briefless, without an opening for advance,
Save facile accident ; would such might chance.
Out of the world should some weak erring switch
Leaders off rails on circuit rudely twitch,
Juniors would by opening prospect thrilled,
On case advising, vouch them all, " Well killed."
Cupid himself to bar called, luckless child,
Might weary waiting, and, appalled, wax wild ;
Long road to fortune finding blocked, essay,
Scorning all aid of time, to clear quick way ;
With arrows sure pierce many a senior gizzard ;
And hang for murder then, the minim wizard.
So cynically pondering, I strayed
In Temple Gardens washed by Thames, and prayed,
That I might rather suicide commit
And drown myself, than get such perquisite.
Then in my note-book, to contrast the scenes,
Rapid I sketched them—Cupid in his teens
Shooting down Erskine, Follett, many more
Here named not, it would make them feel so sore :
Thereafter, heels to heaven, my lofty aims
And downward head stuck in the mud of Thames
I traced, and then another on the bank
Heartily laughing at me as I sank—
A friend of whom I stood not much in awe,
Who questioned with his eyes the things he saw.

A Canon of St. Paul's, a sage divine,

Who, friend of Lucy's father and of mine,
Had both of us baptized, in us retained
An interest unfailing as unfeigned.
Once for the bar he read, but soon withdrew,
Thinking in church to find the good and true.
The ills of law had caused his soul unrest ;
These he to me at times too forcibly confessed.
By him invited, Lucy came to spend
In the great city days too soon to end.
At Temple Church we on the Sunday met,
And after service I, with cute regret
That she our friend had brought, its story told ;
They in my chambers lunched, and he waxed bold.
Free thought was his excuse for speech at need
Beyond strict bounds of custom and of creed.
Sketches of Cupid shooting, and of me
   Committing suicide, which Lucy saw,
Her laughter drew him to her side to see ;
   He smiled, and thus splenetic spoke of law.

CANON.

" Blest he who has for entering court no cause,
Save wish to scan fine features of sage laws—
Some Ellesmere face."

LUCY.

   " Say, Edward in his gown,
And wig, not all of course his very own."

CANON.

" Edward will do ; though conscientious praise
Is due the legal face, not shifty ways.
Knavery drives in law's state coach-and-six
Through best intentions, drawn by shrewdest tricks,
And over-runneth justice in the breach.
Unlooked for circumstance, imperfect speech,
Spite lavish fortunes waste on points of doubt
Too small for men or mice to fight about.
Whatever law forbiddeth not, we try

Turn it to ill advantage well awry ;
Even governments wrest law to factious uses ;
Religion, order oft are state abuses."

LUCY.

" But bad is wind, that bloweth good to none ;
The lawyer profit makes, and frugal fun.
And next to being lucky one to lead,
It must be good to hear him forceful plead ;
Erskine or Follett, grandly different
Each nobly leading to approved event."

EDWARD.

"There are who parliamentary renown
Above forensic eminently crown ;
But breathes not God from any Pitt or Fox
More Orpheus into stolid hearts of rocks,
Than from the man who innocence defends,
And argues law for honourable ends."

CANON.

"Yet what is law ?   Not justice, and I shame
To think it reason, or by other name
Than ' Pluto-crazy ' to design what comes
Of beating Judge and Jury tympanums.
Statutes fix nothing ; custom varies worse ;
Law-equity is still the longest purse.
Juries and Judges seem to hold the reins,
But argument so muddles all their brains,
That not a fact or law to guide remains.
Verdicts in doubt, new trials are decreed ;
Wealth wins, which longer may than penury plead ;
And usurpation by bad law, wealth, might,
Against all public good makes private right.
Even general principles, elastic strong,
Cannot be stretched to an exceptional wrong ;
And suitors must dishonoured feel, who find
Their special right on principle declined.
Strange that profoundest, widest, wisest law,

In finite matters active, seems to flaw :
For general good heaven, freezing winter's marrow
And sleety weeping, starves the poorhouse sparrow."

LUCY.

" Counsel, a man of mind by matter bought,
His brief his only right, and proof sole thought,
Good counsel, errs not when by facts a cause
He proves to be according to our laws,
Right being as is proof, and all belief,
Beyond proved facts, unrighteous as a thief."

EDWARD.

" Would any man his fellows so entrust,
As let them look beneath fact's surface crust?
All knowing God below may scan the right,
But in surmise law sees estray of night ;
And legal honour has no other bar
Than facts and laws, however bad they are.
Here moral right or wrong can nothing stint :
Even should stubborn conscience prickly hint
The partial facts to be impartial lies,
Our leader burketh unavailing sighs ;
Nor less his joy and mine when awkward facts
He, leading forth, so marshals, that each acts,
All logically linked, his case sustaining,
And argues unto point of timeous gaining,
Legal, not moral ; factually wins,
Careless of lawless moral hidden sins,
Which heaven only knows.   It would not pay
To wait for latent facts The Judgment day ;
By things unproved, unknown though likely shown,
To stultify or falsify things known ;
Make right and wrong mere pensioners of chance,
And truth to be a bubble of romance."

LUCY.

" By human laws, that judge within their ken,
He not at bar of God wins, but of men,

Who do their little best, confess their faults
And think humanity, not justice, halts."

CANON.

"Watching some clever spider weave
    To catch each vagrant fly of thought,
From strenuous morn to limber eve
    In court I sit, at times distraught
By matters crowding mote-like small
As Lilliputs, who a giant seize,
Or snuffs, which only make him sneeze,
    Yet under laws that govern all:
Occasionally pondering, to wit,
How, frightened to a jelly or a fit,
Brow-beaten witnesses know what to tell,
Or judge and counsel never overswell
Their own and justice' tempers, till they flaw
In too ungoverned zeal for gain or law—
Vide Judge Lamson versus Sheriff Gray,
Which courtliest in manners, who shall say?

EDWARD.

" Once Tenterden so pondered, and in youth
Exalted satire as free-lance of Truth."

CANON.

" Satyrs rude valets were of gods : we claim
For human satire straight descent from them.
The Satyr, Myron's Marsyas, was fain
    To lift the lute Athéné cast away ;
And who, that knows what we by satire gain,
    Will doubt the wisdom which now lets it play ?
Sixth Adrian thought he would Marphorio
And Pasquin bold in yellow Tiber throw,
But stayed, when warned how all the frogs might croak ;
Had burned them, but a Cardinal wiser spoke,
"Their dust will flying bite the world's wide eye,
And partisans aroused for vengeance cry."
Therefore Marphorio and Pasquin lived.

EDWARD.

" So let all clever satires be reprieved.
For good are pungent scent and taste
  Not to be eaten up of gnats ;
Chester put arsenic in the paste,
  And paper giants saved from rats."

LUCY.

" Young Dizzy too was guilty of contempt
  Not really of court, but advocate,
And said, ' Such should not hanged be, but well hemped
  For bounce extravagate.' "

I winced not, though the Canon roared :
Lucy a hit had surely scored.
Yet whether he, or I was it,
Surpassed the fathom of my wit :
Perchance she both of us had meant to hit,
And had him there, though he perceived it not—
To be discovered in an after thought.
For nothing know I bounceful more than is
So learned opinion, save that thundering quiz
As the " Times " posturing well.   We parting then,
The sad to-morrow took her home again.

But leisure, with sport now concurring.
  Solicits shy birds to be slain ;
Moors lonely alive are, and stirring
  Hid partridge under close grain ;
Where uplands in open heaven wander,
  And lowlands by zephyrous sea,
And wild reeds, than Syrinx fonder,
  Woo Pan to melody.
Lucy beckons to fly the city ;
  Cares vanish while I obey,
As mists in sun-smiled pity
  Meltingly fade away,
And this involuntary ditty
  Makes my compartment gay.

EDWARD *sings.*

" Fancy, still young, has never ceased
    To deem Hesperian islands blest;
Even to find his golden East
    Columbus sailing steered due west.
My heart is in the west too, there
    At home, and not with maidens here;
Treasure I find and pleasure, where
    The maiden lives to me most dear.
Though suns in Nipon orient rise,
    They run to win the occident,
Nor spacious round of steepy skies,
    Nor clouds opposing may prevent;
And running west am I with Sun,
    But to more pleasing Nereid arms
Than shall receive, when day is done,
    And welcome him to blushing charms.

" Machin, for love of Anna haled
    To prison by her lordly sire,
Escaping, France-ward with her sailed;
    But, westering in tempest dire,
Discovering Madeira isle,
    They feeble landed—she to die,
Nor did he long survive her smile,
    Though under so benignant sky.
Thence gods and men gold apples shook
    Through long milleniums too brief;
And Hercules himself partook
    From dragon-tree of Teneriffe
Late felled by winds, by fires consumed,
    Fresh story of it still survives:
So fruit our loves may tardy doomed,
    And still in song outlive long lives,
Both God and man of us possessing part,
Our souls with God, with man our truth of heart."

Not all of the Muses, the Nine indeed
    With Echo could utter my beautiful maiden.

Ah ! would that an Angel from heaven might read,
And touching the chords of my heart to my need,
   Would render the music with which they are laden.
For sure my love is in my heart
Music of overpowering art,
Such as Israfel, the Angel, makes,
   Who, heavenly legends say,
Is skilfullest, and captive takes
   All hearts that hear him play ;
Yes, an Israfel harmony is she,
And every feature a melody.
I feel her in the air as round her home
In the decline of day I aimless roam,
And wonder, " Is she conscious I am come ? "

Twilight dims Luna's full fair face,
Which brightening draws night on apace.
Round it, now dazzling my fixed gaze,
There grows and dwells a darkening haze
Descending on a cloud below—
A snowy cloud still all aglow—
Where loose it spreads like locks of night
Dishevelled on a bosom white.
Rising to the supreme occasion,
Fancy completes a new creation.
An emanation grand of air,
Systaltic breathing, I image there,
My maid, her most divine of faces,
Her radiant cheeks, her raven tresses,
Her snowdrift bosom swelled in breasts
Ambrosial as Olympian crests.
The while Immortals, crazed to wed,
Are gazing on my dearest dread,
Whose robe descends to wormlike me
Kissing her feet.   All this I see,
And is unworldly music played,
Else might I not create that maid ;
For an Israfel harmony is she,
And every feature a melody.

The lyre of Orpheus, starred 'mongst stars, whose dance
It stringful leads, and holds the gods in trance,
She holds, and songfully appears,
As she choirs with the seraphic spheres,
The lovely legend too of lay
Conducting their effulgent way.

LEGEND OF THE LAY.

"Follow us ; we light the road,
And are marching on to God."

CANTO VI.

IN palaces by Pallas piled
Let Pallas dwell,.we roam the wild,
Where equal gods have loved and sported,
And Dardan Paris long resorted,
And lion findeth wolf, wolf goat,
    Goat flowering Cytisus, I pleasure
In Lucy, whose surpassing sote,
    Dispensed to me, is my full measure.
There shades indifferent are blind,
    And for all common use too lone ;
There winds are soft, and beams are kind—
    Sole smiles and sighs save lovers' known
In woods, which over hill and valley
    Unanimous and secret run,
While, now and then with sudden sally
    From warbling shade to lyric sun,
Pour purfled streamlets undefiled
As purest note in wood and wild.
Not Cephalus more proud approved,
E'er jealousy so fatal moved,
Not happier woods with Procris roved—
Kew Arboretum out to play

"Over the hills and far away,"
Wood-sanctuary, world of arches,
Incloistered glades, and open marches,
Beech, birch, ash, elm, lime, sycamore,
Oak, chestnut, larch, pine, poplar hoar,
Hazel, and alders where the rivers pour,
Rude rock, rough grot, rilled brawling fall,
And graces unadorned adorning all.

With Lucy vagabonding there,
Social in solitude, I hear
The chorus of Humanity,
    Although in ready rhyme,
The order of the passing day,
    And feeling of all time.

CHORUS OF HUMANITY.

" Happy the hours, when hearts at ease
Wish to be pleased and want to please,
And none but feelings, that are kind,
Control the play of mind with mind.
Life's cogs and wheels, all oiled, begin
With light'ning rapture round to spin.
Credible augury to youth
That care is dead now in good sooth,
A sense of perfect recreation
Crows in babes of the fourth generation,
While eld in myrtle crowned appears,
Unburdened by distressful years,
Dreaming no more of plumes and hearses,
 And sings, ' Of Ætna I am Thyrsis.'
Harmony sheathes the seraph's sword,
Paradise is to man restored.
Earth, as she ought to be, at last
Through Lethé and Eunoé passed,
All sadness from her bosom shaking,
    Ambrosial nectar quaffs,
And round God's heaven dances breaking
    Into a thousand laughs."

From Paris, while stern judgment nigh
Still lingered in the pitiful sky,
To England, embassied by France,
Journeying, as though in a romance,
Linked with associates choice and true,
Even Talleyrand such moments knew.
But love to spirit, sun to blood and clod,
Are vicegerents of Eternal God ;
Sun, constant fire and kindly day
   To dark chilled worlds bright power sole
Enlivening us and them, as they,
   Controlled to dance, around it roll ;
And love, joy-maker, more than Sun,
All hearts embracing, and of twain making one ;
By love and sun to frolic led,
Mercurial man and Cyprian maid,
Free, wandering intermissive shade,
With whole extatic souls invent
Some uttermost abandonment.
Join innocence, and never throb
So-ever wild shall cause a sob :
The crystal pure will, nothing shy,
Focus the glow of Phœbus' eye ;
More than on heart of altar shine,
Will kindle there a flame divine.

Great Montmorenci blushed to carry
Jean d'Albret much too young to marry :
I dry o'er brooks lift Lucy's way,
   Blessing the brook so happy crossed ;
Her feet the bog unshaken stray,
   And leave no print on fields embossed,
Saffron, and scented camomile,
And everlasting love, which smile,
And daisies, blushing as at dawn
When swallows sweep the dewy lawn—
They spring with tint and taint more sweet
From nimble trip of lissom feet ;
Her step now breaking into dance,
Her curve of neck, and sidelong glance

Taught by her swans, when, rippling the lake,
They, with obeisance food to take,
Superfluitant lilies shake.

We heaths have culled, and thymes, and bells
Blue, succories, and asphodels,
Mayweed, spurrey, and mignonette,
  Elecampane, and marigold,
And Codlings-and-cream, and not forget
  A water-lily, pure if cold,
And agremony, and parnassian grass,
  And with them a golden rod combine,
And she is careful not to pass
  Rare and purple Helleborine.
Pines overhead, we sit on rock
Hard by source sacred, which with shock
Headlong from higher pool to lower
Allays us with invisible shower.
Far hooteth owl, but lark on high
Warbles, and finches answer nigh,
And turtle plaintive coos for us,
Bees golden circling with a buzz
Waters petillant at our feet,
And autumn breathing largest sweet.

There in not shadeless Edenwold,
Reposing from adventures bold,
Most seemlily I Lucy crown
With daisies of hope's fair renown—
Flowers, daint as Anasuya kind
In glossy hair of Sita twined,
If wild yet pure, more choice a quest
Than gems on hand, wrist, neck, or breast.
A Flora over meads with Spring
Tripping light when birds first sing,
Or young rustic Queen of May
Blushing under eyes-of-day,
Seems she, like Alcestes true,
Turned into a daisy too ;
And she rosily crowned me,

G

As Liesce her own Deduit.
Wild flowers all to heaven owe :
'Tis why lovers love them so.
I see one from the water's brink
   Reflected in the water's glass :
The image seems to rise, not drink.
I close my eyelids, just to think
What flower it is ; a single wink,
   When, living wonder to surpass,
It takes another form of lymph,
And now appears to me a nymph.

NYMPH OF THE WILD FLOWER.

" On finger, wrist, neck, ears, and hair,
   And robes, encrusted down to shoe,
Lollia Poulinas gems may wear
   Worth half a million, which some owe,
And move with light Crotalian clang,
As though themselves were bells, that rang,
Or billows far, that rippled o'er
Playing with gems, they washed ashore :
Ruthless as Alva, who once found
Peruvian mines on Belgic ground,
May indolently cruel boast
On Cingalese or Persian coast
For each dear pearl some diver lost ;
May noble brows and tresses fret
Neath velvet-lined gemmed coronet,
Or diamond tiar seeming morn
Glittering on crown of dew-dropped thorn,
Though in Brazil three hundred miles
Lie wasted where such mirage smiles :
But what hath lovely worldly woman,
Patched spotted vanity, in common
With flowers, whose seeds owe nought to earth,
Save death preceding heavenly birth ;
Whose purity must sweetly linger
Cultured by never mortal finger ?
God's hand alone hath wrought and nursed

And taught the bud to blow and burst ;
His breath in gentle fragrance dwells ;
  In simple bloom his smile is given ;
And elegance unconscious tells
  Of art divine and dews from heaven :
And who should rival daisied sod,
Save such fresh modest child of God
As Lucy is, who might have been
  A shepherdess, in old Bretagne,
Crowned by her swain upon the green
And harping to him, or such queen
  As was to Lewis noble Anne ?
Raising a blush on young Victoria grand,
As knelt the royal uncles to her hand,
Humility and modesty conspired
To make her Queen of Hearts, all bosoms fired :
Not crown nor Kohinoor so charmed,
But maidenhood by virtues armed."

Seeing such virtue in my Lucy's face,
I on her breast the flower attracted place,
And dream that it is happy there :
Nothing may touch her but a thing so fair.
Alas ! methought a stag turned full ;
Or did I see a raging bull,
Or was it not a tiger fled
  From some menagerie ?
And flocks of sheep were lying dead,
  And herds of Kine ; and she—
It saw and sprang at her I love.
  I on the instant leapt between,
And with the monster bleeding strove,
  When from a friendly hand unseen
A shot passed whizzing. With a yell
Dead at my feet the tiger fell.
I swooned with uttermost of pain,
  And as I woke, oh, waking blessed,
And myself saw her face again,
  My head was on her lap at rest—

Not long.   A friendly stranger seemed
To raise me, but I knew I dreamed.
There nothing was, not even a snake,
To kill or brave for Lucy's sake,
Nor wound, nor stranger with a gun,
Nor sign, sound, smoke, nor smell of one.

Nor were we senselessly so " ceevil "
As deem our lips could meet for evil.
If in our cups there may be slips,
There is no lapsus in our lips—
Tongues do more damage far by trips,
And though no peril frayed my fair—
No seven-headed dragon there,
Whose force with valour to attaint,
And act the Knight, if less the Saint,
Still helpful I.   And Prospero,
The one-eyed Cyclops, louted not too low.
Ne'er knew he Bacchus with the Graces
So flower a way through desert spaces,
While each unweeting after-comer
Started to see long trails of summer :
She blessed each vague weird-sister waste
Her passage remanently graced—
A fable kernelling truth most sweet
   In polished shell of allegory.
Though nature blossomed not 'neath Lucy's feet
Kind flowers of thought shall, and to me repeat,
   Revisiting, the story
Of all we said and did in stress
Of idlesby's unruliness.

No more may young Arcadians chase,
Insulting, o'er this desert space ;
Sacred to bliss, may nothing daunt,
But nymphs and graces hither haunt,
Venus conduct their dance to end,
And no blood-letting thorn offend ;
Never distracted Cian rites,

In search of Hylas, storm these heights;
Never disconsolate lover here
Cause sympathetic oak one tear,
Or pity-smitten rock to gush,
But all be folatry and hush.

So witless or of time or weather,
We roamed mid-wilderness together
Bewraying not heart-depths, that stole
Down profound channels broad of soul,
Soothingly full of speechless love ;
   With words that dance, and thoughts that flower,
And tongue and spirit playing, strove
   To please each pauseless minute of the hour.
While Lucy's many-sided mind,
   Varied in stores as powers of thought,
So brilliant flashed, I could not find
A lightning to express the blind
   Dumb wonder that it in me wrought,
As we together read with praise
The volumes, nature open lays
Enchanting so our dear unrest,
Not the less wise for being blest.
Thus too I, e'er we further fared,
The Voice of Nature inly heard,

VOICE OF NATURE.

" Now alpine climbers, travellers—faithful wives
And sisters head the roll of noble lives.
On games Olympic, famed of yore,
Argesil, foul contempt to pour
And with a female victor end,
Procured Cynisca to contend.
Winning, she woman crowned, and shames
Manly competitors, not games.
Where white horsed Dioscuri rode
   At Lake Regillus, charging close,
Hoof-prints in stone Rome after showed,
   Since vanished : but Carshalton knows,

Refreshing still, a living source
Spring from where trod Anne Boleyn's horse.
Soft beauty, indolent as air
In August's palpitating glare,
On couch dissolving ; passionate,
Aglow with love, aflame with hate,
O'er fulsome tale of life high-wrought,
And yet low-bred ; her every thought
Sensation nursed, sensation thrilled,
Till earth seems heaven sublimed, or hell distilled :
Let her arise, walk, run, mount, ride,
Earth under-tread.   Each pace, each stride
Shall shake her fancy-free, and chase
The vapours too from Nature's face ;
In such old channels course her blood
As when God called his creature good.
From every step in open skies
Well-springs of limpid pleasure rise.
And far from fashion, far from folly,
Vice, misery, or melancholy,
Although with man, who loves to grow
Exotics in his heaven below,
And houri his seraglio,
Fond Lucy wanders, free and wild
God's daisy daughter, nature's child."

Bright Nature so with inspiration meet
Roused to fresh energy our forward feet
All was the land filled full of faierie,
  In rays of orthodoxy lingering motes,
When as fat friars here made prairie,
  And game of manikins, for God or groats
Blessing hill, dale, and heath and holt,
  River, holm, farm, barn, stable, kitchen,
Castle, and hall, door, lock, and bolt,
  And thorpe and town-land past bewitchen,
Till not a fairy might abide,
Save in far places lone and wide :
One such we knew, rare wilderness,

Too poor to beg of, or to bless.
There unoppressed with shadow,
  In unobtrusive glen,
Along insinuant meadow,
  Beyond all haunt of men,
Where kine are never driven,
  And pine-clad heights command,
While sun held high the heaven,
  We wandered fairy land.
Nature its happiest looked : each scent
  Elves found it heaven to quaff ;
Couched harmony awoke, content
  Only with eyes to laugh.

And life it was : for life is love—
  The life of all true good ;
And nothing in that glen, mead, grove
  To any sense was rude.
From humid cave now blowing,
  Dark Auster softly flew :
And fairy folk not showing,
  Yet there were happy too.
Like rustling leaves and merry
  Singing by day they danced,
As we with steps unwary
  Towards their round advanced.
The little people smiling
  Beheld us debonair,
Old time of scythe beguiling ;
  And Lucy was so fair.
Titania, hasting from high place,
Saluted more supernal grace,
While pigmy muses swept spare shells ;
Fairy-caps bowing rang dumb bells ;
Autumn in balmy breezes,
  Breathed profound blandishment ;
And all in day that pleases,
  Exulted—to repent.

Fat as lark Dunstable, canorous
As was Lablache, if less sonorous,
That fays their ring compact and whist
Some neat-herd Damon's song to list,
Herrick dreams : but he never folle
Had trespassed on a warlock knoll.
There sudden paled grave faces
  With passion deep and strong,
When, scorning their good graces—
  Invisible, though throng,
As Cross-bills on pines Pyrenean,
Or Gryliddæ in grass Crimean—
  'Mid them we sate on circle green,
And, making mountains of mole-hills,
Pried into secrets of small ills :
  For, since our troth had plighted been,
Came the first doubt.   It was a fairy ;
Angered at our intrusion there, he
Whispered it into Lucy's ear.
To me it almost seemed a jeer,
But thus she laughed—

LUCY.

      " They, Edward, say
That law is a long game to play,
Its winnings small, or won at last
When life is weary and joy past.
Heigh ho ! you see that I am growing
Very particularly knowing.
How many briefs now have you had, if any ? "
  Her hands ten-fingered she upheld,
As though to ask me, if so many.
  But to say " briefless " all my tongue rebelled,
Sang therefore this evasive song,
Sufficient answer if a trifle long.

EDWARD.

" Prop not I thy pride too much,
Lest it stiffen to a crutch ;
All my thoughts confess to thee,

Let all thine be given to me :
For thy dearest love might pall,
If thou gavest not it all,
And retained an unexpressed
Grudge in a discordant breast.

" Am I not myself enow ?
Must the world before thee bow ?
What might have enhancing smile,
May enticingly beguile.
Deem not flesh and blood I fear :
None to thee as mine so dear,
But with God I on the throne
Of thy heart must sit alone.

" God, love, good, are all as one.
Surely we have well begun.
Hope, we may each other grace,
Holds the heaven, I embrace :
May'st thou, looking through hope's door,
Turn yet from a heaven so poor ?
Answer not, I thee entreat :
All I hazard at thy feet."

But hope, though venturesome, was not so strong,
As in my shaky and untimely song,
No fitting sequel to the fairy's own,
  " Da Luan, da Mort, da Luan, da Mort."
Oberon shouting from his throne,
  Around him all his fays resort—
Bull-beggars, Kit-wi-cansticks, Urchins, Hags,
Hell-wains, Fire-drakes, Pucks, Bugs, and Boneless wags,
All spiteful minions learned in Oberon's tricks,
Crickets, Orlandos, Pigwiggins, and Pricks,
And who on Tita tend—Hops, Mops, Pips, Trips,
All frisking elves, skip-jacks, and wanton chips—
Inhuman spawn of sportive night, they may
Visit the lights and shadows of the day.
More than when waspish bees buzz all about,

Mysterious nature eerily puts me out.
Sure they were nothing but my silly fears ;
Though some may have been worse than now appears.

Not Bashikouay ants could in attack
Be dread, as so invisible a pack,
Though for the time averted.   The delay,
Unkindly purposed to augment dismay,
Eventuated happily in flight
From what we held in thought, if not in sight.
Fly thy small follies and their little struts :
Gulliver was o'ercome by Lilliputs :
One may unnoticed trip thee, and the rest,
That fallen instant, swarm upon thy breast.
Oberon, master of the revels, sought
To speak with me, who knew not of his thought.
When as he once with Huon spake
He blew his horn, so now with equal shake
He blows and thunders all the heavens rend.
   Not as to safe Olympus roaring fled,
Through gathering clouds, that ill intend,
   Mars wounded sore by Diomed,
But glad, as children freed from school,
With headlong haste and laughterful,
Not chased by such black dog as storming broke
Into the Church of Bungay, killing folk,
And trailed round Faustus' fire, that made no smoke,
Her home we gain
   In spite of storm,
Out-stripping rain,
   And in good form,
No care of double hump to sadden,
Like what weighed heavy on Jack Madden,
While grateful the recoiling door
Smart lash of rain complacent bore,
On eye of lightning closed and thunder roar.

Storms madden Lears, with bodeful croon
   Prostrate St. Chads, wrap Sauls in night,

But also lyre of David tune,
Thrill Burns with inspiration boon ;
  While love's ubiquitous delight,
Heavingly calm in reverent awe
Of vehemence controlled by law,
Knowing God ride on sorest storm,
An in-door paradise can form,
And multiply the happiness
With that enchanted board of chess,
Whereon fair lady always wins
The man, who once to play with her begins.

Up to the third heaven we are caught,
And modern and ancient thought
Dœdal—Icarus-ly explore—
One now behind, and now before.
Upon no foggy bank to strand,
Our spirits wing o'er sea and land ;
Now travel, leaving earth afar,
In comet course from star to star ;
Now drop down soul profundities,
Assumpt thence on philosophies
To view, from wisdom's heights sublime,
God, man, eternity and time.
Minerva, Venus, gods both, prove
Wisdom is female as is Love.
But, lo, the passing storm is overpast,
And sun possesses cloudless heaven at last.
Nor grudge I chess the game by Lucy won,
But, grieving it has been so quickly done,
I have no further cause for stay ;
  And she this afternoon shall go
To join a yachting party gay
  Headed by one, I little know ;
Alas, that little is too much
To know of any, but one such non-such.

Friend Canon had our town brief visit paid :
" Come yesterday, this morning goes," one said.

I met him going.   We of Lucy spake,
Or rather woman for dear Lucy's sake.

CANON.

" Arts, letters, science, commerce, trade,
Councils, professions court now woman's aid."

EDWARD.

" Frail she of old by her own genius fired
Oracular appeared as one inspired ;
Of nature but a weakling was believed,
Yet first by simples miracles achieved.
Felicia, wandering the fragrant mead,
   Knew every virtue of each root,
Herb, flower, stone, gems of various glede,
   And sorceries, men thought she could commute.
In fears and mysteries of Pan
Most deep instructed partisan,
King Henry Adeliza taught
Of all he had in Woodstook wrought ;
She with Albini loved to spell
The wilderness of Arun-dell.
And woman, now man's learned fere,
Prattles of flower, but also sphere.
The apple, which led Eve astray,
To Newton pointed nature's lawful way,
Where male and female equal walk to day ;
May yet on wings electric dare
To worst the very Prince of Air,
Each gay meridian patrol,
And hang love-garlands round from pole to pole."

CANON.

" La bella Eleanora held
The seal of England, and excelled.
Wessex might Queen's abolish, cast
On France an Offal one—at last
Graceless in Pavia to rot ;
But Gwendolen, though dead, still taught ;

Alfred survived in Ethelfled,
Nor is Elizabeth yet dead—
Victoria lives, and o'er our graves,
Britannia still shall rule the waves,
For whose brave purity with pride,
A Boadicea bleeding died.
And more as art makes weakness strong,
   And heart is honoured, growing wise
To rule itself and sway the throng,
   Mothers in Israel may rise ;
God, holding up a woman's hand,
May by Deborahs judge and rule the land."

EDWARD.

" Like Genii of caves retired
By echo of world-bruit inspired,
In rude and mediæval youth
   Of an impitiable earth,
In tower of strength, or cell of ruth,
Adelaides, Maries, Claires, in all good sooth,
Woman brought love and learning both to birth.
Dipping his brush in pitchy evil,
   Juvenal may, on purple ground,
Paint her more black than any devil,
   Solomon in his " legion " found ;
Yet in cute Greek have Jews evangels,
Where more than man she nears the angels.
A very sun our Northern woman is,
Light in her eye, and ardour in her kiss ;
Thunders of Odin slept in Friggas arms ;
Soothed Loki's ills were by Signaya's charms.
If frail was Adam's rib, twice human,
Thrice lost are we, men, born of woman ;
Our hearts she claims, nor can we bind,
By Salic law, her powers of mind."

I said and heard what doubtful may appear
   On worthless paper scrawled with common ink ;

And some may question, for I am no seer,
  What still to me is beautiful to think.
I further now the parting Canon asked
Concerning fairies, orthodoxy tasked.
On superstition casting slight and light,
He passes to my pen the verdict, I indite.

CANON.

" Men can no moment reckon to be theirs,
Yet cumber burdened powers with needless cares.
Their wits and wishes no true limit keep,
See in clear shallows an unfathomed deep ;
And though instructed, grounded, edified,
And stripped of early scaffolding, when tried,
The soul in all its being feels, ill-timed,
The past of being, out of which it climbed,
The superstitions of a bye-gone year,
The lightning heats of faulty hope and fear.
Small follies thus play most prodigious parts,
In corners dark of utter craven hearts,
While fancy has an ague-fit of dance
Upon the tremulous boards of ignorance.
A fairy sure is nothing but a spark
Out of man's folly flashing in the dark ;
But spark, though small, may fire a powder-train ;
A little folly scatters many a brain."

CANTO VII.

AFTER an hour of play with Sophocles,
Before my mind's eye rose two choruses,
Of Ancients one, seen now and heard with awe
  By Moderns answering ; and, though contrasting,
They complemental seemed controlled by law,
  And each a chant of the One Everlasting.

CHORUS OF ANCIENTS.

" Implicit fates to life's lone end,
On man and ruling Jove attend :
Veiled, but accompanied by hope,
They life to crowding mortals ope,
Whose fortunes are as Jove disposes,
  Some dropped like Melibœan Kids,
Others on mingled lilies and roses.
  Loves the lips kiss, and hopes the lids,
Unsealing only for a day ;
What the fates give, they take away.
Soon by their rapid coursers drawn,
Past dreaded night and looked-for dawn,
Beyond inquietude, we gain
Justice, and there with doom remain."

CHORUS OF MODERNS.

" But wrongs can ne'er by stripes be quitted,
Or, save by penitence, remitted
With loving words—God's highest Laws,
To give committal fullest pause.
And never good to be renied,
Was sparely lent, except to pride
That could conceive no love in God,
And only justice in His Nod.
All thanks are due for what is given,
And what renied allures to heaven.
Celestial spirits can do all ;
The dice of Jupiter always happy fall."

Of justice provident, fixed fate,
Doom, or a judgment coming late,
Small heed one roystering gallant took—
Nephew, but nothing more, of Duke ;
Soldier, but with no seaming scars,
Though soft at heart, and pinked as Mars.
To Lucy, more to him than glory,
In vain he told love's fresh old story ;

But deemed, frail pity yet might move
Gentle womanliness to love :
All various feelings are so kin,
To tears of goodness sighs of sin,
Which so of virtue thaw the ice,
It melts in tears of love for vice.

Owned he a yacht, light, dainty thing,
As ever skimmed, on canvas wing,
Irremeable path of sea,
More than delighted to be free,
As was its master, and to toy—
Trundling the world-round hoop of joy ;
Too pretty craft for ugly deed,
But swift and ready still at need,
As Arab bark on Sciote wave—
Eudora's altar pyre and grave.

Where secret up, or devious out
    Ran pirate cove in lovely error,
Half mile from town, or there about,
    The yacht lay, and, a pretty terror,
Giddy to sight and strange to thought,
Hung, keel to keel, its double yacht
Mid mirrored beeches, grasses, flowers,
Towering and pendant cliffs and bowers
    To perching crow minuter given,
All below appended to all above,
All poised, as by an equal love,
    'Twixt an over and an under heaven,
The sea, which should appear between,
So glassy as to be unseen.

That afternoon chance, guiding whim,
    Showed Lucy issuing nigh from wood,
And with her him.   Why only him,
    Whose cutter, wounding friendly flood,
And distancing reclaim of shore,
Out to the yacht my Lucy bore ?

Fair winds, caressing tremulous trees,
  Fill every spreading swelling sail.
The breath of God in happy breeze,
That bloweth all the world to please,
May serve a villain on the seas,
  And infamy prevail.

A groom, there lingering, I sought—
A country clown, his groom, distraught
With care for Lucy, as it proved ;
He had known her long as I had loved.
But love for her his master crazed,
Which had in him suspicion raised.
With much fair company to sail,
Had been his master's idle tale,
Over-persuading her I knew.
" It had," he said, " at first been true,
But falsified—" I cared not how,
Unknown to Lucy even now,
  Or only known, when now too late,
With what excuse he chose to make
Of chance suspense, or day's mistake,
  Embarked with him alone and fate.
" For Lundy Castle they are bound ;
By the coast-road some six leagues round,
Nearer across the buxom bay.
  Homeward to drive a drag attends ;
But," the groom smiles, " a night's delay
  And danger to avert impends.
Some screw a-loose, or other gier,
Some accident will hap, I fear."
Then rose that dastard to my view,
That evil man I vainly knew,
  And yacht receding now, like bark
Of gallant bearing, and brave show,
Whose timbers, we have learned to know,
  Lie rotting in the dark.
On Lucy's conquest madly bent,
No ill more cruel may be meant,

H

What cannot hours together do
Alone, and out on ocean too ?
What may not night avail, detained
In solitary shelter feigned ?
For so the story runs ; but then,
The last unutterable pain,
Should these no more advantage gain,
Repute may, soon a light-lied thing,
In after-fight show mammering.
Plot is it, whose infernal art
Must gladden all damnation's heart.

As maiden, who hath died in grace,
With speaking beauty on her face,
And quickly then embalmed hath been—
What some may fancy, but I have seen—
That beauty lives, and changeth not,
Fixed as her soul's eternal lot,
The spirit to hail with returning wraith
And the very look it left at death :
Even so my Being, sudden calmed,
Deeply seemed, lastingly embalmed,
With one intent that maid to save
Out on the weary waste of wave.
Lo ! out, still further out, far sail
Looks wing of bird on tail of gale :
Even should he round now, many a tack
Shall fetch him late to Lundy back.

Quickly to home and horse, away
Behind me soon the township lay ;
Villas, farms, moorlands, past I go,
Like breeze, and on its foremost blow.
And now above me, like a death,
Tall headlands awful frowned, but breath
I drew not : clearly shock on shock
Struck upon cold and infinite rock
With iteration—like a knell
Ringing out of an iron bell,

And sense of loneness, such as clung
Even to my soul so sternly strung,
As hoof on hoof I hurried by,
Nor glanced aside a forward eye.
The cape, which hid the yacht, I gain,
And, passing, then a moment rein,
Hope with fair prospect not to buoy,
  Nature to me was one eclipse ;
Blind I, as St. Bernard, to its joy :
But foam my steed, and for a toy
  Winds snatch it out of champing lips.
Sol has forsaken crimsoned west ;
Stars glimmer out of darkening east,
Whence shade creeps over heaven : and still
Those outward sails foul breezes fill.
She doubtless oft "Return" hath prayed ;
"A little further," he hath said.
Impatient still "Return" she cries ;
"The wind preventeth," then he lies.
Ha ! he hath rounded now, and, lo !
No longer foul, fair breezes blow.

O'er heaven and earth is shadow cast ;
  Only spare shimmer lingers yet,
Where lids of day are closing fast,
  Their lashes more than met.   ;
As loosened rock from hill-top sent,
  With furious speed away I went :
Darker than eve, a lonely sound,
With shock on shock and bound on bound,
It frighteth eye and stunneth ear,
So I, to any gazer near,
Distinct through all obscuring light,
Clangingly held a flashing flight ;
By startled farm, hamlet, that wondered,
With chanceful haste and reckless thundered ;
Back beat the panting earth, and still
On, heedless, passed wood, mansion, hill,
Bridge, crag, beach, precipice, and reined

At Lundy Inn. I stayed not, prating,
But man and phaeton apt retained,
    Drove, and the drag found ready waiting.
True story is that villain plot, ·
And not far distant now the yacht.

Almost an island in the flood,
The gloomy ruin frowning stood ;
It had not known, nor promised grace,
And looked a scar upon the face,
Even of that bleak and lonely place.
Awhile I walked a cooling mead,
    And kindlier grew the castle's mien,
Stout monument of many a deed
    Of bravery. I could have been
Enamoured of its very stones,
    Had they sole echoed knightly cheers—
Ah ! throats as well of murder's groans,
    And grimed, though hallowed now by years ;
And as they rose in gaping walls,
Lone towers, bare gables, sideless halls,
Strange groups apart, each indiscreet
Seemed, on its ever during seat,
Shaping such things as happened here—
Ghoul ghosts of deeds, which man should fear :
For good or bad the hand was ruddy,
That dipped in times, though bold, so bloody.

I had determined there to stay,
As I had chanced to ride that way,
And hearing of their coming thought
    Their company in driving back
Pleasant to me, if mine unsought.
Nearer and nearer drew the yacht,
    Night settling on its homeward track ;
So have I seen, for witless fly,
In nook of web grim spider lie.

While thus I watched, and land they neared—
I since have learned what then I feared—

She the deck quitting to her cost,
He followed, badly playing host.
As gambler, luckless in the past,
To win will honour lose at last,
So hours gone he had sought to please,
And warmer waxed by sure degrees :
For, as she chilled, he gathered flame,
   Till sick for home, and angered sore,
And fearful of an evil name,
   She barely now his presence bore,
And quit the deck.   Head lost as heart,
Dropping an ill-succeeding part,
His cloven foot began to show,
And hell looked ardent on her woe.

NOBLE SOLDIER.
" Behold me kneel, who never knelt
To man or maiden ; hard one melt,
And list the prayer-sigh of soul
Longing to know thy soft control.
I thee adore, and life each hour
Hold abject to thy gracious power ;
Take me, and make me all thou wilt.
Reject me, rather to the hilt— "
He touched a dagger there, that lay,
A foreign thing, for show or play—
" This weapon quiver in my breast,
'Twere living death to live unblest.
Already would my sun be set,
And in swift death I might forget."

Fool ! deemed he so that she would yield,
   And set all sail to gusts of breath ?
No idle dream, alas ! revealed,
   This fierce confession of false faith.
When he assumed her hand to grasp,
As poisoned by an angry wasp
Backward she stepping, trembling, shook
The creature off with quick rebuke—

LUCY.

" In an unseasonable chance,
    When time and place are an offence,
So eloquent is circumstance,
    Few words are asked of common sense ;
Rise, or for ever rid my heart."

Thus answered she with sudden art,
By terror taught of startled hour,
Alone and in the dastard's power,
To leave him not to blank despair.
    But vain her cunning, worse than vain,
Leading wild hopes to further dare,
    In trust of further gain.

NOBLE SOLDIER.

" Think twice ere you a knave discover,
And never blame an honest lover ;
There is no reason in thy fears,
    Since I nor foul, nor false to thee ;
Eyes are more critical than ears,
    Let us believe in what we see ;
Thy beauty is my love's excuse,
Lucy ; that love no more refuse."

Still temporizing was her cry,
    Though palm-like proud with head erect.

LUCY.

" Nor here, nor now, demand reply.
    My trust thou, failing to respect,
Hast it, and thine own honour broken."

NOBLE SOLDIER.

" Honour, nay, thou hast thoughtless spoken,
Shall honour legislate to love ?

Love has no laws, but gentle dove
And eagle fierce impulsive moves
  To call that hungry woos :
And shall our as irrational loves
  A straiter method choose?
Love unaccountable, self-willed,
  Gloweth in very worm and fly
Fired by a wish to be fulfilled,
A hope, no vitex ever chilled :
  Yet all are not so fond as I.
Did ever woman please all men?
God Himself cannot ; who may then?
Each in his several breast rejoices ;
Taste differentiates our choices ;
And thou art mine, and wouldest be,
Should heaven and earth for once agree,
And equally my cause disown.
  Love, its own heaven, can look up
To bliss it envies not, and down
On foes, which it defies, whose frown
  Can never dash a winning cup.
What feareth it save only ' Nay,'
And thou that word wilt never say."

LUCY.

" Yea ; for I never can be thine,"
Ah! she was only woman still,
Although with all a virgin's will,
  And trembled.

NOBLE SOLDIER.

" But thou shalt be mine
Sooner or later ; be it now
My lovely one, so dear art thou.
Be tender as surpassing dear :
Forget now, Lucy, we are here.
Think us ashore, Oh ! anywhere,
So thou art only loving there,
  And willing to be happy too.
Thee I would win, and wear as woo."

LUCY.

" Woo some one else, since lost on me
Wishes and words by land and sea."

NOBLE SOLDIER.

" Nay, love like mine knows no defeat.
Obstruction gives renitent heat,
Which swam broad Hellespont for love ;
Could gods contentious, Grecians move,
Cohorts and fleets, inflaming Troy ;
Later hath in impetuous joy
Each social bond, diviner link,
With Edwys sundered, and on brink
Of ruin or perdition found,
Wherever love was, holy ground ;
With Bevises for Josyans kind,
Discomfiting, chased hosts combined,
Brute and man monsters, sorcerers, fiends ;
And, upon reinless wings of winds
Riding Cleopatras to throne,
Worlds won, and dropped for love alone.
Venus reflects sole self-same ray
    In sunshine as by night,
Changed but in title ; and to-day
    Love hath its ancient might,
And will, while man shall man remain,
Its toils and triumphs prove again."

LUCY.

" Womanly triumphs, male defeats,
Powers female prove, if manly heats.
I would not have you lose in hope to gain
One, for whom you at least must sigh in vain."
She angered daring him to beard,
A frown upon his brow appeared.

NOBLE SOLDIER.

" Since then it must, it shall be borne
    In plainer words, than well may please,

How heeding not the coldest scorn,
  Which bliss has ardour to unfreeze,
Love hath a lofty innate force
To carry a resistless course,
Snatch to its breast the shrieking fair,
And worlds of angry matrons dare.
Tales thou hast read."
          But here he stayed,
Knowing to have himself betrayed,
 Changed countenance, and seeming sad,
" Forgive me," crying, " I am mad."
On deck rushed.   Lucy followed, there
Secure again in open air,
And, like lone dove from ark abroad,
Beholding land anigh praised God.

As on sea-rock, when day is past,
  A booby foldeth mighty wings,
The yacht with gear of bow, boom, mast,
  And spar, and rattling falls of rings,
Gathered the canvas, as it shook ;
Yet all to me more image took
Of spectre on its own grave-stone
Dropping the shroud from its skeleton.
As from such vision surely creep
  Wild somethings to the gazer's soul,
Advancing boat-ful oars the deep ;
Attendant unto shore I leap,
  While hours in minutes seem to roll ;
And now it touches.   Never I
Shall lose the fragrance of her sigh,
The revelry in Lucy's eye,
The rapture which confessed me there,
  And took my hand, and leapt ashore ;
Oh, it made heaven and earth too fair,
  And told of love for evermore.

And when I said how I had waited,
  She " In kind charge myself receive."

Then turning to that soldier rated,
 "Your yacht demands you, and I leave."
Proud was her mien ; her parting bow
Looked haughty. "I am mistress now
Of self at least, and as for thee
Be thy defeat thy misery."
And such it was though lightly shown
By mock humility alone.
For in his eye a wicked light,
 A burning pallor on his face,
A tremour brief of lip and slight,
 Discrediting much manly grace,
Falsified quite all humble show ;
And while they told of inward woe,
Love, anger, hate, all three in one,
A tempest not without some sun,
Revealed in more than words of wind
The dangerous outwitted fiend.
Lost, worse than lost, the chance contrived,
So opportunely I arrived.
Though night might have lost day retrieved,
I had of hope even night bereaved.
One glance on me he bent so filled
 With concentration of all hate,
Sure if it could, it would have killed ;
 And back on him I glanced its mate.

With Lucy by my side, I drove—
The very horses ran for love,
Happy to speed her timeous home.
Little she said.   Her mind would roam,
Natheless all effort, to the scene
Where she had late a trembler been ;
Though nothing now her lips revealed,
They could not be to a mother sealed.
I trust not quite the mother, not to say, blame ;
Love has in mutual hearts oft kindlier flame
Than burns in kindred ones, which more profess,
Yet, more self-seeking, falsely render less.

Some, while most seeming amiable, are
  As sleek and purring venerable cats ;
Nor try, nor trust them ; even the dancing bear
  Will sometimes hug to death, or kill with pats.
But here in night—for night descended—
  Heaven, air, and earth, and placid sea
And stars, inextricably blended,
  All deep in love seemed one to me,
While Nereus' daughters azure-eyed
Floated with Halcyons by their side.
Her thoughts from wandering would return,
  And flow in words of such sweet leave
In such kind accents, that I burn
  To lengthen out the slender eve.
Then I—

EDWARD.

  " Indefinite longings, springing
  Ever in yearning breast of man,
Are not in vain, good tidings bringing,
  Convincing that soul never can,
Be dust, which unto dust returneth,
While, longing so, it ever burneth
With inextinguishable thirst
For something God hath never cursed,
And sends warm core forth in desires
That seem like deeds, though sometimes fires
Blazing and going out in night.
Oh ! yet man hopes for strange delight,
When wishes shall have act, express
  Most instant will of consequence,
With nothing human in excess,
  Command accordant providence,
That so he may all future harm
For ever and a day disarm."
Then Lucy—

LUCY.

  " Love has stirring life,
And, with its weakness most at strife,

Fain would from heaven the power acquire,
Which there is native to desire,
So soon as thought, each bliss to throw
Around a Pysche's pleasing woe ;
Each adverse chance at wish unsting,
And make her instant sorrow sing;
Cause joy to slough off care, and be
A rising, lasting extasy.
Dreams ! but if idle they, still blest
    As hours to earth so kindly given,
When stars upon her hilltops rest,
And double in her ocean's breast,
    Till she conceives herself all heaven."

Mine eyes on horses ; in mine ears
Music of lips and chance of spheres ;
If mixed my thoughts, beyond recall,
My heart made tender concert of it all—
Unutterable song, with sense
Of rapture wakeful, while intense.
Like clouds dispersed by burning rays,
If speech dissolved, I was all paraphrase.
'Twas night, yet in my soul was day—
High day, when Moslems stoop to pray,
And tremour dazes air and hour,
    Earth dreaming in Apollo's arms.
I have no tongue, if tongue no power
    To tell how saved from more than harms
Her an embracing mother pressed,
And I was more than either blessed
With bliss, no bulbul could express,
Nor ever Angel more than guess.

Ourselves with joy too thrilled to part,
My tongue recovered its lost art.
When both that morn on fairy ring
Had wickedly sate trespassing
Fay angry had in Lucy moved
Doubt of my legal powers unproved,

And with grave thunders chased us thence ;
  And after surely more bewrayed
And stirred my rival to offence
  So foul, though failingly essayed,
Addling my brains ; and now, as when Macbeth
Saw what his Lady not, an eerie breath,
Nor felt, nor seen by Lucy, secret stole
With wizard music on my soul
Conscious of fresh and growing storm.
Impelled to give the magic in it form
And so enhance our bliss with zest of fear,
I tricked with fancies strange her invaded ear,
When, calling fairy ring to mind,
She the lore questioned, doubtful of fay-kind.

EDWARD.

" Hark ! how the tempest roars, till now
By me unheeded : for I vow,
The heaven within me put to rout
The evil sense of storm without.
Yet what the fays are doing there,
  Phantasy, glozing now mine eyes,
Bids me behold, and cries, " Beware ! "

LUCY.

" What think you, hear you, see—to scare."

EDWARD.

" Listen, and I will make thee wise.
Dark muster mantling shadows,
  Young Chaos to enthrone.
They gather drear on meadows ;
  In glens they gather lone ;
And hushed is awed devotion,
  And silent giddy mirth,
And wildest night on ocean,
  And weirdest night on earth.
Black clouds in heaven are keeping
  Kind stars from looking through ;

And loneliness is sleeping
  Spangled with drops of dew,
And in a strange light dreaming
  Far from all haunts of men,
Where fairy fires are gleaming
  In the deserted glen.

" From thunder spouting fountain,
  And where spent lightnings urn ;
From hollow-hearted mountain,
  And where gnomes metals churn ;
From riff-raff of flame-feathered
  And flapping demon wing,
They have culled, and they have gathered,
  And formed their fay-fire ring.
Some, plumed grass-lances riding,
  Hang out a smileful frown ;
Some, gentler sprites, abide in
  Flower-cups, and lie on down ;
Sage some, round circle lounging,
  Revolve orations grand ;
And some, in hare-bells plunging,
  Look forth with head on hand.
From hollow fox peers, stealing
  Back into furthest den ;
Eagle in clouds concealing
  To eyrie screams again,
As drawn from elfin treasure,
  Which dark-charmed waters lave,
Sceptre, by Fairy leisure
  Fashioned in glistening cave,
Grave monarch, proud parading,
  Commands— "

FAIRY KING.

    " We meet to try
Those who our ring invading,
  Have wronged us ; Shall they die ? "

" And owlet bats are bounding
　About the scorchless light ;
And slow-worms huge, surrounding,
　Lie out all length in sight ;
And air seems breathless eager,
　For a whisper, 'tis so still,
When a small Skrymmorie, meagre
　As sigh may bursting kill,
Who, rancours wont to cherish,
　Is miserably thin,
Cries— "

SMALL SKRYMMORIE.

" Let them peak, pine, perish :
　We pardon not such sin."

" Then not Chyppynutie mildly
　Counsels frolic to pursue— "

NOT CHYPPYNUTIE.

" Let us do nothing wildly,
　Or what we would undo.
Kitchens to storm or dairies,
　But not cause mortal pain,
Is proper work for fairies :
　Leave man to murder men."

" But Puck— "

PUCK.

　　" Quick tempest brewing,
　Oh, King !　I fiercely toiled,
Hence chased them trespass rueing,
　And guilty pleasure spoiled ;
Heated, and now would cool them,
　Making frail ardours wan.
Leave folly, Puck, to fool them,
　And punish maid and man.

"In council deep, that fairy
  Commission they to go;
And a thing he is so airy,
  That may come, and we not know:
Lord Nann, and Lady, Bretons tell,
Died when Nann troubled fairy well."

Lucy.

"But what are fairy strokes and pinches
Save frailties of our own small inches?
Our silly hearts their fumes and frets
Attribute to these wayward pets."

Edward.

"And neither need we Mab to heed,"

Lucy.

"Nor Oberon, nor Puck, nor Pede?"

Edward.

"Nor spell nor spite—"

Lucy.

"Nor spook nor sprite?"

Edward.

"While head is clear, and heart is right.
Thunder itself whose vivid glances,
At Chartres smiting English lances,
Brought Edward conscience—stricken low
To parley with his much-wronged foe;
Drove Montespan in terror wild
To cover of an innocent child,
Thinking it spared the undefiled;
Thunder to us shall kindly prove—
Only to tenderer passion move,
As when its voice with turquoise fills
Caverns of yearning Candia hills."

LUCY.

" Had Thor no sacred rowan found,
He had in swelling Vimar drowned."

EDWARD.

" But ordering our own spirits well,
We may defeat uprising hell.

LUCY.

" These weighty words, commanding eye and ear,
Now shut out Phantasy and banish Fear—
Fear, lovely trembler, weak as water swept
By rippling breeze, and Phantasy inept,
If grand as storm-tossed ocean, both, by bomb
Of clear-eyed truth pursued, meet instant doom.

EDWARD.

" Dear truth, fair settler of disputes,
    And ruthless spoiler of the play
Of man's imaginings, what lutes
    Has she not broken, and cast away ?
No more is Helicon a faith :
    Gods don't now on Olympus dwell—
Gods, who have died a natural death,
    Or been exiled to reign in hell.
Celtic, Teutonic, myth in vain,
    On the key of an empty stable door,
Would any whistle to life again ;
Giants and dragons have quit Spain ;
Whatever was of wizard strain,
Fays, fairies, knights, and kings of men
    Are going, to return no more.
Clouds now are clouds, not herds of Sol ;
And rainbow hopes have had a fall.
Yet more than tricks of fancy, truth
I still have loved from earliest youth ;
And learning on the heavens to look,
And know a world in every nook—

I

No cresset trimmed by Seraph hand—
  I long to see imagination,
Perched hawk-like upon her right hand,
Ready to soar with insight grand
To fresh discovery—expand,
  And joy in her ovation."

So extasy was in the bliss,
That trembled in our parting kiss ;
Still in that tremble did I hear
The whisper of a latent lasting fear ?

THE LATENT FEAR.

" What depths of folly heart may show,
No man sees deep enough to know.
A Richter mouse brings forth a mountain
  Easily as a mountain a mouse ;
Grand Burns himself once turned a fountain
  Of song upon the site of a louse ;
And who his proper soul may school ?
Sage Florence could with Pisa fool
About a dog ; Great Peter's sire
With Poland war, in mortal ire
That it had nicked him in the vitals,
Dropping a syllable from his titles ;
Slight thorn may prick Napoleon sore ;
Small hound attack Black Forest boar ;
Mere weasel throttle Althorpe bull,
Tear Windsor hart all antlerful ;
And, Puck or no, creation's fine
Not Aristotle could divine :
So reason may have thought too soon,
The Fairy is a musharoon.
To Thracian birds, obscuring heaven,
May all the pigmy folk be given ;
The victor cranes descend, nor spare,
But rend the Manikins in air :
  Yet sorcery laughed, when Dosithœus stroke
Through Simon Magus passed, as though through smoke."

CANTO VIII.

WE parted.   I my trappings find
With eyes wide staring and yet blind,
Entranced by her I leave behind ;
Then quit her roomy home of light
And stand, with not a star in sight,
Alone in presence of mirk Night
From Hades risen, where Shades dwell,
And joined by Furies, from profounder Hell,
Who with impetuous whistling breeze
Angry scourge the roaring seas
Which, as I homeward shoreway roam,
Shake the ground, and foam.
Yet, tempering body with ozone, the storm
Breathes its stout spirit into man's frail form.
Though Puck is out on cloud-capped spray,
Having his own mad way ;
Though with lightning rod fierce Tlaloc times
His thunder peals, and crashing chimes ;
Thou art not fearful, Ocean God,
  But curlier so and comelier far
Than Clyde, or Cove, or Yarmouth Road
When calm with lighted ships abroad,
  And under azure, pranked with star ;
Man with thy bomb now charming more,
While black night falls thy snowed foam o'er
And the wild winds roar.

Love and Adventure, Spirits always brave,
  Upon my Guardian Sprite attending near,
Foreseeing danger in both wind and wave,
  Inspiring words commend to my tent ear.

SPIRITS OF LOVE AND ADVENTURE.

" Danger, disaster, death, and doom,
Your dread, most threatening forms assume
Imperious sway of vigorous man,
Who in your presence finds he can,
By land and sea to manhood true,
More than he recked of, dare and do.
Jean Sobieski lone afield
Covered all Europe with his shield ;
Prince William with Sea-beggar-men
Discomfited Imperial Spain."

GUARDIAN SPRITE.

Like orbs that spinning roll, and yet,
    Unconscious of activity,
See only sun, themselves forget,
And sing round him, in harmony
Flashing along wide azure way
To glory, greater than all day,
Man the mere rapture of desire disdains,
But not its goal ; superior to pains,
At whitest heat of action cool
Accomplishes the wonderful.
Yet first-born Titan, Ocean, spare
The weak who still to trust thee dare.
Sir Humphrey felt, when tempest driven,
As near by sea as land to heaven ; .
The love of Man and fear of God
Turn not from lions in the road.
And should some foundering bark appear
    Upon our coast to-night, may we
By grace of God find Britons here
Brave as was Christiern of St. Nazire,
    And Britain vie with Britannie."

There how it lightened, God of grace !
    Not thunder, but a gun

Signals from sea brief desperate race,
  Sands not immortal run.
No Ursula with maiden swarm
Embraces feet of spurning storm ;
Yet winds are burdened with a wail,
And deaf to pity Ariel.
I unto life-boat station haste.
Bold men, as England ever praised,
Or ocean nursed, stand half amazed,
Half daunted, round the readier boat :
Whom joining, instantly afloat
We, fully manned, quit shivering shore
Mid prayers deafened by hoarse roar,
And tumult wild of maddened waves
That droop around, like closing graves,
Or tombstones tall, which weirdly nod
Over of churchyard rolling sod,
Or demons, who our doom conspire
And, crested bright with ominous fire,
Leap, falling on us : while undaunted
We, stern with thought of shipwreck haunted,
Urged by heart happiness at home,
Forward unswamping drive flaked foam.

At times from lift of sidelong swell,
  Or Gorgon billow's hissing crest,
In cannon flash, or fire from heaven that fell,
In an instant momentary hell
  Is wreck full manifest.
Brave mainmast gone seems by the board ;
  But fore and mizzen hang dropped heads
In shrouds dishevelled, whose loose cord
  Lashes the canvas held in tangled shreds ;
Then darkling will with hushing stun
Through awe-struck tempest boom a gun,
Whose after lapse of sullen gloom
  Lightnings revivify, that thunder
May know to dart sure bolts of doom,
  And wake the world to weep, and wonder

Who, all but home, or lately parted,
Perish or e'er arrived, or rightly started.

Ah ! there is gladness,
More awful than the ocean madness,
Hope's last suspense in that spurned ship,
While smothered shrieks on every lip.
First women few with children come ;
Then men ; though doubt I not, that some
Now from behind press sore to front,
Struggle for life their natural wont.
Leap they, or rushing drop down ladder :
Escape was never fiercer, madder,
Of steam from lifted valve of steamer,
Or nightmare shriek from waking dreamer ;
  All underneath one lonely lamp.
Like avalanche, falling from the moon,
By peasant seen, whose cot may soon
  Be buried, they our boat may swamp.
Crowded we leave, and on the wide,
Roaring, roystering, greedy tide,
As from fired city rush on spears
Or girding moats more horrid fears,
Many despairing towards us leap,
Or riven bulwarks cross like sheep,
  Tossed tumbling upon waves like rain,
Or, from sore-shuddering shaking deck,
See hope row with us from that wreck,
  And call to us,—to God in vain :
Shrill utterance wild of whose despair
Might heaven from fast foundations scare ;
So fierce, so terrible, and drear,
Hell riots in each listening ear.

Coastward we oar, and toss awhile ;
  Trees never in wild whirl of wind,
Or good men in wide world of guile,
  More desperate tossed. Before, behind,
As when o'er seas fire-flaked.

The Phœnix flew
On Cuba to be wrecked,
   But save her crew,
Above, beneath, hate closes us round—
One rushing roaring vent of sound,
Groan hungry angry muttering doom,
And stertorous sullen horrid bomb
Of breakers far in shore.
No more?

Exultant breezes raising giant waves
To war on earth, heaven fulminating raves ;
And once a clear, near, piercing cry,
As of sea-mew shrilling by,
But with most unearthly tone,
Ghost to haunt one all alone,
Lifting every stiffened hair
As at thing accursed there.
Ah, then scared sea thrice thirty men
Engulfs to render not again,
And back down sinks the mighty ship—
A secret, which dark depths shall keep,
Till judgments shrilling trump invades
Their else impenetrable shades—
Gone with a wail, but to no tomb :
Earth grudges greener burying room.

As, when the Fiend affronted Death,
Hell self-oblivious held its breath,
The rowers half forget to pull,
   Remembering not the desperate place :
Like statues, looking for a soul,
   Look we each other in the face,
But momentarily ; more fleet
Each wildered heart's returning beat.
And as strong oaks full-leafed, once tall,
   Fast down Niagara's rapids reeling,
By airs from the great waterfall,
And headlong speed, beyond recall,

Each quiver of motion stilling,
In every leaf are backward tossed,
With trembling only now when crossed
To some new current, or now lost
In some wild whirl, or now pell-mell .
Hurled from an unusual swell,
Most desperate quiet damps each brow,
White-crested Grææ raging near us now,
And barking Scyllas not far off our prow.
Each nerve too feverish efforts wring,
As borne along anon we swing
On some cross-wave, or mad with lunge
A crested one will forward plunge,
Whole Proteus herds leviathan
  Bellowing down on man fore-spent,
As buffaloes innumerous span
  Earth-quaking half a continent :
And nearer and nearer that roaring stun.
Oh, for a momentary sun !
And we like weeds with rubble and sand
Out-cast are up on rock-ribbed strand
In no Eidophusicon mortal hath painted,
But by the hand of God, and well-nigh sainted,
While lightnings flash, and from outrageous sea
Kind ready hands withdraw unconscious me.

Though not succumbing to the Trident's shock
Like Locrian Ajax on Gyrœan rock,
Not Sceptre Buddle at Cape Hope
Had close as I with death to cope,
Lift by ninth wave, and headlong cast
Beaten to nothingness, my last
Thought " Lucy " still.   And yet restored
Euridycé, to Orpheus gored
By scorned Bacchantes, made amends ;
So I can sing of pain that ends
To tell how she will often come,
And never find me " not at home."
Belles Isondes many sinless stole

The hearts of bodies, they made whole ;
Angels on earth in Brescia bound
Of Bayard the victorious wound ;
Seeming from heaven to descend
Now Nightingales our ails attend ;
In sickness Lucy did not fail
To be my angel Isonde Nightingale.

Heaven scarcely can be fairer truth,
Than woman in her modest youth
Denying self, and making thee
Object of her fair chivalry.
True, heaven may enemies befriend ;
   But it is also heavenly feeling,
That prompts a maid to condescend,
   Fond weakness in bold strength revealing,
Round sickness ministrant to hover,
Nurse sickness sore of grateful lover.
Thinking of Lucy as so sent by heaven,
Heaven opening, the much forgiven,
And female voices, more than male,
I heard around the mount prevail,
Where God sits throned, and by His side
Christ, who for love had lived and died.

The Seraph, at heaven's outer gate,
I questioned of the heavenly state ;
But, what was said, not dare rehearse—
Unutterable words, in rhyming verse,
Sing only in low level strain
Of the dear solace of my pain.
For soon she entered, and that vision passed,
But in another manner seemed to last.
The heaven was now about me, not above ;
I was within the certainty of love,
And sight of Lucy, my enamoured angel,
  Herself my one and she her own evangel.

LUCY.

" Thy mother says, her baby boy
   On furrowed face of Ocean smiled ;
That quitting frivolous game or toy,
To plough it soon became a joy,
   Rising to rapture in the child ;
That student too, on Isis thronged
And racing Thames, for Ocean longed,
Till pleased, as babe by father tossed,
He on its broad back, which he crossed,
The circuit of the world had run,
Chasing the chariot of the Sun."

EDWARD.

" Through forms unfixed it, giant-wise,
   Like circus-rider casting dress,
Revelled in Protean surprise,
   Or, calm, delighted me not less
Through weeks progressing though delayed,
Moving, yet seeming central stayed
In luxury of careless ease
Upon the thoughtless bookless seas.
And habit made it royal weal
Not only to behold, but feel,
Throned upon silence, Infinitude balmy,
Ame—no—mi—na—ka—nushi—no—kami ;
Or, tumult heaving all its breast,
To rise and fall in wild unrest ;
Or through the billows dash on dash
Go, glancing through them like a flash."

LUCY.

" There Cookes adventurous have found
   Open undesecrated grave :
Gilberts and Hawkins, Drakes renowned
There hammocked sleep, still overground,
   With best and bravest of our brave."

EDWARD.

"And there my father : so more dear
The unplumbed, secret, vasty mere,
Than sward or mounded viking-ship,
Which worms, or men, or storms may strip ;
While nothing goes to dust in thee,
Too fond of Shelleys, songful Old Sea."

LUCY.

" Ah, read, or heard of with pale pain,
 Wrecks have to me been fearfully grand,
All wrecks, even when blue pride of Spain
Sank round our coasts, and ne'er again
 Uplifted head by sea, or land.
Little I thought, when we had bid " Good night "
 And Titan tempest roaring stormed the house,
Opening lids sleepless upon levin light,
 While strident thunders waked all heaven with rouse,
Seas pounding earth as shuddering I lay,—
Little I thought, while longing for slow day,
That thou on foundering billows then wast tossed.
What had become of me, hadst thou been lost,
 Thou, honourably so, yet hardly fair ?
Mine had the worse loss been alive to bear.
But waking happy on a shining morrow,
It lighted me, alas ! to splendid sorrow.
And yet still more I love, that thou hast proved
By man, as woman, worthy to be loved."

EDWARD.

" Weak woman, Darling was her proper name,
Sharing a father's risk, earned deathless fame ;
And not by fairy follies is attired,
But armed by angel graces, when, inspired,
Heading a forlorn hope she risks her prime
To snatch some other from a desperate time.
Shall greater strength of manhood show more fear ;
By man humanity be held less dear ? "

LUCY.

" With Birkenhead went Tommy Atkins down,
That others might to boat pass, stood to drown,
Noble, though humble."

EDWARD.

        " Shall his betters fail,
Where duty calls, the rank and file prevail ?
I saw them, as through Cove of Cork they sailed,
   Saluted by manned yards of Amiral.
I had been sorely sick, and sickly wailed,
   " Each is a billet for some fated ball."
I little knew, how they on British story
Could shed a bolder and humaner glory.
And, Christ's first followers, humble fishermen
All images of death disdain :
Whitby, Holm, Goodwin, Point of Ayre,
Show round our coasts what such can dare—
   North Foreland, how in winter wild,
One after other life-boats three
Surmounted unabating sea,
   Till safe returning honour smiled,
And fame o'er ocean blew the tale,
And brave Columbia shouted back, " All hail ! "
S'death !   Gallic Vernet for mere art
In storm and wreck, on deck, apart,
To stump desireful lashed, thence bold,
Pencil in hand, the storm controlled,
And upon canvas living threw,
Immortalizing what he drew.
No art, but heart itself me braved to prove,
   Life hazarding and end of all our hopes,
How deeply set and founded in true love
   Was I, beyond all mere impassioned tropes,
Willing for others, more for thee to die,
Else had I feared again to meet thine eye."

LUCY.

" A ministering angel I : although
More mortal, thou hast passed angelic show.
Yes, some in others peril may
Both hands and voice uplift to pray,
Direct, command, but are too little wont
To share the danger they so much affront."

EDWARD.

" Humanity, God-made and like,
Of no mean worth, though fallen sick,
Yet rises to occasion great.
The eagle spirit, captive late
  To selfish cares, disdains their bars,
And unconfined, unfretted, straight
  Soars to the stars."

LUCY.

" Good birth and breeding need not blush :
Still honoured, to the fore they rush.
As healthy babe proves wiser nurse,
Good crews show better officers
From danger last with life to part,
True heroes after God's own heart."

EDWARD.

" Apollo Dixon, Banks of Hindostan,
  And Persian Bertram, Anson Lydiard, they
Athenienne Raynsford, Dœdalus Maxwell, fan
  On wings of glory heaven's highest day.
Invincible Rennie, Bland of Flora, grand
  Burgess of Thetis, Magpie Smith were men
To die, or better living to command ;
  Baker of Drake heroic more than ten.
Ay, of the roll, that honours thee,
The name is " Legion," holy Sea !
Still broods God's spirit on thy wave,
Wet nurse of all most bright and brave,

Thy breast not sordid, and thy breath
Devotion Godward, manward death.
Since earth arose, and long hath wailed and groaned,
Wind-swept, and cleft by billows thunder-toned,
Time with no scythe hath laid the fierce commotion
Unreaped, unharvested, of tossing ocean.
Mortals upon the heaving fissured plain
Apt hands may lift, but lay not to retain
Though harrow with Armadas, selves so rending,
The mighty bosom not offending
Into which worlds have sunk, accursed
   Cities and empires, and abide,
Or airy bubbles rising burst
   Shed by the winds on moonlit tide,
Wherever leaps the affluent flood
   On continents that under meet,
Or mirroring Chimborazo's altitude,
   Or laving blackened Etna-feet,
Or rounding Cape of Hope or Horne,
   Or channelling Darien or Suez,
Whether Pacific Isles adorn,
Or Austral where Verde rains are born,
Through Cancer and through Capricorn,
   Or where the years are polar days,
Enamouring each vain blown wind
Chasing it never more to bind.
Round Arctic and Antarctic pole
   Fortune, its only mistress, leads
Whither floes drive and billows roll:
   And stern necessity concedes
The haughty range of trackless space,
To power all mighty."

LUCY.

     " And all sovereign grace.
Refreshing nature's sweetened heart,
Purging by winds and waves most tart,
And giving unto streams new birth,
To heaven clouds, and showers to earth,

While hidden lie Atlantas still,
Which Time shall show us yet to till,
And unrecovered Paradise,
Skied by the floods, or crystal-walled by ice,
Ocean, which mothered, bosoms continents
Linked in the mighty current of events.
Servant of nations too, Britannia braves,
And, to protect the whole world, rules the waves.
If stormy, very kindly thus is sea,
Mother of all things and most womanly.
Than air, or water, any gentler thing
Hath God created, or doth poet sing?
Air, which men see and feel, but hardly know ;
Most witlessly still breathe, and ever grow
To love its universal bounds, fresh air,
Is life to man, and heaven everywhere.
Water, more visible, more felt, is still
Pure as free grace, and tender as good will
Spilt from the source of some large loving heart—
Earth drinking, laving, sings beyond all art.
Yet God can freight them both for wilder course,
And rides the wind and billow roaring hoarse :
They are informed with force of his intent
To cleanse the chastened earth and firmament,
Which well accomplished, air and water then
Are, as they were, most gentle things again."

We oft thus amorous debate,
   Joust as in tournament.   For I,
To public room restored, in state
   On couch, now convalescent lie.
Now, further convalescing, books I bring ;
Needle or pencil she.   And she will sing
Pleased to my faltering lute, while I, not strong,
   All eyes and ears for her to whom I play,
Feast on her beauty, and drink in her song,
   Till her dear song and self take all my breath away.
Then, as I lapse into dumb approbation,
She probes the secret of my admiration.

LUCY.

"Some creatures male deem lightly woman
Less than immortal—barely human;
While others yield, divinely taught,
    Heaven to her wishes, but deny
All depth, range, energy of thought
    To one, to whom mere butterfly
Existence in man's hours of leisure,
Favours, and smiles is perfect pleasure.
What say you, Edward?"

EDWARD.

    "What can I
More, than await your own more wise reply."

LUCY.

"Four times Corinna, fairer none,
Poetic palm from Pindar won,
Not as it was to Nero sold
And Dionysius for gold.
Therefore no idle ornament, nor jest,
But God's own last and complemental best,
Eve, wanting, Adam had been purely wasted,
And not till she was made God gladly rested.
Shall man his perfect make enthrall,
Not rather be her pedestal?"

EDWARD.

"While different to Adam gentler Eve,
Of either why inferior conceive?
And yet though dames for patriot Zisca spread,
    Not linen upon washing-green or furze,
But upon field, soon strewed with hostile dead,
    Renownéd kerchiefs tripping knightly spurs,
Needs not a woman Joanne d'Arc to be,
Nor an Hypatia to master me.
Andromaché, with needle tracing Hector,
Fed too his horses surely upon nectar;

Tanaquil, of best Tarquin better queen,
Could public honours shrewd with distaff win ;
Bertha, of Charles future mother, wrought
Such winsome work in lowly woodland cot,
Her entertainers took her for a fay ;
And Mher-ul-nyssa, in still humbler way
Painting, embroidering silk, so true and brave,
Rose to Sultana from seraglio slave.
For spindle-rib was drawn from Adam's side,
Not burly spear, to be his help and pride ;
And long was woman known in Saxon tongue
' Weaver of Peace '—the name is Even-song.
Ediths, Mathildes, with shaded threads could please,
Adorning homes, and robing lords for ease ;
John of Bretagne deemed maiden cute enough,
Proper for Duchess, knowing shirt from ruff."

LUCY.

" Enough ! you would not have me frill your linen,
Nor take impromptu to the art of spinnin' ? "

EDWARD.

" Heaven made its heavenliest creature soft,
Mother or spouse, a family croft,
Yielding herself to whom God fates her,
Giddy or wise as love relates her.
For, woman, man is all thy world, and even,
Though less than God, yet more to thee than heaven."

LUCY.

" And yet not so ; or ever so
Both bliss and blessing to bestow.
Helena, good by grace divine,
Greatened her bad son Constantine ;
Fortune forsook Third Edward's side,
Glory paled, when Philippa died ;
Metro-didactos should sirname,
And wives have nursed Carlyles to fame."

K

EDWARD.

" A mother's portrait crowns the head
Of Garibaldi's wandering bed ;
Whate'er is best in him she wrought,
Nor is Anita once forgot.
And sooner would I cast vain crown
Of virile lordliness straight down,
Than say or deem, that she whose fears,
Hopes, smiles, and sighs mine infant years
To manhood trained, was, in her snood,
Unworthy God's emphatic good ;
Or she, who stirs my soul with passion,
Not of His best and happiest creation."

My guardian Sprite then to my soul drew near ;
His were the words I poured in Lucy's ear.

Prompted by GUARDIAN SPRITE.

" Man would indeed be lost, ah ! more than cursed,
Were not his fall by such good angel nursed
As could sire, husband, all but self surpass
For now Cleombrotus, now Leonidas ;
Be brighter with Sabinus caverned lone,
Than in Vespasian court, or on his throne ;
For Count Alberti all the world resign,
Choose living death with him in Idria mine ;
Forget for Condé Montmorenci pride,
In Bastille and disease young beauty hide.
These all were earthly.   Cast thine eye below ;
There even thou shalt find in willing woe
Siguna stand, of Loki pitiful wife,
Stopping gall-gouts, that fall to scorch his life.
Gladly from Eden Adam went with Eve ;
She bore her own and more than half his prieve,
Bearing him Cain who lived when Abel died,
And there is nothing woman will not bide ;
Pain, sorrow, want, disease, disaster, shame,

Nought can her love remove, or daunt, or tame;
Not oceans quench the ardour of its sun,
Blistered by lifelong tears dropped one by one:
Unfailing help she of male helplessness,
In scorn supporting, soothing in distress,
Risking or sacrificing self to prove
The passion, that endures in woman's love."

Shall I deny, that Lucy could accord,
Due to such sentiment, untold reward?
But wherefore pen, save to retain; unfold,
Save to recall, embraces not yet cold?
Sportive as frolic lambs we, ardent more
Than summer lightnings on a tropic shore.
I, on my convalescent couch now lying,
As on a bed of roses trying
Sebastian febrifuge, not dying,
But eyelids drooped in show of sleep,
Fond vigil closely sagely keep
  Through lashes thinnest seamed.
So quiet she sits, as though a move
Had murdered me, and such full love
  From mines of lustre streamed,
At heaven starred in deeps I gaze,
Till even happiness acraze
In pleasure more than earthly sweet,
  Feels as though up to heaven has flown
My soul her soul to meet,
  And we are in it there alone.
And, drunk with love, mine arms extending,
  Her blushes spread I on my breast;
Then, over upturned glances bending,
  All pain forget, so blest,
And browse on Hybla honey-dewed.
But she, as overcharged with good,
Disembracing, says that I am well,
And dearer things than I may tell,
Then smiling goes: the while I roam,
In fancy following her home.

Surrey saw his Geraldine
By sorcerer raised, I mine
By fancy in a beam
Light-gliding, as in primal dream
To God Himself she first appeared,
E'er His creative word insphered,
Such adumbration of the maid
    Apotheosized in tranced view,
As may like ray on æther tread,
No whorl on lubric waters spread,
From wild flowers not one tint pearl shed
    Of their illustrious dew.

Perchance I neither see, nor hear,
And my own thoughts are eye and ear ;
But minding Lucy shall with eve return,
Rare fresh conceptions of her in me burn.
As over Bethlehem on Shepherds first
A glory-blossom full of angels burst,
So I a vision have of virgins fair
With flowing robes, and streaming flotand hair,
And faces, guiltless of all down,
Seeming their own most sage renown,
Each with a look of Lucy, and a spell
From the entrancing Sistine Raphael.
Gabriel, that Seraph once to Mary sent,
Above them to his trump gives sudden vent.

GABRIEL.

" Behold how goodly these : all praise accord.
For such was Mary, mother of our Lord."

With awe I praise, with awe I gaze :
But while both eyes and lips I wistful raise,
The vision fadeth into twilight gloom,
Not gloomy long.   For lighted is the room,
When absent Lucy now returning spreads
A glow of rapture, through the dying shades
Dispersed by lamp, and clock in sonorous chime.

And not amiss our evening waste of time ;
Most trivial incidents of idle night
Are ample cause of recondite delight.
When she again has most untimely gone,
And mother, too, in closing night withdrawn,
Extinguishing the lamp, I swear
Meaning to follow, I sink there
Into deep comfort of a huge armchair,
And, in a dream, I see again
The fire-ringed green in Fairy Glen,
And Puck refuting some, who say
His brave commission lacketh way.
Ha! then by mine own phantasy aroused,
The wakeful trenching on the drowsed,
That Fairy Glen I see no more,
But in the fire-light on my own room floor
A queer and very little red-capped man—
Whew! Puck again.   His tongue thus ran.

PUCK.

" Eluding storm, averting scaith,
   You think to have outwitted me.
But spare mine ears, and thine own breath :
I never have proposed thy death,
   And if yet Lucy loveth thee,
Bah! will it last?   By her own show
Is she not anxious now to know
How many briefs you may have had?
Ponder that question well, my lad.
For she whom thy sore sickness
   Makes tender now to nurse,
May find in thy gathering sleekness
   Cause to tender thee worse.
You therefore must not, too much humble, be
A honey bag without a sting in thee
Foxes are still at home with chickens met,
Castles in Spain, and heads with rooms to let.
Cupid Jocose, pure pity's terror,

Child is of Venus, Mars, and Error;
So love has many sours, to dwine
And make daint sweetness fain as fine."

Disturbed by a strange dread intense,
I see no longer Puck in any sense,
But my too foolish beating heart
With sleep to calm at once depart.
Ah! heavy, and most vicious strong,
He sits upon me all night long,
Or so I in the morning dream,
And longer may have slept than it may seem,
For, when I woke, the sun shone bright;
    Now all my room is ringing
With music from a caged delight;
The bird is mocking mine affright:
    I catch myself too singing.

EDWARD'S SONG.

"Warbler, wild if captive, thy notes are thrilling:
Sing of her—of something though proud yet willing:
Mocking bird, trill—trill me the blisses filling
        Breasts of the loving.

"Wine-dark ocean glowingly sunny minds me
Of the eyes bright, whose necromancy binds me—
Swimming glad eyes bathed in a light that blinds me,
        Light of the loving.

"Jet as night's own, beautiful are her tresses,
Soft as starlight, shining, and, like caresses,
Round her hanging—hanging in lovely places,
        Tempting me loving.

"Fruits and blossoms heavy on tree of Eden,
Seemeth she all cupids in flowers half hidden,
Gladding me, not filled with a bliss forbidden,
        Looking and loving.

" Roses pale blow over her cheeks of lily ;
Manna snows fresh lie on her bosom hilly ;
Morning, noon, eve tint her, and, willy nilly,
      Kill me with loving.

" But should chance her sorcery cease, a wave of
Hell will sweep wild over the earth.   I crave of
God but Lucy, or the untimely grave of
      One too much loving."

CANTO I.

GRATEFUL is darkness lighting stars,
  That show to men God's love.
The wildest storms, by day or night,
  To tender mercy move ;
Great creatures dumb together crowd,
  Small burrow, feathered nest,
And human strays are welcomed
  To shelter, warmth, and rest.
But, tempest gone, the gatherings part,
  In sore distress begun ;
And with the darkness pass the stars,
  All dying in the sun.
And calmer she and colder now,
  Whom much my suffering moved ;
My sunny convalescence
  Has all her fires reproved.
I rather would be tossing
  Once more on couch of pain,
And see the pity of it
  In eyes of love again.

Lest earth should, more than heaven, to love be dear,
Love's course has never run too smoothly here.
Rough ups and downs, still rude, deform the way,
And to-day hap mishaps of yesterday.
Now upon full-blown hopes, well washed with tears,
Are fondly set my risen watchful fears.
Perchance to Puck I may the feeling owe
Of frailty in my saint, yet God can show
Not sole on earth the hoof-prints of the devil,

But on high heaven itself like hints of evil.
Alas, what evil eye, on Lucy staid,
Has quelled the sovereign grace she once displayed ?
Much wonder I, and, when we early meet,
Rouse her dulled fires, and fret her into heat.

EDWARD.

" Now warm, now cold, by fits and starts,
You act, I trust, the chilling parts.
Or is thy love, as fizgig slow,
 Which oft with powder sprinkling rash,
One once too oft may fiercely blow,
 And blasted be by instant flash ?
Ah, whither has that true love flown,
 Which painted in thy lighted eyes
Mine image, worshipped by thee lone,
 Now banished from those impious skies.
Nothing infallible but Peter's dome,
Who most have hoped are most deceived in Rome."

LUCY.

" More knave, than 'naive,' is thy tongue.
Lag would the year all bloom and song :
With seasonable ivy crown
Flower feasts of Antisterion ;
But, be not uncanonical,
Let carême follow carnival."

EDWARD.

" Yet hunger chases wolf from wood ;
Thebaid sands of solitude
Lionlike raven for the prey,
 I for my far more dainty fair,
Not so to take her life away,
 Only her love with none to share."

LUCY.

" Continual ringing cracks the bell ;
 Too soon the pitcher comes to break

By going always to the well;
   Wine we should sip, and little take;
Love, when half starved, is dear anticipation,
Whose longing wanteth no commiseration,
Happy half satisfied to be,
And never know satiety."

EDWARD.

" In proverb ne'er was woman dumb;
Man also can be Tuppersome.
Put not on to-morrow, nor leave to another,
   What to-day and your own better self can do.
Strike iron while hot; of fortune the mother,
   Occasion once gone will seldom renew.
In the old game of sphere playing king now, now as,
On the board of this world stagy man is, alas!
Like Adalbert, fugitive found after battle,
Late more than a Marquis, now stalled among cattle.
So nigh to grave is man, at birth
Of nothing more naked than of mirth,
He never draws a fleeting breath
Beyond the touch of certain death.
Light's stars, life's sparks, while seeming bright,
Are sad reflections upon death and night."

LUCY.

"Your breathings as a furnace are to me.
   I am as one who walks on coals ashed over,
And, looking down thereon, can thorough see
   A too combustious lover.
You would inflame, spoil, murder my dear peace.
We should not flay our sheep, although we fleece;
Plucking our fowls, we should disdain
To pillow on one cry of pain.
Perhaps you snarl with sword between your legs,
Hang merest morals upon idle pegs.
Who sings to a distempered heart,
   With nitre mixes vinegar:
I will not act so folle a part.

Besides, thou nothing would'st so tart ;
Thy brave distemper is fine art
   To colour me, but not to mar ;
Thou would'st but put me to the pain
Of washing it all off again.
Nay, since thy fancies have thee crazed,
Lay thou the ghost, which thou hast raised :
Confess, sir, I am wise as true,
And that I have out-proverbed you."

And loud she laughed, and well she might ;
I also could have laughed outright,
Glad to be buried so in chaff,
And hear her so outrageous laugh ;
When,

LUCY.

" Pardon me, Edward, you are too absurd.
Alone together long, two miss a third.
If we were all the world, would'st stay long in it ? "

EDWARD.

" I know, I should have loved to so begin it.
   Oh, for a lodge in some far wilderness,
Where we—— "

LUCY.

" Where you might be companionless."

EDWARD.

" Nay, human nature clings to love for love,
And can no utter solitude approve ;
But holds it safe with not a mortal near,
Save only her most fair, who is most dear,
With whom to follow bliss in savage ways.
The thought of losing love is enough to craze?
Oh ! for a lodge in some far wilderness,
Where we might give and take secure caress ;
No Clytian eye to search, no raven tongue

Secrets too dear with faytorous croak to wrong ;
No snake-like Aquitaine through maze to hiss,
And rout with baleful chase an envied bliss ;
Beyond all wing of Cupid's leaden dart ;
Nor god, nor mortal to draw either heart
From other, where is found its better part;
No hope, but love ; no wish, but still to be
I good to Lucy, and she kind to me.
To run away with you myself I seem,
Wing-heeled like Hermes, in a flighty dream."

LUCY.

" A flighty dream, a fancy blown balloon :
Manage it carefully, and drop it soon."

EDWARD.

" From meadow-dance, in darkness-cap,
King Laurin gentle Kimbeld stole,
For his Rose Garden in Tyrole,
　On which rare wanderer still may hap ;
But me you follow, love-beguiled,
While I conduct you, wild to wild,
No trembling fawn that, lost with brother,
Through formidable woods seeks mother,
Now startled by leaf-rustling breeze,
Now adder loosening joints of knees ;
But as with Rama Sita roamed
To where the Godavari Dandak tresses combed.
Hark ! Now, or is it mortal gladness
Made sport of amiable madness,
We hear and seem to wander grove
Which gentle airs and waters rove ?
There soon on an inviting swell,
　Girdled by stream and forest lone,
I lodging find, or build, and never tell
　A far-off mocking world, where we have flown.
Once for Fifth James Earth Athole raised
Palace of boughs, which after blazed,
That it might show like fairy thing,

Of fishing, hunting, hawking, what
Prioress Juliana taught ; "

EDWARD.

" No sad Sulpicia, but one wont
With her Cerinthus pleased to hunt,
Varied sports and fresh wilds seeking,
Sweetly laughing, sweetly speaking ;
Lalagean hours of love
Close and open days, that rove."

LUCY.

" Gos-hawking gay with prancing pride,
Beating the river, forth we ride,
Recovering abandoned skill."

EDWARD.

" Thy bird unhooded, soaring still
To strike far quarry from specked skies,
In sudden contempt of ready prize
To thy hand returns with hasty dart.
Thy beauty then disturbs my heart
And fancy so, although no rukh,
Which may an elephant up-pluck,
    That falcon is, I anguished see
It, wizard-wise changing into knight
Like Maldumarec, vanish with you quite,
    As Pluto with Persephone.
Wildly the lost one seeking, I awake,"

LUCY.

" No more to dream, but courage to retake.
Ah, vision false, could Lucy know delight
In bloody sport, or Maldumarec knight ?
And thinketh any man, when brutes expire,
They senseless flicker out, and die like fire ?
Perhaps : but who can think, and nothing fear ?
Who thinks so, that hath seen and slain a deer ?
Tongue quivering besmeared with ruddy flow,
Eyes raised beseeching out of depths of woe,

Sob, droop, and shudder, all one tale deplore,
' I quit a world of joy to joy no more.'
No more ?   They have no spirit proof, nor plan
To antidote death's dreaded sumpitan.
Yet there may be where ox shall feel no goad,
Hare never start, and gun no more explode ;
My bird, my dog, my horse may yet behold,
The streams flow honey, and the bowers drop gold ;
And I may welcome there from lustral woe
The brute companions, which I loved below :
Behold, so great a heart was in his hound,
Where is Sir Roger, may not it be found ?
Nor shall thy Lucy e'er with any ghost—
And sorcerers are nowhere—once be lost ;
Beneath exists not, nor above,
The Ghostly warmth to exorcise true-love."

And gay she laughed.   I rather would in chaff
Again have buried been, than miss that laugh.
But is she gone ?   Of purpose fled
　　On visit to a distant friend,
She nothing of it prior said :
　　Is this, then, the beginning of the end ?
Oh, how I long her secrets to surprise,
Lifted by prayer up to God's own eyes ;
Her wanderings wantonly astray,
Where sun and stars alone can say.
Ha, is she with her confidante
Laughing, and mocking while I rant ?
Marine and doveless Venus, brought
　　By Tritons from her parent Sea,
Has his inconstant manners taught
　　Unto her boy Cupidity,
Who drives us with unlooked-for storms,
　　With unexpected calms delays,
With horrid mists now all deforms,
　　Now blinds us with excessive rays.
He wickedly and slyly mocks ;
　　I mock myself, and should him seize

By the one ear, the other box
  Until he ceased to teaze.
No sooner thought of than well done :
  I catch him, but don't clip his wings ;
I dare not harm the little one
  Confessing, as he sings.

MY CUPID.

"As Lucy fair is but one thing,
  Worthy of her, the truth you bring,
Truth having eyes
  Piercing the night,
Scales, and a sword,
  Justice and might ;
Truth, bright as sun
  And without spot,
Pure as the day
  Hid in a grot ;
Truth, the sweet life,
  Breath of all troth,
And the one thing
  Good in an oath."

She did not deem one rosebud wrong.
I send her now another with that song,
And this.

Song sent.

" Let others sing the rose so gay,
  Others the grape so juicy ;
One tuneful theme have I, and may
  Sing ever only ' Lucy.'
The rose ' a duchess ' without peer
  May be, the grape 'Sans Souci ;'
But neither has a kiss so dear,
  Or smile so bright as Lucy.

" The breeze may blow now east, now west,
  Now thaw you, and now freeze you ;

But Lucy still will do her best,
  And look her best to please you.
With changeless truth for me, her heart
  Has warmth for every comer:
'Tis night, but starry, when we part;
  To meet is sun, and summer."

And lest she should it too familiar deem,
And I too certain of her favour seem,
Was added yet this other, to beguile
A flush of ardour o'er her dimpling smile.

Other song sent.

" Go thou, where ocean oft with pebbles playeth,
  That necklace earth, his willing paramour;
Go, when a billow, which some cliff bewrayeth,
  Heart-broken hangeth on the bosom dour,
          And think of me.

" Go, where in wilderness oft Zephyr sigheth,
  Meeting with Iris, and dear love is born;
Go, when a roe-deer tame, their sobbing dieth,
  Strayed, since its mistress cast it out forlorn,
          And think of me.

" Go, where in twilight earth is heaven inviting
  Into its shades so happy, lone, and deep;
Go, when Diana may be seen alighting
  Close to Endymion lovely and asleep,
          And think of me.

" Appear to me in vision not to scare,
But with thy lovely presence to repair
Unlovely loneliness, where now I plain,
To notes of birds tuning my woes as fain,
          Singing of thee."

  I had a silly song fore-writ,
  And how I silly was as it,

But sent the others : for I said,
She may conceive me off my head.
And truly since she went from me,
 It might have been to far Hong-Kong ;
For I am absent as weed, tea,
 Pot, cup, and pipe were in this unsent song.

Song unsent.

" My pipe and my teapot charging indeed,
 But thinking the while of thee,
I into the teapot put the weed,
 And into the pipe the tea,
Thinking of thee, Ah ! only of thee.

" Both charging again, and there was no moon,
 But thinking the while of thee,
I filling my cup took my pipe for a spoon,
 And with it stirred the tea,
Thinking of thee, Ah ! only of thee.

" Rinsed cup refilled to sweeten I stopped ;
 But thinking the while of thee,
In the spittoon now the sugar dropped,
 And after poured the tea,
Thinking of thee, Ah ! only of thee.

" What is to be done ? I sate, and thought,
 Still thinking ever of thee ;
I must in my haste have my hat forgot,
 But here I am, to see,
Not think, Ah ! not only think of thee."

I go not there ; she comes not here,
 Nor yet to rose, nor song replies,
Nor may return, till doubt and fear
 Have lost the hope that in them lies,
And law has townward cruel called me hence.
A sudden horror of suspense
 O'ershadows me, with chill to freeze,

As, e'er autumnal leaves are dun,
Beams shorn at noon are from brief sun
    At Cauterets in Pyrenees.
Nay ! now Apollo filleth air
With radiant prophecy.   Fly, care,
Scattered upon the winds : for, lo,
Lucy is coming home.   I know
The very time.   The train I wait ;
Alas ! the train is coming late.
Say, is she in it beautiful with grace ?
Are all as eager to behold her face ?
For wont she was to draw admiring eyes,
As when on Cuzco suns—on Iran rise.
Good hope I have : but Hope may me deceive,
    And Lucy other be, than hope beseems :
That both are false I will not now believe ;
    If but to dream, hope is most sweet of dreams.
What time I long ago her coming stayed,
    One of the outside throng about the door,
And for the ball appeared my trysted maid,
    While I was looking if my rose she bore,
How admiration buzzed, and fixed at last
Each sweet regard, as through the throng she passed :
Then was I thrilled with awed delight, and shame,
That I should one so many charming claim.
My pious wishes God will speed ;
Mine are her wishes, mine her need.
Unconscious of a base desire,
Or impious thought, my soul on fire
Could metal barriers solve undone :
Love has resolved us into one.
For now is she returned, restored
With fresh old love and more toward,
I almost glad as resurrected sod
Living, and winged to be at last with God.

Tibullus, by the Muses taught,
    Inscribed his name upon a song,
With which they his Neœra sought,

Who loved him for it, though not long :
But uninscribed my Lucy guessed,
And modest song has boldly blessed.
Her beauty o'er my chaos vaunting,
Its sacred looks the tumult daunting,
My swelling soul with passion spent
Is laid in absolute content.
Love, leaping lively from the past,
Routs the doubt-demon crossed and cast,
And can be just as well as blind.
Oh ! if brief doubt can die so kind—
And often death is seen to smile—
I care not what tempestuous style
Of rage may pass to still my soul
Under so rapturous control.

Thus was our strangeness passing strange.
Her sun eclipsed had brought no change,
But open heaven now beguiles
With beams unshorn, and day all smiles.
As fires which to each other turn,
To meet to-day we fondly burn,
And shall to share again to-morrow
Joy's which, though fleeting, still can borrow
Immortal virtue from excess
Of rapture in brief tenderness.
Such moments seem seraphic years,
    Yet make to heaven no pretence,
And, preyed upon by after fears,
    Still thrill fond memory with sense
Of kisses many, as stars bright
In amplitude of summer night.
Holy are partings, which reveal
How much is common in our weal,
Preserved, but half enjoyed apart,
In muniments of secret heart ;
Conned, missal-wise illuminated
By monk, to third high heaven translated,
When he again his darling meets,

And she his joy with hers completes :
They fain would never part, but must in twain.
They kiss to go, and come to kiss again.

Dim shines the sun, the year grows cold ;
　　Winter at hand a shadow casts.
Now bared are gardens, fields and meads no more
By Flora visited, and rivers roar,
　　While clouded heaven weeps, and blasts
With tree-spoils gorge dark puddled mould ;
Colourless nature shudders at its fate,
And quitting Lucy I am desolate.

She seemed, with an unfailing bliss,
　　Spring, summer, vintage to prolong,
And ward the dusk of stormed and dying year,
When winter lays it lone on ragged bier
　　Of flower and fruit, of sun and song :
And while it parting pleasure is
In sacred depth of earnest eyes to view
One's portrait warded by a spirit true,

Yet should my heart less know of sorrow,
　　Than nature who lost sunshine weeps?
From her to part is late Octobral thought ;
And in the deed shall winter be.　Will nought
　　Drug weary Saturn, till he sleeps,
That so to-day may tide to-morrow ?
Fate sleepless watches him, and time may never
Nod at fixed moment doomed the blest to sever.

And yet to part is not to range.
　　True as is needle unto pole,
However parted true unto lone, last,
Wild quiver, as dire final fires speed past,
　　Time may, not distance, deaden soul ;
And change of heart alone is change.
Will Lucy feel it, and forget first love,
Quitting the ark, an unreturning dove ?

Puck with a sudden bound in air appears
On wing suspended, answering my fears.

PUCK.

" Ha, ha, the driveller old though fain,
  Time cannot thee from Lucy sever.
Joys, that are fleeting, shall in fancy last ;
Thou often shalt in fancy live the past ;
  And by her absence painèd ever
Shalt thou repeat—' We'll meet again,
And, love's choice grapes in joys own chalice pressing,
To Cupid drink, while Venus smiles all blessing.' "

CANTO II.

I, a barrister briefless, in court undertasked,
  Overburdened with care am, as belle
Who, longing to dance, sits in ballroom unasked,
  Rocked, like Inch-cape, by each passing swell.
The solicitors coming, and going elsewhere,
  Not one thinks of soliciting me ;
Like a cabman who waits all in vain for a fare,
  I too wait all in vain for a fee.
Now in court I sit hard on each long drawn out case,
  And look sage as the judge, who presides,
But feel, fast flying by me, the winged years of grace
  Upon which opportunity rides :
Then I, weary, consulting stars fateful that rise,
  And intrude upon study's limp night,
Hear oracular twinkles, that mock me, advise
  In time's darkest hour to be bright,
" All things come to those who wait."
But though distant views of fate
May enchant, and heart grow fonder,
  Sickening with hope deferred,

On success in life I ponder,
  Bitter with gall black and stirred.
Is it due to little sense,
  Brazen flash, and tinny thunder,
Part a trick of confidence,
  Part of never knocking under?
Yet, if gained by power and toil,
With judicious waste of oil,
Puck haunts me with opposing fears,
That I myself am slow as law appears.

PUCK.

" Art not self too slow, a crick
In an age and life too quick?
Shalt thou ever happy be,
Till death comes and quickens thee?
From want of brains and lack of enterprise
Failure and shame are thine, and law is wise."

EDWARD.

" Nay, I have only entered—not begun,
Not yet had chance of start the course to run."

Not reckoning that to be has right to be,
Love, though pur-blind itself, still makes us see ;
With a most touching tenderness prevails,
And, opening all our ears to all that wails,
Whate'er may stand in its despite impleads,
And mostly law, not fashioned to our needs.
Now dim in dumpish ill oil-'lumined room,
Yet under mystic influence, the gloom
Was suddenly informed with shady being
  Of calf and vellum wraiths, a lettered swarm,
Which out of open books and shelved, worth seeing,
  Came east-by-north addressing me sans form.

SHADY LEGAL BEINGS.

" Despond not, old boy ; we know a trick or two
Worth that—the stayer wins, though law is long to woo.
Holt, youthful called, to manhood prime attained,

While still his wizard wits unfee'd remained ;
Blackstone on briefless law commented long,
Harmonious and dear, though cheap as song ;
Thurlow round circuit took on trial horses,
Nights swilled to dissipate day's idle forces ;
Kenyon for better living secret prayed,
And dined on pence, which also fee'd the maid ;
Grant in Acadia aimless musket bore ;
Scott to become provincial almost swore,
And God forgave him ; Romilly arose
As plains and prairies slowly swell, till close
On Rocky mountains—grandly soaring then ;
And Brougham, most volatile of flighty men,
Consuming life in dread of sputtering socket,
Sudden to heaven whizzed a bursting rocket.
Most lawyers great discovered are by chance :
Patience prime motor is of all advance.
With patient labour then for chance prepare,
That, when it haps, thou mayest safely dare.
Learning, if slow-acquired and later shown,
Is sure, and, coming into, holds its own :
Solid at least, may thine be brilliant too,
Sage justice can be beautiful as true ;
Such Mansfield—"

              Tall talk this, and vague as vain.
   A gust of chimney-smoke obscured the crowd,
Till, clearing off, I saw amidst them then
   Another shade, but in substantial shroud.
He was a strange old man as I have seen,
May very well the Wandering Jew have been :
For the old fellow in his features showed
All times, all places, and not one abode,
Though not in garb, or look, one hint of Jew.
He was a man much like and more than you,
Like everybody, commonplace indeed,
But wise beyond the very Apostles' Creed.
Before he spoke, he passed his card to me,
" Public Opinion ; " thus of Mansfield,

PUBLIC OPINION.

                     " He,
By birth, and rank too, fructuously graced,
Early by fortune favouring embraced,
Not curbed, nor cowed, prevailed well-pleased to show,
How equity and law can kiss and go.
But lesser men and slower must parade,
Plod, and manœuvre, lie in ambuscade ;
With cares and fears, that drag the years that roll,
Wan-faced grow, high in voice, and low in soul ;
Briefless, or devilling like any sieve,
At least two lustres to expectance give—
Camden gave going three still genitive.
And what of love?   Even Mansfield lost his first
By friends o'er-ruled, but not by Pope uncursed :
Westminster Hall too small for full content,
She broader acres chose to circumvent."

So saying he, smoke-loving, in a loop
Of cloud from pipe fresh-lit involved the troop,
Or indistinguishable now, or only
Forgotten, while he thus addressed me lonely.

PUBLIC OPINION.

" Through Parliament might you success surprise ;
On state, not statute, bags of wind arise?
Court favour may no more the bench disgrace,
Finches, Scraggs, Jeffries there, or Wrights misplace ;
But members rise to it, and think to rule,
More fit for bench or copy-book at school.
Or upon winged debate invoking Sun,
Astreal minor place may well be won,
In pensioned calm digesting law and plunder ;
    Though higher perch can rarely any gain,
Up screaming eagle-like through Commons' thunder,
    Save greatly learned, who greater show as men ;
And such may wait, and parliament retire,
Till office calls them there, and thence yet higher.

Then shall you wait?   If Lucy would, you might
The wonted decade dedicate to night,
And study, and yet briefless miss the mark.
Ye gods ! was ever night so utter dark,
As this of law through which each aimless road,
With rubbish littered, lies with ruin strewed,
Like orbits, which star-embers shall immerse—
Ashing all heaven, cindering the Universe."

In form of " Public Opinion " was it " Puck,"
That paled my bravery?   But all a-muck,
Echoing these ghostly thoughts, the shades again,
Who could not moon-light elves be in my den,
Ashy appeared : each haggard volume quick
A shade contributed, the air grew thick
So I in breathing it seemed, breathing them,
To labour with their thoughts and not condemn ;
While he expressive was, with equal voice
They companied applausive, with no noise.

PUBLIC OPINION.

" In France, or far America, or near
In Scotland law digested is, not here.
England approves concealment : countless screens
Raised are to hide what law or statute means ;
Coke upon Littleton, dross heaped on that,
Pelions piled on Ossas were more flat ;
Clouds upon clouds, in air Porphyrionic,
Attainting gods, whose thunders would be tonic.
Counsel, attorney, court on court, here, there,
Nowhere may law be found, since everywhere.
And thus the public in mysterious need
All round consulting, still despairing bleed.
And matters of small moment yet become
Momentous, when the oracle is dumb,
Or double mystery—a kind of play,
And by the legal guild got up to pay.
Courts of pie-powder are no longer found :
Dust gathers upon justice by the pound.

"Chaos confined is nothing ; loosed to reign,
To nothingness restores creation vain.
Fiends through his void vast falling there would dwell,
But organized disorder is their hell,
Where wrathful faces, veiled in fiery lies,
And more pitch-foul caliginosities,
Sept are in ranks of orderous dissent,
Each known for its own special devilment.
And such the law—Cimmerian darkness, lit
Enough to show us justice lost in it ;
Cruel and false, but handy for a fight,
Where still most dexterous is still most right.
Discordant laws and judgments wide oppose,
Right changing sides with wrong as victory goes ;
The old the new assails, the high the low,
The legal winds from every quarter blow,
In a tornado meet, with dreadful steven,
And whirl importunate justice up to heaven.
In Iceland, where is Hecla and contend
Remorseless frost and fire, and neither end,
Thing-valla mountain girt shows arid, brent
By streams volcanic, indurated, rent,
Piled lava-masses here, there yawning chasms ;
Nature immortal fixed in mortal spasms ;
On horrid precipice stands Lôdberg crowned
With doomring huge, whose mystic stones surround
Of human justice such the fittest fane—
Al-thing, where fools think God makes laws in vain.
From densest night educing limpid day,
Order creating from stark disarray,
A labour this a kingly heart to fire :
Great Alfred come, and Britain re-inspire.
Edward First, Burnet, Wolsey, Bacon, Hale,
Clarendon, Cromwell here conspired to fail ;
Most real and most equitable crams,
Sir Parnynges, Ellesmeres, Hardwickes, Nottinghams,
And thirteen hundred years of chancellors,
Quacking, have physicked law from bad to worse.
Noblesse commands law—lords increasing fast,

" Offspring of law, to reverence its past,
Which they into the future worse prolong,
Or only change to make it newly wrong.
Why lords of law create, but to maintain
Subsisting privilege, not right wronged men ?
  Law, as church, lords are of state-craft mere fudges
Stuffed to mislead, misrepresent the judges :
To such poor issue of no public good
Enrich we, and ennoble legal brood,
Kenyons, Gibbs, Eldons, Ellenboroughs learn
To bow to laws, which titled fortunes earn ;
Budding in Inns, in Commons then they blossom,
Fruit in the Lords, and drop on Abraham's bosom."

And here occurred a wonderfullest thing.
For one and all the shades began to sing,
Though not so Desmond-old, yet taking breath
To sing out of the very lips of death
A song, they had made, and called, " The Old Governor's
  Song,"
For an old gentleman, well-preserved, not too long.

Sung by LEGAL SHADES.

" I have turned the leaf yellow and sear ;
   Had no reason my birth to regret ;
Mine age now cannot say to a year ;
   If I could, would be foolish to let
            The fates know.
Hush ! let not the fates know
            How aged I am,
Or they may dismiss me to
            Father Abraham.

" Lights my days are and livers of grace :
   For of time overdue is the bill.
So I wear a grave smile on my face,
   Lest the fates should present it.   But will
            The fates know ?

Hush ! let not the fates know
      How aged I am,
Or they may dismiss me to
      Father Abraham.

" In life's web weaving thread upon thread,
   They may miss, or neglect to cut one,
And a mortal, who ought to be dead,
   To his thread dangle on, till the fun
      The fates know.
Hush ! let not the fates know
      How aged I am,
Or they may dismiss me to
      Father Abraham.

" Thanks, then, whether to grace or neglect,
   I have over-reached three score and ten,
Looking out now for death, and expect
   To be introduced to him, when
      The fates know.
Hush ! let not the fates know
      How aged I am.
Or they may dismiss me to
      Father Abraham."

But he had more to say, and deemed the time
Proper to move the shades to passionate rhyme.
The Book of Judges they had interluded,
He, their Choragus, sternly now concluded.

PUBLIC OPINION.

" Our judges, tottering on each senile year,
Salaried or pensioned, will change nothing here.
Dreading all large reform, they small deride,
And knotting still more gnarl their staff of pride.
The dog, by Erskine dressed for consultations,
Growl had less brutal than their stern frustrations
Of his, or Romilly's so trembling hope :

M

Our wish has more than Coleridgian scope.
Russo-Germanic Empress Catherine could
In this direction look, and promise good ;
Napoleon ape Justinian ; shall we less,
Still under law to general lawlessness,
By our revolted Jonathan surpassed
In children, lands, and laws, in all save caste ?
Shall wrong endure, disorder reign, because
These once were law, and still exist in laws ?
Such with a bugbear fright us, who pretend,
Since change is chanceful, all reform should end.
To regulate old mischief lack we nerve ?
We rot, with what we weakly so conserve.
Better cut out a tumour with a cry,
And take our risk of life, than surely die.
Cut deep enough, or it again will swell ;
Deep, deep, the mischief has its roots in hell.
The body politic and common weal,
To sense of ill excite, and wound to heal.
Man to himself is plague enough ; we add
The pest of lawless law, and drive him mad ;
While land—a search for title !   Oh, ye powers,
Was ever land on earth so cursed as ours,
So much at sea with all its false renown ?
We dare not yet our legal Flambard drown ;
Though die he would unpitied save in song,
That deemed it pity he had lived so long."

Such fervour pleased, but had so warmed the shades,
They dissipated to their vellum beds—
Each in his tome ; while made of coarser stuff,
" Public Opinion," tired of cutting up rough,
Vanished in smoke.   I also took to puff,
But not the law once loved, both old and new,
How full of folly, monstrous and untrue,
Inveterate quack, with nothing more of duck,
Profound humbug, too proud of its good-luck,
Blowing both hot and cold, so many-sided
Not treacherous spring itself shows more divided.

And looking for chance in abounding strife,
I wonder and ponder the struggle for life.
Have we, in our wisdom, worse wrong to restrain,
Legalizing injustice, protected bad men?
Is evil profound and extreme in law?
Such questions confront me, oppressive with awe,
As now from the Temple courts I pass
To Newgate and Guildhall; back, alas,
By Mansion House, Bank, Exchange, and then
By Holborn Hill purlieus and Fetter Lane
With scent of the refuse drained from the city
As open to search as patent to pity:
Or, swinging again like a pendulum,
By Fleet Street and Strand to West Minster come,
And back by the palace, parks, clubs, and then
Seven Dials, St. Giles, and Drury Lane,
Through rear of the race from the blatant van,
And always the tragedy of man?

Here are parks where flow streams of fashion,
Where the poor too ventilate passion;
Here streets and squares, almost of palace
    Where pomp is well wedded to state,
And loiter brisk lacqueys and valets,
    And gather gross wealthy and great,
Whom only deliberate malice
    Can speak of as subject to fate.

The Normans all sons were of thunder,
    And grandeur not wanting in grace,
With hoards of rich, fortified, plunder;
    And the Anglo-Saxonian race
Can work without knowing a wonder,
    Till seen in some foreigner's face.
This curvant symmetrical street
    With multitudes blocking its flow,
Where cabs and carts, carriages meet,
And not shocked from each other retreat,
    But circulate still although slow

As eddyful currents of feet
   That travel the pavements below ;
This wilderness modern of brick,
   Which, stuccoed, they paint to a splendour
Of ugliness rare, that no trick
   Of forcible language could render,
Is London, with only a creak
   Of vasty deep sea to defend her.

Pierce that row of gay shops, my Lud,
   Or step out of your own back door,
You will find—may you chew the cud
Of grave-digging reflection, my Lud—
You will stand in the ruck, and mud,
   And filthier scum of the poor.
Paid poorly, ill lodged, and worse fed,
   Despised they, now owning defeat,
Are thieves, who our houses invade,
   And garotters, who prowl the street.
Self-help is a beautiful thing,
   A fair blossom which ought to blow
In each poor man's pane : to no king,
But his own brave poor should he cling,
And not himself help to a swing
   By helping himself with a blow.
But know-nothing-ful indolence
   With waste now both vice breeds and crime
And rates high and wrongful expense.
So justice, which courts common-sense,
Soon visits law's lightest offence,
Despatching it anywhere hence
   To better our country and time.
One may a chum bruise, if he will,
   Or wife, if he cannot well drop her,
But another's hand-kerchief to steal
   Is as criminal as improper :
The former some plaster may heal,
For the latter the commonweal
   Demands a long Newgate-made stopper.

You now hearts of the poor explore,
  Of drivers of cabs and of carts,
Costermongering people, and sore
You fancy they feel to the core
  Of sad, almost quite broken hearts.
Recalling what sin has ill-wrought,
  Since Adam turned Time's first brief page,
And feeling what is, but ought not,
  To be acted upon our stage,
How refreshing to weary thought
  Is a dream of the Golden Age.
How welcome such dream with a kiss
  To smooth the deep furrowing frown,
Which lengthens whenever we miss
What some others possess of bliss ;
They might help us all up to bliss,
  Or all smilingly let it down,
But rule for themselves, or recline
  To unkind reflection a prey,
Life having most truly divine
But frolicsome quite as new wine,
  That fretteth its fresh skin away.
Quick also as rise the aspiring,
  Their small world with their wealth expands ;
Fresh prospects, fresh objects admiring,
  On their means making fresh demands,
They round self with self-love untiring
  Revolve all the works of their hands,
And nothing can spare for another
  Save what self can hardly refuse,
The wisdom in using a brother,
  If possible not to abuse.
Of themselves they boastfully speak
  With a consciousness born of merit,
Convinced, and convincing the weak,
Who loud praise the success all seek,
  And dream, perhaps even they share it.
Yes, well the world speaks of the man,
  Who knows for himself to do well,

To live, and let live him who can
  And stand, where, alas! Adam fell.
While science can plan and art limn,
  Sings your rich man, sleek in his mirth,
" Come fill up the cup, come fill to the brim,
  With the bounty and beauty of earth."
And as greenest by far the sod
  Overlying no empty tomb,
With means and capacity, God !
  How pleasant it is to consume
What others produce, and grow broad
  On corses and curses till doom.

I once, in Paris hostel of past day,
A fellow Briton met, wont there to stay,
With whom conversing, much from him I learned
Of workers hard for wage too dearly earned,
And intermittent fever of reform
Shaking both France and England, passing storm,
With need of steadier, larger, mightier change
Not only wrong to right, but right rearrange.
I christened him " The Partisan," and we
On top of our discourse were doomed to see
Struggle more deadly for young Liberty.
In France, enlightened, patriots have by word
More served the cause of freedom than by sword ;
Exiled, in prison, or on scaffold given
To country their last breath, in face of heaven.
Yet there in flow of blood I first confessed
The God in Christ, and knew Him ever blessed ;
Found too in ravages of plague true faith,
Saw a church ministrant—Christ conquering death.
And here at home me, meditating still
The passion of the world, and fearful ill,
The Canon of St. Paul's wise counsel lends,
" To make St. Giles and Drury Lane my friends."
Pity too urging leisure to this end,
I many hours in visitation spend,
Till habit grows to open purse and heart ;

Make woe a study, horror a fine art.
Cellar, and attic, alley, court, and lane,
Street I explore, not once but oft again.
With foul and vile familiar, I lose sense
Of all but pity waxing more intense.
But when I ponder to reform the ways
Of poor and wretched fallen waifs and strays,
And speak to them of God, and think to prove,
That He exists and is a God of Love,
I can their ears, not understanding, reach,
Until I doubt not God, but human speech ;
And question, " Can we reason doubt away ? "
And ask the Canon of St. Paul's to say.

CANON.

" Doubt only is, that we may think it out,
And know both what and whom we think about :
Our God is knowable beyond a doubt.
Conscious of self, and other force abroad,
We intuition have of very God,
In Nature uniform a reign of Law,
And Power above all Cause.   With growing awe
We first affirm Him ; after, fear we lie,
Yet do not in so doing Him deny :
For all are constituted to adore.
We doubt our knowledge of Him ; nothing more.
That He is known through Christ, approves Him chief :
Why doubt God's Goodness come to our relief ?
Formed in His Image, and by Him inspired,
What more is left to do, or be desired,
Than up to His Ideal, with His aid,
To grow what He intended, when He made,
So by His means becoming what He meant ;
A voluntary task intelligent.
As we from God come, we His greatness show ;
But none is greater than another so.
This is our greatness, not that we remain
What God created, but more high attain ;
By full development of powers first given,

More than He made us we become for heaven,
And His approval win ; nor low, nor high,
Appearing great, or good in God's just eye
Where high and low, and more and less appear
Each alike goodly, active in its sphere."

So had I help with Easter Time at hand,
But Winter clinging still to half the land.

CANTO III.

NURSE, comely but cruel,
  Spring grudges babe years
The pitiful fuel
  Of sunshine in tears ;
With kisses half biting,
  Gives freezy caress ;
Like Balaam affrighting,
  Gins cursing to bless.
In park, square, and street may
  Man shiver, bird, bush ;
It overhead sleet may,
  May underfoot slush ;
Love still keeps heart glowing,
  And fancy ice-free,
And hope its flowers blowing
  In gardens of glee.

Oh, for more senses, or another ear,
Or these to open trancingly to hear
The springs of being welling from below,
And coursing from above ; the roots that go
Ravening through savoury loam ; the leaves that draw
Carbonic draughts from air, and back by law
Give it in oxygen to brutes again,
So re-arranging all for good of men ;

The microscopic wisdom, that within
Keepeth all busy in a nebulous din,
As rind on rind expands, cracks, grows the bark,
Begins the bough, the bud forsakes the dark,
While wax the leaves unnumbered, and the root
Shoots into midnight millionary shoot.
This could I hear, Sh! what a world of sound
Would swell in wonder up from underground
Through spiked and pillared space all leafed abroad,
And rise in anthem thunderous to God.
Could I too hear the heart of Lucy beat
    For me, and only me, in this spring-time,
Her blood flow pulsing, then, all praise as meet,
    I would the laws of nature own sublime,
And, town for home quitting,
    Sharp arrow-like dart,
No murder committing,
    To Lucy's true heart.
I straight to Lucy thus repair,
Making one draught of intervening air,
And ushered in expectant stand
Of rapture in my Holy Land.
Meek Moses died in view of his ;
Eve fell in hers ; shall I in this?
Still, that old Jesuit, the Devil,
Promising good, proposes evil,
And now commissions, lo, another,
Not my dear maiden, but her mother
To interview me.

LUCY'S MOTHER.

        " Grieved I speak :
For silence now would show me weak.
Fortune you may through years dispute,
To find it mocking strict pursuit ;
Maze, like old labyrinth of Crete,
Where you some Minotaur may meet.
A loving heart and constant will
'Twere folly then to fire, worse ill

To strain, distempering to strife,
Bad modelling a hoped for wife.
Myself not young, I can be bold
To teach young lovers to look cold.
For soon the world begins to talk,
And modesty should sagely walk :
Nay, one may change, and people scorn
The love another once hath worn ;
And strictly armed for turns of fate
Must be my child, since doomed to wait.
Your meetings must be few.   Lucy, to whom
I have my views exposed, is 'not at home.'"

I nothing argued.   Hope intense
Balloon-like bursting fell immense,
But noiseless on encumbered care.
   So utterly discomfited,
I may have pleasured her, who there
   To show it was too finely bred.
And Lucy "not at home," I went
Scotched with most motherly intent :
While in my ear Puck, gravely to my face,
Thus put my foolish, not uncommon, case.

PUCK.

" Oft by a worm in the bud the rose is blighted ;
   You think to know what to your eyes is held,
Yet secret foes deceive close friends far-sighted.
   The rhyming Douglas, Bishop of Dunkeld,
Saw within view of palaced Honour dwell
Sinone and Achitophel."

Oft budding spring is nipped by rime ;
   Not full-blown summer.   Love confessed,
Not spring of passion but its summer time,
   Should glow with ardour unrepressed.
Still summer may in thunder storm
Hail, or grow cold, as it was warm,
When strands upon Acadian shore

An iceberg drift from Labradore.
Such storm has risen in our love,
Whose chill I fear will lasting prove ;
An iceberg loosed, unmelting, driven
Into warm bayou of our heaven.

Restrained at first like deer to park,
Then kennelled like mere hounds to bark,
Then "not at home" not always so,
Our meetings rare angelic grow.
Upon us, too, with no one nigh,
We ever feel, or fear an eye,
Not that aloft—for who in love
Hails not the eye of God above—
But insecurity in air,
When tell-tale pyes we witless scare :
While mother sits in inquisition
  On what has nothing to repent,
As winds, that blow upon their mission
Nature to chill and stay fruition,
To suns of ever more ignition
  Are irksome, though no ill is meant.
Sad Jocus 'gan a song to sing,
  Not a psalm of Tait and Brady ;
There's no religion in the thing ;
  The mother is the lady,
Whom he would send to Jericho
To take a little arsenic.

SONG OF JOCUS.

" When pretty maidens do no more
    Than seem to love too blindly,
And mothers feel a little sore,
    True lovers then should kindly
The mothers send to Jericho
To take a little arsenic.

" If the first thimbleful, too spare,
    Quietus not the mother,

Be comforted : myself I swear
    To swallow quick another.
Then let her go to Jericho
And take a little arsenic."

Privacy may no longer be invaded.
Restraint has home, as well as park, blockaded.
Alas ! do I in Lucy change discover ?
Will she the mother please, confound the lover ?
When-as Domitian case to courtiers put,
"What say ye, fathers ; shall this fish be cut ?"
Has mother questioned Lucy so of me ;
And answered been, " That would unhandsome be ; "
Yet gently wrought her, " Let us then surprise,
And crush him in a net of ampler size,
Within whose tightening meshes helpless may
His swelling passion vainly think to play."
Have maid and mother both combined,
And can their purpose be unkind ?
As, scorched with scrutiny too ramp,
Frayed Cupid fled fond Psyche's lamp ;
So fails her love, whose eager kiss
Once nectared more than honeyed bliss ;
Was prompt as stars, which laughing rise
Dim night to light through lustred skies ;
And fonder than Eve's tender breeze
Constant to fanned Hesperides.
Turbid the truth, which limpid pure,
Once deep, calm, floated me secure,
While gentle thoughts without a care,
And heaven lay embosomed there.
Obscured the innocence, whose joy,
Once, like wine sparkling and not coy,
To feast invited with rapt zeal,
And made intemperance common-weal ;
Sharing the appetite it roused,
Fêted the guest, and self caroused.
These memories are as Indian isles
In palmy seas, where nature smiles

With moon and stars of warmer ray,
While, riding in sequestered bay,
Joys, dangers passed have made too dear,
Safe thrill on lip of buccaneer.

" Can lip of mortal taste a bliss
Inalterable, and still his,
Too pure to pall, too full to fail,
Which western song and eastern scent regale,
While peacocks perched nod proud consent,
    And doves round crooding turrets play,
Tinted like comely clouds, that tent
    The closing eye of failing day,
And dewdrops, lustreless as grief,
Course cheeks of closing lotus leaf?"

So Eloise, through window barred,
Breathed her warm soul to Abelard ;
I thus to Lucy mine in a lament
Set to old plaintive music with it sent.

EDWARD'S LAMENT.

" Libations to the Unknown God
    Athenians vaguely poured,
Breathing their souls in vows abroad
    To ignorance adored.
The God, whom witlessly they loved,
    More honoured was when known,
But all my dreams have real proved
    As idle dreams alone :
And now true image of my thought
    I hope no more to find ;
Fancy is false, and must be taught,
    That Lucy is unkind."

Declining faith small matters sized,
While Eastern Churches analysed,
Losing, the light of Transfiguration
In their own light of speculation.

And doubting now I rate her public smile
A shivery brightness only to beguile
A heart, which frozen is, and flung
Back to me "good as new," or hung
Dangling, not dropped but sorely wrung,
Sunned by a look of Russian weather,
When beards, saluting, freeze together.
And off my balance, reeling to recover
A pace sedate, I nigh forget the lover,
Impetuous on Lucy fain would push,
And win fair footing with ignoble rush.
Failing of private now, I form
Public occasion, and, with storm
Of an emotion fearless strong,
Rapid from circumambient throng
Draw her, as currents awry guide
Vessel, whose swelling fullest pride
Of canvas, soon an idle boast,
Is drifting on an iron coast,
Where cliffs magnetic awful seem to bend
The stubborn sails towards the fatal end.

I with her wonder warning blended
Asking—

EDWARD.
" In what have I so deep offended?"

LUCY.
" Offence can scarce be given, when not taken."

EDWARD.
"I know not : but I feel as one forsaken.
Between us snow wide chilling lies."

LUCY.
" Lies blackly, if it love denies."

EDWARD.
" Lies deeply, if it love professes."

LUCY.

" Lies not at all, save in your guesses.
I feel we both are waxing warm."

EDWARD.

" Warmth sometimes comes with a snowstorm.
Forbidden all but public bliss,
How can our loves in the open kiss ?
Low Germans, steaming Lake Maggiore,
Publish by shows their speechless story,
And to a demonstration prove
Their light-worn, light-come, light-gone love :
    But sunsmit coal-fires cease to blaze ;
Stars, which in night for-gathering glow,
In day-light darkening cease to show ;
    British hearts close to public gaze.
As birds, in utter songful prieves,
Court shadiest secrecy of leaves,
True manly passion is most dear
Lone whispered in deep covert's ear."

LUCY.

" Wouldst have me turn then from my mother's door,
Smitten by conscience ragged and forlore ? "

EDWARD.

" Should now your mother mean deceit,
We may in secret fairly meet."

LUCY.

" Rodney could hold his fleets in hand,
Not boys and girls off Gretna land.
You once proposed to run away with me."

EDWARD.

" Yes, I so early judged, the need might be."

LUCY.

" Such danger gives my mother pause.
I fear we could not live upon the laws."

EDWARD.

" Thou can'st not give me back my heart :
Would'st break it quite, say ; shall we part ? "

LUCY.

" Not part, but go I must, and yet,
Believe me, never to forget.
Still credit not mine airy oath,
    Which only is a promise due ;
Trust rather me, who plight my troth ;
    I rather am, than am thought true.
Mirage is splendid to deceive ;
But rainbowed clouds we should believe.
Still love me, Edward ; wisely prove
Deserving of sore proof of love."

Has Lucy sworn no trusty vow ?
Is falsehood penal ?   Look you, now
If one black speck on one pearl tooth
Has witnessed to her perjured youth.
Nay, she is fairer than before,
And suitors throng her more and more ;
While I, who scorn to be her sport,
One of her crowd but not her court,
Unreckoned stand amid the throng,
Till word of mine low, faint, yet strong,
Taking her apprehensive ear,
Moves to responsive tremour dear
Sternly by prideful will subdued
Into a calm, that bodes no good,
And brief, as stir of passing breath
On lips of life at touch of death.
Loves she the lover, she forsakes ;
Or pities but the heart, she breaks ?

In Satan's tears, ah ! who can tell
What drop is heaven, and what drop hell ?
I fancy Mephistopheles by her side
With baleful learing lips stretched ear-wise wide.

MEPHISTOPHELES.

" Old servant brave for Laird of Keir
Could, trusting God, himself fore-swear ;
So sworn in reverential mood,
His falsest oath gained Stirling good.
Swear, lady, then by parish spire,
By vault ancestral for good hire,
By nightish signs, which speechless burn,
By heaven all deaf as taciturn,
By God Himself, and swearing well
Grow to be fair, if false, as hell.
You may by Dian arrows true,
    And by Minerva locks one oath
Swear false all round, and painless too :
    These gods permit once broken troth.
Fear not thy words, which Jove with glee
Strews upon winds o'er land and sea.
Venus laughs ; Cupid too, who whets
On sanguined stone his ardent jets ;
Tibullus ; Horace, on whose sooth
Time blunts in vain edacious tooth ;
Wise Merlin is convulsed, as when
    The leaf from Gunieda hair
Fond Roderick took, conceiving then
    That his queen honest was as fair,
To hear, and scarce their ears believe,
How oaths can laugh in Lucy's sleeve."

As sailors, ringed with calm, the heavens—
Each cloud consult, and very swevens,
For answering passion, veiled with grace,
Search I chance open heaven of Lucy's face
Not Argus-guarded Io more distressed
Jove, whom to heart she once not brutal pressed.

N

And, as Vertumnus long Pomona sought
Entering by wile her orchard lot ;
To find my love alone at last
Her threshold late unwished I passed,
Though rather had furred Ruthon fronted,
Who cloak of royal beards once vaunted,
Demanding Arthur's from his face
To give it there more honoured place.

EDWARD.

" Estrangement and assumed surprise
Give sorry welcome in dilated eyes.
Reproach me not for coming ; 'tis no wrong,
Or one to pardon.   I have suffered long."

LUCY.

" The bond between us is not broken.
My mother hath sufficient spoken."

EDWARD.

" Less fond than when we others greet,
We willing part, and fear to meet."

LUCY.

" And taught I am to think, that so
We best avoid conclusive woe."

EDWARD.

" By thus beginning to be sad ?
Nay, Lucy, wilt thou make me mad ?
As Noy of law, you may of love
Profounder knowledge think to prove,
Ruling it other than conceived,
And noy-ful more than we believed.
But love's such seeming last excess
    Shows as when justice most appals,
Hangs victim up in evening dress,
    Burns priest in full canonicals,
Or kills, with courtesy japanned,
By one's own sword in friendly hand."

LUCY.

"Wouldst have mine eyes breed waste of water,
For that I am my mother's daughter;
Obeying ruefully her hest,
Be to please thee a world's fair jest?
Weeds, which become a widow, may
Languish on heart already gay,
And graced that Chinese widow shrewd,
Whose dying spouse had prayed she would,
While moist his coverlet of sod,
Confess him still her household god;
Quick to fan-dry his turf she ran,
And handed suitor fresh a twin-wide fan."

EDWARD.

" Dost thou disdain for me then feign,
　And only cloak, not shroud esteem;
'Neath smiles for others hide a true disdain?
　Art contrary to all you seem?
Though in appearance fat and florid,
　'Tis said of San de Paula, he
Was no profanity so horrid,
　But skin and bone invisibly;
His chubbiness, or what you please,
But greater gift of grace, not grease.
Lest, then, I doubt the very creed,
Let me not hear thee prayers read,
Nor Scripture eke, it were such pain
To think that Abel murdered Cain."

LUCY.

" To reason with such folly sad
Would prove me melancholy mad."

EDWARD.

'In salves for and assaults of hearts
　I do confess myself unschooled—
A ready butt for idle darts:
　But am I worthy to be fooled?

Glassing thy moods for weal, for woe,
  Like ocean bosom-bared to heaven,
I unto thee a mirror show,
  Wearing thy frowns as favours even.
Does generous confidence invite
Selfish disdain, ungenerous slight?
Thy smile might, bright as spring,
Move melting rock to sing,
Like morn auroraing
  Memnon no longer granite ;
Alas ! now thy regard,
Gorgonian and hard
As coral, has ill-starred—
  Not sunning more its planet.
No more for sun's bright rise
Dismantled Memnon sighs ;
Blind are his stony eyes,
  His stony heart past breaking :
But be it bliss or woe,
Thy will I long to know ;
  Though suns may cease to glow,
Hearts should have no forsaking."

LUCY.

" To save Parmenio's hoary head
Not seventy years of service weighed
With great, but hasty, Alexander
Against a breath of passing slander:
Even friends, like Edwin and Cadwallo,
Parted were by suspicion callow.
But charity conceives no guile ;
  And love is real stedfast power,
Not whim chameleon-like to wile,
  And take its colour from the hour.
Am I, then, what these should not be,
  Only the slave of waxen sense,
Melting to every passing he,
  Fusile and fluxile as intense ;
Double, if blessed uncertain whether,

And fickle as wild wind and weather :
Most true to nature, when untrue,
Fooling myself, or fooling you ?
' Ho, Akhab ! where do you put up to-night ? '
　　The Arab shouts ; and, as it rolls, it cries
' Still with the wind ; ' and think you, I am trite
　　To every whirlwind gust of masculine sighs ? "

　　Tears further answered me drawing near.
As clouds by thunder questioned, why
They darken all a daylight sky,
　　Showering affrighted, disappear ;
She, too, was on the instant gone,
And I in agony alone,
As wretch, in lull of growing harm,
Who has trusted to a failing charm,
And round whom silence spreads increased alarm ;
Or Orpheus when, hell quitting conqueror, he
　　Revolving eye of loving fear or doubt,
Looked back and lost forlorn Euridyce.
　　What then availed his harp, that stout
It had mollified Cerberian ire,
Though hundred serpents salient sowed
　　The ferial head uncouth,
And tetter-breath and sanies flowed
　　From the trilingual mouth ?
Pluto was stern ; her mother is more dire,
And I awaited not her ominous tire.
Satan half-heaven in his fall withdrew ;
From forfeit paradise passed two.
But, thus attempting bliss forbidden,
I lone was routed from my Eden :
And in full sense of some alones
Such outer desolation moans,
That one would rather life depart.
A fluttering hope I took to heart :
As string long stretched needs tuning rest,
May Lucy be but over-blest,
And, o'er my songs of love to crood,

Seek memorable solitude?
The rock, when riven in twain, will show
   Two faces similarly scarred,
Proving to each, such parting blow
   Has been alike heart-breaking hard,
And that they will thus marred remain,
Till love-fires solve them one again:
So Lucy, whom I grieved am leaving,
May sit bereft too, as bereaving:
And till that hour I had conceived
Expectance, born to be believed.
I in my soul—for always she was there—
Compose, and offer up to her a prayer;
May such have written, but now cannot swear.

THE PRAYER.

"Forget me not, I pray,
   As ocean proud doth bark
Washed with its furrow lone away;
   But meeting bright in dark
Of fancy fond, not blind,
   Let us embrace in thought,
Renewing hours that were so kind,
   We can forget them not.
So shall our memories sweet
   Holy Communion take,
As hails, which not despairing greet
   Over an angry lake.
The waves shall surely fall:
   My labour, waiting long,
Cross the wide waters to thy call,
   And join us; or should song
Be here to hopes untrue—
   And meeting not be given,
Our faithful spirits may renew
   And join their vows in heaven."

Ah! with pangs of doubtful fight
All my coward heart is white;

All its promises are pale,
Faint with fears, which more prevail,
Blanched as stars, which trembling pray
Dying out of dawning day.
Is some ill chance at work?   Have I by Puck
Sudden with fairy wand been lightly struck,
And changed into an aspen-silly crook
With head erect, but wanting heart of oak?
Like quiet breezes that expire
In high sun's meridian fire,
Valour in me seems to die
In full glory of her eye,
Boldening others to oppress
Me alone with shamefacedness—
Me, poor clerk of Brittanie
Longing for his Rose-Marie.

Timid, as Endymion
When Diana on him shone,
At a dance, where all were glad,
I only was exceeding sad.
Though gayest orb of all was mine,
   Bright in that galaxy for all,
It seemed not there for me to shine :
   Why went I to that lonely ball?
Ever to dance with her forbidden,
I dared refusal, and, unchidden,
Even now I feel
Returning weal,
Walking in thought that prim quadrille.
Then, in the flame it loved and neared
As the goat lost its frowzy beard,
My passion frizzled in her smile,
And shivery bravery failed me, while,
Upon mine arm, she loitered round
Looking queen lady of the ground—
Beauty receiving dues of splendour,
Whose homage easy was to render.
Eye and flesh lust, and life's most pride

Seemed duties in and to such wished-for bride ;
I was as nothing by her side.
I know not all I said, nor how I said it ;
Nor if excuse I made, nor how I made it :
Or was it Puck that spake, and did she hear ?
Or did he only speak in mine own ear ?

PUCK *or* EDWARD.

"Accursed be he, who first for orient pearls
Dived, or, now buying, barters them for girls ;
Imports from Afric diamonds, till sun
By rival rays invidious is outdone,
And belles of seasons his rude aspect shun.
Accursed be gems, and luxury, French robes,
Or Coan, Tyrian dyes, lace flouncing globes,
Enormities of value as of dress
With trains like tails of Comets measureless.
Accursed be modish homes of exquisite taste,
Where all is reckless cost, though nothing waste,
Italian, Louis Quinze, our own Queen Anne,
Or Mediæval Moor or Allemagne ;
Rare articles of vertue everywhere,
More rare than vertuous, fanciful than rare ;
Ancient and modern master, decoration,
And entertainment rising to ovation.
Accursed be very flowers, too liberal strewn,
Dying on velvet like a honeymoon.
Accursed be fashion, thus demanding wealth
To keep a woman more than in good health.
Ah, woman velveted can go the pace,
Though man no deer in velvet cares to chase.
Purse too, too small, for exigence of style,
Dooms man a benedict to yellow bile,
While only sterling worth can win the fair,
And arts of love and moneymaking pair,
Or tinsel title. Imogens in play,
Paulines in act are rare, and little weigh.
Wedding Demetrius, called Ivan's son,
Marina Mniszeck throne of Russia won.

He fell; she then a fresh Demetrius found.
When he too fell, she sought another round,
Eager her vanished honours to regain,
Till they in Volga drowned her pride and pain."

Reseating her, I, fallen from grace,
  By sense of mine own faults made dumb,
Now yield to rival Earl in chase
  Claiming her for the waltz to come :
Like Spains-Hall Kempe, from speech shall I
For seven long years my tongue deny ?
On him she leans in dance, as vine
Round elm lithe tendrils may entwine,
While loves among the branches play,
Till elm and vine look equal gay,
But dazzled by her sunshine free,
Enhancing each dark tray in me,
I feel as though all black to be,
And should descend through Avaiki
To the bottom of Te-enua-teki ;
As Te-matua fond with Vari,
Stick by my parent and not marry ;
Or, in Mute-land, where dance is noiseless,
  And gift of speech itself unknown,
Taught the fine art of living voiceless,
  Remount to woo by sighs alone :
So to unrein my mortal tongue
Was to my goddess tantalizing wrong.
Yet, as in Waltz she round me flew,
To me the measure songful grew.

SONG OF THE WALTZ.

" Flickering fire-fly !
    Whither so gay
  Planet-like sparkling,
    When sun's away ?
  Hither and thither
    Glancing, thou
  Flickering fire-fly,

Whither now?
Not as any meteor
   Beam of delight
Shining but a moment
   Through a long night,
Thou hast a brilliance
   Upon wing
All through many a night-time
   Flickering.
More than one shall chase thee
   Fondly and fast :
Hast thou been taken
   Fly-like at last?
Cease then to sparkle
   Flitting : nay,
Flickering fire-fly,
   Flit my way."

Glad child, in evening sports engaged,
'Twixt concave palms a fire-fly caged,
Yet full of fear, lest flame impressed
Should restive scorch, or die caressed ;
From hands unlocked the flying joy
Secured was by a bolder boy.
Can I look for safer bliss
To reward man's cowardice?
Vainly I urge discouraged heart.
As labouring bark, whose pumps we start,
But on whose hull hard ocean gains,
Tasks baffled hours and ebbing pains,
And sinks with mighty sough,
   And most balloon-like bubbles,
Leaving tossed billows o'er its trough ;
   So in unsparing troubles
My sinking heart with bursting sigh
   And after gulps, that will not drown,
Spraying and blinding each shocked eye,
   Most lifelessly goes down.

I quit the room : and, now to me

The cynosure of memory,
Lucy, is future hope o'ercast
With sighs repentant of the past.
Much like as when an angel shines
  Sore heart to heal, big tear to dry
Of mortal, who despairing pines,
  With so great glory in his eye
Bewildered man affrighted flies ;
  No harms arresting, stays, and turns :
But fadingly the vision dies.
  He runs, and kneels, and loudly mourns,
"Come back ;" but back for all his moan
It will not come : he is alone
Wishing now he had not fled
Glory, though faint life had sped,
As from Semélé to prove
Love of unconcealing Jove.
That courtly Earl can dance and fool with skill :
I am a poor, slow driver of a quill.

CANTO IV.

Now upon visit, welcome to my mother,
Came her sole living and still bachelor brother,
Who, somewhile rich from India safe returned,
Nor fashions had, nor folks provincial spurned,
But in a neighbour county settled, where
He to a good estate had fallen heir.
Much travelled he, much pondered had, much felt,
And yet his smile was bright, and eye could melt :
For on his soul remained the dew of youth ;
Trial had only wrought a world of ruth.
With him our Christmas-tide was seemly glad :
Shall now through me his spring with us be sad ?
Cause of my noted sorrow soon to view,

With cunning, kind as curious, forth he drew—
My story, to the passing moment told,
Of one in wisdom young for years so old.
My doubts he heard, enduring passion guessed,
And situation warm thus cool addressed.

UNCLE.

"When fortune level favour minces,
A part to each, then all are princes.
And knowing rival none supreme,
  Since thou hast Lucy's troth apart,
Wherefore thy fortune misesteem?"

EDWARD.

"Doubt may, discreet, be no fool art,
But safety beacon of the wise.
Illuming truth, exposing lies,
Its reasons are the very spans
And inches of our bravest plans."

UNCLE.

"Yet faint and crooked as St. Kinéd
By his own fearful prayers repinéd,
All huddled into formless heap
The Hodge will never sow, nor reap,
While winds and clouds for bad results
He superstitiously consults.
Woodpecker tap, or cheap of chick,
Gnawing of mouse, or beetle-tick,
Are thunder in so abject ears
Admitting only horrid fears.
Though fickle are law and the fair,
  Upon the brave future still borrow."

EDWARD.

"But to-day is so irksome to bear,
  That I fain would put off to-morrow:
To-morrow will errors disclose
  In to-day's and yesterday's action,

And add other error to those
 For another to-morrow's distraction.
On Niagara currents, 'tis told,
 As fallward is garbage floated,
Darts the bird, which fierce rapids hold
 In strict embraces, devoted.
In vain would it rise upon wing
 Too weak now to burst a bubble,
And is whirled like some human thing
 To the leap, that ends all trouble."

UNCLE.

" Still he who never makes mistakes,
Never anything better makes :
And sloth is most cowardly sin.
 On trial success may be waiting :
For he, who can lose, may win.
 And since ardour knows no abating,
Though fickle are law and the fair,
 For joy on near future still borrow ;
Though to-day is irksome to bear,
 Hope on for more lively to-morrow.
Let others to her love resort,
And with it confidently sport :
Playing them false, she still may be
True upon law's long road to thee,
As was to Prince of Troubadours
Berengaria mid amours—
She temptation-proof, however
 He in heart might change or mind ;
She a vane that was fixed for ever,
 He chance failing wind."

EDWARD.

" You do not doubt my truth ? "

UNCLE.

 " Nay, nay :
But what if Lucy sometimes may ?

Hilda lonely sat and sighed,
Plight to Guy and yet denied.
He, to win her nobler hand,
Nobly fought in Holy Land.
Fell a beauteous Paynim maid
Captive to his Christian blade,
Which enamoured wed renown :
Hilda sits and sighs alone.
She, false fortune ante-dating,
  Hopeful sees days vapid run,
Danceful springs revolve unmating,
  Vainer summers parched with sun ;
Till, fruitless bloom now gone and dying
  Chill after-glow, without a date,
Breath, become all one waste of sighing,
  Gusts life's last leaf off without mate.
Has Lucy no such thought, nor care ;
Let her be happy, or you worse may fare."

EDWARD.

" I all things to my love would be,
Such needful misery is she to me.
  And if a falsehood blinds mine eye,
Its colours flying, as ne'er Reynolds painted,
Nor Iris wove, nor hope herself invented,
  Show all so lovely as to look no lie."

UNCLE.

" Be strong, and still trust ;
Be bold, and be just.
Though dances Asiatic
  With piety grew
To action dramatic
  And poesy too ;
Though with ark Zion-nearing
  The King danced and praised,
And Sundays God-fearing
  Round May-poles we raised ;
Though Bess, having fancies,

Could Perrotts neglect,
Who showed Hatton dances
    A brave disrespect ;
Leave dancing and dangling
    To carpet-made knights,
And ogling and angling
    To love parasites—
De Grammonts, De Orsays,
    Hewetts-demme, and Nashes,
Most weakly of forces,
    If brightest of flashes.
To courts—not Provençal
    Of soft Languedoc,
Where troubadours chance all
    And ladies don't mock—
Law calls thee.   Cease sighing ;
    Forget vain alarms ;
Snatch fortune defying
    To labour's strong arms,
Not saying with Hatton,
    That even Queen Bess
The heart, she once sate on,
    Could never redress.
Thy failure perplexes,
    Chills Lucy to snow.
Success to her sex is
    Law, light, love, and glow.
She were but less human
    To honour it less ;
So gifted a woman,
    Herself is success."

EDWARD.

" Shall I dismiss my watchful fears
Despite maternal daunts and jeers,
Advancing and opposing years,
Rank, wealth, each countervailing voice
Of worldly charm, and wiser choice ? "

UNCLE.

" Assembly of proud argument,
   Uniting with delusive force—
Which gods forbid and maids repent—
   Life from affection to divorce ;
Despite it all, may she be given
To faith and thee, to love and heaven,
As Perdita to Florizel,
Both true—which most, Truth could not tell—
True ! Olave sprang from Abbey wall
To Talbot arms, which stayed her fall ;
True ! nine feet wide and sixty deep
From tower to tower, the Lady leap
Grim Castle Ruthven shows to prove,
How lady-feet are winged by love."

I took the lesson fond to heart,
Having a feeling for high art,
And now my brighter hopes believe ;
Even Cumming saints could earth reprieve,
As Jonah Nineveh, and date
Leases beyond fixed hour of fate
In scripture scrolls, by them unfurled,
Dooming this perishable world.
Law, deigning me one cheerful smile
Could all my latest fears beguile :
And I, to woo it, now from Lucy part
With a light fancy, though a heavy heart.

Beyond thought's plummet, 'neath Pacific waves,
O'er drowned volcanoes filling early graves,
Through darkness never chased by shafts of day,
Worms coralline entomb their upward way.
With generations piled of creamy cells,
Slow monument interminable swells ;
E'er island germ disdainful chafes vexed tide,
Young earth has aged, and ages old have died :
What strength must faith have thus to root, and rise
Through myriad night to hail and base clear skies.

So I through one long darkness Lucy seek.
In court, in chambers, days become a week,
And week to week, and month to month succeeds,
And still I study, while some other pleads.
In twenty guineas when shall brief be mailed?
Am I myself a rap to counter nailed?
Puck seized the cue, and cannoned round the table;
The game was in his hand : he said—

PUCK.

"Diable!
What if out, in, long briefless years all pass,
Till weakening sight you fortify with glass;
A wayworn barrister no longer brave,
Are drifting, drooping, dropping, to the grave,
Lone, needy, shiftless, nerveless, sad, a waif,
Which life will never miss, but death make safe?
Death save? ha, ha! if mercy in the deed,
What horrid dark in fatal depth of need :
Life wasted, mis-employed, and run to seed;
Powers mis-directed; a mis-take, alas!
Which with attorneys wise may never pass.
Is your faith froth of bubbles bursting dumb,
Foam settling, seething, hissing into scum?"

This surely was, by Puck or said or no,
The track on which my thoughts concurred to go.
As one, on journey far adventuring blind,
Long travels but no thankful rest to find—
Unlikely now, since further walk depressed,
Sinking or rising, wanders marsh, or waste,
Ponder I erring start, or missing way.
Have I misled, or chosen road astray—
Profession wrong, yet now for loved one lost
Would dare, like Euthymas, the fiend almost,
And in extreme of earth cavernous storm
For golden apples Hesiodic worm?

Rare faculty have I of second sight
Dark formless thought to clothe in shapely light:
O

For not alone is sense on soul depicted,
But also sense by soul at once convicted.
Who wields such power, can never truly say :
For all will real seem as noon of day.
So now in cleft Parnassian bestowed
And grove of Helicon in sun that glowed,
The Muses nine and orderly appeared
Headed by her, to me the most endeared,
Who thus addressed me answering, the while
Apollo distant harped with shaded smile ;
She spoke like any modern to surprise—
Perhaps they all were Christian—gods are wise.

CALLIOPE.

" I rocked thy cradle, Neptune watching me
And trident shaking in mad sport at thee.
Athéné led, till Themis taught thy years ;
Yet open unto me were all thine ears,
And I am sad to see thee now to-day
Standing uncertain of thy further way."

EDWARD.

" Burke, Sheridan, quit bar to rise on crupper—
But I would not—of ten or thousand Upper,
And scorn like Stephen, though an alien king,
Ever to be an abdicated thing."

CALLIOPE.

" Still Christian, floundering through sloughed despond,
Thence issuing not more wished safe path beyond,
Forsook the way of faith, and took to law—
His grand mistake—soon eager to withdraw.
You may a bye-way choose with better gain,
Avoid straight desert, strike highroad amain ;
Lawyer by day, by night a writer, be
Such sleepless man as Homer thought to see,
Now neat-herd, and now shepherding white flocks
For double gain on Loestrygonian rocks.
A clever friend, in infancy of mark

Enamoured now of owl and now of lark,
The artful windy lawyer, Hermes, taught
His well-strung shell sweet music full of thought :
Littleton, Somers, Mansfield, Blackstone, Jones,
Davies, law's David if not Helicon's,
Hardwicke himself could with the Muse prevail,
And on irreverent circuit Powis hail— "

Here I broke in : for sudden on my head
Minerva's helm unseen I felt ; I said—

EDWARD.

" He on Parnassus found, with pools to search,
Nothing so rich as a Westminster perch.
On law and learning deep constrained to doat,
And having taken Fancy by the throat,
Now shall I liberate it chance to be
A waste Castalian source of poesy ?
But may I now ?   And, if to try so bold,
Would fount of song from hearts of rock draw gold,
Not rather copper dropped in passing scorn
On wasteful torrent, brawling night and morn—
To Hamlet and the Ghost a thousand pence ;
Double to Paradise Lost, munificence ?
Would congregations Ruer now approve,
For saintly hymns accept his songs of love,
Whatever the Salvation Army may,
Priests grant a pulpit to the science gay,
And with whole after offertory pay ?
Though Charles gave to Marot hundreds two
For thrice ten psalms of David frenched like new,
Genevese nothing giving, when he died,
Stole and embalmed them in their creed with pride.
Though Alexander doned, for each great line,
To Cherilus a golden Philippine,
Mahmoud, like promising to Firdusi, paid
Silver instead, despised for the mean trade.
Poet should, when inspired or in a fret,
Spurn the base gold of Sovereigns, and yet

Yourselves to Æschylus were false, when fell
Upon his head, and broke it, your live shell.
Spenser starved ; Dryden prostituted wit ;
Otway of hunger died in eating fit ;
Camœns, Burns, Chatterton were plumed, but plucked
Poetic bones, from which brave juice we sucked,
Sparing our purse, to marrow them with fame :
God grant to no poor poet such dear shame.
To please may Rogers write, but most to live
Needs most demand what publishers will give—
If anything at all, for Collins lays
Less than St. James for well-sung ballad pays.
Poetic stock is reckoned brains too tender,
Less valuable than sheep's-head remainder,
Poor pittance for rare Lucy with bewild'ring,
If happy, possibilities of children.
Venus craves opulence of vulgar things,
Cares neither what God says, nor poet sings.
On purple lock—his sole—hung Nisus' life,
And immortality takes song to wife ;
Yet how has time mostly meanly reckoned art,
Now girls have golden locks, and diamonds more at heart.
Avaunt, ye Muses, if of no avail,
Not winning gold, ye only please to fail ! "

Calliope hinted here of compromise.

CALLIOPE.

" Prose is more paying."

EDWARD.

　　　　　" That's about the size :
But so to please the public as to pay
Is not for all at once, nor every day.
Niggard this modish world, and must be gulled ;
If trained and taught yields ruts, when you are hulled.
Nay, let me lawful live, and swanlike die :
When nearing heaven I may sing, or try,
Like Desdemona, or Ophelia mad,

Portentously and overwisely glad.
Mine eyes not yet are purged, nor pinions plumed
To soar in, see, and sing pure truth illumed :
Song else must perish, and be less than one,
Who fain would sing for ever—not for fun.
Oh, Calliope, only less than Lucy, dear !
For her fond sake I leave thee, rapt by fear
Of wronging thee and her with love too blind :
Law, my strict master, be no more unkind."

By Calliope summoned then, Polymnia straight
Advancing, I was ware of coming fate.

POLYMNIA.

" As time's last trump shall void the grave,
  And Hades rout with fateful breath,
So men have been, whose voice could save,
  Piercing the ear of moral death,
A nation civilly to raise
From lowest blame to highest praise ;
And died, but not their words, which thrill
Down hollow ages echoing still.
With glory growing, not to end
  Boreal in a midnight sky,
Their shapes majestical distend
  Pupil of time's reverted eye,
And Rome articulate appears,
Forum and Rostra, crowds and cheers,
But chief the man, whom one might know,
Even in his dust, for Cicero.
In Capitol you Venus guess
Uncertain if a Grace, or less :
But who in Vatican once sees,
In marble knows, Demosthenes."

EDWARD.

" Such for a purpose seeming small,
Milonian or Coronal,
Catch, holding wide, time's ravished ear."

POLYMNIA.

" No idle talk was e'er so dear.
Not many genius have, or art
To tongue the passion-stops of heart,
In words of power the soul reveal,
Make reason see, and conscience feel.
Of varied accent but one speech,
   Webster, and Erskine, Grattan, Bright
English the rounded world, and teach
   With pentecostal tongues of light."

Her finger from her lips Polymnia taking
Laid on my mouth, so frenzied for speech-making.

POLYMNIA.

" Known have I how, when heaven and ocean
Were mingling in perpetual motion,
One stood on rock, whence nought was green—
All churning tempest, nothing seen
'Twixt pallid waves and leaden skies
Save dipping oft the gull, whose cries
Pierce through hoarse roaring fierce of storm,
That with sea-foam besprayed him warm
Outstanding upon venturous rock,
Which shuddered under shock on shock
Of angry billow following billow.
Strong winds, that wreathed huge waves like willow,
Wroth shouldered failing him to move,
Who earth, sea, air had come to prove,
Against them all his own stout voice,
And in mad tempest did rejoice.
And, mate for eagles, sometimes he
Would mountain lightly climb, and see
Crags fallen to drossy dust far seamed
With silver threads, and unto streamed
Magnificence, and forests wide,
And rivered plains where towns abide,
Things glorious rehearse, his soul
With nature's mingling so, the whole

Her words might be, he could not know,
But like a whirlwind would they come,
And like long roll of thunder-drum,
    When gods assemble, would they go."

Polymnia so whispered, whom insane
I now had foolishly upon the brain.
In higher background still Apollo hove
By Hermes joined, thither despatched by Jove.
With wingéd cap and on Talarean feet,
Now Hermes at a bound alighted neat,
And, with Caduceus, touching, breathed on me.
Thalia, Calliope, Melpoméné,
Together talking, turned a farewell glance.
A parting strain Euterpé played, and dance
Terpsichoré began.   While Cleio full
Noted what passed, Erato, only dull,
Seemed with Eurania in the clouds, when I
Sudden was blinded by Apollo nigh.
Of some propitious chance he prophesied ;
Then faded all, and there was none beside
Myself.   And what are these then?   Love and Puck.
These ? Law and Caw. And these ? Life, Luck, and Pluck.

CANTO V.

BLACKSTONES by lecturing attain
Also to judge and sentence men ;
Mitfords to print a practice owe,
Illumine law, and selves fore-show ;
But senior bags may happen still
On junior a brief to spill ;
Or time, or other bird to slay
In neighbour court, one's leader may
Absent himself, be gouty ; in brief,

Dunnings still watch the falling leaf.
Each moment burdened is with fate,
And chance may come to those who wait.
Goal is not always unto pace,
    Nor victory to strength, nor bread
To understanding, neither grace
    Nor honour unto skill; but, shed
Heaven's sun and rain with equal fall,
Time happeneth and chance to all.
The happy chance, alas, to me
Was others' time of dire necessity.

While strikes, like scoriæ clouds, disclose
High winds of passion in strong blows,
Plague also with unequal hand
Distempers the penurious land.
Prodigal famine ravening roams
    With drought, low wages, and less food;
And broken hearts in desolate homes
    Doubt if God lives, or can be good.
To fool despair, and laughter cause,
Tickling it with political straws,
In feignéd issue loud contend
Rich liberal and tory friend.
Passed in new session, seeming vain,
At the Lords' mercy once again,
Some people's Bill, or parchment drum
Is beaten now by other some
Rallying with pretentious sound
To change, that overleaps the bound;
While unions, gatheringly derne,
With firm-set purpose grim wax stern.
Trade—manufacture—commerce—bank
Business is palsied to a blank;
And on a Monday—call it Black,
And never again to London back—
From every quarter bannered march
Processionals through either arch
To meet in Park, and thence to stream,

Passing the Lords and the Lion-hearted
With due salute, and, like a dream
  Of Babels, upon all sides parted,
Each several course on homeward way
With speech in chosen hall to close the day.

" Drop old-world systems to abysm
Of Dynamite and Nihilism ! "
From vagrant outside groups arise,
" Down with the Lords ! " and other cries.
Hell is abroad, and rage and fear
Permeate lurid atmosphere
Frenzied with a prophetic power
Perpending horror's natal hour,
While on it Dirœ sail, and breathe
Approaching wrath, and threatening death :
For beggars have Erinnyes,
And vengeance tracks who wrong even these.

One homeward line long threads the massed
  Embankment, and Blackfriars straight
Up Ludgate to St. Paul's, and past
  Upon this side ; and thither late
From Court in Guildhall having come,
  I on St. Paul's fore spacious landing
Watched thoughtfully the steady march home.
  The doors behind, still open standing,
Had some concluded service seen
Of schools, or other ; and, within,
The nave was scaffolded and benched,
  The transept benched and chaired,
And, where the nave on transept trenched,
  A dais due prepared ;
When came the march to sudden pause,
Blocked by invisible strong cause.
Above the space, now crushing rude,
Near with his aides a leader stood
To organize a fresh advance ;
When sudden the cry rose, " What a chance !

Let's hold a meeting in St. Paul's."
And one to other shouting calls,
" Let's hold a meeting in St. Paul's."
And with fierce haste, beyond our stem,
They rushed, and forced us, heading them,
Into the church, and up the nave
To the dais, which we seized to save,
My friend and his aides directing thence
To calm the ordered turbulence,
Till the vast temple showed one sea of faces
Under the whispering gallery's lonelinesses.

High flaming thoughts the soul inspired,
By pressing need alarming fired.
None cared to first, yet one to speak
  Forward upon the dais stepped ;
And with a voice, that seemed too weak
  For understanding strong, he crept
Through living tragedy, and prosed
Anatomizing, while some dosed.
Audience vague, restless as a sea,
That heaves, though seeming calm to be,
And breaks up on an arid beach,
Drowned in long groan the heavy preach
Empty to ear, as laid to eye:
So, learned in grain but husky dry,
At Bolton once one came to close,
Chaffed by the crowd, till Paulton rose.

The various mystery of wrong
  Now become master of my heart,
And stirring me like mournful song,
I grieved to know the frustrate throng
As birds, which, at a window long,
  Thence crumbless in mid-winter part.
Heart with emotion, meant not to unman,
Maketh its feeling way, as best it can.
Yet are there issues various of heart :
Though good in all, not all the better part.
For passion, sometimes masterful in mood,

A wrong may wrongly right, and miss the good.
Better the heart by reason not disdained,
But in its hate of hates still wisely reined,
Going its kind instinctive way, but ruled,
Bearing, forbearing, yet not once befooled.
With eyes whence streams of passion fiery flowed,
A fixed white face beside me glowed.
Impulsive through his spirit poured
Large argument, which speech implored,
Strong feeling straitened unto pain,
Whose utterance never comes in vain :
For that, whose force compels to speak,
If sometimes bad, is never weak.
Great Cæsar's wounds were tongued so well,
Rome never rose from where he fell ;
Uneasy, too, still lies the mace,
Which Cromwell baubled out of place :—
And while I pondered, lo ! the Partisan rose.

PARTISAN.

" Let's have a talk, my friends, about our foes.
I as a workman speak, and to his like
Out on a holiday, or say a strike
Against the laws.   Who made them ?   What sustains,
That they should stand, when a whole nation strains ? "

FIRST WORKMAN.

" Peter and Paul say ' God.' "

SECOND WORKMAN.

"' The Devil ' I."

PARTISAN.

" You have well said.   Oh, hardy villainy !
Cruel as Spartans, and without their grace,
A riotous, self-indulgent, robber race,
Normans, sea-vikings, veriest land-sharks,
Our island overran, forsook their barks,
And made their feudal lord, stout sovereign,

Master of our legitimate domain.
Him, too, in time they stripped, and selves attained
To all his crown had in our state-right feigned.
Our legislators these ; they rule us still
By veto on the National good will ;
And were and are, without our own consent,
Makers of laws, that have but one intent—
Their own immoral self-aggrandisement,
Spite of the ten commandments to subdue,
And hold the many abject to the few.
They bishops gave to church, and lords to bar ;
Ennobling swords, made state-craft out of war ;
Till battle, law, religion to be feared,
Were right well cozened having been well peered.
Beer, banking, shipping, manufacture, trade
With agriculture they conservative made,
And to their rally fervid gallow-glasses
Paid, privileged to spoil the labouring classes.
And had they only been less cunning strong,
We had not been their treasures-trove so long."

Second Workman.

"The irresponsible Lords ! Ah, there's the rub."

Third Workman.

" The House of Commons is no poor man's club."

Partisan.

" The Commons first we forced, with Lords conceding,
To strip mere commerce of its special pleading,
So long as privilege remained to rent,
Which stayed, conserved even when the Corn Laws went
The Commons, though not Lords too, we reformed ;
Ramparts of slavery and monopoly stormed ;
Religious tests annulled, and criminal laws,
Themselves most criminal ; made good our cause
In master contracts—wage, not rent, equations ;
Ousted the Holy Alliance from the nations ;
And all effected 'gainst unfailing ban

And gross majorities of Privileged Man,
Whose bloated body feeds on all it may
From the general good abstract to make shrewd privilege
    pay."

THIRD WORKMAN.

" It smells too rank.   Its days of grace are passed."

PARTISAN.

" And yet you suffer the vile pest to last,
While ancient laws—not ours, but of our Lords
Enslaving us—upheld are by their swords.
For though power place has changed, and now resides
In ballot votes, their veto still o'er-rides
Forceful in this dragooned, boycotted, primrosed land,
Whose standing armies are at their command
To turn against ourselves, and not our foes,
And with our own arms our own breasts oppose.
Force still is master of the fretful hour,
   Conserves ill-gotten gains by fraudful might,
Reading new laws to suit the past of power,
   And making legal wrong of moral right.
Not to reform are any judges paid,
But backward read the law with counsel's aid :
Apt, too, they are, how learned soe'er more coarse,
On slight offence to drop with seven-fold force.
And try-and-do-the-poor-for-nothing fudges
Try 'em, and do 'em with decemviral grudges,
Deface the scutcheon of our state and times,
While making virtue of their virtual crimes.
Even paid magistrates read law to play
Into the hands, which give them place and pay.
And, martial law ! What is it, but a will
Which, failing to impose, is going to kill
Men, who in strictest right combined might stand
Against the powers of wrong in all the land.
To rouse by batons is their little game,
And then by shot the British lion tame."

THIRD WORKMAN.

" Away with armies, Lords, and Commons too,
Magistrates, lawyers, the whole cursed crew."

PARTISAN.

" Peace, friends.   No more than what is just, we seek :
Ask what we think is due from strong to weak.
Behold the Island Emerald—a gem,
But in a swine's snout, governed by them.
Called to account, law-making might
Law-wrong sustains as legal right,
In worst believes as shade of best ;
' Submit,' it cries, and unredressed
Yet scourges whom it would set free,
As Pilot Christ, and you and me
An Arabi and Araby.
Stern hypocrite, on strong demand
Law frowning can itself command
   Peterloo massacres, and then
Thistlewood plots ; itself transgress,
And own it, yet forgivingless,
E'er doing right, still more repress,
And look for gratitude.   God pity men !
For states are pitiless, our loss their gain."

SECOND WORKMAN.

" Then down with privilege !   By that we stand."

THIRD WORKMAN.

" Fair equal government, that's what we demand :
And we will have our rights."

PARTISAN.

                " Do you not prate?
Know you not, wrongs to the many are rights of state?
God seems to frown on Erin's isle,
And Britain scans with fading smile.
Yet slowly we progress in spite of lords,
Laws, barracks, muskets, bayonets, guns, swords.

If it were surely, we might trust the slow ;
But is it an advance, whose greatest show
Still eminence accords to wealth and name
Beyond misfortune raised, above all shame ;
And can the multitudes despised forget,
And crown some letters of the Alphabet ?
The landless many, from the soil divorced,
To emigrate or root in towns enforced,
Owners of land grow rich, whoe'er may fail,
Its unearned increment their due blackmail.
Rents and rates rising our stint wages trap,
Labour and enterprise so handicap ;
Our hope of earth but a brief lease of grave,
Which shall our bones eject, dust only save."

FIRST WORKMAN.

" To bung a beer-barrel with it.   Let it go :
Hamlet disposed of Alexander's so."

SECOND WORKMAN.

" And Cæsar's own to-day may have become
Skin for a revolutionary drum."

PARTISAN.

" To use a common fellow, not improve,
Our great ones reckon constitutional love.
Though when they die the grave respects them not,
And their great names as well as bodies rot,
Now they advance, if we poor folks regress ;
They frame our laws, and thus our ills redress.
Some half-starved wretch is day-hired for a crust,
Or for a leak hard-worked, since taken on trust,
And not his own, he gets for it seven years ;
Genius and virtue, dulled by cares and fears,
Are mocked by fools as each sublimely blind,
The first before its time, the last behind ;
To labour capital assistance lends,
And sweats us for it, kills its poor dear friends ;
Puppies are pampered on the public purse ;

And surely were forgotten by the curse
Those very fortunate, who trace a name
From royal minion, barber, footman, flame.
Rank raised to dignity where wisdom stood,
Meanness a sin, and wealth the chiefest good,
Stoled is your bishop for good cause, since great,
To prove that providence has ordered state.
' Blesséd the sheep, that hunger in our folds,'
The Bishop preaches, and the church upholds
The order of the day."

SECOND WORKMAN.

> " Sheer slavery that.
We're not machines."

THIRD WORKMAN.

> " Ay, give us eight hours pat,
Old England's day."

PARTISAN.

> " And still shall ruling powers
To fill deep bishop-pockets dip into ours.
They once the church robbed, now paid slave retain ;
Armies and navies ponderous ordain,
Embassies, wars, that babes and brothers may
Be happy in receipt of public pay ;
Enlist the Commons in the strengthened peers,
Attracting and controlling high careers,
So he, who nobly man to champion stood,
Soon for an order strikes with hardihood ;
Till, warped against itself, the general aim
To rise to lawful fortune, lawful fame,
The wish becomes, in mean though master mind,
While man still, to be parted from mankind,
Where freedom ends, and privilege begins,
And rank claims pardon full of all its sins.
And such is British life."

FIRST WORKMAN.

" And such is British life ; curséd liberty ! "

SECOND WORKMAN.

" Privilege masks and honours robbery."

PARTISAN.

" Friends, know you not, any one to state may rise—
So boast they of this constitution wise—
And make his heirs for ever lordly here,
Above each common man and native peer ?
Will none take car then in this fine balloon ?
Why should we prick good hope so sagely blown ?
Why?   Because mighty men have weakly sons,
    And genius seldom propagates its fires ;
So we are governed by degenerate ones,
    Whose powers of mind, exhausted in their sires,
Show they, mere noodles, are chance-nobs of state,
As small by nature, as their sires were great.
If we had reason good the sires to exalt,
For reason bad the sons should suffer default,
Since the rare dolts conceive the common weal
And their own privilege incompatible—
True, so would still conserve their own good graces
By force of arms and legal common-places.
Oh, what a vampire sucks our blood !   In all
Hell, when concerted to make Adam fall,
Milton shows ne'er on his immortal page,
So fell a fiend as My Lord Privilege."

FIRST WORKMAN.

" No privilege ! "

SECOND WORKMAN.

        " Down with the Lords ! "

P

THIRD WORKMAN.

" Give us liberty ! "

PARTISAN.

" Cease to be slaves and your own freed men be.
Our masters dread us not—a wretched rabble ;
    And so they turn on us a haughty back.
For they are men of honour, we, unstable
    And without honour, simple Gill and Jack,
Life-climbers, who have tumbled down the hill—
Been thither kicked, or who at bottom still
As we were born, unenvied plebs remain
Dishonoured by our honourable gain.
For honourable they, since well-to-do
Barons, who made the Magna Charta too ;
Pocket the general rent and dues, to wit,
Of crown and country, and don't swing for it,
Nay, pose as patriots, while they drop, and lay
On landless masses taxes, lands should pay."

FIRST WORKMAN.

" We are too cowardly."

SECOND WORKMAN.

" And they too bold."

THIRD WORKMAN.

" The wrong is ancient."

FOURTH WORKMAN.

" Aye, the land is old."

PARTISAN.

" Let's talk a little, friends, about this land.
    God-given, was it not both made and meant
For common use, or leased in private hand
    To pay the public revenue a rent

Out of what sole is private—fruits of toil?
The state inalienably owns the soil.
Could Kings bestow it then in lasting fee,
Or save conditioned upon trust to be
For national defence—an old makeshift—
With the condition also lapsed the gift?
Law has no virtue to create a right
Wronging a nation in its own despite.
God only can eternal things indent :
Nor may a temporary parliament
Do more than pledge a generation's rent.
Pensions of money to no end of time,
Eternal claims to land through trust or crime,
Like those to thrones, exploded now with ease,
   Or those to heaven based on endless hell—
Clerkly inventions, not divine decrees—
Are, quite beyond the range of human pleas,
   Mere usurpations of the infidel,
Yet, as our lawyers now interpret law,
To be regarded both with faith and awe,
The longer, too, enjoyed more just to show ;
As though years virtue could on crime bestow,
Or grapes on thorns, or figs on thistles grow.
Is England of all common-sense bereft?
Is wrongful occupation now no theft?
Must you walk off with land, which you would take?
To ward off others, is not that to fake?
Does he not steal, who pockets all the gain
Of wrongly holding land by might and main,
Or legal quackery, or worse chicane,
Trespasses permanently, claims, receives,
And lordly on the rents of nations lives?
If one king wrong the many, shall he not
   Make restitution to the multitude ;
Much more, if ten or eke ten thousand plot
   The public right to wrong for private good?
A public wrong, then, shall we weakly spare,
That some usurpers may the better fare ;
Be seeming weak, as we are real strong ;

Rather than right ourselves, our country wrong?
Or shall we wrong these honourable men—
Bring down the law upon them : and what then?
Our arms, if they defy the magistrate.
Rights of the many now are rights of state ;
And, if we still would have our empire stand,
We must begin at once to right the land."

FIRST WORKMAN.

" Let's tax the holders."

SECOND WORKMAN.

" Skin their precious teeth."

THIRD WORKMAN.

" Make them their prey disgorge."

PARTISAN.

" Perchance their swords unsheath.
They have in battle headed us, they say,
Made soldiers of us.   Who have had the pay?
The rank and file, the Chelsea pensioners
And Greenwich ; or the Lords and Officers?
Now government by all must be for all—
A general rise, if with particular fall.
We by our votes amazing into awe
May now interpret right, or change the law.
But such right will these men of honour yield?
Might is their right, its law the battle-field.
They know no other parliament of man :
Take is their foible still, and keep, who can.
Such honour ne'er will self of spoil unpack,
Save in the struggle for a bigger stack.
The sword has ever been, and still may be,
Their arbiter—not always victory.
Surely no man here will refuse to fight
To give these good men might, which unto them is right?'

FIRST WORKMAN.

" We will refuse."

SECOND WORKMAN.

   " None here will swerve.
Down with all privileges ! "

THIRD WORKMAN.

" Perish the traitors, who will serve
 The people's enemies."

PARTISAN.

" Perish the wrongs based on a hundred fights,
Old territorial and political rights,
Which, obsolete now, men as ills endure.
 Abuses unreformed, and wrongs maintained
Are greatly more volcanic than the poor,
 Who, always humble, have been easy chained,
As dog domestic, which may yet go mad,
If you draw tight the chain, and feed it bad.
A gest is told of an Emperor quitting his throne,
How he to others parted all his own.
His nobles asked and got his wealth and lands :
His people found him then with empty hands.
But he was kind, and in a happy hour
To them delivered his Imperial Power,
For that his nobles should by these do right
To whom he so had given absolute might.
If by the Emperor, God was meant, His will
Unto our nobles must unknown be still."

SECOND WORKMAN.

" Their pride and ignorance are equal rank :
Bah ! let us club our pence, and break their bank."

PARTISAN.

" A heart embittered may my reason warp,
A discord drawing from a once sweet harp ;
But over me at times a passion comes,

Which seems to beat innumerable drums
To riot sounding, when I see, how spare
The chances of the poor are and how rare.
Honours, lands, wealth, in several centres massed,
By fashion, as by law, bound grimly fast,
Lo ! family gods in disproportion rise
Above the pigmy brothers, they despise,
And meaner mortals, mentioned not in Dodd,
The multitudes known only unto God.
Their lordly woods and country mansions grand
Cover the amplitude of half the land,
And while St. Giles not even sniffs the fare
Of lungs aristocratic, lifesome air,
St. Jameses, revelling in rural joy,
Themselves at will intoxicate to cloy.
At ease they live, or fast from move to move
O'er earth at pleasure vagabonding rove
Sipping the essence rectified of bliss,
And deeming fortune quite a comely miss ;
From spleen recovering, regaining health,
For selfish ends alone employing wealth.
And when at length to towns they condescend,
Their pompous chariots far from misery wend ;
In purer air and under brighter skies,
Than east affords, their palaces arise.
For rank and riches have at their command
The most delectable of all the land ;
In cellars need not house, nor bed in dirt,
Nor in some mill's warm gutter wash a shirt ;
In pestilential closes need not dwell,
Nor bound for heaven make a start from hell,
Tell as a wonder, that an oak they've seen,
Nor only fancy, that the fields are green,
Nor hapless want dilapidated cows,
For slaughter bound, to mind them of the knowes,
Down which they used to roll, where they were born,
'Midst vocal verdure of a summer's morn.
Work we demand of them, not feather beds,
And needs must lift our hands to raise our heads."

SECOND WORKMAN.

" Ready, ay ready, are our hands, but how
Best raise our heads is the plagued question now."

THIRD WORKMAN.

" Must we for mere life wear existence out ? "

PARTISAN.

" I cannot think it ; flowers make me doubt.
With grinding toil and mad forced mirth,
    Say, shall the million poor wax wan ?
Is there no hope on ageing earth ;
With our humanity of birth
    No felt community of man?
 Is masterful solitude self-possession,
And brotherhood always its repression ?
May we not all with heart and mind
Intelligently join, and find,
On power's own field, the means to be
A merciful Political Economy ?
We need the secular good, which knowledge brings,
And the morality of common things.
The truth we want, and not a loose bold lie ;
Virtue in act, and not hypocrisy ;
Right, and not might ; reason, and not a dare-
Devil authority rampant everywhere.
Though sometimes false our theories, and crude
Our varied fancies of the right and good,
Yet method in the madness of the cries,
When pain and anger blind a people's eyes.
A frown is gathering on the national brow ;
My Lords, to timeous warning hearken now.
Irish and English peasant, Scotch, Welsh too,
The workman, and the thinker, all blame you.
The franchise trick, played out, won't serve your hand.
Why for your pleasure, sport, or gain is land
Estranged from us now forced in towns to fold,
Fleeced by your rents and rates, to slavery sold ?
                                                    —

Look to your title deeds ! For them show cause
More just than conquest and unequal laws,
Which hold us in the dust, whence once we sprung—
Nay, rose to fall, when this Old World was young.
Crushed, there we now, but shall no longer lie
Patient beneath oppression, fond to die.
If thence we ever sprung, we thence again
Upspringing shall renew the race of men,
Nature's nobility, to stand, and thrust
The spurious species back to virgin dust.
They, hearing not, or careless of the groan
With which we let them hold a nation's own,
Have of state-lands had each mad dog his day,
For any service past sufficient pay,
While deeming us ordained to live and die
On crust unmoistened in a worse than sty.
Combining now, we claim a nation's right,
If need be over-matching stubborn fight—
Their stern example following.   What, ho !
They vanish from the shadow of a blow."

Pin lightly dropped, or heavier-lifted sigh
   Had overcome the hush severe,
In which those numbers still and spell-bound lie,
   Then burst into a free-born cheer
Rare in that dome.   The Duke's dust under
Indignant stirs with curious wonder.
And fearful, is it not, to feel
The pulse-beat of the common-weal ?
Strange, too, is breath whose vapours fade,
Nor blunt nor break or glass or blade,
Yet wordy offspring have of power
To temper misery's maddest hour,
Or raise its barricade and man
With patriot, or partisan.

CANTO VI.

ST. PAUL, an orator if saint,
Had trembled, listening to the plaint
That wailed, as though it wailed in vain,
  And ran around his sacred wall,
A cry of more than passing pain,
  Appalling and yet rousing all.
Not Louis Blanc, nor Lamartine
Had voice of perfect discipline
To stir the sense of wrong aright,
And lead with rein impassioned might.
In times, which had already known
Epaminondas and Timoleon,
Even philosophic Dion quailed
Before the breath he had exhaled.
For multitudinous scatterlings
Themis alone has leading strings,
And rarely trusts them to another,
Although Mazzinis fondly hail her, " Mother."
Phaethon of his awful Sire
Essayed the chariot, set the world on fire,
And perished, like Desmoulins, young,
Striving to rein, ashamed of his own wrong.

Then came the leader whispering to me,
" Oil thou the waves : I count on thee."
Rising, in silence falling fast,
One to fore-front of dais passed.
As drops from heaven commissioned rain
To lay an overturbulent main,
Out of himself constrained he broke
Upon that audience ; surely spoke
The very heart of him displayed,
Compassionating to dissuade
From riot pricking angry might,
And erring road to sacred right.

Third Speaker : Edward.

" In name of God I in this temple rise,
And hence all evil passions exorcise.
When midnight tempest in Helvetia raged,
Its fury they with clang of bells assuaged ;
Urgent in churches many voices choired
And organs swelled, and prayers to heaven aspired.
The powers of evil stayed at heaven's nod,
Worship was followed by the peace of God :
And may a reverend awe now timely chase
Unholy passion from this goodly place.
Reason alone secure on sands of time,
Opposed to winds of passion, stands sublime ;
Firm in its own not brief authority,
Taking precedence of priority,
Not striking, speaks, and, better to persuade,
Heart to convert convinces first the head.
But not all law from reason hails :
The custom of strong ill prevails,
Whether now rich men grind the poor,
   Or these in turn, though suffering long,
Revengeful smite at every door ;
   Selfishness goes so blindly wrong.
Whom egoism sways, is fair
Surface for float of any snare :
Seeking to lead, he is not man enough
To self command, but of impulsive stuff,
By self-love moulded now for good, now bad.
Let us be reasonable, and not mad."

First Workman.

" We are not mad, most noble Felix, you
Forget yourself."

Edward.

            " I say but what is true.
Who reckon rivalry man's proper mood,
Seeking their own without another's good,

Each for himself and hindmost to the devil,
Are the most subtle ministers of evil,
Or rich, or poor, or lords or sons of toil,
Disintegrate the race to rule and spoil.
Indifferent to curses as to woes,
Such take and profit by what neighbours lose.
They say, "possession is nine-tenths of law,"
Not reckoning the missing tenth a flaw,
But right of taking, then by law holding fast—
Hard old-world wisdom : its good time is past.
Great heart begins to question it at last ;
In its authority sees might
Imposing on a world, as right ;
The man of power an institute,
More cunning selfish than the brute.
His ancient ways, though mended, still
Pursuing, thinking to conceal
He masterly his gains defends,
Blind trust demands and ignorance commends ;
Divided counsels, ignorant trust,
Making men victims of his force and lust."

FIRST WORKMAN.

"Tools he of fellows makes, of women trulls."

SECOND WORKMAN.

"We are not British lions : we are gulls."

EDWARD.

"Think how, by public means both built and run,
    Our railways the land-rents and values raise ;
How water-rates and drainage make of town
Street-veins of gold for landlords, pursy grown,
    While other rates maintain our common ways ;
Think, too, of all our industries, and thus
How much by land is gained though owed to us,
Our true creation : for how grievous small
The wealthy landlord's enterprise in all,
Save when extortion, greed, and secret hate

In opposition make him grossly great ; '
Think how the tradesman's late and early toil
Business creates to be his landlord's spoil,
Who takes the gilt of it in rising rent,
And in his pocket drops it—cent per cent ;
Think, is it just, land values so should rise,
And the whole increment become the prize
Of men, who no laborious finger move,
But override to mar the land, which we improve."

FIRST WORKMAN.

" Mean robbers they by legal stratagem."

SECOND WORKMAN.

" By laws they taxed our loaves, and let us clem."

THIRD WORKMAN.

" Employers of labour, what of them ? "

EDWARD.

" By thought and labour money made is seed,
Which rightly sown should reap its proper meed.
Yet can we greed of capital forget,
Taking its pound of flesh and extra suet,
For eight hours wages ten or more of toil,
Bating the pay to aggravate the spoil.
On heels of progress poverty thus treads :
Wealth gutter-basements has and attic leads,
Landlords and cottars, full and empty coffers,
Parasites princely and abandoned loafers :"

FIRST WORKMAN.

" Predestined sphere of Charity, some say."

SECOND WORKMAN.

" Should the worker then pay, that the idler may play ? "

EDWARD.

" We must, at least, to princes give their dues :
Though so we should fair charity abuse

Supporting idle hands, our laws have made :
Even poor-laws may their objects more degrade.
A self-restrained, most law-abiding race,
Whose senators were lords, whose censors grace,
Whose consuls worthy kings, whose laws, some just
And golden still, are current without rust,
Romans, whose sires like ours had 'mongst them carved
The common lands, till ousted commons starved ;
Luxurious infamous become, the while
Guardians of poor, without the style,
Granting to popular need and cry
A sporting dole of Charity,
So weakened all, supine at length,
Unused and vitiated strength,
Unfit a vigorous War-god to oppose
Fell with the Empire low beneath His blows."

THIRD WORKMAN.

"They'd have us in the work-house.   Damn their alms."

FOURTH WORKMAN.

"Away with all such charitable crams."

EDWARD.

"But what then of the slums, where shame is dead,
And homeless penury to vice is wed?
Ah, let us, high and low, confess and face
The miseries and failures of our race."

FIRST WORKMAN.

"Sometimes our miseries feel present hell :
But like a book you speak."

EDWARD.

                    "All, that ends well, is well.
Good-will and clearer insight may attend
Time, in the future, wrong to right and end.
Yet here behold that too despisèd fate
Owed to ourselves.   Mere hangers on of State,

We look that it for us should surely do,
What we ourselves could, if to selves more true :
Or reason not, but vaguely weary grope,
And ignorantly stay our flickering hope
On brilliant parts and subtle specious lies
Of noble men and masters worldly wise.
Helpful and providential powers of state
May all instruct, and many educate ;
Open the wells of thought, and to their brink
Lead ignorance athirst with joy to drink ;
Let knowledge to and fro, and hand in hand
With wisdom run through an enlightened land ;
But most great men, distrustful, lag behind,
Drags on the wheels of progress and mankind.
Not from the Lords of sublunary things,
But The Almighty Father, King of kings,
Comes the True Love that, slaying Giant Despair,
Emboldens us the worst of ills to dare.
Let us, my fellow labourers, strike hands ;
Our case good Fellowship and sage demands."

First Workman.

" Most truly said.   Apart we are poor slaves.
Of drops make Ocean : ocean will make waves."

Edward.

" Taught by experience, in division weak,
    Humble but many, lo ! the mighty mass
Begins its strength in unity to seek ;
    From land to land its emissaries pass,
Excite the multitudes to think and plan,
And agitate the brotherhood of man.
Well done, if wisely : but with growing strength
Our sense of wrong may grow to madden at length ;
Rights preach and wrongs in words not meant to burn,
Which yet may into fiery action turn,
And o'er a nation's ashes freedom mourn.
Ah ! who shall magazine, and who control
The dynamite forces of the popular soul

Ready for any outcast moment dark
To strike, and with its tick to wreck our stately bark?
Our native land, must it too rise and fall,
Once groves be groves again, or, bared of all,
Be less than when woad Britons roving bold
Stormed in far haunts almighty brutes of old?
Must nations uphill progress roll, and then
Be crushed beneath it rolling down again?
Is none that, great now, shall continue grand,
Improving ever more a Promised Land;
Not righting human wrongs with inhuman force
Despotic, or patriotic—which is the worse?"

THIRD WORKMAN.

" Each good may on occasion be the better."

FOURTH WORKMAN.

" Cromwell protector now, and now dictator."

EDWARD.

" Nor patriot, nor despot knows
To lift the burden of our woes.
Lo! forms despotic take the helm
    To steer the ship of state to Eldorado;
In deluges of blood o'erwhelm,
And cast across a subject realm
    Their lurid, darkening, and gigantic shadow
Yet promise first, disarming hate,
    To better and enrich the world.
For which of them, now styled " The Great,"
    Did not on banner broad unfurled
" Goodwill to man," brave words, inscribe,
And followers to glory bribe.
Death-smitten at due stroke of time,
Which stoops not to a port sublime,
Into distended jaws of hell
He with his sudden empire fell;
Or that in burst of open smile
And riot seemed hell risen a while.
If God, outwitting then the devil,

And drawing foul black teeth of evil,
Bettered what tyranny had begun,
Of many nations making one,
God's was the good.   The tyrant still
Must answer for the tyrant ill :
He at the best a butcher here,
Hereafter has the bloody score to clear."

FIRST WORKMAN.

" Sometimes to do it sent is by a bomb."

SECOND WORKMAN.

" How good it sounds, God's truth, the tyrant's doom."

EDWARD.

" In battle such may revel, weep ·
For still new worlds with fire and sword to sweep,
But passing strange, that freedom fair
In blood should birth, in murder lair,
Commanding horror in the van,
Advance to right the wrongs of man.
Strange, though for gain, or rank, or power
He would not redden one rash hour,
A Garibaldi still will go,
Wherever freedom has a foe,
Lend to despair a brain to plan
And soul to dare—a loyal man,
Who dominating hardiest needs,
Matching great dreams with mightier deeds,
Thinks soon on an acclaiming world
Liberty's banner broad unfurled
To root, and still in heaven to wave
   The glory of each happy nation.
Until with the good it shall perish and brave
   In the general final conflagration."

FIRST WORKMAN.

" By sword the tyrant reigns, and by the sword
May rightly perish."

SECOND WORKMAN.
"It is God's own word."

EDWARD.

"For freedom men have risen to do
Deeds, that fanned hell to whiter glow ;
Moved heaven to strike the dastards down,
And give a tyrant back his crown ;
Poor, not forgotten, blood, whose stain
    Earth would not hide, nor heaven cleanse,
Have deluged from a bluer vein,
For poorer blood to dye again,
    The land one hecatomb immense ;
In freedom's name done freedom shame,
Till strange she to that land became.
Mere brute inevitable force,
    Or patriot, or tyrant, reigns
By right of might ; and each in course
    Is subject to the other's chains.
The sword, while powerful to enslave,
    Alone can make no people free ;
But often blindly leads the brave
Now to the dungeon, now the grave,
    Or if to misnamed liberty,
Which soars itself above all laws,
Drowning in blood a righteous cause,
Although of human force the best,
Must still by stronger be in turn suppressed."

FIRST WORKMAN.
"'Tis very pitiful."

SECOND WORKMAN.
"And cruel too."

THIRD WORKMAN.
"'Tis very strange, but not more strange than true."

Q

EDWARD.

" Now meditate with me the power
Of him, whom the eleventh hour
Of revolution finds its master
Commanding back a feared disaster.
Who in time's hinder ocean dives,
Finds few such pearls—few swordless lives,
Brains, but with moral, not main, force
Shaping of history the course.
When, imminent on glorious faults,
Hither and thither swaying halts
   On utmost verge of swift decline
A nation, and such saviour breeds,
Whose majesty makes words worth deeds,
   Who of the morrow shall divine ?
Behold he cometh, whom, to rear,
That nation from its earliest year
Hath struggled ; hoping, comes in right
Of all the virtues, that are bright
Along that nation's fervent way,
In him attained to shadeless day.
Blossom of ages, welcomed he
By the perfection yet to be.
Hope waxes in his people bold ;
God favouring regards. Behold !
So comes he to arrest the fall,
And perishes in vain for all ;
A welcome tomb with freedom shares,
And lives not even in his heirs.
Yes, for the vices of the race
Burst also into blossom : space
Too narrow is for both to blow,
And Cæsar murders Cicero."

FIRST WORKMAN.

" Another Cæsar fell by Brutus hand."

EDWARD.

" 'Twas a Brute blow that felled him, if a grand :

Yet cute Augustus rose the world to enslave,
And a Tiberius followed to deprave."

THIRD WORKMAN.

" Czars now outdo them ; Cæsars beyond the Drave."

EDWARD.

" My God ! is this wild world Divine ?
Are all men like, and works of Thine ?
What ! none predestined to disdain ;
None ruling here predoomed in hell to reign ?
Pardon a cry, man's woe makes bold.
Father of liberty ! behold
Thy children, in thine image formed,
By thine own love of freedom warmed,
Enslaved and rolling in the dust,
Or, panders to some tyrant's lust,
Hounding him on to giddier crime ;
Hell surely hath a lease of time ;
Though heaven bendeth over all,
This fallen world seems still to fall."

FOURTH WORKMAN.

" Why should it ? "

FIFTH WORKMAN.

" Can't we raise it ? "

EDWARD.

" Yes, and such
Our mission is. We here are at a touch
The schoolmaster abroad and vulgar ? more
Outworth a noble's blood and even as ? ? now
While labour with philosophy ? ? ? ?
The shrewdest state ? ? ? ? ? ? ? ? ?

FIFTH WORKMAN.

" And well deserve ? ? ? ? ? ? ? ? ? ?

EDWARD.

"And though the poor wise man despised may be,
Goethe, Grote, Bancroft well the truth confess,
  ' Man's humbler class is highest God's most high.
Patience, endurance, temperance there embrace,
  And live with sister virtues, not to die.'
Ours is a life thus ordered still to show ;
  To quench our own Gehennahs Dead Seas drain ;
Not raise the world by laying others low,
  While heights we level where the few still reign.
License, though boasting it is free,
Is lawlessness—not liberty.
Hell's luring masquerading stole,
Flower of all evil to the soul,
Fiend in the garb of seeming heaven,
Most damned of all the unforgiven,
With promises of earth's fruition
Still cheating man to his perdition,
  Most practical and heartless joke,
Of all things least the thing it seems,
Most vain and flightiest of dreams,
  That ever day's chill morning broke !
Avaunt, thou Fiend ! thy spell hath power
Even in time's fresh running hour,
Though all the blackness of thine art
Might teach how false thy cruel heart."

FIRST WORKMAN.

"We want no license.   We are temperate."

SECOND WORKMAN.

"The House for lawless ones is a palace of state."

EDWARD.

"As from mooned waste of night an Alp
  In unobscured and lonely height
Lifteth to heaven its snowy scalp
  Sublime in meditative light,

So rising eminent at last
In the pale light of all the past,
And viewing heaven, and as well
Earth, whose deep roots are part in Hell—
Virtue in peasant, and in peer,
Weak, and the world full of fear,
With broad upon its ample brow
The brand of serfdom burning now ;
And realizing heights supreme
Beyond an angel's wing or dream,
Heights, which with Christ we may attempt,
Hope, not from bitterness exempt,
Smiles at the manner of our state,
Whose privilege is profligate,
Raising, that we may heaven climb,
Ladders, whose rounds are steps of crime."

FIRST WORKMAN.

" Down with the lords ! "

SECOND WORKMAN.

" Away with privilege."

THIRD WORKMAN.

" They are too old, and we have come of age."

FOURTH WORKMAN.

" All must vote equal."

EDWARD.

" And all equal feel.
Then may a general sense of common weal
Win over such as now fair progress bar ;
With vice and ignorance alone make war,
On the long march to a safe happy home:
For surely is a good time here to come.
Clouds melt off in showers, whose every drop
   Is no sooner born in the upper air
Than it shines in heaven's rainbow a token of hope,

So the sad lower world may cease to despair ;
Our struggle for life well may ills endure,
To which pitiful heaven gives good hope of cure.
Since each to self was all in all, his own
Workman and husbandman, a savage lone·
Uniting with his tribe to hunt or fight,
Seizing new lands, or holding old by might,
Divided labour hath with commerce reigned ;
Each now on each, all mutual depend ;
Coals from the west and spices from the east
To all fair profit yield and frugal feast ;
This nation studies matter, that the soul,
And southern genius charms at the northern pole ;
The New World is the Old One's complement;
All heaven roofs alike each continent :
Adjust the pieces, work their puzzle out,
They fit, not rasp, though wealth, waste, want may doubt.
A shadow of doom, forecast by the masses
On the tinsel moonshiny upper classes,
About to shroud them in lasting night,
Is only a threat, and passes quite,
Like the shadow of earth from its satellite moon ;
The classes may mate with the masses soon.
This truth is growing in the land,
    Truth upon truth, to rise and tall
With cap of liberty to stand
    Within sight, hail, and touch of all."

SECOND WORKMAN.

" We grant the hail and sight, but touch we doubt.
What touches Russia most ? "

EDWARD.

                            " I fear the knout.
Though wrong may sadden still, oppression scare,
Contempt and infamy be everywhere,
Inheritors of earth, which is for you,
Like the Redeemer rise and raise it too.
Uplift the nations.   Patience, temperance

Endure with sister virtues and advance
With charity, and intermarrying
Are ever fresh-born as Eternal spring,
And safe among the peoples find a home.
Uplift the nations : Christ to them has come.
Seldom has good on earth struck root to grow
Save in a lowly soil, but, spreading so
Through willing masses, has to purpose pushed,
Else had the seedling by the powers been crushed ;
All silently unnoticed has made head,
Where humbly causing rampant ill no dread ;
Wider and wider, slowly, surely, fair
Cheated the outwitted devil unaware.
Uplift the nations.   What if great men fall,
Good in the multitude is God in all.
We want no war to stay us on our march ;
Hope has in nature storms enough to arch.
Not that a true defensive fight is wrong,
   Or madder revolution out of date ;
But this the burden of my song,
That with God's love in us most strong
   Then most The Lord of Hosts is great.
And the whole people's voice I hear
So full of God, I little fear :
No ruffian Jingo-party cry,
But consensus of humanity
Helping a nation in its need,
   Whether it be to hold its own,
Uproot an oligarchic weed,
   Or cease to prop a tottering throne,
The fullest voice of God is still
The lovingmost—the people's grand good-will."

FIRST WORKMAN.

" Three cheers for the people ! "

SECOND WORKMAN.

               " Three for old England."

THIRD WORKMAN.
                    " Three
For the Nations all."

EDWARD.
                    " And peace, and amity.
The rich begin to lift the burdens dropped
On weighted shoulders, they should sooner have propped ;
The poor to find assured redress
In a united helpfulness ;
Most dire necessity, at length
Mothering invention, proves true strength.
Harrison, Arkwright, Brindley, Watt,
Franklin, and Stevenson have taught
Material force to yield to thought.
Laws economic cease to fight,
Meet, and, dissolving into right,
Join battle with their foes disgraced—
Political privilege, financial waste.
Labour and capital no longer hate,
Chambers of commerce with trades-unions mate ;
Machinery makes time to think ;
Thought grows on thought ; we seem to drink
The present, and beyond to play ;
To-morrow supersedes to-day.
So let the race all rich and poor combine ;
Each helping all propitiate laws divine;
Quell with united heart each witching charm,
And with united will oppression stayed disarm.
Then when the few no privilege acquire
Over the many, none for rule conspire ;
When seeking others' good one finds his own,
Contentment shall be near to fill her vacant throne.
With patient wisdom learning to unite,
Divine with human force, and rule with right,
Nations shall federate, co-operate men,
And labour find in peace fair rest and gain.
Man weapons moulding into forms of peace,

Taxes declining as debts national cease,
Wealth shall, with few accumulating now,
Then, by the many shared, diurnal grow,
For all enough, enough for every day,
And weak and wayward helped upon their way.
Wrung from the many, riches by the few
Now on church squandered, state, camp, court, and stew,
Shall by those ministered, who know the worth,
Instruct, redeem, regenerate the earth.
So unity advances to embrace,
And rule omnipotent the human race;
Call it democracy, or what you will,
The brotherhood of man progresses still.
Time was, when showy progress grand
Seemed dawning on one favoured land;
Now all—night fled, and flag of day unfurled—
Live in the early morning of the world,
From which our paths fresh dews receive;
That their Redeemer lives, the nations now believe."

The instant mass arose, and, cheering me,
Warmed my glad heart with ready three times three.
I then was by the Canon followed, who,
    Known by his reverend face and sober cloth,
Coming upon the dais, not to woo,
    Nor sanctimonious to fluster wrath,
But deeming it a favourable time,
Rang with rare soul and voice a holier chime
Than Bow-bells ever sounded, or e'er fell
From Paul's own many miracles of bell
Sprinkling all London round and air abroad—
Such a full sense of harmony and God,
As Catharine at Ledbury heard, or dreamed
And waited in; it coming heaven seemed.

CANON.

" Your ears to lend me, friends, your hearts incline;
I love a friendly hearing; be it mine.

Yet love, God's true interpreter, shall right
And overmaster all immoral might.
Deflected nature with persistent force
And spring eterne attempts its primal course ;
Although in error oft, and oft in rue,
Retaining its resolved and native hue,
Gives back to man the rights which, constant, prove
That they are laws of an Eternal Love.

" One parting word—it is God's own
Gathered from steps that mount to His throne.
He who in ought would any wrong,
In his own right stands never strong ;
But who fears God, to God endeared,
Is a foe worthy to be feared.
Therefore may suffering good well wait
On exigency of debate.
You change not spirit by a blow,
Nor speed you justice, sure though slow.
Years make not right of wrong, nor can
Law give it virtue, nor yet man.
Justice is never once at stake ;
In time, may time-made wrong un-make ;
While sensitive as churl to hell
Is bluest blood though watered well,
And upon whom doom waits to fall
Gods knows when they deserve it all.

" Kings, ministers, ambassadors have erred.
And public interests slightingly deferred
To ceremony, private pique,
Or party speech, and Kalends greek.
Even Gods now in Japan may spend
A yearly month with their good friend,
The Emperor, temples abdicate,
And leave a nation to its fate.
But Christ, our Lord, is with the poorest here
Through every moment of the livelong year :
Trust Him.   All else is idle talk ;

Though in the chaff a slender stalk
Of golden grain may serve to show
Beyond what mathematics know,
Less is it than a babe may list
To gather from the lips of Christ."

And with a prayer and blessing all were sped,
Happy as many sheep by the bell-wether led.
My friend, the Canon, loved his brother man
And shook the hand of my bold partisan,
Whom the march-home too soon abrupt recalls :
Thanking the Canon, we together leave St. Paul's.

CANTO VII.

To morn, which rose aglow with shame,
Newspapers and reflection came.
Lucy may scorn me for speech-making,
Occasionless and briefless speaking,
The public double badly playing
Of noted Bright.   Grave doubt, dismaying,
Insinuated sure perdition
To the unheedful rhetorician,
As when Thersites cursed the great
And by Odysseus was beset,
Or Cola di Rienzi, though
He doubled back Colonna blow.

Not Erskine, dragging peer to court,
Made safer gain of dangerous sport.
    A brief that day came, then a rich
Recurring sprinkle, which, as showers
In spring develop natural flowers,
    In me quick raises lucky flowers of speech
Opening hearts of rock, controlling

Gnome-like solicitors and treasure,
Judges and juries button-holing,
And making law a business pleasure.
And now, with flutter of expanded wings,
A golden bee-like business pleasure sings
A song, which I to Lucy send, in trust
  Its breath of promise may her mother shame;
Dull torch of hope revive; enhance with gust
  Low spark of love, and kindle it to flame.

SONG OF BUSINESS PLEASURE.

"Unrestful repose
  No more I know,
Prelusive throes
  Of struggling flow.
Flood quick is making,
  And high I ride
On billow taking
  Spring-top of Prime-tide.

"Well mounted by chance
  In the favour of law,
The success to enhance,
  No rein I draw.
Let others rein,
  I ride for life.
Relaxless strain
  Of vigorous strife
Is hope revived;
  Is one wild bliss:
I never lived,
  Until like this.
While fine frenzy of soul
  From love-lighted eyes
Sees already near goal,
  And Lucy my prize."

My song unanswered she, as soon as read,
Dropped upon fire, whose hungry flames it fed.

Ah, should she be lost,
  I may regret
She has idly cost
  Such Pythian sweat.
Not a stride will I less :
  As flashing across
High road to success
  Comes her possible loss,
I will harder spur,
  Mischance to outride
And in work forget her—
  Another's bride.

In sense of employ
  And power to run,
Oh ! is there not joy—
  In work well done ?
Though Potter, brave painter,
  So swiftly he ran,
Grew momently fainter,
  Young, died like a man ;
Though snake dissipation,
  Seen killing to lurk
In fast recreation,
  Shows faster in work,
Rest, rest will I none ;
  If but sooner to die,
I would live at a run,
  Or hope weary to fly,
Praying fortune, inhuman,
  Unfair in the past,
To be now, all the woman,
  Kind, true to the last.

Though helping gaol-birds to escape their cage
  Is scurvy practice, Law without remorse
I pleased delude. Its selfish cruel rage
Late swung the forger from its gallows-stage,
  And stealer of chick, sheep, or nobler horse ;

And is to small offences cruel still,
While itself guilty of much graver ill,
Licensing palaces of drink to prime
Weak human souls to madness and to crime.
Some I from pains may rescue, none reform ;
Rather I feel companion of poor worm,
That wriggles in corruption, 'tis so clear
Drink and debauch prelude crime's fell career :
Woman at lusty evil shameless winks,
And hell boils over fearless, when she drinks.
Crime, when conceived, unacted is till sin
Is fortified by beer and drugged by gin
For trade distilled and brewed, and taxed for State,
Which cares not paying evils to abate.
But Bulstrode Whitelock could renie the sport ;
Like him I now explore the civil court,
Yet find few briefs there.   Upon favouring wave
   And crest of fortune, late I mocked despair :
Now struggling in its violent grave
   Am hurried back to briefless care.
I correspondence ne'er with Lucy held.
   The bold, triumphant, though forbidden pen,
Of my late song, unanswering she quelled ;
   Yet now, vacation near, I sing again,
With purpose double still, but now to prove
Despondent as of law, so too of love.

EDWARD'S SONG.

" To lank lean-bellied death
   Euridyce's sail
Going down in a breath,
   Sweet home within hail.
Miners all moil
   And pitmen to perish
Burrowing soil,
   They cease not to cherish.
Kirke-White bows breaking,
   Winged arrows drop,
Not overtaking

Vanishing hope.
Wherefore, oh ! wherefore
Labour and pain—
Labour, and therefore
Prayer, in vain ?
My present brief-support is in decline
And passing slender : give me hope in thine.

" Kensington Gardens flowerless seem,
    But their flowers are trees :
He, who peacefully would dream,
    Favours flowers like these.
Pleasing shadows he affects,
    Daylight strong will shun :
For the castles, he erects,
    Build not in the sun.
Early mid bird-twitter of song
    Roams he with the sheep,
While the future seems one long
    Jubilee to keep ;
And when dewy eve descends
    Rosy in the west,
Here his day of labour ends
    In a dream of rest.
Oh ! for shades where we might rove,
    And fond fancies weave,
And the fancies that we wove
    Might unfooled believe."

Prompt to my need comes answer kind and wise ;
Of law or love, it may of both advise.

LUCY'S ANSWER.

" When Boreal rays give nightly warning
    Of coming wars and doom to Kings,
Hope only sees untimely morning,
    In winter always coming Springs.
Hope then, and believe in

R

> To-morrow to-day,
> And patience will even
> Ill-fortune outplay.
> Thus lighten thy labour
> And sing at the yoke :
> The flash of the sabre
> Is half of the stroke."

No mention made of love, I deem she could,
If false to it, still wish me legal good.
Vacation come now, stray are seen
Folletts, like Spenser's Verdant Green,
Killing, with no great loss, time dying
At Baden-Baden, butterflying.
At least vacation well employ,
Gathering up remains of joy.
Since constant work might wear at last,
Cease to complain of victory past.
Time now is good for crushing grape ;
  The storm-tossed galley beached awhile,
Idling in sunny shade to shape
  Cares wreathed into a smile ;
And, on shy grass reclined, to praise
Lucy in songful holidays.

The Time of Year then shaped itself for me
  In accents so familiar, that I knew
And could the spirit feel, and almost see,
  All was to me so natural and true—
A universal word, and thus conveyed
To senses, which approved it, as it said—

TIME OF YEAR.

"Copses hazel, spreads of bramble,
  Furze, fern, dew-dropped gossamers ;
Shades, where startful squirrels gambol ;
  Stubbles, whence plump partridge whirrs ;
Pheasants, stalking out of cover,
  Regal as now dying wood ;

Leaping salmon ; gentle rover
  Lightly lashing run and flood ;
Lowing kine, full udders bringing ;
  Sheep, that bleat o'er field and fell ;
Birds, not full spring-throated singing,
  Only whistling sweet ' Farewell; '
Hoofs that ring, and shouts that clearly
  Through dew cool of sunset sound ;
Spiral smokes slow rising, yearly
  Dead leaves fluttering slow to ground;
All are dear, but dearer lonely
  Sunshine hushed, when all appears
Dreamy, breathless, stirless, only
  Feeling exquisite in tears,
Colour rainbowing broad forest,
Green and yellow, gold and sere,
Russet, brown, and blood-red—sorest
  Heart's blood of the dying year."

And with feeling of all-over,
  Surely never felt before
By a leal true-hearted lover
  Upon journey to adore,
I to Lucy now am hieing,
  And with song, but sad, I fear :
Can it be her love is lying
  Dying with the dying year ?
And though harvest golden-tinted
Is the bounteous season, which
Bursteth granaries, if love stinted
  While the glad round world grew rich,
Only love and Lucy needing
  Could I deem a brief success
Other than a golden fading,
  Should I find her loving less?

Pride, thy bravery revealing,
  Manliness to me restore ;
Though autumnal sadness feeling,

Through my veins like vintage pour.
Let me match her pride inflated,
   Sing, though I should wind oppose,
Only, reed-like agitated,
   Murmur as it comes and goes.

EDWARD SINGS.

" Time is a bitter draught, unless
   Its sweetness love impart ;
Eternity will fail to bless
   The breast without a heart.
For God himself—for time below,
   Eternity above,
Earth can no other joy bestow,
   And paradise is love.

" A slave am I to love and bliss :
   I Lucy love, and she ?
God keep her ever as she is,
   If Lucy still loves me.
Let those, who cannot love, forego
   Bliss here and bliss above :
Earth can no other joy bestow,
   And paradise is love.

" But should she cease to love me, while
   I change not any way,
She may some other fool beguile
   For some such other day,
A heartless wretched flirt below,
   A blissless ghost above ;
Earth can no other joy bestow,
   And paradise is love.

" Love will forget what cannot love ;
   Oblivion to be
Will seek and find another dove,
   That will but coo to me,
While they, who cannot love, forego

Bliss here and bliss above :
Earth can no other joy bestow,
  And paradise is love.

" But wherefore sing I doleful song,
  Singing of Lucy ?   Be
My love for Lucy ever strong,
  If Lucy still loves me.
We'll love for ever, nor forego
  Bliss here and bliss above :
Earth can no other joy bestow,
  And paradise is love."

Thus to myself I sing a prouder roll
Than e'er before I noted in my soul.
Day following night of my return,
The while I fear approaching cause to mourn,
Lucy with unobservant eye,
As lone I walk, rides blindly by,
And proud between us her high-landed Earl
  Parting as Pyrenees from Spain part France.
I no Durandol have aloft to swirl,
  Nor do I think she sees my slow advance ;
But now no longer is the Earl despised.
Truth has my inmost soul surprised ;
His triumph now is undisguised,
And Puck, who hates me much, but ne'er forsakes,
Invades my ear, and purposed tempest makes.

PUCK.

" If like that Epirotus pool,
Which fired approaching torch, then cool
Hissed round the plunging darkling light,
Lucy now scorns the love she chose to excite ;
Still as the torch, extinct in vain,
Withdrawing was inflamed again,
By disregard should thy desire
Provoked be into fiercer fire.
Rejected meteors, once at birth

Phlogistic in atomic earth,
But soon mere ashen stones apart
Not gathered to its hardening heart,
Then flashing sword-like on it fall
To stay, but strike first and appal."

EDWARD.

" Such meteors firebrands are, some say,
Wherewith true angels drive the false away."

But now a gleam of conscience wondrous clear
Shows jealousy to be the Puck at my ear,
And, seeming darkness falling on my soul,
Rises the cry, as conscious thunders roll—

EDWARD.

" Come, thickest night of Hades, close
　　Around my jealous rage, and hide
Immortal tortures, that expose
　　The weakness of Typhœan pride !"

Stirred by my ravings, piteous moved,
Trees overhead my storm reproved :
And from their midst a zephyr kind
Leaf-rustling came, like thought to mind,
And might in air such angel be,
　　As on Bethesda pool descended
Moving the waters healingly,
A touch of nature kin to me,
　　That with my railing spirit blended
Its better spirit to engage
And whisper classic soothing.

ZEPHYR.

　　　　　　　　" Cease to rage,
Or her with bitter tongue assail :
　　Smile down her scorn, which now may be
Nearer to shame, a greater ail
　　And sorer to herself than thee.

Neath lava crusts and shows of snow
Volcanoes proud and prisoned glow.
Her love may soon irruptive prove,
And flight from her be loss of love—
A loss, which you would seem to choose,
Flying from her you fear to lose."

I could not to such noble merit
Encourage my distracted spirit,
But drooped, like torch extinct on broken column,
Crooning a tattered lay from grief's old volume.

TATTERED LAY.

" Teach me, ye days chasing nights still returning ;
   Winds that, for rest sighing, nowhere remain ;
Wandering billows, which earth still is spurning,
   Breaking to wander, be broken again ;
Teach me all nature is restless and fleeting,
   Every bright bubble-like world soon shall burst,
Hearts are all shaken, some broken by beating,
   And the soon broken may not suffer worst.
Yet kindly flowers in wilderness blooming ;
   Birds, that most dearly in solitudes sing ;
Teach me, that nought lacketh some faint perfuming,
   Silences even with harmonies ring.
Rivers far flowing and ceaselessly, going,
   Running with song to be lost in the main.
And there forgotten, ye teach me so knowing
   Love may not lost be, if loss for her gain."

" Loss, for her gain ! " I made refrain ;
And has it come to this now, " Loss, for her gain ? "
The zephyr took the thought so full of doubt,
And shook it, till I heard it all about,
" Loss, for her gain," and still, " Loss, for her gain."
Loss, for her gain ; while, him, coming and cooing
   Earl, have I noted rich, noble, and stern ;
Gentle to her now, but over the wooing?
   Then shall brief summer have winter to learn.

Nor can she care for him, yet may she marry :
　Men are so courteous, and women so slight.
Bide but a little, love : time will not tarry ;
　Hope in the future will make it fly light.
If hope must perish, be it later on :
　Till then at least what seeming chance there is.
Though the conclusion may be now foregone,
　The lengthened Life of doubt is hope of bliss.

Yet is my sore heart in my troubled breast
Horrid with angry wounds and all unrest.
Rage, misbegot of love, green-eyed
　Jealousy, seeing love's self green,
Drinking love's very nectar dyed
　Into obnoxious draught of spleen,
On self so feeding, superinducing
On cups of love its own verjuicing ;
Envy most jaundiced, bitterest malice
Mingling in love's all poisoned chalice,
It fouls the fountain-head of good,
Corrupts the heart and vitiates the blood.

As night Plutonic caverned wages
　Battle with whirling fires, and snows,
And wind, that from each quarter rages,
　So is my heart the sport of woes,
Now stirred by love, and now by hate,
Between them tossed, their bleeding bait,
And very shuttlecock for fleers
Of passions, all one round of spears.
But mad because that rival is approved,
Whose love I doubt and whom I think unloved ;
And thoughtful of the general weal,
I cease my own wrong most to feel,
And gather all self torture's ire
In one fierce wish for taloned fire
To gird the gorgon in love's path,
And rend him with unutterable wrath.
Their open doors may wooers throng,

Infamy make them here its song,
And tenfold curses wait them dead,
Who now astray to marriage bed,
From pure and plighted troth, displaced,
Woo woman by their bribes disgraced,
Write " Cozener " on love's whimpering face,
And wreck the faith of half the race.

Soon at a picnic in the fairy glen—
So changed, alas, to me—we met again.
We, and not it, had changed : the ring was there,
Though fairy land no more, or full of care.
Of the chief caterer, I and others guest
And uncle, first arrived, await the rest,
Who various, Lucy with her mother, came,
And with them that proud Earl, I now not choose to name.
One too appeared, I had not thought to see—
The soldier, who had stolen her once from me :
Whence had he now returned with look so bold,
And his attempt not yet so very old?

I menue not the feast, from hampers drawn
Far borne by narrow path to that spare lawn.
Though busy I, as with no sense of teen
My soul in meats and drinks had festive been,
Yet did I not neglect the meanest call,
But of all work was servant unto all,
Save Lucy.　She was cared for by her Earl,
Who often as I passed was in some peril,
To her so gracious he, to me so civil,
My hands so itched to pitch him to the devil,
As did that soldier, too, upon whose face
I saw a nameless wistfulness of grace :
For yet he was but nephew and not duke,
Else might the proud earl now have chanced to lose his hook.

Each exquisite in his way, the Earl a flat,
The warrior a sharp, or more than that,
Dogs o'er his shirt front coursing a vain rat

Not à la D'Orsay ; but the outward other
You might have taken for Count D'Orsay's brother.
Nor doubt this showed, nor that a late dejection,
But both superb assumption of perfection,
Dumbly but surely each so letting all
Know, by himself he stood and not to fall.

THOUGHTS OF A MAN OF RANK.

" I am alone : I am myself, and feel
I owe no member to the tailor's steel.
Indeed, but tell it not, I rather think
Of all that's possible I am the pink.
May-hap it puzzles you to fathom, why
Fashion should have me always in her eye :
These outer rags of hers may be her loan,
But upward, downward, inward to the bone
A gentleman should all my features pair,
My person to nail-tips and tops of hair.
Something there is, too, in my special gait
Demonstrative of honourable state,
In all my motions, as my every act,
Noting the gentleman, and him intact.
Should I, suppose it, rage, a storm each word
Whose syllables are ' trilled not by a bird : '
But should I sigh, there is a glance around
To find an angel dropped unfallen on the ground."

What of their talk to her !   Shall I report ?
Something there was of state, and more of sport,
But most of fashion and the great world's ways,
And with it more insinuated praise.
The flat was condescending ; but the sharp
Upon a heart could play an 'twere a harp,
Yet could he nothing win : for she could glow
Not yet so fiery as his breath would blow.
They maddened me : but none was let to see
Visage of my consummate misery,
Save Lucy ; for I think she saw it all,
And gave me one more chance, and one more fall.

When, through some wall's fast closing door,
A dog has sudden missed his lord
Evanished and without a word:
    Now on the left it will explore,
And now that failing try the right:
Now at the door it howls despite,
Now right and left, again to stray
Back ever to that door closed way:
So Lucy lost, from me estranged,
    The busy picnic round and through
And o'er again I roamed deranged,
    And still towards her ever drew,
    For that my love was hidden there I knew;
Till parting all in several ways
    As favour, whim, or fortune sped,
I stood at length by chance, or craze,
    And lonely mused beside the bed
    Of waters broken by a fall.
Methought—what thought I?   Many, many things,
And each one pricked me with a thousand stings.
    Cloudless the sky, the wood was musical:
With arms outstretched o'er rocky brink
It blessed the stream, that singing gave it drink.
And in a grot, just such a place indeed,
And time, as love would choose his cause to plead,
Lucy I saw : how came she there, or why?
And had I followed with incurious eye?
But wherefore be a fool again to show,
How heights of love o'erhang streamed depths of woe?
Anguish and sudden wrath, those linkéd passions
    To whom to seem and be are equal right,
In the distroubled sprite forget vain fashions,
    And had resolved me upon any slight,
That might to anger move her haughty heart,
For which soft touches have no happy art.
Hate is in woman of love the wild brother ;
    Would that I could even anger engage :
Scorning the one, and fast freezing the other,
    Ice to my sighs she is, rock to my rage.

And thus I open unavailing speech
With pitch of voice her ear alone to reach.

EDWARD.

" This life is worth the living to adore,
To love and hope for love, if nothing more ;
On wings of love and hope to sing lark sweet
At sunrise, noon, or set, when incomplete
Horned moon is then itself enough delight,
Or hidden stars are credited to night :
True love and hope have thoughts in darkness even
Starring and nightingaling ravaged heaven.
True love is hope's own lung-inspiring breath,
   Of patient years the very milk and nurse,
And it admits the article of death
   In creed, but only to abolish curse,
So that true love itself may never die,
And hope in it have all futurity."

LUCY.

" Yes, Edward : here and now how mild thou speakest,
Whose looks and actions else are none of the meekest.
To-day I had in mind a hundred times
To tell thee of thy too apparent crimes,
Not against God and man, but love, and me
'Gainst whom thine anger burns too visibly.
Thou goest ever about like a roaring lion
Seeking both whom to devour, and first to spy on:
Nor I, nor any round me staying, but stand
In momentary dread of thee at hand."

EDWARD.

" What mean you ?   Have my feelings so appeared ?
Do they distress you ?   Are they to be feared ?
If you are false, then must you dread my truth ;
If you are cruel, feel a touch of ruth."

LUCY.

" Thou art at liberty to think, or say
What likes thee best, but look another way,

Or with less unction : for I am resolved,
I cannot be thus openly involved."

EDWARD.

"What further thou intendest, is too clear :
That cannot be far off, which looks so near.
More Jew than Jessica, thou art worldly wise,
And wouldest love, not money, martyrize.
For I, no Cockerell out to sea,
  Washed overboard by angry wave,
By next washed back again to be
  Restored as from a living grave,
Am of thy falsehood full assured :
Thou for the world hast me abjured."

LUCY.

" Nay, but thy hungry, jealous flame
  Would with like ardour me inspire,
And spend itself in cruel blame,
  Which moves to pity, not to ire.
If thou from Satan wouldest fly,
Fly thou from this fond jealousy—
Strange passion, ofttimes loving well
The loved ones longed for life to quell,
As waves love ships with clingings close,
And rather crush than fear to lose.
The robe, by Dejanira sent,
Horrid was, although loving meant,
Lernœan venom in it turning
All sense of love to death most burning.
Brunhildas burn, while Sigurds bleed
In many a well-sung lay and Lied ;
And ancient song is modern deed.
But these were women.   Men should prove
Both less in hate, and more in love."

EDWARD.

" Dog, smarting sore with scourge too rash,
Still licks the hand that sways the lash ;

Sweet unto it is sourest crumb,
Which from a master's board may come.
Yet that will chafe, whose owner dear
No more desires its presence near.
If blessed privacy atoned,
Public offence were well condoned :
But not now lost in light and heaven,
I, not by night remembered even,
Ne'er glowing lone with Luna fond
In circle of her argent pond,
Nor first to greet refulgent sun
And shine awhile to see him run,
A planet am so far away,
Although it once was bright with day,
Light out hath cast it, like a spark
To shiver into utter dark."

LUCY.

" Art thou so perfect then, my friend,
As I am faulty, not to mend ?
Favours in viewless ink you write
  On heart unwarmed by love's feigned fire,
Yet wrongs tattoo, and keep in sight
  On palms of hands, that itch with ire.
Would'st wring my neck, as thou my heart hast done ?
It were an easier death, myself to drown—
Not yet.   We die but once, so Caumont found.
And he was hanged, alas, not pleasantly drowned."

With this she went, as though a stour
Upon a wind that passed a boor,
Who could not stay it going by,
Filling with stour each watering eye.
And dark from near future falls shadow o'er me,
  Ah, what may be coming I trouble to know :
For it swells, and, and looming up fearful before me,
  Outstretches quite over me hands full of woe.
They are dripping and dropping their burden upon me—
  And I shivering shudder, and cannot escape ;

Now into a huddle of horror have drawn me,
　Though I cannot distinguish a possible shape.
What is it but fortune in horrible state ;
And evil it is as Lucy, my mate.
No need have I her path untrue
With Leucophyllian reed to strew :
Fortune less froward is than she,
Who makes my fortune froward be.

CANTO VIII.

"WE die but once.　So Caumont found :
And he was hanged, alas, not pleasantly drowned."
Can this be Puck, that now is buzzing round ?
In Rigoletto, always charming me,
Recurs "la donna é mobile ;"
These other words, but swelling full of pain,
In eddying thought return upon my brain.
As flowers, that from cliff-crevice shoot,
　While beautifying, rend the rock
With deep descending bitter root,
　Lip and eye services but mock.
Obeisances of dumb politeness,
Phrases, whose falsehood is their brightness,
With ostentation of good-will
The piquancy of hate reveal,
Truth double may most biting tell,
Flatter like heaven, feel like hell.
As tinted clouds, when night is nigh,
Approach upon a loving sky,
Playing with lightnings, keeping under
For coming storm dark threatened thunder,
　Francesca Bentivoglio
Manfredi may to couch invite,

And, when assassins show weak fight,
  Herself will lay him low.

Soon gentler thoughts my spirit sway,
Apart and in decline of day
Musing in that fairy glen,
Which is traditioned among men
E'er Christian to have pagan been,
An ancient Delphi, now a fairy scene;
While rumbles in its inmost dell
An intermittent source of hell.
Thence narrowing the glen ascends
  Nursing a wooded torrent's ire,
Till entering the pass it ends
  Where moors expand, and hills retire,
And water for the town's supply
Is dammed in reservoir on high :
Puck may have built it to burst by-and-by.
Ah, once more sensuous were these woods and rills,
Alluring even now with classic thrills :
Anacreon or Ovid tune the lute,
Or Sappho warbles, and I listen mute,
While through the leafed and labyrinthine gloom,
O'er meadows silent as a grassy tomb,
Forms wizard wander, and the glowing dead
Promiscuous mingle with the gods they made,
And metamorphosize the world of shade.
Why are our hallowed groves thus taught to be
The ministers of classic lechery?
Again with eager cry of scenting hound,
Methinks, the startled solitudes resound.
From flowery caverned slopes, and groves, and glades
With Artemis comes all her train of maids,
Fresh arrows at the strings of half-bent bows,
And beauty kept for pools, no mortal knows.
Methinks, Pan tunes again his reeds that please,
And Hamadryads issue from the trees,
Oreads, Naiads, Limniads too throng,
And Fauns and Sylvans, and with shout and song

Sportively join, and whirling in the dance
Rich nectar quaff of many a sidelong glance ;
Till quaintly spied, as bard once, I am chased
And ringed by nymphs, who flout me unembraced,
And toss elated, as when billows leap
Round ship embosomed struggling in the deep.

Ah, here and now I long for Lucy still ;
And all my longing senses troubled thrill,
When sudden Dian through the circle breaks
Leading dear Lucy, who me partner takes,
And in the general dance renewed we whirl.
Now boils my blood ; all over, too, I thirl,
And whirl, and whirl.   The Wandering Jew, when driven
By breath of fury, ages out of heaven,
Might have forgotten the too distant grace,
If favoured by such dance in such embrace ;
Till irrepressible my reckless bliss
Refrains not what is so a parting kiss—
Too hot for Dian, as when Huon dared
To leap the bounds by Oberon declared.

Ha, Oberon and his followers haunt this glade.
    Fancied or seen, they upon man intrude
Promptings of folly, mostly by Puck made,
    Whispers that are imperative in mood,
Such small untutored inches pert are fairies.
Creatures of feeling, reasonless vagaries,
Some in their nature wicked, others show
Heedless of friend, as fearless, too, of foe ;
Uncanny all—for little folly reigns
With little effort over largest brains
Misgoverned by heart.   Some say, indeed,
That they are Gods, of an exploded creed,
Dwarfed like those fossils huge, whose modern swarms
Hide their diminished heads in lizard forms.
And while, though capering, gallant is a meet
Of fairy horsemen for a midnight heat,

S

What if with hell-hounds and prolonged halloo,
As fiends the Rhinegrave, they should men pursue ?

In flower-embroidered verdancy arrayed
And silver shoon, their elfin locks with braid
Of starry glitter bound, and combs of gold,
Their quivers full of arrows, and, behold !
Shaking a lance, or bow, ha ! mounted brave
On mettled steeds, whose tails and manes long wave
Storming the face of night, hark ! how they wake
Their silver whistles with unearthly shake
Into field minstrelsy, and hounds untied
Bound eager for the chase : thus full in pride
Of bravery they gathering forward ride.
Light, wan as moonshine, crowns each rider's head,
Moves with his motion, and with him hath sped.
Swift through wild woods they go on wizard track
Of wondrous game, nor linger, nor look back,
But ever forward blow the silver horn,
And cull an echo from each cranny lorn.
Ha ! now along the mountain side they sweep ;
Ha ! turn and gallop up its wildering steep ;
And now like falling stars more swift descend
To vanish underground : so some contend.

Twilight was fading when I inward glanced,
  Though it seemed outward, to their fairy ring.
Fancy or fact, and night or day, there danced,
  While was a strange weird light on everything,
Innumerable fays ; till wonder grew,
And overhead poised Puck, I knew.
And round him, winged for the occasion,
A host of devils of the bee-persuasion,
Most minim-showing mighty influences,
All little passions that provoke offences,
The spawn of anger, hate, revenge, and scaith,
Of envy, malice, jealousy, and death,
Pride, and ambition, covetous desire,
Lust, and each form of it : and all conspire.

Seemed it a Pandemonium alive
With legionary fiends in crowded hive,
And like to Satan with those gods of men,
Beelzebub, Chemosh, Moloch, all his train,
Ashtaroth, Thammuz, Dagon, Rimmon, him
Called Belial, Isis, Orus, Baalim;
And all in consult gathered to deceive
Lucy and me, as they had erst done Eve,
But me to special wrong: for in God's plan
I folly should have worsted—I, a man.

I knew not what their plans, if now completed;
But suddenly in air the Lords were seated,
While lesser fays still underneath them danced.
Puck impishly on me then fixedly glanced,
And, as I watched him, suffered curious change.
The observed of all observers, thing most strange,
In hellish fancy's mystic music hall,
And a Gladstonian dicky, seeming tall,
He with a startling strident " Hem " begins
A sportive song of his, and vilely grins.

PUCK.

" Skin beauty most seemly may lie without taint,
    Or any refreshing dissemblance of art :
For sans powder or brush lying spirit may paint
    Fair words on the tongue, which are false to the heart.
            Beware of the paint.

" At a fancy-dress ball one, impeaching the rose,
    O'er her flower-festooned robe wore a skeleton hoop ;
Man approaching her saw, with a fear to fore-close,
    This visible on it, as loud as a whoop,
            ' Beware of the paint ! '

" Such hoop parabolic on Lucy would show :
    All perfection without, her offence is within.
Ah ! she, who would love without flattery know,
    Should, simple and true from the heart to the skin,
            Know nothing of paint."

The Lords acclaimed wherein they thought to see
The growing success of his strategy :
He also entertained me, to enrage,
With fooleries upon his modern stage,
While on profounder trickery intent,
To have immediate disambushment.
Sudden by rush of sound mine ears were stormed,
And eager eyes of secret cause informed.
From the dark pass and summit of the glen
Poured a Niagara ; and I knew, that then
The mighty reservoir its dam had forced :
Stones, rocks, and trees were from the soil divorced,
Borne on the waters of the raging flood.
I turned, ran, shouted, through the twilight wood,
And o'er the vale, where still the stream made song,
Rounded a knoll, and burst upon the throng.
Cleared had the feast been, yet the crowd delayed :
Loiterers towards their equipages strayed.
Instant the dread news spread ; and with a stride
I mother's brother found, and was by Lucy's side.

The cunning soldier had to win the maid,
Proffered her mother his availing aid,
And to her peer left Lucy, who disdained
The poor solicitude, I nothing feigned.
In ready cart, coach, carriage all depart ;
While uncle, I, and several mounting start
By other road in danger's front to ride,
And warn, who haply may the warning bide.
Upon its course, by ocean only stayed,
That headlong flood no human life allayed.
It swept the fairy glen, then fields o'erspread,
Descending still, but, in its river bed ;
Now down a wooded hollow found the shore
Distant from town, and was a flood no more.
Past us it raged with many a tossing tree ;
And wreck both left behind, and bore to sea ;
Spoiled fields, swept cattle, bridges down, and graves
Plundered upon its journey to the waves.

Had Puck conceived the thing to overwhelm,
And purge of us his desecrated realm ;
Or only so again our sport to spoil,
And wash of evil steps his fairy soil ?
I know not ; but with unexpected worst
I hope on him and his the waters burst ;
Yet think that folly has too many lives,
Drowned or compounded serpent-like survives,
More fell than Orillo, whom Astolpho share—
His life dependent on a single hair ;
Worse than Caligorant, for no horn you bray
Will blow the mighty gossamer away.

I sad as eve with uncle lone, alack !
Revolved the luckless day on homeward track.
" Why so downhearted, Edward ? "
                  questioned Nuncle.
I answered—

EDWARD.

      " Wherefore ask to learn
What you already know, good uncle ? "

UNCLE.

" In part."

EDWARD.

      " The ending is too dern.
I might have borne to see my rose
Rifled by every wind that blows ;
Its honied fragrancies and dyes
Taverning vagrant butterflies ;
From one so richly dowered to please
Not warded even swarming bees,
Though every sip had stung me mad
With melancholy over-sad.
I might in rage have wildly spoken,
Been scorned, yet deemed her faith unbroken :

For she indifferently proud
Might scorn, too, while she pleased the crowd.
But now a glitter and worm appears,
A snake its coronal uprears,
And forks her with its baneful tongue,
   And fixes with its baleful eye,
And hath such fascination strong
   As star malign and very high.
Though I in moment mad may scoff,
I cannot shake the terror off ;
I feel the fated hour is born
To blight my love's too radiant morn,
Yet little force have to protest,
No charm to save whom I love best.
What can I, if a prey she go
Willing to Mammon throned below,
When Ceres' self with aid of heaven
Back could not win her daughter even,
Save yearly for a nine months' stay,
Though Proserpine loved upper day ?"

UNCLE.

" Edward, give heed unto my common-places,
Though I should ride to death their fluent paces.
Heart-burning with desire of gold,
Colouring often young as old,
Rich-skinned as Iber's fleecy flocks
Drinking of springs from quartzose rocks,
All something gain to live, some live to gain ;
Profit and loss is God-almain.
Medœa, Amidas, alike
Wronging and wronged, for gold still strike.
Shylock, Malbecco, wife or treasure,
Daughter or ducats ; which is pleasure ?
Spousal, fraternal, filial love,
Gold will parental, too, remove.
For poverty is worst of living,
And love a sin of overgiving.

Timon, not Eusthenes, is fate;
Friends flow and ebb with our estate.
Fortune with canvases unfurled
  Catches, and circumnavigates
Fair-breezy praises of the world;
  Misfortune levies for the rates,
Turning us out of home and heart.
So we for gain with conscience part,
In graceless rivalry contend
To rise on shoulder-shotten friend,
And rush all jostling in each others' way!
This passes t'other without even ' Good day,'
And then we fight; one calls another proud,
Who, having cause, confesses it aloud;
And then we lie, each whispering to his set
With what a host of devils he has met.
Ye jovial spirits and Plutonian powers!
Has God another life like this of ours?"

EDWARD.

" 'Tis passing strange, and more surpassing sad;
If better than it feels, must still be bad."

UNCLE.

" Suppose we sum the universe as well
Into a rather more extensive hell,
And own, the Prince of all the Air has sway;
And there is everywhere the Devil to pay,
And money needed for the dirty job;
That one can't amble on a priestly cob
Anywhere through the crowd, but rough-shod ride
Over some others, or be thrust aside;
Confess, and in a word, this world is good
Only for him, who for himself is shrewd,
And careless of the cost to others will
Empty their pockets, so his own to fill;
That Hermes, bringing luck and purse in hand,
Might for our proper devil-worship stand,

Our potent Hœmony, our sacred Moly,
Of Holies most esteemed our inner Holy ;
Is Lucy's action perdurably worse
Than others' ne'er a mortal cares to curse,
Or wanting more than carnival disguise,
If, failing thee, she books a higher prize?"

EDWARD.

" Disparaged love feels doubly spilt,
When trumped by less than love—by gilt ;
When beauteous Frances broke her word,
Sir Rodney fell upon his sword."

UNCLE.

" But faulty Derham, less a coward,
Flouted a greater frailer Howard.
With flashing scorn then shame thy sorrow,
And from the light fresh courage borrow ;
From peril draw, from worse despair,
Strength grown by Samson with his hair.
Though any simpleton may see,
Whatever may true beauty be,
Worth is not merely opportunity.
Beset by nettles, if you will,
A myrtle is a myrtle still ;
The plum, which blossoming once promised fruit,
Though nipped by frost may be unchanged at root.
Jove, prudent too of future times,
Issues conceals from prophet rhymes
In night caliginose of fate,
And laughs, when lawless Paul Prys trepidate."

EDWARD.

" Hee-Haw ;
Yes, from her I cannot part,
More than body may from heart ;
Immortality is bond
For true feeling, when once fond ;
Hee-Haw.

"See-Saw;
Never level, smile or frown,
Tetter-totter up and down,
I am up, but not to stop,
Now am down, and with a flop,
See-Saw.

"He-Haw;
She is certainly inhuman;
Softer I than man or woman.
Since I cannot welcome neigh,
Ass am I here still to bray,
Hee-Haw."

So we our homeward way beguile,
Pondering, though with a clouded smile,
How great soever female error
Man will not fill her soul with terror,
Unless he be such saracen
As burned my Lady Villaren.
"Make thyself Christian, I will make thee Knight;"
St. Louis said to Moslemite:
For knights swore women to defend,
And Christians' grace to foes extend.
And when another Childe of France
Satirists of himself forgave,
He warned them not to couch like lance
Against his queen, or they should dance
On nothing to the grave.
Even Thor, when beating horrid wives
Of Giant Ills, that wrecked men's lives,
Pleaded, they all were wolves inhuman,
His thunder-hand ne'er fell on woman.
And thus the Nabob with a twinkling eye—

UNCLE.

"Cease like a lover lorn to sigh.
Let Lucy pass forgotten, or,
If thou hast courage of a Thor,

In honour cloak poor cowardice
Fearing a future void of bliss ;
Instant senility arrest ;
Tickle despondency with jest.
Grants in their Wilderness know not defeat ;
  Wellingtons also, who hate it as sin,
Pass it unknowing, or, fearing to meet,
  Yielding at Quatrebras, Waterloos win.
First may be last, and withal not be worst :
  Charles the Fifth, in power grateful decreed,
That of the shoe-trade the cobbler goes first :
  Many in triumph so Cæsar precede.
Now last of night and first of day,
  Now last of day and first of night,
And ever looking either way
  Is boon twilight.
Be thou as gay ;
In the leaden and gray,
Sing and play."

Advice so sage unanswering I hear ;
For, seeing golden Silence standing near,
I take the hint now in her speaking eyes,
And, meditating action, look as deeply wise.

BOOK III.

CANTO I.

WITH thrice five hundred comrades in his train,
The Lord of Love in Florence knew to reign.
One revel long through ardent months prevailed,
And princely strangers glad the concourse hailed,
While bannered streets were gay, and crowded halls,
With feasts, processions, tournaments, and balls.
Nor did he less in iced Bologna glow
Hollowing azure halls 'neath hills of snow,
Or building high, as doth at Mont—Réal
Acadia, holding winter Carnival,
Routing with pleasures, warm as sun-browned lark,
Invasive frosts, bleak day, and dismal dark :
Now I with equal zeal and zest conspire
'Neath Lucy's dainty snows to light love's fire.
With music, dance, and laughter as of Gods
Convulsing heaven, whose fast foundation nods,
I now assume to worship other where,
Till she to open ears invite my prayer.
Gudrana, widowed oft, at last a nun,
Confessed to her inquiring fervid son,
That of her wooers she had loved him most,
To whom she wrongly seemed least well-disposed.
My slackening chase now may her flight retard ;
    Ah, bold, if not strong, I have ceased to pursue,
Neither her frost, nor heat latent regard,
    Seemingly careless, if lastingly true ;
Not disregarding warm glances of any,
    Pleased when they smile, giving smiles in return,
Dark unto her am, but bright with the many,
    Ceasing to blow at a torch that won't burn ;

Sunshine in any form wildly desiring,
  Changed not, nor wayward, but chilled quite to heart,
Into gay crowd of warm beauty retiring,
  That she may miss me, I win her by art.
Yet am I ware of warning on the right,
Dropped in my ear by mine own Guardian Sprite,
Answered by me, while Puck, the bantling deft,
Crows with an after-chuckle on the left.

Guardian Sprite.

" You think with folly soon to master love,
  But should at least the cap and bells remove ;
Else of the two you may the greater fool
Seem, serving openly the Lord of Misrule."

Edward.

" Eight hundred exiles, scaling air,
  On Vaudois vallies dropped below
Recovering right to altars there,
And homes entrapped by ducal snare
From Cottian Alps of wolf and bear
  To citied plains of winding Po.
None ever fought, yet loved so well ;
Such spirit ne'er showed infidel ;
Vaudois, though fighting when betrayed,
Still for their faithless princes prayed."

Puck.

" The saddest of all sage old cures
Is that insipid sprite of yours.
Give him the slip, and, bond to none,
Enjoy thyself with every one."

    Her distance apeing,
      Like shadow true
    Mockingly shaping
      Itself on you ;
    With reckless daring,
      That wholly lies,

And pride of bearing,
  That bursts with sighs ;
A coward, facing
  But fearing facts,
Part by hints expressing
  And part by acts ;
I, lack-a-day,
  Suspecting change,
Defiantly gay,
  Sing as I range ;
Though upon wing,
Of Lucy sing.

FIRST SONG.

" Sweet, sweet though not long,
  Thou of love once wast singing—
Of love, that was young
  And around us too winging ;
And I heard, as it flew,
The sweet song : was it true ?

" Sweet, sweet, all alone
  It was with us abiding :
Away it hath flown.
  And, oh ! where is it hiding ?
May its far image dwell
In some paradise shell ?

" A vision of light,
  Full of soul-hushing story,
It hung in my sight
  In a loose robe of glory :
Say, then, can it have gone
To the porch of the sun ?

" A beautiful love,
  From my longing devotion
It floated above
  With a beckoning motion ;

Happy cherubs may fly
Round its tent in the sky.

" It rose upon earth
    In the twilight of even ;
Thy voice gave it birth
    Just to vanish in heaven,
And a proud mother smiled
On the death of her child.

" When young Ibrahim died,
    Mohammed could say,
Bliss was nursing his pride
    Now in paradise-day :
But false songs are inventions
Paving hell's east extensions."

SECOND SONG.

" Did we love, when we say we love,
    As we hate when we say we hate,
Time and tide, which untiring move,
    Would on love seem to wait.

" But this love was and is a cheat,
    Like clairvoyance of early skies,
Which, assuring us days of heat,
    Is but fair-weather wise.

" Love is fickle as vagrant breeze,
    Which now hot, and now chilling blows ;
Changes quarters with happy ease,
    But expires in repose.

" How one's love then more surely prove,
    Gain more faith for it, lady fair,
Than by singing thus ' love may rove,'
    With the burden, ' Beware ! ' "

THIRD SONG.

" I know for whom was blowing,
  And dying late a rose.
I've plucked it, and am going
  To Maude, whose mirror shows
Than Lucy's face a fairer,
  Who will have much content,
When rose and I declare her
  To be our sentiment.

" A wilderness I know, and
  Am going to invade
With Grace, whose lint-locks glow, and
  Illumine all the shade.
Though Lucy may disown me,
  Grace beaming now is seen
Flower-crowned, where I have thrown me
  At the feet of my new queen.

" Madge nothing finds to fear in
  The fairy-ring, we stand
And are together dear in ;
  All earth is fairyland.
Let Lucy dread the fairies ;
  Madge only laughs.   Ah, me !
With three and more such Maries
  I shall too happy be."

FOURTH SONG.

" Bright glowed the suns, all radiant, while
I guileless saw in thee no guile,
And faith rewarded every vow—
Augustan suns were these ; but now
Thy light of love has lost its vigour,
Touched with a more than Arctic rigour.
I therefore, too, am cold, and feel
More hard than flint to flash of steel,
Insensible to cold regard.

T

Maiden, farewell.   I am so hard
That, though thou soon mayest long for me,
I shall have neither eye, nor ear for thee ;
Yet might perchance to-day, or never more,
Welcome returning ardour, and adore.
Ah, trust not thou to colour : locks of night
Are sooner sprinkled gray, than shocks of light.
Some prefer buttercups to paler daisies
Although all crimson-lipped : 'tis as love crazes—
Love, which may range.   Trust not too much to love :
He in him more of serpent has than dove,
Eyes full of speculation ; lives on change ;
Not his own mother is more given to range.
Trust not to beauty fêted, soon to fast.
Trust not to love ; you shall not be his last.
Amphion so, beside melodious fount,
Sang to his flocks on Acarynthus mount."

FIFTH SONG.

" Herodias' daughter dancing won
From oath of Herod head of John,
At wish of Mother fierce as frail ;
Will Lucy ape that evil tale,
And win an Earl, my heart to break,
Dance to him for a mother's sake ?
Horace, by lyre of Chloé lured,
A while his Lydia abjured,
Whom Calais prevailed to scorch,
Consuming with commutual torch.
Die Horace could to Chloé save ;
Calais for Lydia death twice brave.
But ancient Venus fresh returned :
Though Calais more than star-bright burned,
Lighter than cork might Horace be,
More passionate than Adria's sea ;
Yet when his door, on Chloé closed,
Open to Lydia he exposed,
.She stayed not doubting to forgive
    Him, worthy of her sigh ;

But could with Horace loving live,
   And, God permitting, die."

Thus lilting on my way, with dubious gains
From ready spilth of wonted amorous strains,
A proper man, I thought to live for girls,
   And not inglorious roused their leaguered camp ;
Now willow-hang a lyre fatigued with dirls,
   And under sit a threadbare heart to vamp,
Which in this war has coward been, as hare
Beating a tabour in Bartholomew Fair,
Gay but in seeming, bold but with despair.
She with a show of fine command
Bated my braggery off-hand.
'Twas in act fifth of my mad play
Her purpose, one black-letter day,
Sealed came, she could so cruel be,
Dismissing quite all thought of me,
Forbidding future meet or speech,
Even writing now would fail to reach,
Or be returned unread, and move
To more disdain, but no more love.
Has Puck, or devil fooled us ? She,
   Seizing the apt and sorry chance,
Deemed a prompt riddance rude of me
   A heavenly deliverance.

Uncle, when parting, had compassionated
And with his sister all my love debated.
I since had noted her too curious eye
Brooding upon me, and a motherly sigh
Heaviest when I showed lightest. She had seen
How joy's sun glinted off grief's evergreen ;
Now questioning learned what, I with shame disclosed;
And, though to pity dearly-well disposed,
Thus blamed.

MOTHER.

" With Lucy, Edward, thou hast broken."

EDWARD.

"I?"

MOTHER.

"Yes, if thou in verity hast spoken :
Truth scorns the folly stooping to a lie ;
Love trusts not love, that can pretend to die."

EDWARD.

"But have I sinned, then, more than she
With lukewarm passion sickening me?
As inland sea bars turbid pride
Of affluent Nilus from its tide ;
And ocean, rising, backward drives
   Reluctant and coquettish stream,
That hesitates before it dives,
   Indulging many a haughty dream ;
So niceness suits not love in spate,
And coyness may make love too late.
I had excuse for holding off ;
She might have better done than scoff,
And, smiling on the time to come,
Not banished me her heart and home."

MOTHER.

"Have you for jealousy, my son,
Sufficient reason had, or none?
What if she, also jealous now,
Angry hath taken back her vow,
And like to Hamlet, who could flout
His father's scaly ghost with doubt,
Now reckoneth love a ruthless feeling
Idolatry of self concealing;
Zephyr pursuing its own sigh,
Which roses only magnify ;
Itself, pursuer and pursued,
Attaining never any good ;
Vanity of too huge a cost,

Self not possessed, and all else lost?
Who digs a ditch, or sets a gin,
May catch or fall himself therein;
Perillus bellowed like a fool,
First in his own perilous bull."

EDWARD.

"I may have jealous been, not proud;
And to her will too long have bowed.
Her gusty pride hath swelling tossed
    The sea of love, till faith and hope,
Their light extinct, their anchor lost,
    No more can with the tempest cope."

MOTHER.

"Good form within and not without,
    My son, is grace, and prudence praise,
And virtue fame with no brass-shout
    Of trumpet in the public ways.
And these, obscured or held in fear,
    By pride eclipsed, perhaps to show
More evident and doubly dear
    In fires of penitential woe,
Appealing unto soul, not sense,
These have prevailing eloquence;
Afar or near their beauty shines,
Living or dead attracts, refines;
Laith Socrates made loathlier death
Beautiful with his parting breath;
And something of all this I see
In Lucy, howe'er false she be.
If false she be, how pitiful for you;
And the more pity, if that she is true."

EDWARD.

"Bleeding with love's afflictive smart,
As rosebud torn, my redder heart;
Black as her hair my day; like coal
'Twixt fire and water my drossed soul."

MOTHER.

"Yet smouldering fires are quick to light,
And love's may at a sigh ignite."

EDWARD.

"Ah, when we last as strangers passed,
It might be innocence harassed,
Or purposed guilt, or sudden ire—
For blame will righteous flush hell-fire,
And wrongful ruby virtue's cheek—
Would that the tell-tale blood might speak ;
But love, by look not tongue arraigned,
No surer recognition deigned
Than spoke in blushing front, which paled,
Showing her cold, as when hath failed
    Sunset from off far Alpine snows.
God help the lone one left abroad
Lost upon such chill heights untrod :
    Even so she leaves me and my woes,
Well knowing I would freeze to stone
In any arms, but her dear own.
Would some good angel might release
A Felix Saint to sue my peace,
And cause that bramble grapes to grow,
Whose only wine can glad my woe,
Make forms all rhythmic, day all smiles,
Night a Cleopatra without her wiles."

MOTHER.

"Mere flattering awe with pretty art
Is all she owes that Earl, not heart :
And, if love wins in marriage play,
Seven is thy chance, his cink and trei.
Hark to a parable, which shrewd
Read rightly may be true as good.
Geronica to church refusing
Geneviéve, and conscience losing,
    Was stricken blind, nor walked abroad,

Till, in her darling's tears of pain
Washing blind eyes, she saw again
   And gave Geneviéve to God ;
In thy suspected tears her eyes
Lucy so washing may grow wise,
Smarting herself to think how sore
For her and self thou art, and more—
All that a coronet will cost,
Should faith and love with thee be final lost."

EDWARD.

" Oh ! had I been Sir Martin Dove,
   And she poor Adelaide,
I could have seemed to die for love,
   And straight in shell been laid,
And, to her prison-cloister borne
For burial, have heard her mourn,
And pitying risen, embraced, and fled
With her, who had believed me dead :
For could she see, or think me so,
And not repent of all our woe ?
Yet Lucy Sacheverel wed,
When rumour false spake Lovelace dead—
Recovering only to be slain,
Handsome and brave, alas ! in vain,
Killed by her falsehood more abhorred
And cruel than the foeman's sword."

MOTHER.

" My words, boy, on thy spirit fall,
As chaff on breeze dispersing all.
Wronging the heart he prizes most,
And to his own eternal cost,
Man jealous sees in friendship's show
Smiles of dishonest ardour glow,
In squint suspicion shameless proof,
In virtue's footprint Satan's hoof.
Yet Guido through his colour-grind
   His beautiful Magdalen achieved,
Leaving the lubber coarseness far behind ;

The Model only helps the mind
　To embody, what it has conceived.
Grant her a somewhat erring one .
Of whose dread loss you danger run,
Still faith would be the better reason :
　For faith will often shame a lie,
While doubt, unto fair truth high treason,
　Yet something credits treachery.
Although idolatry most broad
Of wood alone, or stone makes God,
If value lies not in our will,
　Still private need is value sure ;
Want of some worthless thing may kill,
　Possession of it cure."

EDWARD.

" As bore up tidal river strides,
Ever on front of memory rides
Surge of recurring misery
　Greater a thousand times than tears.
Can she be well so ill to me,
　Or that be good which bad appears ?"

MOTHER.

" Self, Edward, bounding blinds our view
　Of all without its ring :
Within it partial we, untrue,
One-sided, see nor through and through,
　Nor all round anything,
And sins of others bear in mind,
Our own unfelt on backs purblind.
Nor Lucy, nor uncertain chance,
Nor man, nor God, nor circumstance,
　But folly blame without impeach
Of love, which thou mayest keep—not losing :
For that is still within thy choosing,
　And she not yet beyond thy reach.
And, praying thee to shun illusions,
I leave thee to no rash conclusions."

I lone then mother's counsel meditate.
  Has neither truly played the other false?
Was I with frantic folly rash to mate?
  Shall I repent—assent to passion's calls?
More eblouissant to behold
Once Lucy was, not then too cold.
Her face, by love illuminated,
  So like to heaven shows, that hell
In awe of it might stand amated,
  And God Himself forget, Eve fell.
And let her only smile again,
I shall be more than ever fain,
Eager as fire, which spouting flowed
  From bachelor-barge of Lincoln's Inn,
When Elizabeth, red rose, was snowed
  And twined with white, and crowned its queen:
Bold as Ghirardo, when they said,
  Blanche now was dead to all his woe,
Raised coverlid of narrow bed,
And kissing trance from lips still red,
Opened her ears to words, that fed
  With rapture the returning glow.
And now my thoughts took counsel with themselves.
  From craniol hollows rose a whispered strain
Of under-music, as from airy elves;
  Out of each lobe and hemisphere of brain,
Not fairy-fancy musical good-for-noughts,
Nor Cupids, much less men, but angel thoughts,
Issuing to the wizard music, under control,
From either hand upon the stage of my soul,
Joined their processions twin, and joining turned,
In concave crescent which most moonlike burned,
Eyes full upon me, the Choragus still
Centreing and guiding song, as thus, at will.

CHORAGUS.

" Who ever by our Lord stood strong
As woman, when the faith was young?
Mohammed owned Codijah true

Beyond what he prophetic knew;
Cromwell's Eliza was so good,
She seemed her father's holy rood;
Flora, than all her Stuarts dearer,
　Sweet scents foul memory of that race,
Haloes corruption, though too near her,
　And laughs dishonour in the face.
The very negress black as night,
With soul by glow of heart made light,
Never on lonely Mungo Park
Turned look inhospitably dark :
Men have she-devils feigned, but then
Such have been angels to some men."

LEFT.

" Wantons may spit upon thy shield,
　As on Sir Marhaus' seeing he,
So true himself, would never yield
　To dally with an infamy :
But had you reed of Dorco-strain,
Spoiling the pirate of his gain,
A symphony you might invent,
And rive gold bars with your lament.
By love, with minstrelsy to aid,
Proud Lady Malfred's pretty maid
A gallant lord in wedlock won—
Against the mother's will the son :
Like Signalil thou shouldest sing,
And Lucy to thine arbour bring."

RIGHT.

" Would'st rather measure take of time ;
　Above it rise, and, mastering fate,
Then set to Solomonic rhyme
　Triumphant ? "

LEFT.

　　　　　　　" What if then too late.
The past is milk to-day must cream,
Futurity a skimless dream."

RIGHT.

"Yet may the boldest pause and think
On great occasions imminent brink."

LEFT.

"But, unarmed Pompey doubting on,
Cæsar had crossed the Rubicon."

CHORAGUS.

"Time by the forelock of occasion,
    Unmeasured, seize without delay,
Or that, which hung upon a hair's persuasion,
    Chains may not unpropitious stay ;
    Courage itself may ooze away.
Beneath all stones lie scorpions for cowards,
And fortune ever is to such untowards.
If Henry's horse at New Ford quails,
By Ryd Pencarn he enters Wales,
And with him one to rescue fair
Captive Adelaide St. Clair."

ALL TOGETHER.

"Love should be nothing, or dare all ;
If losing, gallant to its fall.
Peril asks no deliberation ;
The present is its one occasion.
Write, sing of love—no grovelling strain—
And her esteem at least retain.
When time is passing, he who keens
A simple woe yet something means.
Larks would escape, did heaven not goodly cage them ;
And men would songless be, did love not rage them."

When tempest compassless abroad
Obscures star-crested front of God,
Samoyede strips delusive snow
From mossy face of earth, to know
Lost secret signs, his course to guide ;

So I in night of stormy pride
With more than Samoyedish skill
Through melting snows would read her will ;
Therefore would touch each choicest string,
  Accomplice of Glaskerion bard ;
Therefore a dearer song would sing
  Than love yet sang, or princess heard ;
Would heaven like Israfel impart,
  Like Orpheus hell subdue with lyre,
In song and rapture all my heart
  Uttering attract her whole desire.
To Lucy and myself alone
Covertly making moan,
A sombre nightingale,
Syllabled I my inky wail,
Not as St. Valentine, who goes
  With thousand and ten thousand loves
Attendant rustling tiny bows
  And wings as of St. Mark's tame doves :
For Blackstone died upon his day,
And sad my song as bitter hay,
Sounds, as of night the gushing tears,
Holding all her obstinate ears,
Filling her eyes, too, as with stars that fall,
Since my ink is made of gall.

EDWARD TO LUCY.

" All farewells are not with weeping ;
  Knells not every parting bell ;
Yet death living is, and reaping
  Bliss with each farewell.
Speak not once that dread unholy
  Word : the drawn sword in its breath
Murders hope, and melancholy
  Maddens at the death,
Seeing joys, the past had brought us,
  Perish ; those the future said,
It would certainly allot us,
  All with hope now dead.

"Will you, dust to dust returning,
  Lay yon future with that past ?
Pride may nerve you now to spurning,
  But it cannot last.
Say 'farewell' you cannot, maiden :
  Faltering stays the rebel tongue ;
Mute the bosom sorrow-laden,
  As moist harp loose-strung.
See your lover : for, believe him,
  Song his suffering cannot tell.
Say, you love him, and forgive him ;
  Do not add 'farewell.'

"Air first heard it, when the fallen
  Watched the hues of heaven fade ;
Earth first heard it, when the fallen
  Went from Eden shade.
'Tis a word of sin and sorrow
  Only for the unforgiven :
Speak it not but let to-morrow
  Still believe in heaven."

As Vehmgericht from secresy
  Brief summoned traitor sharp to doom,
She lenten and forbiddingly
  Meeting assigned me at her home.
Had Venus fain not looked condign,
I should have prayed of her a sign,
And, though with token of delay,
Been happy Palamon that day.
But day of Mercury was named,
For sleights and subtle speeches famed.
To show at bar of Lords and gain
Place honourable, Cowper fain
In dread of public ordeal crazed :
I Lords ten thousand had outfaced,
And quailed less, ay, if there had stood
Great Thor in prejudicial mood,
As when he lady-like unveiled,

And wives of Giant Gods assailed.
Goddess more dread of human speech
Is Lucy, and not less a witch.

Ah ! there a grandeur vague with awe,
As Rome in ruin tombed, I saw.
Nought can unchanging skies protest,
    Nor man dissemble, nor earth hide
Its mighty past, though now confessed
A wraith of glory at the best,
A present night-mare on the breast,
    The torment and despair of pride.
    She gave me pause.   As pilgrim falls
Into continuous prostrations,
Sighting the Niobe of nations,
    And knees his way through opening walls
Into God's temple, so, awed fear
Sorely restraining, I drew near.
Like Jephthab, whom false honour led
His daughter's dancing blood to shed,
Stood her resolve all naked, bare
    Pride sacrificing rival love :
Such fierce self-worship I might dare,
    But natheless with small hope to move.
All diffident of blood her cheek,
Has she a heart of marble without streak?
Calm she, dread, unembarrassed, pale,
Stern, looking all the speechless tale
Of happy days returning never,
And hopes behind her cast for ever ;
Caged eagle, lily-white and tame,
With eyes of sodden fire, whose flame
May not be roused, or to your shame.
What my first trembling accents told,
    While turtle-like I cooing quaked,
Or how I waxed in pleading bold,
    Rough as down-trodden earth fresh-raked,
Memory fails me.   Ocean deep,
    Unnoticed through Batavian stakes,

First trickling, then with forceful sweep,
  Invasive over province breaks :
So gathered into noted flow
Billows of memorable woe
More strenuous than pitiful,
  But perilous far more than all,
Last hazard of true love to rule,
  Or be a hapless hopeless thrall.

CANTO II.

LUCY.

" The heart-sore wants too much redress,
Which you incurable confess.
Pity, for so far gone a love
I am not hospital enough :
Though strong my weakness old to try,
And drop with this last tear, out of mine eye
Falling, not now in my defence,
But rebel to reason's continence."

EDWARD.

" Ah ! thinkest thou, that our desires
Are flickers of ignoble fires,
Or to be reasoned out of flame,
Or covered with an ash of shame?
Nay, these aglow, indulged to-day,
Would eager for to-morrow pray,
And find fresh joy in it new-born
As dawn to dance on Easter morn.
It was never meant that ought should sever
  Two hearts for each other created,
That they should long, and pine, and never
  In this world dare to be mated,

Or circumstance untoward ban
Heartiest vows of maid and man."

LUCY.

" Deemest thou, I am prone to dance
Attendant upon circumstance ? "

EDWARD.

" Then never tell me, I have swerved
So from allegiance as deserved
    Dismissal ; never tell me how
Thy virgin heart its joy achieved,
Yet falsely no true love conceived,
    But wind of words—a thoughtless vow.
Shent were I, you, by other won,
Might fail him, too, and cling to none ;
All favouring be loving-less ;
Want heart for all you might confess.
With such Celimene, I would not pair
To be another Moliére.
Vows given thou art free to thwart,
    Or back recall.   I have no thought
To win thee save from loss of heart,
    Or bind thee if thou wouldest not."

LUCY.

" I would, but will not.   Thou hast shown
Nature to jealousy too prone,
Nor in thyself, nor me that trust,
Which manhood should, and lover must :
No Celimene I, thou confessed
Weaker art jealous as Alceste.
I will not to a lover cling,
    Whose very virtue shows like vice,
Darting me off as with a sting,
    Making me hate one over-nice,
Yet loose as some rain-letting roof,
And pervious to every proof.
Doubting in law as thus in love,

Wasting thy prime in songs and sighs
With hopes of idle treasure-trove,
Thinkest thou others will approve,
  When thou dost so thyself despise?
Forgive me, but I never can :
A woman seeks to wed a man."

EDWARD.

" If I have jealous seemed, hast thou ·
Given no cause?   Take back thy vow,
Take back thyself ; and yet thy heart
From mine shall never more depart—
It is too true.   In this do I
Too jealous seem, or only lie?
But more than heart now, circumstance
Artful controlling love's romance
And civilizing even hate,
Marriages *à la mode* debate
Betwixt not fond but worldly wishes,
And misery dines off golden dishes."

LUCY.

" Think you with love a herbal feast
Better, than flesh with Beauty's Princely Beast?"

EDWARD.

" Safe the proverbial well-stalled ox.
But, if the wisdom of the fox
To brute success gives precedence,
I to thy hand make still some small pretence.
Midnight is past : the Cross to bend
Begins, and sunward to ascend ;
And, ere another year shall end,
Thee I may claim.   Wilt thou not wait?
Or shall success soon come too late?
Ha ! dumb as Anaxarété?
To stone then harden too, as she."

U

LUCY.

"Statue on pedestal to stand,
  Till I on thee have ceased to frown,
A god-like warning in the land,
  To grace admitted stepping down,
Like her who loved Pygmalion
For having raised her out of stone.
Yet my down-stepping would not be
From rise, which thou hadst wrought in me,
But to a block in mine own way,
And the proverbial delay
Of law, and opposition strict
Of my late father's derelict."

EDWARD.

"Though much is ill which well may please,
  Yet liking free alone is blest:
For God on high free-will decrees,
  And liking, freely willed, is best.
Then free as air be heart and mind;
  And, following whither these may tend,
Still let us be our own fair wind,
  And happiness approve the end."

LUCY.

"May not such love be, in excess,
An ill-considered selfishness?
To mother, friends, society
I duty owe—to more than thee,
To the world; and heart may sacrifice
To self-esteem, for woman's price—
So call it, if you will—such place
As hope expects with right to grace.
Loved Anna wedded Donne too dear—
Discarded by my Lord Ellesmere,
And due to friends his daily beer:
Therefore he curious was of fame,
That she might love his empty name.

But own I will to nobler pride
Of influence over circle wide ;
Have ever deemed Elfrida wronged,
So cheated of a king who longed ;
If planet only of some sun,
Would be a satellited one ;
Contracting not my natal sphere,
Would rather wed my more than peer,
And you are something less, I fear,
Or may be, what I know not yet,
I know not when, and me forget."

EDWARD.

" Thee ! "

LUCY.

"Yes, and you :
We are but two."

EDWARD.

" Forget thee !   Look you, were I now
Tenfold more opulent than thou,
   And higher placed, some social star
Like Raphael, or Goethe famed,
Who were not of their loves ashamed,
   I could not happy glow afar,
Till I had coupled bliss with thine,
A double star in heaven to shine.
Orpyne upon Midsummer Eve
May wrongly bend, not I deceive :
You, sowing hempseed, look behind
With other hope than me to find."

LUCY.

" To purpose small for thee I sow
Good-wishes, which to nothing grow."

EDWARD.

" Cheating the time for chance to throw me over,
Which you accept now in a noble lover.

But art a will-o'-wisp, whose light
Bewrays the compass of my night,
My fire thy flame must follow still,
And, mingling, steady its wild will."

LUCY.

" My will mine own is, thou shalt find ;
Woman does sometimes know her mind."

EDWARD.

" Yet would I have thee, as God would,
Simple to evil, wise to good,
Not having won thee erst for love
To see and hear thee scornful prove.
If once a demigod to thee,
Therefore thy love was won by me,
So Damayanti Bala loved ;
But when he only mortal proved,
Unheavenly, dusty, weak, footsore,
A tottering shadow cast on polished floor,
Sweat on his brow, a god no more,
Her hand to him went willing prize,
Though sought by gods of Indra skies ;
With flowers she wreathed his toil-stained brows,
Saying, 'Beloved, I am thy spouse.'"

LUCY.

" I can't make that example good."

EDWARD.

" Bad could not make it, if you would.
For what is station, title, fame,
   Power, wealth, even pleasure without heart?
I'd rather be the valley stream,
   Clear, fresh, bright thing, that hath the art
Of song and heaven in its breast,
Than any lordly lofty crest
Of any Blanc, on which the sun
Glitters, as though he had undone

A casket of his jewels rare,
A thousand of his rainbows there;
'Tis lifeless cold, however fair."

LUCY.

" Ice it may be, not lifeless cold :
I know at least those on it bold,
Adventuresome, and vigourful."

EDWARD.

" But not to stay."

LUCY.

                " Ay, always cool :
I would not sweltering below,
When I could climb, through valleys go."

EDWARD.

" Then climb with me thine Alpine guide.
Heights know I higher than thy pride,
Heights not of fashion but of toil,
Fresh heights, whose winning shall be spoil,
And, won for thee, not less than heaven :
Without thee—Say, I am forgiven :
Daring the future, no alarm
May in it then unnerve this arm.
Not Chanticleer with Pertelote
More readily his fears forgot,
Inspired all dangers to embrace,
Frayed only by the beauty of her face :
Yet him she scornful misesteemed,
Conceiving that he only dreamed."

LUCY.

" Dost more? For surely little comes
Of all this beating of ear-drums.
And what if I alone dare win
At once, what you but now begin ;

Be mine own stroke, and trust no more
A feeble and unsteady rower ? "

EDWARD.

" Harpest thou still upon that string,
  And undertone of all thy plaint ?
Goliath fell by David sling,
  But from it was a stone well sent ;
Thy pointless dart is homeless borne,
Winged by airs idle of feigned scorn,
Whose quaint despite I all forgive.
  'Tis natural, thou should'st not know
Life difficult : for so to live
  As thou, is as with flood to flow.
But would'st thou rise than flood-tide higher,
To mountain tops cloud-capped aspire ?
Fear not to quit thy foolish plenty
  And bliss thou hast no need to woo.
Its dolce far niente,
  And nothing else to do,
Exchange for pleasure brighter far,
Which poortith makes and cannot mar,
While woman's love on man attends,
And he is active for high ends.
Yea, by thy girdle-end with me
Thou mightest lead the dragon poverty,
And sing, like Enid touching fate,
' Though small our hoard, our hearts are great.' "

LUCY.

" Becoming picture ! minds me much
Of Belisarius, and such
As blindly follow dogs, that lead
Following their noses, which precede.
Better a single life, than brief
To double it, and have double cause for grief."

EDWARD.

" A Marvell, water-drunk, was he,
Who could unmated double see

Two paradises in his one
Twice happy, being shared with none.
Women there are, who never wed,
Illustrious living, noble dead,
Who chosen have the general heart
And ocean of a public part,
Virgins like Queen Elizabeth,
Or she Gavona—Rosa to her death,
Or Nightingale, or Martineau,
Or simpler Martin only known to woe ;
But thou would'st make wise marriage pay,
　Heart sacrifice for wealth and rank,
Exchange for gold thy tinted clay,
　Adorn a coronet or bank.
I know such objects may be dear :
Yet who the owner of a sphere
Mates—his, not him to so possess,
Weds poorly for a rich address.
Sidney's dear Stella here may preach :
She poorly wedded my Lord Rich—
No cure for heart-disease, which, aching still,
Unhandsomely ejects the golden pill."

LUCY.

" Ha ! who of me may so conceive
Will falsely.   Hand may I not give
With or without heart—counterfeit,
　When most impassioned then least wise ? "

EDWARD.

" Escheat thyself to be a cheat,
　And no trust-worthy prize.
Ah, Lucy, I do fear to prove
The battle not of life, but love ;
And, strong, though faint at heart, still hold
And deem faint heart worth sumless gold.
So I my faults, and love confess,
And plead love's all forgivingness
In whose great mercy virtue shows,

And graces spring, and honour glows.
Thus every mastered wayward mood
Composed into beatitude,
Who love, and have their faults forgiven,
Are surely verging upon heaven.
I trow, that God Himself would deem
    His bliss, his heaven incomplete,
Should every creature thing blaspheme,
No sinner have heart-home for Him.
    And what are we, that we should treat
With more disdain the love of others
Even in their faults our very brothers ;
Use them like Eastern potsherds cheap,
Not cleansed when foul, but cast on heap
So broken, that no sherd remains
To carry fire, or gather rains.
Divinest love white-flaming yet may quell
The red heart-hate of legionary hell ? "

LUCY.

" In me, alas ! is no disdain,
But a whole stricken world of pain,
While fancies in dissolving view
And hopes decline, once based on you ;
As mists on Nevis melting reel
To the low bed of quiet Loch Eil.
But life is stern, and longer than romance.
That we have had and lost our chance,
My fault may be, or thine.   Forgive,
If mine : if thine, forget, and live
Proving in uncontrolled career,
That thou wert worthy to be dear—
An Orellana, whose erosion
Drains Andes to Atlantic ocean.
With me, companion of the race,
You would but drag a weighted pace
Both need all powers untrammelled, each
Some halting midmost aim to reach.
Then part we.   Vigour fresh will prove

Sure antidote to scurvy love ;
My discontent its bud might kill,
Or turn away its honest will.
Most hard to self is heart when, wise,
To love for love it self denies."

EDWARD.

"'Gainst Cyclades by Philip sent,
Admiral of the Fleet low bent
Before two Altars, new invent,
That they might his abettors be—
Injustice and Impiety.
But you, soliciting them base,
From self conceal your own disgrace ;
Mother revere ; the world adore ;
And fleer at me with sacred lore.
As Nero cast on Christians guilt
   Cruel of conflagrated Rome,
You on high principle have spilt
   The blood of our twin martyrdom.
But what am I, that I should covet
Such hardy merit ?   I don't love it."

LUCY.

" For double fee in vain had tried
Isocrates thy tongue to guide,
Which lacketh power of winning speech,
Or sense in silence to beseech.
Who sole self pleases with his glikes,
Shall list to what he whole mislikes.
Who good hath spoken, good shall hear ;
But malice well may malice fear,
And with its own tongue try to stop its ear.
Good motive, if not obvious deed,
Is meaningful my cause to plead."

EDWARD.

" Thee to thyself without disguise
   Shall I unmask ?   Thou scarce could'st know

Thy proper self: thou art too wise,
  And too enamoured of thy woe.
Edward his crown to Harold gave,
But ruin with it : and, though brave,
Thou hast no strength grim war to wage
On Love, and all his baronage.
Not quite into the purple born,
Thou wert not made thy heart to scorn ;
No Marie Louise, for a time
Happy, Napoleon's couch to climb ;
Not of the moderate bloodless hue,
Which to ambition can be true ;
What glitters in thy mental eye,
Soul cheating, won't heart satisfy ;
False shall the world, a hollow crust,
In thy strong grasp collapse to dust.
But as Macklin, who could betray
Her full proportions in a play,
Hid them from lance of pure good-will,
To die of a too modest ill ;
So to thyself thou mayest be unkind.
  Wisdom indeed to profit us may chide ;
But, though a man born blind may rule the blind,
  Who have no mind to be guided none may guide."

LUCY.

" Long, as some fasting Howe, you pray and preach,
  And cull from History reproach
Irrelevant as pictures, which
  Panel a Queen Anne coach.
Thou art to me so babillard,
Not Abrahamic scold more hard
Shaking out double-tooth of Og—
Giant, whose head was in the fog
Whence rained the deluge not to rise
Above his ankles, such his size :
Long-lived too, burying Noah old,
Outliving Abraham and his scold."

EDWARD.

" If I in this be idle found,
Then under, not now overground.
Dost mantle of Tegau prefer,
At least to my Padarn threadbare ?
Is there such cancer in thy breast ?
Then would I Lully it to rest.
I cannot let thee go, but feel
Equal to thy consummate weal,
Thy woe else.   Do not from me take,
And lose thyself, my heart to break.
Long years must sorely surely grieve
Hearts, which by love knit, cease to cleave ;
As orbs, when parting from their sun,
Reel into darkness strayed undone.
When Jane and Irving loved in sooth,
But earlier fancy claimed his truth,
Say, was it well of them to part
For show of truth then false to heart ?
Irving that other marrying died mad :
Jane wed her pride, Carlyle, and sad
Drudged for him, yet he took no blame,
And nursed him up to lasting fame ;
Then for a dog died.   Ah, few knew
How grandly, miserably true,
When Scottish Jane and Irving parted,
Both had been dumbly brokenhearted.
Dear Cowper, too, one long true sigh,
Love's martyr maddened, doubting God on high.
And what of Richard, son of Burke ?
   He humble love and true, but human,
Forsook for more ambitious work,
   Feeble in this as any woman,
Because his proud blind parents willed
   Unweeting how his heart still pined.
Heaven on his cheeks its roses spilled,
   But Zama blueing lips slow signed,

Kissing them softly, loath to dwine
The fond sole hope of Burke's brief line."

LUCY.

" I have not yet so quite lost heart,
As fail of blood.   I have no art
To humbly act a feeble part."

EDWARD.

" Who truly cherish noble blood,
Are niggard of the meanest good.
In fallen fortunes of her house
   Grimani could with double pride,
Happy, rejecting rank, espouse
   Another actor, Young, and died,
Young, twelve months after : in the grave
He buried all he could not save,
Through fifty years of fame to be
Still wedded to her sweet young memory.
When Phoceus darling Phillis saw,
   He deemed her parents could not shame,
Gentle though poor, a son-in-law,
   Who might be honoured owning them ;
So fine a strain her breeding showed,
That truth to troth was all it owed.
   This neither idle tale nor artless,
Our situation has reversed.
True wilt thou be as Phoceus erst,
   Or, more than man and pagan, heartless ?"

LUCY.

" Stay thy reproaches ; they are blind,
In heart I am not changed, but mind."

EDWARD.

" Might it another Lucy be,
A changeling, who now speaks to me :
But since thou art thyself, I would

Thou still unto thyself wert good.
As sun material things embraces,
And warms from orb to orb all spaces,
Hearts should in love's fond ardours blend
From Adam to the world's far end,
And were not meant to dwell apart :
For we are magnets heart of heart.
As hot simoon sweeps desert stour,
Dull Spaniard fled from fiery Moor ;
But Douglas put his heart away
In casket where the Bruce's lay,
Then, o'er the foe high hurled the twain,
And died to win both back again.
So having sent my heart before
With thine, I fate for both explore,
Careless of hostile flags unfurled
In this, but not the other world.
Woman, too, where her heart is given,
Should herself follow—there is heaven,
Nor doubting wait to count the cost,
Knowing, if heart is, all is lost.
As once said France, or Shakespeare on her part,
  ' Glory grows guilty of detested crimes,
When for fame-sake she counter-worketh heart ;
  Indulges it for play at idle times,
Contriving, when more serious, to spill
Blood of poor deer to which is meant none ill.'
Thou horned as Hunter Herne should'st be ;
But wherefore so thyself abuse and me ? "

LUCY.

" Thou sugarest not thy creamless curds,
  Effectless acid, whey-milk diet ;
And nothing dainty art in words,
  But piping like a peeping pyet,
Pottering and plaining round and round,
There is no end to thy poor sound.
I have forgotten the beginning ;
Seems to me 'twas of mutual sinning,

While you confessed to something more—
The latest act, if not the longest score."

EDWARD.

" So sore my grief to have offended,
Has sorrow nothing me commended ?
Penitent humblesse oils to shine,
So salving, hurtled pride ; and thine
Should droop its eagle wing unbroken,
All by my pain and sorrow stroken.
For, as in Censer grain of rue,
Heart in this breast is bitter true :
Here I no face have to remain,
No heart to go, though that were gain.
Poor dog, I watch the fast closed door
Of thine affection, hoping sore
Thou open wilt to my return,
And not my love for ever spurn.
If cold as Christmas, still for yuling
Throw crumbs of comfort to my puling.
Drop touch of pity on distress ;
Pity o'erflows in gentilesse.
Blushes my cheek like beggar fain
In presence of a sovereign ;
Incurable disease addresses
Thy generous curative caresses ;
No sovereign such beggar sure
Would scorn, and quit without a cure.
Light of these woeful eyes and blind,
Balm of this ulcerated mind,
Leaves art thou from Al Tuba tree,
And streams from Salsabil to me."

LUCY.

" Enough ; if more, thou must address another ;
Shall I go, send, or come again with mother ? "

EDWARD.

" Stay : one, who steals into another's heart,
False hope in sport to raise, may light depart

Killing the fluttering hope, and, from the corse,
See living hatred rise, and feel its force,
And soon, too late, memorial remorse.
And, ah, thou gavest me leave to woo ;
 Thou gavest me lips to kiss ;
Thou madest me think thy love was true
 By all that loving is.
Upon a lute may others faint,
 I die upon thy voice,
There is such rigour in the saint
 Of its constrainéd choice.
Loyola praying had sincere
Gift of apparent wanton tear ;
The teardrops are not in mine eye,
But throat.   I cannot weep, I cry.
Could I like Syrian recluses sleep
Two hundred years, and wake again, I'd weep ;
All, too, might know the cause deploring,
Thou would'st in heaven be then, I here adoring—
Not letting fall with unspent blow
A hand raised once to smite thee, ah ! so long ago."

LUCY.

" Edward, forbear ! I would not hate
The man, whom I once hoped to mate."

EDWARD.

" But, Lucy, have you not a heart,
And can you from your lover part,
A loveless future choose and be
And make a wreck of it and me ?
As painter back retires a space
Effect of his own work to trace,
Thyself and work far off behold
In me far more than words have told.
I would thy last touch deprecate ;
What finished is becomes as fate.
Time is a bitter draught, unless
 Its sweetness love impart ;

Eternity will fail to bless
  The breast without a heart :
For God Himself—for time below,
  Eternity above,
Earth can no other joy bestow,
  And paradise is love."

CANTO III.

LIKE lightnings quenched and thunders drowned
  In showering heaven, now appears
Her fury, late all flame and sound,
  Dumb in a blind passion of tears.
Then waxing white as Hecla, though
Her heart was like the fires below,
Pride her drooped head imperious raised
Struggling, until she fell, nigh crazed
And sobbing, by mine arms embraced,
Whose eager fondness made them bold
To hold her, and not cease to hold,
But lip to lip wild strain prolong,
As echo clings to parting song.
Though nought but snow with fervent kiss
From face of rock I melt, it yet is bliss
The tears to drink, as sun fresh-born
Drinks Pleiads and night-dews from face of morn.
Ha ! pride anon its throne resumed.
Withdrawn, erect, and pale as doomed,
Like bark, inclined to gust of breeze,
Rising ruisselant from frothed seas
While snowy canvas spreads new-driven
Steady the vertical peaks in heaven,
She said, and thought to fly apace.

LUCY.

"It cannot be ; I cannot face
Your future :"

    Words like these :

       "Good-bye."

Yet was it such, and not a lie ?
 For she again was at my side,
Fired by the passion she withstood,
By mine—her own despair subdued,
Taking farewell of all her good :
 God ! that we both might then have died.
Merciless love, and miserable me !
Longheaded wisdom can hardhearted be.

From Val de Pistre rises wild,
 In Neustria, a mountain lone
Whose king a daughter had—sole child,
 More highly valued than his throne.
Who woos, to win her must that hill upbreast,
And haltless bear her to its skiey crest.
And many tried, and many failed,
When one, she loved, the steep assailed
Unbreathing, till far summit topped
He, fainting, sudden dying dropped,
But to be folded in embrace
Of her, too, dying on his face :
I envy the dead lover's case.
That cruel doom I could not blame,
Whose equal crack all crushing came ;
No smallage, night-shade, cypress, yew
Then unto death were justments due,
Unnecessary, and consumed
With all, in one destruction tombed.
Thoughts swift, as of a wretch who drowns,
 Contrary course through my despair,
While passion, amorous of frowns,
 Caresses the rude face of care.

         X

Scarcely that contest was more warm,
  When with Saint Michael Satan fought
In close embrace of fiery storm.
  Colour, which glows to hint the thought,
Painting the Devil passing well,
Singes the Saint too sore with hell.
Which she ; which I ; and which shall go to wall ?
Heavens ! how I love her all in all.
As Russia, leaving Moscow fired,
  Transporting all love held most dear,
From coming Buonaparte retired,
Who only ruin thus acquired
  From lingering patriot hate and fear,
The bliss, so being lost, I sought,
  Compressing and extracting then,
To leave my fooled successor nought,
  And in her heart no power again
To love, as it had loved before,
Though heaven should smile, and earth adore—
I, timorous blackbird whistling strong ;
She, adder deaf to all my song.
And still I would the agony prolong.

But like heated sands, whose every grain
Is separate world of stinging pain,
Are the sore scathing words of woman,
When she, besieged, becomes inhuman.
There is no rage of hellish fuel
Cruel as woman over-cruel,
Flaming in faithless Venus high
As flicker Mars himself out of the sky.
One claw for Phidias was enough detail
To draw a lion from ; a shrew in gale
Is as full-tokened by one finger-nail.
Timid as hare she fierce assaults ;
Flying as wolf, with many faults
Putting pursuer out of breath,
Turns on the prey, and gives it death.
Yet if like Leyden Dutch she fought,
I Spaniard-like with dagger wrought,

In helm and breast-plate scooping earth,
To rampart giving hasty birth
'Gainst sudden storm of fire and water,
And arms all dissolute of slaughter ;
I struck, like Ariosto blade
Not knowing when the hand was dead,
That beaten back I still might vie
With my Mary-Ambree enemy.
Then parted we.   Alas, though kissed
Fondly and lingeringly, I was dismissed
Hungry as Esau who, of hope forsaken,
After a burning hunt with nothing taken,
For mess of pottage all his birthright quit ;
So died her troth to me in kissing fit—
One last embrace, now given and now gone,
Put upon love by way of colophon.
Ah, had some Gordon-rival, not a devil,
   Aiming at me, mischanced, and in her breast,
Then interposing, buried the purposed evil,
   And killed her, I had deemed her murder blest
Beyond this spiritual decline from faith,
Which unto me murders her worse than death.

Her doors behind me closed, my heart to break,
Shutting me out ; and lonely way I take
Adown her avenue of trembling shade.
Now calling all my energies to aid,
I stand to fight despair, which always is
Shocking to heavenly Cupidities,
And, while so standing, surely must have crazed :
For some one seemed to speak, and unamazed
I knew my father's voice, and it was so
That all else strangely seemed to fade and go,
Till the whole father, and no saint
But sailor-chief, inspired the plaint.
So had I heard of friends departed
Returning to the broken-hearted ;
Knew one whose brother, lost in foundered bark,
Held converse with him oft.   My father ! Hark !

FATHER'S SPRITE.

" Though some do well to rend blind ties
Impious of imposing lies,
And break with lovers weak as poor,
Till cracking heart-strings they inure,
Listening to reason's wiser voice
Arguing love for better choice ;
Yet women fighting strength adore,
And struggling worth should bind them more.
Wild Rose of Thornhill looked no weed,
Sunning by Hogarth's ingle gleed ;
Not ill did Surtees Bess, eloping
With fitter's son, in Eldon hoping ;
Fair Frances Aylesbury, when Hyde,
Of little lawyer lesser bride,
Appeared in fortune-shifted scenes
Mother and grandmother of queens.

" You, equal with your Lucy born,
Thought creature-force no goddess lorn ;
Though gods are fabled to have mated
With mortals by love elevated.
Cephalus, by Aurora raised,
Melted in heaven, freshly blazed ;
And Thetis unto Peleus bore
Achilles, than his father more,
On Pelion their nuptials splendid,
By all the gods, save one, attended.
But gods for love were never paid ;
Now commerce rules both man and maid,
And marriage has become a trade.
The very church too speculates,
And, as you pay it, loves or hates.
Ashes, but not with papal grace,
Upon Ash-Wednesday Boniface
In eyes of an Archbishop cast,
Saying, ' Ghibelline begone, and fast

With all thy Ghibellines to burn,
Hence ! to slow ashes quick return.'
Yet Guelph could heaven sell disrated
To Ghibelline accursed and hated ;
Pope league with Turk, and Russ with either
For gain of earth and hell together ;
Poor Dick Fitzgerald, church to please
And eke its priest with buxom fees,
Wed Merrow dowered with wealth of seas.
Passion and beauty importune
Are dainties for a silver spoon :
Pewter nor looks, nor feeds so high,
  Or turns the stomach amorous ;
Nigh false as Cressid she, and—"

EDWARD.

"I ?"

FATHER'S SPRITE.

" More guileless true than Troilus."

EDWARD.

" So young my love, while yet was day,
Simmering with stars, all silver-grey,
'Twixt dog and wolf I could not know,
But loved her when I saw her so ;
And, since I might not choose but dwell
In my first fancies, loved too well."

FATHER'S SPRITE.

" Preventing Sun, with Robin bold
As you to morning, dull and cold,
Pipe, may no seeming dog appear,
And prove a wolf, e'er you know fear.
Beware of snakes, too, when the sun is high ;
Some look wreathed flowers, and under such may lie.
A viperous knot the World is—New and Old ;
Men in a snake-boat sail the Azure scrolled,

Like Winnipiseogee, from Red Hill
Seen with its countless islands snaky still.
West Point of Arnold and his wife can tell ;
What Eden wants its serpent tale?   Ah, well !
If all part-fable of a fiend and fall,
But still some snake once sported with some ball,
Mortals so cautioned are to use their eyes :
No Eden safe is from a snake-surprise :
Seek not to dwell in a fool's paradise."

EDWARD.

"One, who has taken, while he dreams,
A seeming good for what it seems,
Waking to find, not what he thought,
   But, of all ills the worst of ill,
Something not sorting with his lot,
   Has evil fancies of free-will.
Can it be fate, or chance fallen out,
Or God, that turns man round-about ?
Who once obeyed may soon in turn command,
Drop woodman-axe for sword in Ducal hand ;
While more than Napoleonic change remains
From rule to servitude, from crowns to chains."

FATHER'S SPRITE.

" Mischances, child, may be God's will,
But injured love is evil ill.
Six hundred years and thirty-four
Not Lion-heart of Richard more
Withered to semblance of leaf faded,
Than love, when false, has heart of faith abraded,
Its spring to Autumn turned, called Fall—
Most truly that, and rot of all."

EDWARD.

" With turn of Inismurry stone
And curses shall I weigh her down,
Or in forgiving mercy shed
Live coals of fire upon her head ?

Yet have I to forgive, or curse?
　Or am I ought, when all are weak,
And fate is dark, and one is worse,
　Who may things better seem to seek?"

FATHER'S SPRITE.

"Let not reflection take so sickly a hue ;
In her false pride thy love was strong and true.
Live full employed, and never whine :
Losels do most with love repine.
Embrace professional renown ;
Keep fond, weak, idle feelings down.
Strive well to act thy proper part ;
Into the man throw all thy heart ;
Forget even Lucy, or recall
Only the pity of it all.
Though now the fates to her seem kind,
　They never yet condoned a lie :
Lucy shall retribution find,
　If long delayed, still ever nigh."

EDWARD.

"Yet, touching heaven with Thalian front,
　Small joy were mine far down to see
Her bear the unforgiving brunt
　Of Providence all smiles for me."

FATHER'S SPRITE.

"Unfaithful gain, like Lucy's, is unsure :
　Though its dishonour lasts.　But virtuous pain,
Whose passion may in thee too long endure,
　Has joy in honour—an eternal gain,
Which, from God's image on its guinea, may
A casual discolourment rub away :
While cold, as dog-star aged shall surely show
Six thousand years hence, bringing frost and snow,
Lucy, instead of lovely, should appear
Bloodless as ivory, verging on the sere,
One yellow stain, till, nothing now dissembled,
She from her own reflection flying trembled."

EDWARD.

" Nay, proud I know she is ; but though she were
Dark as proud Satan, she would still be fair."

My filial questions answered, he, who came
In form of speech, was gone now like a dream.
Through lodge-gates issuing then on homeward way,
I could not take it, nor in the open stay :
But with a broken will and filmèd eye
Seeing no faith on earth, nor trust on high,
Nor gracious chance of healing touch of ruth—
Unprofitable when divorced from truth,
Nor issue other than the common hearse
Processional to the end of the Universe,
I hither thither stumbled, errant, rude
Misery both my burden and my mood ;
Then leapt opposing fence, and shortly hidden,
Whence still was visible my loved lost Eden,
In screen of thick and swarthy broom I fell
Clutching fresh-nibbled sward, while tear-drops well
And dew-like sobless diamond the grass,
Conscious I but of what had come to pass—
Not of my tears, which noting I revoked :
Than weep so, I had rather been so choked.
How many minutes thus I knew not, till,
Now lying on my back, and with no will
Looking to heaven, my rooted lashes dry,
A heavy globule, dropping from a sigh,
Blooded my thoughts, which Puck then, strange to see
At such a time, and whimpering over me,
Put into words—

PUCK.

" In the twinkle
Of an eye
Mortals wrinkle,
Mortals die.
The past a regret,
The future a hope,

The present a sweat
　Up and down a slope
From and to a shore,
Where time is no more ;
No more regret,
　No more hope,
No more sweat,
　No more slope.
In the twinkle
　Of an eye
Mortal wrinkle,
　Mortal die,
And be, when not,
God only knows what,
And I only guess
That more or less
Than now to be
Were good for thee."

As mid foes deadly one who feigneth dead,
While so supine I lay, a breath was shed,
But whence it came, I knew not, over me,
Dulling the lively sting of misery.
Nature may then have thrown me into trance—
Nature, more kindly than all circumstance—
And not into a faint : for, thus out laid,
I still was conscious, that I inly prayed.

EDWARD'S PRAYER.

" Oh ! could I hear not any partridge whirr,
But singing from afar the Swans of Lir,
Then I to sleep might sink, and rise with morrow
Oblivious of cause for tearful sorrow.
Night, worshipfullest night, dispensing sleep,
　Spring not from Erebus but drop from heaven,
Fall soft as dew, such night as angels keep,
More day than night, and all my senses steep,
　Bathe, and enwrap them, veil, and seven times seven

Bury in preternatural repose
Beyond surprise of time and mortal woes ;
That nothing life-recalling on me steal,
Each avenue of dream hermetic seal ;
Too life-like dream itself would wake a sigh,
Let all save gentle breathing in me die,
While sing to me from far the Swans of Lir."

A breathless silence fell.   I did not stir,
But saw and heard, when o'er me sudden grew
An aureole of being bright to view.
By angel-cherubs circled, there appeared
A vision, such as art has oft insphered,
Of mother-hood in Glory—more divine
Than Mary and child in humbler earthly shrine—
Presenting to my mind the love of woman ;
And that love stirring me, my soul grew human,
As thus they sang of it,
Till all air rang of it.

ANGELS AND CHERUBS.

"Oh, love maternal, instinct, what you will,
    Within the mother's breast not found in vain !
Ineffable presence, irresistible
    Sending the heart forth to the son, and then
    Drawing the son's heart to itself again,
Selfless and changeless, fathomless ! we know
    No tenderness to match it among men.
Most infinite of finites ! man must go
To heaven to overmatch such love as mothers show,

"Soothing the son's impatience, and his faults,
    If known, still sorrowful sharing at each fall,
Till evil so constrained first limps, then halts ;
    And hoping, trusting, loving him through all,
    Nurse in his sickness, to his health at call,
His joy the mother's own, she watching still
    To serve his pleasure, though afraid to pall,
Ready to warm him should the cold world chill,
And bless him as he leaves her, leave her when he will."

Then seemed they meaningly on me to gaze,
Seeing ears open to a mother's praise.

ANGEL CHERUBS.

" Home hast thou and a mother here,
  Who never has been unforgiving,
To whom thou art exceeding dear,
  Why doubt God—Father—Love is living ?
Though, far as any sun can show,
Grief may not end, hope on in woe.
God still is good, to issues kind
Controlleth fate obscure and blind,
Groping through shadows dense of time,
And weaving many a seeming crime.
With flashing glance of piercing might
Traversing time, dispersing night,
His love the Infinite expresses,
  Willed only what it should and would,
Is Destiny, and still redresses
  Ill finite with an Infinite Good ;
And wert thou in a desert space,
His ravens still would bring thee grace.
Life entire of evil never
Wrecked good hope, and high endeavour ;
Still hop, step, and skip of bliss
Overleaps, what falls amiss.
Could not man from past-time borrow
Hope sufficient for to-morrow,
He might his quietus make
With a bodkin and a stake ;
Pierce the veil of time, and see
What is in Eternity.
But since being may, when wronged
By self murder, be prolonged,
And to worse grow, man in doubt
Clings to what he knows about :
More its joy than all its pains,
And a better hope remains.
Though your life may never measure

Outmost scope of looked-for pleasure,
Will you war unto the knife
With the giver of your life ?
Should you only store poor mowings ;
Should your food be bitter sowens,
You are camping out in time
'Twixt eternities sublime—
Outing brief, whose hardship's stress,
To the mud-lark happiness,
Higher hearted faith endears
To experience of tears.
Plashy sleets and rains, that run,
Soon are dried by dash of sun ;
Memories of ill by good
Mellowed to a pensive mood ;
And each villain-dark deceit
Proved a shadow, or a cheat."

When ceased these angels, Motherhood insphered,
With lips about to open, disappeared
And all with her.   And yet I knew she was ;
I had such mother, therefore excellent cause.
And now, for heaven was so kind, there came
Around me playing such a lambent flame,
I was electrified when it took form.
The Sprite of Love I knew, it was so warm :
And may my Guardian Sprite have come to glow ?
I yet had scarce recovered wit to know.

SPRITE OF LOVE.

" God meant the universal eye
With beauty to beatify.
Apelles, Phidias, Praxiteles,
   Of Phryné nature honest franions,
With rocks and pigments sought to please,
And artful, recreating these,
   Indivinated boon companions ;
Another Pericles was Jove ;
Young Alcibiades was Love ;

Mortals seemed gods, and men fell prone
To canvas limned and shapes of stone.
For beauty, glorious in face,
In form of such inhuman grace,
Though pure itself, man's lust enrages ;
Controlling kings and fooling sages,
Striking the gazer's forces blind,
Awry leads passions of mankind.
But in thy Lucy limn it all,
Conceived without a let or fall ;
In glowing colours full express
With more than Zeuxian address
Selectest form of loveliness ;
And fail the beautiful to show,
Which we in her have felt, and know
Beyond attainment of design,
Or sense of pigments most divine,
Of stronger and superior charm
To tint of cheek and turn of arm,
Of delicately sweeter strain
Than lutelike voice which dies again,
Foiling expression, though of lip
Which Venus has inspired to sip,
A touch above poetic paint,
A dream of passion for a saint,
A good from God, something in air
   Transcendent hovering, not to fix,
Spite of all evil evident there
   To be approached, though over Styx ;
Buddings of being, that reveal
The blowing beauties, they conceal,
High charactered above mere dust,
And having the immortal gust
Of goodly reason and true grace,
Worthy of love to give them loveliness ;
Powers, virtues, graces, on the wane ?
Nay, though uncrowned now, yet to reign ;
So full of promise, each a sign
Of heights and depths still more divine ;

Ranges of spirit, more and more
Exceeding depth, surmounting soar,
Rising to God to find and share
The nature, they were born to wear ;
Living for Love, and not too late
Forgetting, what it was, to hate.
And such in her and like in thee
Beget what cannot cease to be
A deep response of soul to soul,
  Once voluble though now tongue-tied,
The more that one has broken parole
  By indecorous hush belied,
Yet permeating through and through,
And incommunicably true,
An indestructible delight
In one another, though in fight,
A lingering, lasting, longing to unite."

GUARDIAN SPRITE.

" As earth with heaven, so thy heart
With love can neither hold, nor part.
Alas ! if thou from Lucy must,
Then, tining only loathly lust,
Be love, though tried more than by Eve's first fall,
Thy faith and strength, thy song, thy all.
Stronger and hardier than sense
Is love, that seeks no recompense ;
So shall not patience suffer wreck,
Nor reason quit high quarter-deck.
Windows of joy, that lit the past
Heaven may against thee shutter fast :
In night of sorrows be no wail,
But in its mead such nightingale,
As sang to Orpheus' shade to stir
The ashes in his sepulchre.
Sweetly warbling fondest pain,
Holy gladness trembling feign,
Not, like Prince Edward cast adrift,
Plunge headlong to a timeless shift.

By flying foe and parting friend,
  Brave Robbins, left at Osipee,
His gun for one last shot retained,
  Though himself wounded mortally :
Wounded, forsaken, love may rival hate,
With after-glow the fire of it abate ;
So ne'er may Lucy hide her head,
  Like child alarmed by blab of nurse,
Haunted by ghost of a love lost and dead,
  Or shadowed by a living curse."

With this they vanished : but their song regaled,
Remaining in my heart, and so prevailed.
I was but mortal foolish man,
And soon to hope again began.
Who that hath lost can credit it, or swear
Exactly how he lost, why, when, or where ?
Fools verily have all space for self-deceit :
Catullus-like I could myself so cheat,
Musing in screen of broom, until my mind
Was by mischance resolved to make no find.

CANTO IV.

As when, with thunders big and unborn tears,
The round of heaven undisturbed appears,
But nature prostrate lies below
Faint with anticipated woe,
Comes one quick-swelling cloud o'erstriding all ;
Air still, and stifling to appal,
Is sudden to sirocco changed
  Covering with sand-dust heaven entire,
Obscuring sun, whose rays deranged
  Show prodigies of blood and fire

Supported upon pillars of smoke
Whirled hither, thither, twisted, bent, unbroke ;
Into such passion falls unpoised my soul
And wanders blindly, stumbling to its goal,
With eerie feeling of determined fate,
And self or its familiars in debate,
As with a fresh and growing sore dismay,
I hear a rider beat the impassive way—
The favoured Earl ; and whither bound ?
Puck answers—he was buzzing round—

PUCK.

" To Lucy, who is waiting to be found."

EDWARD.

" Embraced me, not an instant gone,
Loves me, and I love her alone.
Yet while fond memory for years
May oft indulge her bursting tears,
And those, I kissed away but now,
   Burn blistering my lips still white,
She life this very hour may vow
   To that proud fool, who wrongs my right."

PUCK.

" Pooh ! dress a monkey how you will,
A nut shall show it monkey still ;
To dance on hind-feet gown a cat,
A mouse shall make it drop all that.
Low animals can ne'er withstand
Temptation proper and at hand.
E'er time can one slow moment count,
On car of Morgan Muynvhar mount ;
Instantly at her threshold being,
In Arthur veil, unseen but seeing,
Enter and see
Her treachery."

He vanished, with a wicked smile
Going himself to see ; the while

With back to heaven, more blind than mole
Hiding from sun, I, dark in soul,
Supine lay, helpless in embrace
Of evil promise, not of grace ;
Then stirring quit the screen of broom
To front my further way and doom,
Not wishing, God her hopes might wreck,
Too haughty high for me to check,
But doubting, to a wolf was sold
The one ewe-lamb of my heart's fold.
Yet, as when ocean upward lifts
Wild wreckage, that abandoned drifts,
I something dear of Lucy see
On every surge of memory.
Even Richard Third so dearly lay
In memory of North-Country clay,
Small stir, as of light passing breeze,
Roused in its muddy soul his turbid lees.

    Alone once more I wander
      The stilly fairy glen,
    Love's early promise ponder,
      Then folly, falsehood, pain,
    Since storming Puck attacked us
      Driven from the fairy ring,
    And fairy vengeance tracked us.
      Are fairies anything ?

    I, fighting love's sore battle,
      Forgot the fairy fool,
    Fairies are such small cattle :
      Yet little follies rule.
    For subtle germs of evil
      Abroad are everywhere,
    Unseen, in which a devil
      May enter, and not scare
    A soul, that quick believeth
      What lie he may suggest ;

                     Y

While love itself conceiveth
Jealousy in the breast.

Love, as first sung by Lucy there,
Lingering in enchanted air
And taking form of Sprite, appeared,
As though my passing thoughts it heard.

SPRITE OF LOVE.

"Love ne'er was your undoing.
  Puck tempted, not to good,
You overjealous growing,
  And Lucy overshrewd ;
Till small wrongs unforgiven,
  Repeated, waxing great,
She seemed an angry heaven,
  And you a dreaded fate.
Thus folly, bold and bolder,
  To battle going forth,
Triumphed at last, and sold her
  For wealth forgetting worth."

EDWARD.

"Puck may have been worst sinner,
  Are fairies Lilliputs?"

SPRITE OF LOVE.

"Folly at least is winner,
  And now unblushing struts."

Lean crescent Lune, spare-horned and white,
High-risen shone in broad daylight :
Then I asked, with a croon
  From the throat of despair,
How the Man in the Moon
  Ever came to be there.
And thus the story ran
About this man.

SPRITE OF LOVE.

" Of dry faggots old
  One Sunday an armful
He, cutting here bold,
  Not deeming it harmful,
Forked all on a stick,
  And, momently bolder,
Trudged home with them slick,
  Hung out over his shoulder,
When he met on the road
  One who, going to church
In his Sunday's best mode,
  Gave him thus quite a lurch—
'Twas an Angel disguised.
'Ha ! this day of the Lord
  Dost thou break with thy labour ? '
To whom man ill-advised—
' Nay, good faith ! on my word,
  I don't see it, good neighbour.
Or Sunday on earth,
  Or Moonday in heaven,'
He mocked in his mirth,
  ' It is odds but they're even.'

" ' Bear thy sticks then for ever,'
  Was that angel's behest,
' To the Moon, where is never
  A Sunday of rest.'

" With his sticks straight he rose
  To the Moon ; woe betide him !
As the Moon nightly shows.
  Would'st thou up be beside him ?
Then, when God grants thee sun,
  Be thou never contented,
Until, out of it run,
  Thou too late hast repented.
Doubt the sun, and all sunshine

Shall pale in thy thought,
Till to thee all is moonshine— "

EDWARD.

" Heaven only knows what."

My Guardian Sprite, with sympathetic dole,
Wont to attend the motions of my soul,
Commissioned one, himself to supersede
And aid Love's Sprite now in my heart's sore need,
The Voice of Nature, which seductive spake,
  And honoured Lucy in a happier hour ;
Fair, blue-eyed, golden-haired, a glittering snake
  Circled her robe of green embossed with flower.

VOICE OF NATURE.

" Ah ! the heart is sometimes so sore
  With a feeling, as if it would break,
That man thinks it will never-more
  Be whole, or cease to ache.
And the world seems full of woe,
  And no solace may he gain :
For to fly from it were to go
  To another place of pain.
Yet, if God would but take him, he had
  Rather then painlessly die :
For the joy of the world seems mad,
  And he cannot cease to sigh."

EDWARD.

" Once wandering in solemn mood
  Out the Appian Way from Rome,
Far from all living I stood
  In the door of a vaulted tomb,
And, startling the wild repose,
  Came a sigh weird, sad, and lone :
'Twas Rome's telegraph, which goes
Along the highway of woes
  For ever making moan,

As Rome living were mourning Rome dead.
  So round the whole world, with a sigh
Over graves of hearts that have bled,
  In spirit I fly ; cannot dry
The rivers of tears, that are shed
  By the living, who wish to die.
And the heart within me fails
  For the grief in which man is lying,
As the kindly dog that wails
  For utter strangers dying."

VOICE OF NATURE.

" Ha, the breezes fresh, free, and wild
  With their loving sorceries !
You once felt like any child
  In the happy sportive breeze.
'Twas delight like the gull to be
  Borne lightly by the wind
O'er the leaping and shouting sea,
With the wind still fanning thee
  And freshening body and mind ;
And on hill, or dale, anywhere
  To fly, or fight with it even
Blowing through your soul as it were,
Blowing from it sorrow and care,
  As rain and clouds from heaven."

EDWARD.

" For a cure now the winds I try,
  But a chillness they through me dart,
As though spirits were passing by
  Sighing to break my heart."

VOICE OF NATURE.

" Yet the woods have dear charmers been
  With their vast and robed solitudes,
And their mystery deep, but serene,
In warm odours steeped, while unseen
  Over all a felt sun broods ;

The peace of the place,
Like a spirit of grace,
And its glad and sinless loneliness
  Begat in you happiest moods,
While fairest dreamings would come
  To believe soliciting you :
Though on earth you in heaven would roam.
  Till wet with evening dew."

EDWARD.

" I have thither hopefully strayed,
  But chilled now feel among
Sad fancies peopling the shade,
Drear forms, and things from the dead ;
While silenced is woodland song,
Or I hear it not for the trees,
  Which troubled as my own breast,
Sigh, with sound of far-off seas,
Toss and shudder in the breeze,
  Sighing as if for rest.
From the living of life sighs rise,
  And nature has taught us the art ;
The songs of birds we prize,
But the winds and trees are sighs,
And they dim the beautiful skies
With their sighs, with their sighs,
  And break the weary heart."

VOICE OF NATURE.

" The stream now behold, in its play,
Over pebbles rippling, and gay
Sparkling ; and, on as it dashes,
Drawing music from rocks, which it lashes,
And rainbows from falls upon pools ;
Then hiding 'neath trees, where it cools ;
  Then bold in the open out,
Like a sunbeam, among the flocks
Laughing it runs ; "

EDWARD.

"But mocks
With something like a doubt.
The rainbows of weeping skies,
  Though painting hide not sadness ;
And one may a sob surprise
  Mid the gurgle of its gladness.
And can this wild thing be wise?
  And is its joy not madness?
Lo ! now where it spreads in a deep
  Dark pool in a basin of clay
With boughs overhead, that keep
The sun out, and a sweep
  Of darkness deepening away
Into the forest.   Hath
  Any suicide, fond of beauty,
From woe, world-neglect, or wrath
Taken this hasty path
  To bliss, forgetting duty?
And away in the hills I hear
  Where it leaps some precipice lone,
And it sounds in my maddened ear
  An everlasting groan."

VOICE OF NATURE.

"Yet the mountains, with swelling heights
  Sun kissing, seeking no shade,
Seem a land of quiet delights,
  Which no sorrow may invade.
And as these you used to mount,
  Your body seemed melting away,
And your spirit to rise, like a fount
  Beginning at last to play."

EDWARD.

"But fatigued now I feel, e'er I gain
  More than the swell of the base,
And would rest me to sigh, and fain

With Despair's aged self remain,
  And cease young Desire to chase."

VOICE OF NATURE.

" Yet their heads, being lifted high,
  Are nearer heaven than earth :
How shall grief then ascend so nigh
The gates of heaven, and not die
  To give pure gladness birth ? "

EDWARD.

" Hark ! the hills by sad voices sweet
  Are steeped in a plaintive woe :
The lambs and their dams bleat, bleat.
Happiness is false ; I meet
  Sorrow, wherever I go."

VOICE OF NATURE.

" To the fields, oh ! haste then ; away
  To the fields in search of the joy,
Which you found when a boy making hay,
Or a man there roaming all day,
  More gleeful than a boy,
With bright fancy informing the scene,
  Or a friend, and happy youth,
And souls, as the skies serene,
Discoursing like meadows green
  Full of flowers, and the beauty of truth."

EDWARD.

" But nothing now fixed, the hills,
  The vallies too, all seem afloat
Tossing on a sea of ills ;
  The pallid sun remote
Fast failing, and dull of years,
And drowned in tears.
I stay, and stray below
  In the meadows and fields unshorn,

But never away from woe :
There, like sorrow sitting low
And sway-swaying to and fro
Sighing ever-sighing so,
The grass is full of woe,
  And swaying sighs the corn.
And low as I bend an ear,
  I start at the many sighs ;
The lark also, starting to hear,
Seems all in a tremble of fear
  With flutter on flutter to rise—
To rise, but without his song :
  For his tender spirit is crushed
By the terror on him strong,
Or sadness ; or something is wrong,
  Which hath the song in him hushed."

VOICE OF NATURE.

"But up high in æther he sings
  To the gates of heaven nigh.
With rapture quiver his wings ;
From throbbing throat with rapture springs,
And at heaven's gates thrilling rings
Note on note, as though in strings ;
  Nor sob is heard, nor sigh."

EDWARD.

"Fond spirit, spread thy wing
  And soar larkwise to the skies :
This life is too sad to sing
This world is too bad a thing—
Too bad and too sad a thing
  For anything but sighs.
And never, since Adam fell,
  And never, since Eve did wrong,
In most secret dell could sorcery dwell
Ope of seeming bliss a well,
But its bubbles would burst, and break the spell,
  And end in sighs the song.

The good old Pilgrim Fathers came
Unto no new Jerusalem.
Dear Wyoming, asleep for hours
  In Susquehannah vale,
Woke, massacred amid her bowers,
  To perish with a wail.
And here where prettiest lanes
  Lead to hamlets hid in vales fond,
With flowers in the latticed panes
Round a green, where cricket the swains,
  While geese hiss the dog from the pond,
Trim gardens in front, and behind
  Old orchards whose fruit still is new ;
Where the church clad in ivy we find
  Amid graves overshadowed by yew,
Drains naturally and springs
  Run into and out of each other ;
Fevers toss ; and feckless young things
  Prove the love and not strength of the mother.
And the pothouse, famed for its ales,
  The paradise is of the boor :
Swilling till head or purse fails,
He reels to a home, that quails,
  And knocks down the scold at the door.
And pity roams unblest,
  Wandering round the land, to see
Commons parked by lords, confessed
To the manner born, who molest
Grudging space for a last long rest
  To a shilling-a-day peasantry."

Love's Sprite, with an unwonted jeer,
Wantonly intruded here,
Flame-tongued, fire-eyed, and near.

SPRITE OF LOVE.

" Whom the church teaches pretty hymns,
 . And who feast, when an heir is born."

EDWARD.

" Tramps only and poachers have whims
   Beyond the mercy, or scorn
Of a Lucy, who trains a rose
   And cannot care for it long,
Or a lord of men, who knows
Place and power, and overflows
In cruel sport, and throws
   Ditch-water on cries of wrong."

SPRITE OF LOVE.

" Selfish such however mellow,
   Less human than brute, half-breed,
Without one claim to be fellow
   To any creature's need."

EDWARD.

" Bright the sun in country places,
   While shadows of ignorance lie
Upon stagnant human faces—
Shadows, which no sunlight chases ;
Ignorance the lowly debases,
   And want of wisdom the high—
Grand masters of boors and brutes,
God's anointed, baa ! family fools :
England sickens to the roots,
England sickens on the fruits
   Of territorial rules.
And the heart, though it anxiously look
   Lovelorn, can nowhere find
A shepherdess out of a book,
A shepherd without a crook
   In his lot, or with any mind.
And the smokes and smuts of cities
   An earnest spirit rear,
Moved with a thousand pities
For the pastoral life, which in ditties
   And only in ditties is dear."

VOICE OF NATURE.

" Hence then to town : and yet
   For an unhanselled vow
Dost thou nature well delate,
   And no love allow ?
Slow into ocean sinking red,
   When sun from earth turns—soon to return—
Through every lessening glow of shade
   His farewell ardours panting burn,
Till day he seemeth to have taken
From a regardless earth forsaken ;
Still he illumines sable night.
Soon the blue dome of heaven is bright,
Soon lustral majesty of moon,
And courtly stars are shining soon.
Though earth may quench her every fire,
He from his casket thus will tire—
Queen her veiled head with moon and star,
Breathe through night's bosom light from far—
The love he cannot cease to feel,
And be on earth attendant still."

SPRITE OF LOVE.

" And must thou still from Lucy fare,
Be love the light of thy despair—
No passion-flame of sensual bliss,
But ardour hopeful, that she is,
Yet to complete and make thee whole,
Thy future other half of soul,
Whom parting betters to combine,
And fashions to be wholly thine."

Nature now hushed, o'er Blesséd meads
Roved Helios' unharnessed steeds :
And straightening my desultory way,
   Like a spent chase I home regain—
Asylum for my mad and closing day ;
   But in its bosom not to plain.

Grief, emptied in that ear of joy,
Might dull it, and not self destroy.
Yet all my open looks confessed
To mother, who had hoped me blessed,
Read them, and questioning knew all.

MOTHER.

" Woman has had another fall."
Severe she spake, who late so kind
Had fault in Lucy failed to find.

EDWARD.

" Her mother tempted her," I said,
More gently Lucy to upbraid.
" Ah, losing her, I feel as shell,
Whose spirit lone through every cell
Wanders, and in a blind emotion
  Even on Olympus singeth low
Echoes, memorial of wild ocean,
  Chastening feasts of gods with woe."

MOTHER.

" Nay, bide irrevocable loss ;
  And, choking feeble sighs of love,
The tear-drop with indignant toss
  Quick out of passion's eye reprove."

EDWARD.

" Bright Caaba-spar for man alone
  Wept itself black ; but I am human,
And, softer than Mohammed's stone,
  Weep the decline and fall of woman.
Spray clouds in heaven gathering show,
Where falls Niagara below ;
Her lapse from love has sure on high
Brought tears into her angel's eye.
Not heartless although self deceiving,
In wealth and honours misbelieving,

Her soul with them, her heart with me,
With them can Lucy happy be?
Repine she must.   Yet as is flower
Offspring at once of sun and shower,
Kind should her Earl be, fond may grow
Love, purer from a cleansing woe.
This may God grant : for deep I feel
I love her so, I wish her weal.
And though it now my heart may wring
   That he, too, shall the blessing share,
Yet nestled 'neath my loved one's wing
May hope retain the obnoxious thing
There losing power even me to sting,
   While still I lift forgiving prayer."

MOTHER.

" Thy ' God-befriend-her-in-her-need '
Bears judgment in its poor ' God-speed : '
With prophesy of present worse,
To after-bless her you fore-curse.
And faith was never yet forsaken,
   Since Abraham cast Hagar out,
But trust betrayed has vengeance taken
   Raising, that Ishmael, wild doubt
Finding for every hope a dart,
To make a desert of the heart ;
The ruin, which its falsehood wrought,
Attending guilt's remorseful thought,
And injury's forgiving prayer
Drawing judgment down on the betrayer."

EDWARD.

" Strong I a cross with heart to carry ;
Weak she, heart crucifying so, to marry."

MOTHER.

" And yet she deems such marriage gain
At cost of your unreckoned pain.

Ah ! if a prey to grief and slight
All dark was she, could you be bright ;
Pleased, wheel a planetary car,
Were she a cast-off sunless star ?
Could Cupid shake in arms of mirth,
While Psyché wandered lost on earth ? "

EDWARD.

" I had not so considered it."

MOTHER.

" Or rather wert too slow of wit
At once to feel the barb unkind,
That thrust thee out of Lucy's mind."

EDWARD.

" As Suffolk freed from bonds yet done to death,
Me does she exile, too, to greater scaith."

MOTHER.

" Ay, happy as the roving billow,
Which found a shell on some coast-pillow,
A while pleased toyed with, then outcast,
Fickle forsook, forgot it fast,
With saucy leap of libertine
Filling the face of heaven with brine."

Quickly now blank despair and black
O'erspread the passion of my rack
Seeing not sympathy so scant,
Whereon one hope of grace to plant ;
Till I, all overset with rue,
Could have cursed Lucy so untrue.
Yet what sweet dish of poison did she dress,
And who with stannyel wing had checked not at the mess ?

As mother quit my solitary den,
She lingering gazed where hung suspended then

Above the mantel-shelf my father's sword ;
And over it himself, as when aboard
On his own quarterdeck commanding strife,
There painted to the very glorious life,
But now on mother smiling with a look,
Whose grave approval was my stern rebuke :
"Attend her counsel," seemed to be his will.
And when she went, he looked a speaking portrait still.

SPEAKING PORTRAIT.

" When Desdemona, who her sire deceived,
Was after by Othello misbelieved,
And done to death, was that retributive ?
God can, we too may, Lucy safe forgive,
That us she wronged, a mother to obey :
For love and truth unvalued pine to-day.
To guilty luxury peace falls a prey.
Now profligacy enervates the strong ;
The weak and worthless live and breed too long.
Death-rates decline—not vice so much, nor crime,
Which crowd the course, and are the curse of time.
Better the sexual instinct lose, or slight,
Than over-people day and prostitute night.
I know you think to live a perfect life,
Engendering high thought, without a wife ;
But should some other Lucy find you lone,
May she have had a mother like your own."

Return to town was imminent with close
Of autumn vacance, when I fond propose
To ride to Killie Castle six leagues round,
A memorable road, eventful ground.
Far on my way and going easy pace,
I heard behind me, as in coming chase,
Another horseman with accelerate stride,
Which bounding brought him quickly to my side—
The soldier, who had yachted erst that way
Staying to give me evident " Good-day,"

I rather would he then had parted straight;
But 'twas his idle fashion, or deep hate,
Or was it only my most bitter fate
Sent him to ask me, had I heard, or thought
Lucy should wed in early winter? Nought
My passion idly veiling, I descry
A cruel twinkle in his wicked eye,
When to my ignorance confessed he shows,
How shortly she to London also goes,
There to abide her marriage.

NOBLE SOLDIER.

"Will you see?"

EDWARD.

"Nay."

NOBLE SOLDIER.

"But a witness purpose I to be:
She never loved, and never jilted me."

'Twas his revenge; and this I understood,
Replying,

EDWARD.

"Ah! you love her then for good?"

NOBLE SOLDIER.

"For good, or bad I love her. Damn them both,
And you along with them;" was his fierce oath.
For I had hit him hard, and with intent:
And yet he quite as fiercely could relent,
Thus, "Nay, not you, nor her, but that rare fool,
Whom marrying she will hope to make a tool,
Though she may fail: for he is proud, and cool.
So may she hate him: therein lies my chance."

This last he whispered with constraint; his glance
Far in the future looked. His thought I guessed,
But more to know it thus his words addressed:

← z

EDWARD.

" Your chance, what mean you ? "

NOBLE SOLDIER.

" Why, what should I mean,
But that I loved and love her, as you've seen,
And that I mean to have her, if I can:
For she is but a woman, I but man.
A strange confession this : yet hear to end.
You doubtless fain would be her special friend:
Know, then, I enter openly the lists,
And cede no favour to antagonists."

EDWARD.

" Nay, nay, I wish her nothing save pure joy.
In haste you rode, and time I misemploy.
Proceed : or rather I must back.   Good-day."

I turned : he went, but going had his say,
" Love I hold sacred, nothing else but love,
So help me God, if one there be above."
Then mocking hoarse he laughed unkythely mirth,
Which from deep throat of hell came saddening earth,
Angering and maddening, tempting too.   Shall I ?
Shall he?   What horrid possibility,
Whose thought was as a sudden precipice,
And one foot over the abrupt abyss.
Only to think it, was one foot advanced,
Where foot could never rest, or if it chanced
A moment in suspense, to be withdrawn,
Or fall, than Vulcan more, from eve to never dawn.
Amphiaraus, though a seer, too late
Reined headlong steeds on sudden brink of fate.
No more believe I this the heady man,
I once conceived, but one to closer scan—
A thinker, in philosophy as fearless,
As for research in science 'mongst the Lords peerless ;

A devotee of pleasure on the scent
Of knowledge, his supreme, first, last event.
Free thought, morality as free has been
Uncurbed in him by a most cynic spleen.
Philosophy his sport ; and secret pride,
Tempered by manliness, his ruling guide ;
Lucy has conquered him, and touched his heart—
At once his highest, best, his weakest and worst part.
With Love's Sprite, winged and speeding by my side,
I scoffingly discoursed on homeward ride.

EDWARD.

" Evil than good more thorough-going shows,
Ill using friends, abusing foes.
Humanity mere skin becomes,
And hard and hollow, as her drums.
Without a heart, or lovingless,
   Our gifts and graces are inhuman ;
With joy and gain in others stress.
Our heedless mirth is wickedness,
   And trust is lost to man and woman.
Laws ten or more, on granite writ,
Fell with the stone, and broke with it :
Love has a wreck been since the fall.
   Now hate crowned, reigns on the decay :
Wrong comes with seeming right to all,
   Even hope in heaven is lost to-day.
God, if He hears some scoff, some cry,
May chance to smile, or frown on high :
But if His thunderbolts descend,
   The Prince of Air their flight so mars,
They e'er the proper moment end,
   Or strike above the stars."

SPRITE OF LOVE.

" Yet none so bad, in whom blind chance
Knows never hero of romance,
And good omnipotently done,
In depths of hell a heaven begun.

Through hearts of rock to Vindhya skies
Narbadas from shades nether rise.
In water iced by Boreas' breath,
   Find we heat latent under zero ;
A Christian grace in Judas' death ;
   Something of Seneca in Nero ;
Saul with the prophets ; foul and fell
Geraldine with a Christabel ;
Sage guesses dim of Socrates
In a voluptuous Alcibiades,
Whose dog, more worthy to be famed,
For art was saved, when Duncombe flamed."

CANTO V.

NIGHT fell around me on my London way.
At starting I, upon the platform stray
Encountered happily and joined a man
Famous, or infamous, the partisan,
Whom I by speech to temper and convince
Had striven once, in court defended since.
He had been lecturing my native town,
Yet I had nothing heard, read, seen, or known.
Together we the lingering journey speed.
An infidel, one recking his own rede—
Would that all Christians were as good as he—
He talked no infidelity to me,
But of the submerged tenth, and rank and file,
The masses labouring, the grovelling vile,
Discoursed with infinite pity, wisely too :
He so was speaking of the things, he knew,
And I myself was given to explore.
Both knew too much to rant, and felt too sore.

A memorable night : for his discourse
Lifted me out of self, it had such force,
And carried me along upon its chide
Into the desert of afflictions wide,
Ay, as the world, and seemingly so rude
As to be hopeless to immediate good.
Yet, if to future hopeful, 'twere a sin
It should not now endeavour to begin.
The thought still further lifted me ; I rose
Into an active sympathy with woes,
And to forget my own, no longer blind
To the forestalling misery of mankind.
We planned and purposed ventures of reform ;
Proposed to win the world, but not by storm,
By gentle seeming moonshine turn the tide,
Whose hellward lapse more stately craft defied ;
Hope kindle in the dazed eye of despair ;
Let that have light ahead and see to dare ;
And yet, with haste to meet importunate needs,
Our random talk was full of wilder weeds.

EDWARD.

" A magnet of hearts is the city,
With excellent parts—more's the pity—
Hoping, on heights attained
   By earnest aspiring toil,
To find there, not profaned
As when Adam fell, Eden gained,
   And splendour full of spoil."

PARTISAN.

" With seeming voidance of strife,
   How typical of strain
And rush and roar of city life
   Is speed express of train.
On prairie base of Rocky Mountains,
From Colorado Springs and fountains
Railing once in sunset, curious

Round us stars fell, fast and furious,
Fireflies by the million, or
Air one cloud of meteor ;
Sight of wonder to explore,
Never seen on earth before—
Proved, but gleeds of wood blown back
From an engine's chimney-stack :
Such are city stars—a dream,
Dust and ashes kick the beam
In tumble-down Tom-all-alones,
 Whence fever goes out to nurse,
Where famine sits picking men's bones,
While vice does not care to break stones,
 And crime with a terrible curse,
In mock Alexandrine tones,
 Regrets that it cannot wax worse."

EDWARD.

" Once lit town seemed jets of joy
 Sprinkling all and gassing me :
With a shout, like any boy
 Plunging in a summer sea,
In I nightly plunged with coy
 Happiness at liberty.
To me now it looks but a fire
 By woefullest creatures lit
To be the funeral pyre
 Of night, whose brows are knit—
Of night, which will not expire
 As clouds reddening madden it."

PARTISAN.

" Though by toil with ardour shrewd
 To develop oneself, and surpass,
And grow great and honoured feels good—
Good as zest of angel food,
 And draughts of hippocrass ;
Yet Strand's admired most crush,
 If, to a passer-by,

Ardour not needing to blush,
Seeming neither push, nor rush,
　No heart has save to try
And flash to prosperity's crest,
　Like Napoleon, pictured on the prance,
Heedless what cot he burned, or nest,
　Over Alpine circumstance."

EDWARD.

" Tripping up, overreaching in chase,
　Each thinks of himself and no other,
Till the runners grow hard as the pace ;
　And though all are the sons of one mother,
Giles and Drurys find no grace,
There the feeble soon lose place,
Each runs to be first in the race,
　Over-runs or knocks over his brother."

PARTISAN.

" While misery untold,
　And damnation more infinite still
Are in much, that is made and sold,
Out of windows looking bold
Being pinchbeck, or, if gold,
　Made gold by starving skill.
Ah ! the colours, which sometimes throw
　Over Thames a mantle of pride,
Composed of heaven's suns, we know,
And Earth's filth, like glory show,
　While they pollution hide :
So whom fraud and force have crowned
　With gold, may never transpire,
Till at judgment they are bound
With their crowns and coronets, found
　Good only for hell-fire."

EDWARD.

" Yet what dream that ever flew
　Out of golden gates of morn

Making nature, born anew,
Hum with pleasure, seemed more true
	Than the wealthy and high born?
Could the ages have an heir,
	Ever dreamed of, tall to tower
Over wrong, more strong to dare,
Justly nevermore to spare
	Any evil of the hour?"

PARTISAN.

" As early dawn ascends the skies,
	But warms not earth, which it explores
While sun is hidden from our eyes ;
	So wealth with rank, which wealth adores,
May rise and look into the plan
Of social nature, study man,
And thoughts and ways of all unfold.
By ses'amë of rank and gold
Instantly opening every door,
Welcome the whole world to explore,
My Lord from powerful, good, and sage,
All lights and wonders of his age,
May closet friendships cull, and count
On wisdom's waters from their fount.
And every pleasure, heart and mind
	With educated taste approves,
He may command, or ready find
	Within the circle, where he boundless moves."

EDWARD.

" These joys are pure without display,
	Or exercise of selfish power."

PARTISAN.

" The lords have but to wish, or say,
And place is at their feet, and pay ;
And all are eager to obey
	Grand-masters of the hour."

EDWARD.

" Too high they and haughty are
    If not idle, nor useless things.'

PARTISAN.

" O'er their element risen far—
O'er humanity, they don't mar,
    Whether it sighs, or sings.
And although exceptions prove,
There is never a rule for Jove,
With scorn on the poor they look down
    As a useful danger, which may
Be creasingly crushed in a frown,
Or charmed by one going down
    There to make fouler prey,
Where toiling for daily bread,
    And, some say, producing wealth,
Many, envying dogs well fed,
Confess to being bled
    For the good of the great world's health."

EDWARD.

" True godliness may be gain
    With contentment sweet on a crust,
Trusting God, and not in vain,
For the former and latter rain,
    Thirst quenching and laying dust."

PARTISAN.

" Still the Sundays may cost too dear,
    Since so quickly the week-days fly,
That one dares not drop a tear,
    He has no time to dry ;
And the workhouse is so near,
    He fears to waste a sigh.
While to others in viler slum,
    Where in shreds of your cast-off clothing
Squalid misery sits, to its sum

Adding ever some good-for-nothing,
Despair at last may come
  With a sick and deadly loathing.
Then for mercy may cry the proud,
  Should the poor burst forth like a flood
And, ' Down to Hell with the proud,'
Be the cry of the reigning crowd,
' Down, down to Hell with the proud,
  And let us have their blood.' "

Here thought, brimful of horrors, paled
  Before a shrilling new dismay.
Our engine sudden shrieked and wailed,
  Slowed, checked upon its jarring way.
Then, with a jerk ! and crash ! we find
  Ourselves out, safe, upon the line,
But groans and ruin round unkind,
  While now too many make no sign.

On the same curve and line of rails,
  Like dragons, eager for fight,
Panting for battle, with noise and fear
  Filling the quiet night,
Out of the West came our passenger train,
  And out of the East the other,
With engines vomiting flame and smoke
  Unseen by one another ;

Along a broad deep cutting rushed,
  And each its whistle blew,
Whose wild weird shrieks the horror told
  When they each other knew,
The western stoker pressing hard
  The lever at his post
Death rather to confront, than fly
  With sense of honour lost.

Tempting and bright, athwart the night,
  His firelit home arose,
And little ones around the wife

Who, prescient of woes,
With arms outstretched, and head advanced,
    And eyes too fixed to weep,
And lips that moved, but gave no voice,
    Implored him thence to leap—

In vain.   And as when cloud on cloud
    Dashes with thunder peals,
The engine from the east was crushed
    Beneath the west one's wheels ;
And tender was on engine hurled,
    Carriage on carriage piled ;
And heaven wept ; the few stars seen
    All shuddered as they smiled.

Two pyramids of ruin rose,
    Bounded by walls of rock,
Freighted with human beings, few
    Uninjured by the shock,
Some dead, some dying, frantic more
    To quit their living tomb ;
Such shrieks may no man hear again
    Before the day of doom.

Thence lover bore his sweetheart, death
    Still beckoning her back ;
And sore, sad, piteous scenes appeared
    Along that iron track.
A guard his babe saved, out of wreck,
    From its dead mother's breast ;
But why should now no pity move
    The stoker from the west?
The tender on the engine leapt,
    And crushed him, at his post
Of duty, choosing rather death,
    Than life at honour's cost.
Though rough and rude, as if just spilled
    By Chaos from his hod,
The cold clay gave a spirit great
    Up, rising straight, to God.

Oh, Kings ! your honours give away ;
  They neither make, nor mar.
The man, whom men and gods approve,
  Can do without a star.
God has with open arms received,
  To grace in Glory blest,
The humble, noble artisan,
  The stoker from the west.

Surgeons no apter aid there found,
  Than was tendered by my friend.
Till break of day we hold the ground,
  Then sadly seek our journey's end,
How sadly ! Who may sudden so
Taste all extremities of woe,
Suffering and death, hopes dashed with wrecks
Of every age and either sex ;
And in such instant realize
Life only as it grieves and dies,
All being but one heave of sighs,
And deem not that God little knows
The sodden bubble, which he blows.
And now approaching dusk of town,
And running into its renown,
As though the place were God-forsaken
I with a doom's-day feeling was shaken,
Fore-seeing advance of dawn
  On cloud-encumbered sky,
Which dark but lurid shone,
Soon to pale before the dawn,
  And faint upon the eye.

EDWARD.

" What mirky shapes appear
Fiery, and spirits to fear,
Some more than others bright,
But all of night,
Each like a several devil
And so many powers of evil,

Which could I limn, as gathering there
Round the reigning Prince of Air,
Who spans the æther, crowned with starry gold,
Men would cry, ' Hold !
   On such we dare not look— '
Such forms as darkening heaven cheerless spread
O'er the accursed tree, whereon the Christ hung dead."

PARTISAN.

" You speak like any Scripture book ;
Here clouds of life are swollen vice,
Duplicity, sordid avarice,
Pride, ambition, ostentation,
Envy, detraction, adulation,
The morning dreams of Christian town,
Types of City life, and grown
To be the ruling motive powers
Of the world's winning ways and working hours."

We parted.   I fast-breaking late then seek
   To walk down poisoned blood,
But find a broader blacker streak,
As of expiring candle-wick,
   Disheartening the rudd.
On I glide in a living stream,
   But bewildered feel and lone :
Crowds and houses like a bad dream,
A cloud among clouds I seem ;
And the thoroughfares roaring seem
   A never-ending groan.
Though a light and giddy spray,
   Over life's rapids rising,
Flares in the sun all day,
Nightly where none can say
   And there is no good surmising,
All jostle each other unknown ;
   Keep out of the way if you can.
Unknowing, unknown, as a stone
'Mongst many stones you are thrown ;
Nothing is so hard and lone

As the wilderness of man.
If handsome are many and fair,
On the mirror of each soul
You fancy a breath of care,
    Like a ripple over the roll
Of an ocean everywhere,
With a trouble all through air,
    And a sigh from pole to pole.

Rise, oh, song ! from my soul, like a cloud dun of vaporous
    incense,
Holy to God, who rides upon Chaos billowy tossing :
Fill thou its ears, oh, my soul ! with a song to the Lord, the
    Creator,
Isling its baffled abyss, and the maw of wondering nothing.
Albeit mystical whispers from stars newborn now are
    dropping,
Spirit upgirded and lofty pass lightly o'er time and its
    cycles—
Changelings, palaces now, then graves, cathedrals of ages
Startled to hear me hymn the Destroyer, who is the Creator.
Over the rack, and the ruin, from which rose the world re-
    constructed
Carlomans too, and Justinians, and Constantines musty, and
    dusty
Cæsars, and tumble-down gods upon mud exposed of the
    Tiber ;
Temples and Parthenons waste by Jehovah disdained of
    Athenians ;
Ancient Etrurias tombed, and Phenicias masted no longer ;
Sculptureless halls, Sand-heaps, Sphinx marvels, and doom-
    land of deserts ;
Aztec, Pelasgic, and Hidoo colossi of King-pride and priest-
    craft ;
Also the Great-father heaven and Dear-mother earth of the
    Seres,
Stay not to reckon, but hasten, and over the cannibal
    Adams,
Races submerged of Atlantas, and gloaming-of-day acclima-
    tion,

Spirit upgirded undaunted look over the verge of existence.
Darkness and death there, soul, be thou still, and commune
   with the wondrous
Wild blasts hurry and go, each puffing its cargo of tempest,
     While no deep whose briny wave
     Sprayed with tears a Timon's grave,
     But of woe a tumultuous sea,
       Breaking upon eternity,
     Drowning peace and bliss in bree,
       Deluges humanity.

     And eerie day takes flight ;
       Gas flames in the street and flares
   From the windows : the blaze of light
   Bewilders the pensive night,
   Scares the quiet pensive night
     Of nature lit by stars.
But this first night I have in sage advance
Engaged to dinner, opera, and scratch dance,
And take the sequent trio at a run,
Proving a not divine but sorry one.
In small hours after, homeward walk with me
Frivolity, Misanthropy, and she,
As Melancholy known, The Muse of Thought.
No gold could have the weeds of Melancholy bought
Nor art appointed such Misanthropy ;
A heliotrope buttonholed Frivolity.
A flight of fancy caused me passing pain,
" Public Opinion I may meet again,
I—thus accompanied."   But in the dark
He, seeing, well may pass, and not remark.
Not myself sure of being self-possessed,
Now Melancholy was most manifest,
And murmured—

         MELANCHOLY.

        " Company with me,
And make of two one company.
An unmitigated woe

Is the carrion dark and lone ;
But though dark, not lone, the crow
Will in company gossiping go,
 And never woe-begone.
So a gloomy mood to dispel
 The thought of a friend is enough :
Once your hand in his would dwell
 As a saint in bliss above,
And his voice was a marriage bell
 With joy in each note, and love.
Peace may grow between us two ;
Let me company with you."

Deeming this fond one had herself demeaned,
Misanthropy here earnest intervened.

MISANTHROPY.

" With infinity of art
 Manners, only masking men,
Flower about the bitter heart,
 And disguise the soul's disdain
Of self, but lesser than
Of woman : such is man.
Not one will on other depend ;
 Each would occupy the throne,
Sole good, sole great, to lend
 Transmitted light, or none ;
Oneself beginning and end
Of existence, to rule, or rend,
 And be, and perish alone.
And God knoweth, that the race,
 Each repelling and repelled,
Lonely, hating loneliness,
Now would curse Him out of space,
 Against whom it hath rebelled."

MELANCHOLY.

" Ah, since happiness, out of date,
 None can from anything borrow,

Grieving that all have ate
Of Eve's apple, we wish that fate—
Are tempted to wish, that fate
    Would end all on the morrow."

FRIVOLITY.

" Still after a day of toil,
    Or thought, or worse regret,
To dedicate the oil
Of night to joy, and coil
    A garland of flowers round fate,
Choice merry bachelors meet,
    And dainties sauce with wine,
And wisdom lighten with wit,
    Is humanly speaking divine,
Waxing turbulently gay
    As gods when on stars they feast
In a proper state of decay,
    A system of them at least,
With oceans of blue to drain
Till all is blue again."

MISANTHROPY.

" But to fill a void of heart
    Is beyond a Menu, ay,
Of toppest Soyer art,
    And game though heavenly high.
And wine cannot sorrow drown,
    Though it runs till hell is drained,
And you think from the talk of her son,
That woman and sin are one,
    And virtue is only feigned ;
Mid hips, hips, hips, and hurrahs,
    The generous wine, you are quaffing,
Blushing to be the cause
Of such breakage of God's laws,
    And glass, and silly laughing."

2 A

MELANCHOLY.

" Ah, vain is appetite,
  And sensuality vain :
What man falsely calls delight
  Is ecstasy ending in pain,
A flash illumining quite
But with its fork stabbing night,
  Which roars in a tempest of rain."

FRIVOLITY.

" Yet God's inaudible voice,
By which, and with no noise,
Fixed stars to dance are given,
Harmony surely is heaven,
And hath a mortal birth
In opera on earth ?
Ah ! rising and falling still,
  Its billows over you roll,
And almost seem sense to kill :
For you lose all sense of will,
  And no longer possess your soul."

MISANTHROPY.

" By its charms it open steals
  From soul the hidden fire ;
Not creating, it reveals
Only, what the man conceals,
  His innermost desire.
And while it may better the good,
  It maketh the wicked worse :
For evil or good is a mood,
  And music is only the nurse.
That language of heaven, flowing
  From heated lips, can tell
How they only wax more glowing,
  Like the lips of Israfel
  Who though fallen, sings so well,
As dainty heaven blowing
  Fans the flames in the bosom of hell."

MELANCHOLY.

"Yes, opera only wakes
  A slumberous evil to song ;
Harmonizing its many snakes,
  Makes it happy, young, and strong ;
Gives its appetite, which hope slakes
  Without a sense of wrong.
And, around and about, how many
  Of vanity's surfeit dream,
Of ambition, of folly ? Can any
Against the current row, when he
  Afloat is on harmony's stream ?
And your bliss, though tamelessly sweet,
  Ends as ever in a sigh :
A moment, and in retreat
You behold its twinkling feet,
You behold its flying feet,
  How rapidly they fly."

FRIVOLITY.

"What then of the dance, while gay
Is night, and surpasses day,
With colours beyond a Faed
To tempt a Roman raid,
All brilliance around and beauty,
  And folly to night unreined,
And nothing but pleasure a duty,
And the love and worship of beauty,
  Whose worship is unfeigned ?"

MISANTHROPY.

"As stars look down on the tide,
  But care not in it to dwell,
Let only an image abide
  Of lustre on the swell ;
Unknown, or scorned, and fooled
With some proud bright image at heart,
Man calls the thing too bold,

Whose shimmer is so cold
  With all its naked art.
And to matron, whose daughters are plain,
  Strange beauty is no delight
But cause of jealous pain,
As to clouds, that drop mere rain,
  Are sun-sprinkles starring night ;
Or, if young, she may heave some sighs,
  And beside you stands to allure,
While she seems in her husband's eyes,
Which she calls her own bright skies,
  As any angel pure."

MELANCHOLY.

" Passionately all would go
  Conquering, and trumps and drums
Seem to beat and seem to blow
Now ' The Conquering hero, lo ' !
  Now, ' The Conquering heroine comes.'
Though the triumphs are more than half
  Defeats, so killing the paces ;
And, courted mostly with chaff,
  The worse for wear are the graces ;
And the mirth is all in the laugh,
  And the rapture on the faces ;
And the crowd grows denser far,
  Than it ought to for one to be gay,
And you feel as must a star
  In the crush of the Milky Way.
Then, Edward, never let us part ;
Take, and hold me to thy heart."

I crossed the threshold of my open door,
And shut out all of them.   But doubt I sore,
If that they real were unto my senses,
Or more than spiritual influences :
Such last indeed they were, and still remain,
Never have gone, or soon have come again.
Ah ! changed seems life, when love

Has left it, purpose, faith ;
Vain all its interests prove,
And through the world we move
    As worms through realms of death.
The butterfly down is gone ;
    The moth a grub appears ;
And falls the pitiful sun
    In a dissolution of tears,
Each star a dropping one,
    And night through all the years.
And with wisdom's vain conceits
    Puffing flesh and blowing bubbles,
I, life's follies and its cheats
To discover, loose my sheets
    On a tossing sea of troubles,
Sick, for action never strong,
Only knowing all is wrong.

CANTO VI.

LUCY to town has come ; I nothing know
How long to sojourn, or with whom, but, lo,
Great the occasion is, all London gay :
A more important stranger comes its way.
Cleio herself, and with no dreamy eye,
Reviewing things, which still are passing by,
Commends to ear of trumpet-blowing fame
How unto Wales his Alexandra came.

CLEIO.

" For whom on tiptoe doth Britannia stand
    And from her Emerald Isles expectant gaze ?
What new invader would disturb the land,
    And interrupt the peace of halcyon days ?

The Dane, the fair-haired, and the conquering, comes
   Quitting the rigours of the northern main.
Light all the beacon-fires, beat all the drums,
   And let the Isles shout, 'Welcome to the Dane.'
Comes she through peoples, who rejoice to see,
   Escort, and cheer, and bid the Dane be strong.
Ah, can they envy us that liberty,
   We use so well and have enjoyed so long?
Comes the Sea Monarch girt by British keels,
   Whose rocket-stars make space all firmament;
Our queen's own royal yacht obsequious wheels
   The Dane in triumph to the great event.
And England is awake through all the night;
   And Margate hastens with foreflush of dawn
To the fair-haired, who wins without a fight,
   Accepts its homage, and then passes on
Up the rejoicing Thames to Gravesend, where
   Great London and its tributary towns
By rail and river pour to greet the Fair,
   While the Prince waits her with his many crowns.
For this is no red-handed Viking bold
   Coming to take possession and destroy,
But Denmark's daughter, lovelier than gold,
   Affianced to our Prince, who meets with joy
And kisses her.   All England feels the kiss,
   Blessing the Prince who gives it; and the air
Shakes with the rapture of uncommon bliss,
   And roar of cannon and brass-trumpet blare,
And cheer from bannered fort, ship, wharf, and town,
   As Prince from yacht conducts the Royal Maid
O'er scattered blossoms, rows of beauty down,
   And drives through all the holiday of trade
From Gravesend up to Windsor.   Who shall raise
   Pole and triumphal arch in verse august;
Make air all garden; stretch across the ways
   Fresh strings of rags and blossoms; and adjust
Fresh draperies on all houses; and rebuild
   In every vacant place the terraced seat,
And round our churches, while again is filled

Roof, window, balcony, stand, square, and street?
Shall London pour to Gravesend, and again
   Britain to London stream, and thousands grow
To unkempt millions hustled, and remain
   From early dawn to welcome one, none know,
And part asunder, that the maid may pass
   Happy to Windsor from the home she leaves,
Subduing, as she comes, the surging mass,
   And bowing back the homage she receives?
Ah ! 'twas a sight to see, that earnest face
   Fair as the moon, and beaming as the sun,
Pale with emotion, with a perfect grace
   Seeking to please, and pleasing every one
From Gravesend to our Castle, where the Dove
   Of Denmark finds the Mother of our Childe,
Who writes to thank her people for the love,
   Which makes their welcome tender, if as wild
As wondrous.   Who shall tell it ?   Let the might,
   Which elsewhere rules, learn here what love can do.
' God bless her,' is the prayer of all at sight,
   And God looks radiant, smiling through the blue,
To bless her with our Prince, who now around
   The British oak the rose of Denmark twines,
Wedding her royally on hallowed ground
   Sacred to God, home, country, first of shrines.
The nobles and the princes of the land,
   Of Europe and the wide world grace the scene,
And from her closet overhead at hand,
   Clad all in sable vesture, looks the Queen,
And weeps, one missing who had shared her throne :
   For since those Princes gathered round his bier,
No pageant had hither come and gone :
   They meet again his son to wed, and here.
Husbandless mother ! more, oh, Widowed Queen,
   Not unremembered is the Good, though dead :
We cherish thoughts of him, who has not been
   To be forgotten in his narrow bed.
Witness the welcome Alexandra had ;
   The holiday we kept while fife, drum, gun,

Cannon, and trump, and clanging peals, run mad,
  Proclaimed to all the world his wedded son.
And fain we are the day to lengthen out,
  Dispelling shade, illuminating night,
Eclipsing all the stars, with song and shout
  Wandering down rivers of deviceful light.
Each town and city on its flaming streets,
  And London pours its shouting millions forth ;
And in the South afire are all the fleets,
  And Arthur's Seat is blazing in the North."

Along the Mall, whose jets innumerous dance,
With the enraptured crowd I slow advance.
Now in Trafalgar Square I stand, when near
Two ladies and two gentlemen appear,
And one is—can it be—yes—Lucy here :
And that ?   Her Earl : both lost now in the crush.
In single file young ruffians shouting rush,
And pierce the crowd on all sides driven back.
Ah, then the horrid turmoil.   Lucy, alack ;
Bare time have I with force her side to gain
And prop her, falling, else she there had lain
Trampled to death, her parted friends all flown.
I in the crush now am with her alone,
Whom safe conducting, though through danger still,
To quiet stand beyond all push of ill,
I further progress wilfully delay,
She still so trembles, fearful of the way.
With scare of peril past and risk I ran,
Which she more magnifies, her cheek is wan ;
But now recovering blood from calming heart,
Late reeling reason plays a sobered part.
I gladly learn, she, for these festal days,
With friends hard by in Carlton Terrace stays.
Moving to gain it, easy of access,
What now is in her mind I think to guess.
Mine arm, on which she hangs, to which she clings,
She would not drop for flight on swallow wings ;
Though my poor suit has failed her choice to mould,

With tender passion thrills her voice of old,
Heard in too few unmeaning words, whose prose
Could ne'er in so brief space our breach compose.
The crowd we thread ; attain her door at last,
Each other by the hand now holding fast.

LUCY.

" My life I owe you, Edward ; cannot part
Without this farewell kiss,"

EDWARD.

                    " Which breaks my heart
To take,"

LUCY.

        " Rends mine to give."

                              God knows, I should
My cause again have pleaded as we stood,
But she my hand quits ; turns ; rings ; my brains whirl,
When, the door opening, issues thence the Earl.
Thither return to seek her shows some care.
It is his friend's house, and I leave her there.

Trafalgar Square recrossed with Strandward feet,
Another friend, the Partisan, I meet,
Who tells how late he in the crush has been,
And the great Earl escaping from it seen ;
And when I answer, I too saw him there,
Further reports the actions of a peer.

PARTISAN.

" Your native town I know, its neighbourhood,
And something of the Earl, but nothing good."

EDWARD.

" Ill then ? "

PARTISAN.

        " Yet good to know if bad to tell.
Cold hearted and cool headed, hot as hell,
Still in his teens, he lovely sisters twain

Wronged in one year and homestead.   One amain,
Fled e'er suspicion found frail show of proof :
A friend had offered here a humble roof—
That friend my mother.   There she bore a boy,
Reported home as born in wedded joy.
Then pangs of birth the younger sister moved ;
Fruit of her error a fair daughter proved :
But soon an honest farmer wooed and won,
And with her took the daughter for his own.
Rumour, which had the elder falsely wed,
And lied of husband soon and sudden dead,
Bore truer tidings of her own fresh tomb,
When the good farmer had her orphan home.
As cousins reared that boy and girl may marry :
Their secret, dread to keep, is sore to carry."

EDWARD.

" No more such oats the Earl wiser sows."

PARTISAN.

" Let us so hope : but that his God best knows.
Such is the Earl : one such is one too many.
Numerous our peers ; folly alone makes any."

EDWARD.

" Their Prince at least has wedded well to-day."

PARTISAN.

" Perhaps.   But is he not a little gay ? "

EDWARD.

" He now may, dropping boon companions wild,
Live as should Albert's and Victoria's child.
Certain nor Prince, nor Princess in our day
   Shall despot sceptre in this Empire wield ;
But theirs the higher glory to display
   The Majesty of goodness, virtue shield,
And make it princely to be good as great :
   Victoria makes it Queenly.   Like fine parts

In them may serve to sway the moral state,
   And rule the empire of our homes and hearts."

PARTISAN.

" A tactful Prince may compromise, and make
An outward show of goodness for shame's sake ;
So seem the while to make for righteousness,
And mitigate the passion of distress,
While general immorality gives sign
Of final stage in national decline."

EDWARD.

" You pessimistic are ; yet folly real
Possesses our high-hearted common weal.
This, which we call a glad illumination,
To me seems rather love in conflagration.
There is no sweetness in the stifling air :
Let us get out of it to my chambers—anywhere.
Sore is my heart with all this curse of feeling
To no good purpose, while there is no healing
In ought save quiet strength of intellect,
Which finds some joy in what it may dissect,
While too much given too little to respect."

But now we suddenly desert the long
And brilliant Strand and still more wondrous throng,
And plunge into a darkness dull, profound,
And silence weirdly broken by the sound
Of our lone footfalls in the vacant lane :
So great the contrast is, it strikes with pain.
My friend to chambers bears me company ;
And, entering, we find that we are three.
The Canon of St. Paul's, awaiting me,
Had dropped from weary bus, whose journey slow
Was aggravated by mere length of show.
Three, and not one too many : and our speech
I lead to mental power, how wide and far its reach.
The Canon had of my fond trouble heard,
And come to see how now I lonesome fared.

EDWARD.

" Weary of life in time, mysterious play
Constant in every instant of the day,
Whereby each momentary ' Now ' is brief
Disgust supreme, indifference, joy, or grief,
And in one ' Now ' you may with rapture doat,
In bitter next propose to cut your throat,
Ah ! how I cherish that remembered hour,
When on the boy first knowledge rose to power.
All nature full of wonder then appeared
Open to search, and, by discovery cheered,
Soul ventured on a sea without a shore,
And grew in power, discovering ever more.
But soul distracted now, with will supine,
Current upon each drift, how discipline ;
How firm the whole that early peace to find,
Wont to attend the play of powers of mind ?
Though happiness is our unceasing need,
Pleasures are transitory, pains succeed ;
The throne, a falling Angel abdicates,
A demon occupies—lost, worst of states ;
And soured disgust becomes confirmed disdain."

CANON.

" All earnest life, love wanting, palls amain ;
But life of action, motived by true love,
Duty to man below and God above,
A state of Being ruled by principle,
Happiness, is within our own good-will."

PARTISAN.

" Yet very noble is from earliest youth
The joy of knowledge growing up to truth
Attained by exercise of mental power,
And stored for instant use, of strength a tower
Commanding ignorance to hide its face,
And vawarding the progress of the race.
And it is well one should heart's sore annoys
With intellectual pleasures counterpoise,

Who is weary of the reckless waste
   And sore of heart and sense,
The wrongs he cannot right, but taste,
   And vanity's offence."

EDWARD.

" Oh, mind ! unceasing spring
   Of thought wide-spreading, bold,
Absorbing every living thing
   Even as the flood of old,
Insatiably athirst
   And heartless as the grave,
Without a feeling from the first
   To the last topping wave ;
Brave energy of mind,
   Eternally explore,
I would not that thou shouldest find
   Here anywhere a shore.
In thy great need to know
   Let me forget to feel,
Observing every form of woe
   Be careless of its weal.
Be thou in every part
   A peace unwooed, unbought ;
Each pulse of blood and throb of heart
   Calm, and absorb, wise thought.
Intellect is a mill, whose grind at least
Of chaff and grain makes just and equal grist."

CANON.

" Mysterious Mind, from age to age adored,
Capacious, vast, so largely unexplored
Its various phases, some still unbelieved,
Others half-known and many unconceived,
Brave men have studied ; but its province, still
Unmapped, seems bounded only by its will.
With science dwelling much alone, it shines
Into the depths of Nature's opened mines.

There in an atmosphere of blessed calm,
While every feeling is a silent psalm,
With order, unity, and law abroad,
It hath a growing consciousness of God ;
Finds each fore-thought a prospect into plan
Enticing, never satiating man ;
Discovery fresh still bracing, charming still ;
No heartache in it all ; no moral ill ;
Infallibility seen everywhere ;
Inevitable law without a care.
Yet man the while may know a curse apart,
Not aching there but in his own sore heart.
For energy of thought, not joy of find,
Is strict sole property and act of mind,
And fails to please, when heart, with feeling strong,
Freights brain with images of moral wrong."

PARTISAN.

" Activity itself can never cloy,
And pleases even when in misemploy,
Tasking the faculties which, when idle, fret
Or moon and swoon in waste of chilly sweat.
Power inactive waxes powerless,
   All reserve of it is loss ;
Trees don't fruiten that are flowerless ;
   Leafless ones make moss.
Crop a Samson; seize and bind him :
   What with anguish, horror, woe,
And stagnation death will find him
   Heedless of a blow.
Indolence, enthroned and reigning,
   Exercises like control,
Tortures, horrifies, enchaining
   Petrifies the soul."

EDWARD.

" Take the ant, and with it going
   All the realm of nature through,
Nothing find, but, though unknowing,
   Toils its all to do.

Hark ! machines make ceaseless clatter ;
  Brutes and serfs are working blind ;
Ever more in motion, matter
  Can no Sabbath find.
Voyagers mid-ocean staying
  Never meet we.   You and I
Must at top-speed live ; delaying
  Not, at top-speed die.
Man at half-speed is a lonely
  Monster here, a curse abroad
Worse than death, top-speed the only
  Speed for Sons of God."

CANON.

" Yet may power be over-rated.
  Impulse only is mere fate :
Self-possessed, self-regulated
  Power alone is great.
We are drifting logs, not sailing,
  Till we course by compass steer ;
And, 'gainst wind and tide prevailing,
  Steam to port with cheer.
Heart, soul, body, full in action,
  Moved by love of God and man,
We shall find true satisfaction,
  Doing all we can ;
And the sovereignty owing
  Of himself, man, with a will,
From his cradle steady going
  His chief end fulfil,
Shaping destinies of others,
  Forming too his own,
And with sisters and with brothers
  Rising to God's throne.
God has purposed no disaster,
  But that active power shall be
Motived by true love, and master
  Sin and misery.

Let us quit the past, unfearing,
   Trusting love to make us blest,
Working to the utmost, steering
   Till we enter rest.
Such counsel some may now, alas, reject.
Would we had love less reason to suspect.
Yet willing I, one should by trial prove
What may be lost by mitigating love.
Ah, woman herself may discover,
   That the world ill-won has cost
Not only a true-hearted lover,
   But her joy in the winning been lost."

We parted, I in stilly chambers trimmed
The lamp of labour burning long undimmed.
As whom the witch of Endor could recall,
Or shades, Macbeth and Banquo to appal,
Arose a race of spiritual kings
Before me, men who knew and did most things,
Davids and Solomons, Henry Eighths and Quatres,
Richelieus, Wolseys, Emperors, Popes, and Paters,
Governing men, who gained an immortality
For equal powers of mind and immorality,
And though their private lives were badly schooled,
Yet strangely bettered those they strongly ruled,
Most knowing indefatigable men—
Nine tailors make a man, one such makes ten—
And in their midst Economy Political,
Embodied to my mind's eye, throned withal
As Watts has painted Mammon to be feared.
Heavy and strong, and heady he appeared,
Pure intellect to know and use all force
To personal advantage sans remorse.
Obeying what he takes to be the laws
Of his own nature, and the Primal Cause—
Such cause as he at least believes in, lo !
His feet are planted on a world of woe ;
That he no moral weakness has, no flaw
Of foolish sentiment, I felt with awe ;

He has no pity for the world, he crushes ;
False shame upon his cheek has spared its blushes ;
Foreign is weakness to his active mind :
For to his real self he is purblind.
The vision, passing, in my soul was shrined,
    While diligently grows
      The labour to my hand,
    Which, the more energy it shows,
      Finds more at its command
    To fill with sense of power,
    And charm the fleeting hour,
  Sorrow, nor cark, nor care
    Admit I to my heart ;
  Hours unemployed with science share,
    Philosophy, and art ;
  In thought alone would live,
    In work alone would breathe,
  Nor could spare moment, startled, give
    To the approach of death ;
  Live only to forget,
    And gradually know—
Love's sprite here interposed debate.

SPRITE OF LOVE.

" Alas ! but is it not too late— "

EDWARD.

" Forgetfulness of woe."

SPRITE OF LOVE.

" Ha ! wounds there are in the battle of life,
Whose most skinned scars are open strife."

Time hasted with the hour unkind.
And now had passed me out of mind,
But at the instant of event,
I to the Partisan my powers had lent,
And, in the midst of his now winning cause,
Fell for an instant into dream and pause.

2 B

"Who giveth this woman to be wedded to this man?"

I seemed to hear, though far away;

"In the name of the Father and of the Son and of the
          Holy Ghost," it ran.
I could not say,
"Our Father, who art in heaven."   I could not pray,
Yet nothing saw of all the show,
Though since have read, and still more know,
And tale of broken faith resume;
But now with prophesy of doom.

Prophesy ne'er will to misfortune fail;
It was with Jonah in the whale,
Nor could Cassandra wiser rave
As freeborn princess, than as slave.
From head to foot in pearly white,
All veiled it stood but full of light,
Like bridal Morn in gauze of mist
Just to sun wedded and still triste;
And with the Sprite of Love attending,
Their voices sympathetic blending,
It sings, and seems the while to be
The utterance of my woe in me.

PROPHESY ATTENDED BY LOVE'S SPRITE.

"Grand was the marriage following brief betrothal,
   And for it milliners tasked night and day.
Rich presents magic made and papers froth all:
   For even princes went to see the play,
   Which was a sight to make a devil gay,
As church and state together joined their mights,
   And fashion flocked, whence God had turned away,
To bind and bless all future days and nights
Of two so bound and loosed by most unhallowed rites.

"Thy tower of bliss thus based upon a dream—
   Lucy, a ruin round thee strews of lies

Asking, 'What truth is?'   False all prospects seem.
  Thy spirit broken yet its wreck denies,
  And mocks at all a world now deifies,
Seen on the rapid slope to mouth of hell.
  If any feeling in her heart replies
To this in thine, poor comfort ! thou mayest well
Leave her to fate's revenge—it has no heart to sell.

" Nuremberg's iron Virgin Mummiform
  Had inward spikes upon its open door,
Which, closing on some coffined victim warm,
  Pierced, as he upright stood, to quivering core ;
  And needless suffocation choked him more,
Twice killing him ; and down on stream beneath
  Descending virgin shook him from darts sore,
Bubbling the blooded flux with his last breath,
Spiked, suffocated, drowned, barbed by a tripronged death.

" Lucy such iron virgin is to love
  Imprisoned, pierced to heart, and suffocated,
Only expressed by sighs, that latest move ;
  In torrents drowned.   Ah !   Shall her eyes be fated
  To image other loves, more happy mated,
And drown them too, as when from Brutus dire
  Parted fond Portia.   But she abated
Impatient life, swallowing most subtle fire :
Lucy, her passions choked, may not herself expire.

" For being not into the manner born
  Of rule hereditary, she, so great
Only by marriage made, and under scorn
  Even of the lord, who hath her for his mate,
  Or rather sport of lust inordinate
And heartless passion, may his scorn partake,
  And nurse a settled, if a silent hate,
Deeming he only can by lewd mistake
And privilege of laws, which God did never make,

" Rank hold and lands, his ancestors made their own
　By slaying of a deer their side-march stream,
Or rived from Church and Commons, and, rich grown,
　A lofty title won to low esteem.
　Though rank and riches are no empty dream,
Their worth is lessened by a lordly mood,
　Which cannot humble to a lady seem.
Woman, when in the wrong even, ever should
Be tenderly arraigned, not haughtily withstood.

" Ah, what has Lucy wed, if not to be
　Mistress of lord and revenue ; a slave,
If marriage all, to what grim slavery
　Mastered by him?　But she can dare be brave
　Mistress at least of, what she never gave,
Will strong as his, and stubborn to enjoy
　At any rate the world this side the grave :
Not knowing it a dust-filled dressed up toy,
Which love can cast away—the wretched naked boy.

" But when it comes to this, such battle drawn
　Is woman's stout advantage, leaves her free
To every folly fashion fawns upon,
　And men, not husbands, glut with flattery :
　To licence quick fermenting liberty,
Sour grapes producing often raciest wine.
　For, heartless marrying, strength most womanly
In shows of bliss can revel, nor repine,
To pleasure's harlequin a stately Columbine.

" Let her a coronet enjoy, and prove
　The pleasure her self-sacrifice has bought,
And earth and heaven sedulously move
　To occupy, not irk, unrestful thought ;
　So be, as happy as her mother taught,
Insensible to heart, but full of soul
　And beautiful as things, that live on rot,
And frozen worldly as is either pole,
Round which the reckless earth whirls to its fiery goal

" With Helens and their husbands, dead or live,
　　Theseus, and Menelaus, Paris rare,
Deiphobus : for one had four or five,
　　Counting Achilles, though she neither were
　　Of Bath nor Samarie, and had her share
Of blood and rapine, murdering at Troy
　　Eighty-six thousand Greeks, and, more than fair,
Seven hundred thousand Trojans, quite a ploy,
Beauty so conquest loves, and conquers to destroy.

"Venus, of Mars chief mistress, is loved best
　　More damage doing than his steelest pin :
Be heaven witness, when to father breast
　　Unfallen Satan grappled lovely Sin,
　　And there was war in heaven—so hells begin.
Lucy may husbands other have than he,
　　Along with him, and each appear to win :
French and Spenserian allegories three—
Sans-foi, Sans-loi, Sans-joie, and they shall constant be.

" For is so hard experience sometimes wise
　　To undeceive, and teach full littleness
Of what possessed a woman still may prize,
　　But rate now than her bartered self much less—
　　Dear bought at cost of self-esteem's distress,
And loss of love.   Solicitous to hide
　　Head humbled, broken heart, but not confess,
She yet may spread each inch of canvas wide
To pleasure's wooing breeze with more determined pride,

" Making her manly.   Mixture quaintly strange,
　　And very pitiful, like joyous home,
Fond haunt of loves and graces, which sad change
　　With soldiery disturbs, who flaunting roam
　　Showing their uniforms lest the spoiler come.
And for defence she armed will, scorning life,
　　Flash with bright look of metal venturesome,
In part concealing sore intestine strife,
Which in unloving home breeds treason in a wife ;

" Though little practised where occasion halts.
  Politeness comes of virtue in the heart,
But virtue little counts where rank exalts.
  Superior to virtue, rank can part
  With all but polish of collusive art
Burnishing lustre dimmed of haughty name.
  Infamy even cannot noblesse thwart
Obliged to be ' My lady,' not ' My Dame : '
Vulgarity alone can bide no patent shame.

" Thus howsoe'er I search the prospect round,
  It lurid shows for Lucy—wild obscure,
With even now a tremble in the ground,
  A trouble in the air, and evil sure
  With change from bad to worse, and to endure.
But may not he to better change, she led
  By guard and guide, not lord, with kind allure ?
Hope will not live on such mere fancy bred :
Beauty he, she the world, neither hath other wed.

" Her choice is made—rank, affluence, and a lie :
  For truth and love are never bought and sold,
And never can in Lucy wholly die
  Though wraithed in lace, and mummified in gold,
  Their pyramid a palace, where untold
Pomp, revelry, and brilliance cheat the nights,
  But not dispel the livid gloom so cold,
Whose inmate shudders in unfelt delights,
Mocking sad death in life with festive funeral rites.

" Faithless herself, can she in truth believe,
  And not a trust betrayed for ever dread ;
Nor yet reflect, how hope can self-deceive ;
  Nor doubt fair word of bliss, she lied to wed ?
  Lightly may youth forget the lost, the dead,
And she the wrecked inevitable past;
  Still must it have a ghost, that walks unlaid.
Let her enjoy the moments, while they last,
Of unremorseful wrong ; they fly so very fast.

" Though forceful spirits early cribbed austerely
   In mail of circumstance, which none quite doff,
Oft Pharisaic see no whit more clearly
   Than hell by its fireside, where devils scoff,
   Or water-cures, which quake some stout men off,
Or any other narrow-visioned ring
   Of fortunate or unfortunate chance trough
Taking sharp boundary, that clips its wing,
To be the world God made, and meant for everything :

" Sooner should mother with small means go buy
   Cheap winding sheets for daughters, and to make
Teach them, and counsel willingly to die,
   Starve, rather than unlovingly for sake
   Of house and name to cast away, or stake
Happiness on unfettered wanton chance.
   Ah ! many a strong heart, wed, begins to break ;
Would all the pride and pomp of circumstance,
And Eden give for one fond moment of romance."

There trembled on its lips a truceless curse
Meant for the House of Lords and weightier purse ;
When, lo ! the vision, paling out of sight,
Deposed its robes, and wreaths, and wand of light,
Proper to Prophesy, as though it grieved
To be prophetic, and to be believed.
I grasped the falling wand, but in my hand
I saw it not—it was no more a wand,
And yet my tongue was loosed in semblant play
Echoing the soul of Prophesy gone away ;
And Love's own Sprite remained, and lent an ear,
And tongue to argue the occasion dear.

EDWARD.

" As vainly the clansmen O'Donoghue wait,
   To see him ride over again to his halls,
On his prancing spray-steed, to reverse the false fate,
   That has buried his treasures and riven his walls ;
So man, who lost Eden, expecteth the hour,
When love shall descend, and the wilderness flower.

"Where leaden mists molten the lake overspread,
  E'er the sun walks across will O'Donoghue ride,
Fays strewing with roses a path for the dead,
  As Aurora descendeth to usher his pride.
From the wraith which he rides, he alights to behold
  His mist-mantled castle renewed in its might ;
And he enters and wanders his halls as of old,
  And his clansmen are thrilled with a long-lost delight.

" E'er the hosts gray of morning fly arrowy day,
  Back borne he on shimmer of which he is born ;
Then happy the clansmen, who follow, and stray
  Where hollowed out hills cloak the treasure, they mourn.
His lake's darkest depths lined for venturous feet,
  They travel its bosom on pathways of mist,
From those mountain-hid treasures, hope whispering sweet,
  He will graciously give them far more than they wist.

" But morning from castle, lake, valleys, and hills
Hope's visions, night's vapours, dispelling reveals
His fortress in ruins, his lost treasures—where ?
And only a dream of all lingering there.
So love is Night vapour, which daylight disperses,
To Lucy a dream, which life waking reverses :
And loving me, yet other's wife,
  She, fooling least-wise two of three,
Has screaming farce of maiden-life
  Ended to fashionably be
As men who country love, but choose
Party before, and both abuse :
Though Eve lapsed more incontinent,
  An apple ate by serpent bidden,
Promised no coronet, and went,
  But not from Adam, though from Eden."

SPRITE OF LOVE.

" Young and lovely, not demure,
  Lady of the House now, still
May she have some fancies pure
In her heart with holdings sure,

And not tenants at mere will ;
Or are these, plague-stricken too,
Gardens of Boccaccio ?
As from some far Eden blowing,
  All where bee at random feeds,
Zephyrs to a desert going
  Lend strange fragrance unto weeds ;
So some stray imagination
  Of far childhood may redeem,
With a kindly inspiration
Over all her desolation,
Waking into new creation
  Many a young and happy dream.
Of the blossoms childhood bore,
  ' Let those fruiten now,' they sing,
Of the hopes she had of yore.
Ah ! she lets them sing, and soar
Leaving her to self once more—
  A sadder, not a wiser thing.

" For as waters, which into a cove
  By the rushing torrent are chased,
But never thence to rove,
Eddying round still prove
  How irksome can be rest ;
So culture, pomp, and leisure
  Have a whirlpool emptiness ;
Peace is no part of the measure
Of ill-gotten and used power, and treasure ;
  The simmer of fond distress
In over-much leisure and pleasure
  With sighs o'er-tops success."

EDWARD.

" Not Constance, Geoffrey's widow, Arthur's mother,
  Prisoner in Castle of St. Bevron held
By husband gaoler, falser than fierce brother,
  More hated Chester, even in sleep rebelled,

The Noble Soldier now I grave agnize
With less distempered hate, and more surprise.
Admiring science by him pioneered,
I come to honour whom I once had feared,
And join with pleasure, hopeful of new zest,
A bachelor dinner given, of his best ;
Now tell in verse what he of woman taught
And others felt, and I too almost thought.

NOBLE SOLDIER.

" Woman a plaything is, which we put dress on ;
 Toy of a whim, meant to be cast aside ;
Way-flower, to wander and lavish a caress on,
 Pass then, or toss heedless on passing tide.
Woman protests that thus we should amuse her,
 Offer her myrrh, though in a swindling way :
Adam, by Eve vexed, nothing could refuse her ;
 Pleasure them all, each for a single day.
Silliest fellows, seeking a safe treasure,
 Think they can love fix in some pet of pets ;
Wise men contented scatter abroad pleasure,
 Loving all round : Women are all coquettes.
Unto fresh loves you should sing of love,
 ' What is love, and what is beauty ?
Beauty is below as God above.
 And love is duty.
Love to beauty,
 All the world over—
Love is duty,
 And to be a lover,'
You should kneel, and whisper, where you dare,
 ' Stoop thou, as I kneel before thee ;
Kiss me in the ambush of thy hair :
 For I adore thee.
Love to beauty
 All the world over—
Love is duty,
 And to be a lover.'

Sing, she may be bashful in her pride,
   ' Clasp my neck, as I embrace thee :
Charms all glowing on my shoulder hide,
   I cannot face thee.
Love to beauty
   All the world over—
Love is duty,
   And to be a lover.'
Sing, while circling her with arms of love,
   ' Circle me with arms of beauty ;
Kiss me, kiss me into heaven above :
   For love is duty.
Love to beauty
   All the world over—
Love is duty,
   And to be a lover.' "

A brother soldier, giving folly rein,
Talked lightly in this louder strain.

OLD SOLDIER.

   " Round and sound,
   Tuppence a pound,
Cherries, rare ripe cherries ;
   Come and pick,
   Happence a stick,
Cherries, red ripe cherries ;
   Big as plums :
   Who comes, who comes
For rare red ripe cherries ?
   Open ground
   Orchards abound,
Cherries, rare ripe cherries ;
   Kisses thick,
   Lovers, be quick,
Cherries, red ripe cherries ;
   Thumbs don't suck,
   But pluck, pluck, pluck
The rare red ripe cherries.

Lips impound,
Tongues hush around
Cherries, rare ripe cherries ;
Rhetoric
Don't know to pick
Cherries, red ripe cherries ;
Mum's the word,
And bird—true bird
For rare red ripe cherries."

A Noble Sailor, widely known,
With Love thought Bacchus to enthrone.

NOBLE SAILOR.

"Wine hath also charms :
With its kisses wet
Time knows no alarms,
In the future great,
Evil looks so good,
Good, too, so divine ;
Hail men would a flood,
That from heaven rained wine.
Love and wine are best
Helpfully uniting ;
Bacchus is most blest,
Torch of Cupid lighting,
Time will soon be up :
Love, salute the cup."

A Classic Painter of the nude
Answered for Love as woman should.

PAINTER OF THE NUDE.

"I had rather kiss you than the tumbler, my dear :
If there's death in the cup, let us kiss before bier.
Our lips close with a cling
Undespondingly bring,
Then two happiest pairs to a good wassailing."

And after, lo !
Tell me if you the singer know—
"Why doth beauty blush,
  Colouring so high ?
Why that tear about to gush
  Out of beauty's eye ?
Is her lover blind ?
  Must she love in vain ?
Or can she no lover find,
  Whom to love again ?
Surely he is own
  Magnet of her heart
Voyaging the night, and known,
  When the stars depart,
Basking in her sun
  Constant as her sigh :
Whence this gathering-force-to-run
  Tear in beauty's eye,
And that blush then, tell?
  Show they sudden bliss,
Or do love's soft angers swell
  In an eye like this?
'Tis no sudden ray
  In a clouded hour
Flashing vapours from the day
  In a happy shower ;
'Tis no loving rage
  Causing loving woe,
As when doves soft battle wage,
  That hath moved her so.
Doth then grief intrude
  Such a tear unbid
On a blush, that things she should
  She too seldom did ?
Heaven may be won
  By a tear and blush ;
But for what she hath not done,
  She don't care a rush.

"Can disease in bloom
  Look then half so sweet
To surprise, but with a tomb
  Opening at her feet?
Ah! the health is here
  Of an Arab Scheik:
Whence, oh! whence the gathering tear,
  And the blushing cheek?
Beauty seems to me
  Chastely purely bright,
Like a pebble of the sea
  Flashing back the light;
Yet in whispers say,
  Are they born of shame?
Did the moth too eager play
  Round the scorching flame?
Joys there are on earth
  Tempting to the fair,
Know they not that joy and mirth
  Sound in poisoned air?
Lo! the sparkling cup
  Brimming and unquaffed:
Ah! they drink the nectar up
  In one maddening draught.
Tear, I see and sigh;
  Blush, which raises mine;
That the tear of sympathy,
  This the flush of wine."

A pagan M.P. laughed, protesting gay
Against my unobjectionable lay.

PAGAN M.P.

"I would not so of lovely woman speak,
But thus address her, dearest when most weak.
Shrill ancient birds, whose grapes are sour
  Since now too good for them, may sneer;
Deem love an impious, ill-starred power,
  That pops the moment they draw near.

Doves know the kites, the god of birds
  Has changed to owls : they call me, ' Zaney.'
I value their ironic words
  High at the eighth part of a penny.
With Lepithi may Centaurs brawl ;
  Well-tempered cups make us more human,
Inclined to a much kindlier fall,
  Than the Old Serpent gave the Old Woman.
Give me a thousand kisses, then
  A hundred, another thousand pet,
A second hundred, and again
  A thousand more, a hundred yet ;
Till we, confused by many misses,
  Again to count in vain essay,
Then sum past, present, future kisses
  In one repeated one for aye ;
So with good manners by the billion
Blind one another and the million,
And thus, for ever still beginning
  And coming to no end of bliss,
Find no one envy us an inning,
Of which the score, however winning,
From first to last, no heavy sinning
  'Neath Brehmen rose, is one long kiss."

Such was the flow of that wild evening
And others wilder, many following.
Love's Sprite in prayer then I heard.

SPRITE OF LOVE.

                     " Great God,
Show Thyself now with virtue in Thy rod ;
Cleanse Thou a heart, which vagabonding roves
With faint desires to prostitute its loves,
Pursuing wealth, power, culture as it may,
And tasking pleasure to prolong the day."

God not attending, Puck, who hovered near,
With nimble tongue possessed my captive ear.

                    + 2 C

PUCK.

" Ho, merrily quick run the sands of time,
As each moment bright from the globe sublime
   Merrily, oh! merrily, oh!
Shakes out its own appointed grain,
And dies with a laugh and without any pain
   Merrily, merrily, oh!
They just have time to be happy and die,
As into and out of existence they fly
   Merrily, oh! merrily, oh!
Pure pleasure of being begin to feel,
When they die with the feeling about them still
   Merrily, merrily, oh!
Men's lives are made up of moments too,
Then why should they not go merrily through,
   Merrily, oh! merrily, oh!
Laugh with the moments as they fly,
From bright moment to moment live, and die
   Merrily, merrily, oh!"

My Guardian Sprite, by Love's own companied,
All seeing, hearing, testified, and chid.

GUARDIAN SPRITE.

" Sing so the silly,
   Esteeming themselves wise,
While shrinks the lily
   From their fiery eyes;
Even the marigold
Burns in their hot love bold,
   And nightly weeping drowns her sighs,
Tears on the lashes dewing sleep;
So Fulvias in secret weep.
Cleopatras with hotter fire
To Antonys aspire,
Embracing, quench their noontide suns;
And men praise nuns."

EDWARD.

" Yet how sweet the Syrens sing :
　Through and under their high strain
Ocean lapses susurring—
　' Cease of sorrow to complain.
This the world's Port O'Rest,
In whose Inn we serve the guest :
Curs of tumult, burs of toil,
Cark and care we all assoil ;
Lift the curse, and weave the spell,
Without candle, book, or bell.
We are happy ; love is gay.
Love we make, and holiday.
Toilers of the Sea, come play.' "

SPRITE OF LOVE.

" Look out, look out and see
What objects, these may be,
Enforcing so thine ear,
It nothing else may hear ;
Strewing with lusty vows
　The gentle spelling air,
That loves upon it browze.
　Three half-breed wantons bare,
Look out, look out and see—
The Syrens one, two, three :
For ravenous below
Each is a Kytral crow ;
Should croak, not algate lust like virelay.
Seal your ears to their dismay :
They would upon your carcase prey."

And 'twas at home after an evening gay,
" Write," something in me " Write " said, and I could not
　　write a word.
　First I fancied it the champagne, then the port, the
　　sherry then,

Then the ale, which had been rather flat, like some Dun-
    dreary Lord
  With a little effervescence and a very little brain.
So I thought to go to bed, but in me something still said,
    " Write " ;
And I stayed to write, but could not for the life of me know
    what.
And I stirred the fire, and turned up higher the gas to get
    some light
  On the subject, if I so might see to cut the Gordian knot.
But, the knot, it sorely puzzled me : I could not see to cut ;
  I could not even see the knot, and clipped at it in vain.
Then I thought it could not be the ale, nor port, nor sherry,
    but
    A mixture of the one, two, three with rather much
    champagne.
So again I meant to go to bed, but, while I thought of going,
  Out went the fire, and chilled I sought to warm me by
    the gas,
But could not make the burners blaze sufficiently, and,
    knowing
  That something made a fool of me, wrote—" Sir, you are
    an ass."
And when I read what I had written, I knew that I had done it ;
  And, putting out the gas, observed, I could not see ahead,
Resolving that it was the drink, and that I ought to shun it,
  Or mix it less, or otherwise not write, but go to bed.
Yet there I slept, till morning grey
Waked, and I knew it not quite day.

    Gazing blank on the chill cheerless grate,
    Which looked hard, cold and desolate,
      I was sitting solemn as stone.
    It was late—early late,
      And I felt I was sitting alone :
    And right in the mid-sore of dreams of the past
    A vision rose, making my heart beat fast ;
    " Art a Spirit ? " I thought with strange courage at last ;
      And it looked as though meaning, " Thine own."

My body, apparently there,
Had no hold of me, more than the chair :
  Was never such feeling thine own ?
But that air, form of air,
  Seemed not altogether unknown ;
And the vision entranced me, the while a beam
From no earthly sun made it heavenly seem,
And I thought, " I have seen thee before in a dream :
  No spirit art thou but—Mine own ? "

For, like lightning aflame in the night,
Swift a fiery thought took flight
  Through the brightening past, which shone.
"Thou art right, ah ! quite right,
  Kindly ghost ! " thought I then, and anon,
" The ghost of my once happy self thou art,
For I slew him.   Nay, Goodly Spirit, depart
No longer to haunt a desert heart :
  I was once, am no longer, thine own."

And it heard, but in pity remained,
And all my wild spirit enchained
  By its goodness, and sadness, so lone,
Surely pained—sorely pained
  By the change that had come over one
Who had once been so like, but was different, oh,
Now so weary.   Bowing its head blushing low,
For the change that it saw, with a face full of woe
  It beside me stood grieving—"Mine own ! "

Loose hemp might have held me in tether :
For its love broke my heart altogether,
  And remorse embittered my moan
Pondering whether, wondering whether,
  It would leave me for ever alone,
Thinking, " Stay, Spirit, stay : life anew begin.
I am worn without, I am weary within.
Good Spirit, return ; I will let thee in ;
  And a soul repossess—all Thine Own."

Thereat from the face dropped the hands,
And a smile shone, like sun on the lands
   Beyond Jordan, where saints gird the throne,
And in bands, happy bands,
   Sing when prayers are answered.   But soon
The smile with the vision seemed fading away,
As with vanishing sun disappears dear day ;
Still my soul did not sadden, strange to say,
   While I thought, " Leave me not, oh ! mine own."

As the vision faded, I young
And cheerful was growing, and strong
   Fresh-winged life was dawning new-blown,
Full of song, blissful song,
   And incense and glory unknown :
For the vision was into me passing, like rain
Into dry parched ground, and banishing pain,
And my soul to itself was coming again,
   And whispering within, " All thine own ! "

But was it so ; or have I ever been
The Ideal Self so dreamed of, or so seen ?
At least it had my feelings sparing shared,
And is my counsel still within me heard.

IDEAL SELF.

" Though woman sports with man,
   And man makes sport of woman,
Till all heart seems a flash in the pan
   Like the pistol of a show-man,
Flash not thou thy heart away,
Worse—a woman's, and in play.
Let never lie impure thy lips distain :
Whom Lucy quits, may Circé tempt in vain."

The Partisan, my constant client, lone
Seeking advice has sometimes given his own.

My loss of Lucy not from him concealed,
The tumult of my soul had been revealed ;
That of his own he more and more disclosed ;
Though differing still, we are not quite opposed.
His smiles and words, both cynical, intend
No harm to me, when they may most offend.

PARTISAN.

" For self you have perchance done wise and well
To break of Comus, wand and cup and spell.
Let yours be shrewder, if less rapturous bliss.
You may with woman sport, and never kiss,
Her luring arts observe, like me ; and can
While in the world, not of it, study man,
In courts and chambers know his shady ways,
And moderate warm censure with cold praise."

EDWARD.

" As mere winds with subtle ease
Lift to heaven yielding seas,
I, in mental strength elate,
Love had thought to win, and mate ;
And the humble walk began,
   Dedicate to use and law,
And all ways and rights of man,
But with triumphs in the van,
   Filling Saxons with strange awe,"

PARTISAN.

" Glamoured by an Ermine-dress
Covering of craftiness,
Which can, seeming artless, fool
Superseded stole, and rule,
As the church was wont to do,
Still the many by the few ;

Not by Pope and hierarchy,
But by king and oligarchy
Raking out of old Black Letters
Type enough to forge new fetters,
Precedent to loose, or bind
By self-interest inclined ;
Using also church to prate
About ordinance of state.
Yet prize-beauties care no pin
For late triumphs, law may win ;
Passing fancies have for wigs,
Not upon the heads of prigs."

EDWARD.

" Sense loves idols of the den,
Its own shows, not lights of men :
Spirit earns too scanty pay,
Lord, not scullion, of its clay.
Gold, gilding rank, can buy
  False beauty's chill caress ;
Mind is not rated high,
  And love is valueless."

PARTISAN.

"Why woman scorn, whose kiss
  Is given not to rags ?
Since what one has, not is,
Not mind, but means of bliss,
  Titles, and money bags
Form male as female Dis :
  And so the great world wags,"

EDWARD.

"A thing to study, know, not mate ;
Use, if you will ; and, up to date,
Above it in the growing sense
Of wisdom feel omnipotence,

In the vast latency of power
Ready and sure for any hour,
Under the spirit's own control,
And indestructible as soul."

PARTISAN.

" Great is the mind of man, and reigns to-day
Inventive : bracing, profitable play.
For oft with one hand blinding truth you laugh,
And with the other cram its mouth with chaff
By order of the great Chin-Kam-Chi-Ho,
First emperor of Moons, Stars, Suns, and Co.;
Tossing fancies hither, thither,
   Into systems, frail as flighty,
Drifting, no one knoweth whither,
Views dissolving have, and either
   False of man, or An Almighty ;
Think prismatically ; blot
Canvas, whistling for a thought;
Out of scrannel pipes of straw
Light-brained music vent, and draw,
Tear from eye, from throat guffaw ;
With some pepper pot-boil paper,
   And rhymes libertine create ;
Like truth too romance, and vapour ;
   Lie, like history, in state ;
Wisdom, up in a balloon,
Gold prospecting in the moon,
Intellectually proud,
   By the incense vague of praise
Deafened, blinded, in its cloud,
Ravished from the gaping crowd,
   And their too incurious gaze."

EDWARD.

" Charming into life and heart
   Marbles chiselled, colours blent,
Mind by miracles of art
   Makes immortal ravishment ;

Fulmines Greece, and glory fires,
    Or, when banners slumber furled,
Peace woos, smiting tuneful lyres,
    And enrapturing the world ;
Acting history, yet, snatching
    Rare occasion, writes to last ;
Reads the future, genius catching
    Inspiration from the past ;
With predestination close
    Modest walking, as behind,
Never forward to oppose
    Thus the toward march of mind,
Probes the possible, and, choosing
    What shall be, on fate improves,
Kingdoms founds, religious using
    Or inventing onward moves ;
Learning nature to coerce
    Or to follow sagely, steals
Secrets from a universe
    It admires, explores, reveals ;
Gathering up each separate spark
    Into one grand flame of laws,
In excess of brightness dark
    Drawing near the primal cause,
Barely conscious, ravished, awed,
    Quivering like a lambent flame,
Treads on shining skirts of God,
    Uttering His mysterious name,
Who a mighty thing designed,
    When He breathed a soul of powers
Into bodies used by mind
What is knowable to find
    In its tenement of hours,
Drinking wisdom from God's breast,
While fond ardours, gravely blest,
Such as fired the radiant king
Homeward glad the ark to bring,
With a holy rapture dance
Over each grand countenance

In humanity's advance,
As when suns meridian shine
Upon calms, that cross the line."

PARTISAN.

" Young Mind gave birth to all that it confessed ;
And gods appeared by it creatively expressed.
Apollo, son of Jove, could all foresee.
Daughter of heaven and earth, Mnemosyné,
Herself a goddess and her babes divine,
To Zeus, great father, bore the Muses Nine.
To him too Themis, known in Ancient Greece
Goddess of law, gave order, justice, peace,
Seasons, and Parcoe, which with vital rein
The Universe, still falling, still maintain.
What time Jove's head oped wide to Hermian blows,
Thence Wisdom's goddess panoplied arose:
Olympus quaking moved the firm-set land,
Poseidon paled, and with unsteady hand
Helios himself upreined the steeds of light
Dazzled, till Pallas doffed her armour bright.
As the Olympian artist, wise though lame,
Hephæstous, Hera born, was blown by fame
The god, who works in fire, supreme in skill,
All metals moulding pliant to his will :
Venus, his spouse, could heaven itself coerce,
And was The Beauty of the Universe.
All is but as in mind which comes to birth
By exercise of self, builds heaven and earth,
To men and gods their attributes assigns,
Divines their substances, some say sombines,
And never has a thought to daunt its powers,
In the prolonged procession of the hours ;
Adores the gods it makes—its own brave shows,
And yet may worship me.   Ah, who but knows,
That very love itself can hate assay?
Or put it, if you will, the other way—
' Is there no love in hate, no hate of hates :
No lie in truth?   And are not all true mates ? '

Fell fiercest passions have a purposed good ;
And war is peaceful, fairly understood.'
Be charitable, man, and give the devil
His due of all the good, that comes of evil.
Anoint thine eyes with knowledge ; learn to see
Experience reconcile things contrary."

EDWARD.

" That truth is falsehood, not its counterlight,
I may to-morrow see : meanwhile— "

                                    But bright
A somewhere shower with rainbow arched the sky ;
Tears filled mine own and nature's hazy eye ;
Earth seemed to pass, while over heaven wan
Stretched the frail beauty of that wondrous span,
Its ends by Iris grasped, whose radiant grace
Else lone possessed the void and vast of space.
And thus the Partisan disturbed the air.

PARTISAN.

" Having forgotten, or dismissed all care,
Messenger of the gods, lo, idly there,
Regardless of what charges they have given,
Careless of man, and undisturbed by heaven,
Iris is with the rainbow skipping, whiles
Through brightened tears Sad Nature on her smiles,
Its only pleasure to behold, and know
That gods, if such there be, can soon forget man's woe.
Why should they mind it ?   And if One alone
Indifferent He, upon necessitous throne
So shared with none, is powerless to restrain
The good, or evil fates, that rule his reign.
Earth-works and megalithic, world-wide found,
Sepulchral, monumental, or renowned,
Or more obscure, still tell of ages past,
How long ago ! life, death, and dust at last.
What races are commemorated thus ?
Dig deeper, and you stranger sights discuss.

Whence all these monsters winged, or sprawling strown
Gigantic, fossilized to stone in stone,
Or bogged, or in the strata fragmentary,
Leaving no simulachres earth to harry,
Though other living kinds to sigh in vain,
That they too only live to die again.
Dig deeper, penetrate to mother mires,
Liquid and gaseous flames, and central fires,
Confusion worse confounded : then survey
Unfathomed space with universes gay,
And on them all the finger of decay.
Sun, satellite, star, comet slowly burned,
Each, with the ashes of its dead inurned,
Speeds to its laughter-limit ; then is turned
To spatial dust, disorganized at last.
Unnumbered universes so have passed :
Their dissolution is our vital breath :
Life has one source and consummation—death.
Is there a race, improving, not to perish?
Nature no longer can hope wisely cherish.
Think then no more to memorize the grave :
Some fading flowers are all you thence can save."

EDWARD.

" I will not so believe—not though with doubt
I whisper now a faith, which once was stout.
You on recurrent dung-hill chaos crow:
Old fellow, are you happy ?   Say, and go."

He silent disappeared; but, not long gone,
That evening reappears in chambers lone.
Ah, has his spirit always been with mine?
Here now in form he sits, and sips my wine,
We two in lampless gloom,
    Night on its way
Chasing with shades of doom
    Vanishing day.

EDWARD.

" Over the laughing dark
    New heavens for earth,
As from Thor's anvil, spark
    Into bright birth.
Daintiest lights of night,
    Day's true arrears,
Fairiest, little, bright,
    Beautiful spheres !
Clearly they shine, and man,
    Freighted with care,
Purely delighted can
    See them up there."

PARTISAN.

" Your God can make most pretty things :
Some are cheats, and all have wings."

EDWARD.

" I look out now up there, where each star
    In heaven shines down upon me,
Like lights sprinkling ocean afar,
And twinkling, and fair they are
    As angels, and joys to see.
As Luna the tides rules, as thunder
    The breeze and the billow stills,
The vision of glory and wonder
    My calming spirit fills.
These forget-me-nots of the sky
    Show we are not forgotten above.
They are whispers of God to the sigh,
    As it rises : they soothe it with love.
They are drops of concentrated bliss ;
    And their peoples, if peopled they are,
Must surely feel life a kiss
    Delightful, and pure as a star."

PARTISAN.

" Through the olden windows gleam,
    Here and there and all about,

Stars, that happy look, yet seem
  Twinkling, shuddering, to doubt.
For, like any other sphere,
  Bright and beautiful is earth,
Yet men darkness see, and hear
  Very little mirth.
This world is a beautiful lie ;
  What else are those ? Who can say ?
Could you look with a seraph eye,
  You might see them cursing their day.
No comfort I find in the light
  And loveliness of each star ;
Ah ! better were utter night,
Than things deceitfully bright."

EDWARD.

" True, the flames of Hell may be bright
  And beautiful afar.
God, can grace to the heavens high
  Have a brilliant leprosy given,
And with misery blotched them ? I try
Not to hear, though I fancy a cry
  From every star in heaven."

He unto window walks, and there his hand
  Uplifts as though in face of heaven to shake
With unmouthed imprecation, or demand.
  I pray no evil may us overtake.
Storm has begun. Thick darkness now prevails ;
In torrents rains fall, and winds rise in gales.

PARTISAN.

" Look ! the stars have pulled on their cowls
  And the heavens wept themselves blind.
Hark ! I wonder, what is it, howls
  So dolefully in the wind ? "

EDWARD.

" Perchance on the wind has been shed
  A sorrow, which more than kills,
Damns living hope to despair, now fed
  By fancies of worse ills."

PARTISAN.

" Ah, I think, if that wind, as it flies,
  Could gather up into one
The groans, and curses, and sighs,
That rise, or that never rise,
  Yet break the heart of town,
And down this lone lane swell,
  So would the wild sorrow dismay,
As none might live to tell
  The horror unto day.
Though it comes not your heart to break,
  You start.   Can it coming be ? "

EDWARD.

" Nay, the fancy off I shake,
  As a dog shakes off the sea ;
But, oh ! the chill.   The poor dog knows
  To roll, run, bark, and warm it so :
But when to heart the iron goes,
  The curdled blood of man won't flow."

PARTISAN.

" Sunlight of the Cosmos, whole
Sun and centre of the soul,
Faith in an enduring love !
When that fails you, and you prove
That there is no certain stay
In the love of any day,
Waking you as from a dream,
That which could so certain seem—
God and good, love, faith, hope, light
Cheerless fade in starless night."

With such last word the Partisan departs ;
I fear we both have somewhat broken hearts.
And I to Sleep a wakeful breath addressed,
Which could not rest.

EDWARD.

" Kindly sleep, our senses stealing !
   Subtle mockery of death,
So denuding us of feeling,
   While not stinting us of breath,
Rather making night restore
Strength, we lost the day before ;
Sleep, thou thief, yet larger giver,
   Seven hours taking, giving seventeen,
Though our days beyond the river
   Shall not need a sleep between ;
Sleep, to my couch come, lie
   Over me, sleep !
Rover in clover, shy
   Are you to creep
Far to the place, where mid
   Cypresses sorrow
Doseless with closeless lid
   Weepeth till morrow :
Sleep comes not, dreams flow, flow
   Sore dreams, and so,
Weeping or sleeping, woe
   Knoweth but woe.
As in dust the cast-off form
Still is riddled by the worm,
So in sleep the sore-heart's brain
Writhes in images of pain.
Is there any pillow for woe ? "

SLEEP.

" You have now a feather one pressed,
But no poppy pillow below
Can misery find, nor go
   To sleep in an angel's breast."

EDWARD.

" Such a sound, as one hears when high
　O'er some rock-bound billowy coast,
Now sounds in mine ears, as I lie,
Or tumble, and fever, and sigh,
　Or moan, like one tempest-tossed.
Till as south-wind gusty blows
　Into clouded morning and dies,
I late find disturbed repose
　Full of dreams ; and about to rise
From crushed pillow and crumpled bed,
　Like a sun which vapour shrouds,
Both my face and eyes are red,
And, like my heart, my head
　Aches wrapped about with clouds."

SLEEP.

" Yet air a sense of freshening coolness takes ;
A wave of day on the horizon breaks ;
Now rise, immortal, and behold the sun,
And learn of him with energy to run."

By wingéd dreams attended, sleep retires
While chill hours still surround night's waning fires.
　　　Should weary life seem vain,
　　　　And through all the years
　　　One long sense of pain,
　　　Running, never rain
　　　　Off in any tears,
　　　The slowest life is brief,
　　　　Brief the longest ill :
　　　Though hoping little, live,
　　　　Work—it is God's will ;
Seek only facts—to know what is, and must
　Or may be done, not merely ought to be ;
And, if thou hast a heart, not quite distrust
　But ask it to enjoy thy work with thee.

CANTO VIII.

IN country now, while only gentle floods
Make music unto silent hills and woods,
Through dusky œther grayish hues appear
Broad pathway clearing for high sun's career.
Aside they cast shades envious of night,
And bury blinded stars in shrouding light.
Each pointed ray shoots up a panting stream,
While nature drinks strong life from every beam ;
And all along far horizontal line
Ten thousand stars immaculately shine.
Brave sun, uprising from his laughing bed,
Throws off his shoulder-clouds, and bares his head ;
Dissolves rank sluggish mists in ruddy glow,
And pours pure flooding light on all below ;
Ha ! scattering glory through each leafy shade
Glads every haunter fresh of wakeful glade.
Bird, beast, and man, in lively ardour gay,
Frankincense offer upon shrine of day ;
While young delight, too powerful to restrain,
Bursts into sound from all the glowing train,
Pours in a rush of rapture o'er the land,
And swells in triumph at yon sun's command.

I still my days and nights all round pursue,
Peace seeking in the toil, I still renew
With no more passion for the thing that's done
Than locomotives have, which fastest run.
Uncle, who guest has of the Canon been,
Comes to prescribe for my catarrh of spleen.

UNCLE.

"Christmas with me and Easter with thy mother,
Wont to be passed, have missed thee lately."

→

EDWARD.

"Other
Distractions not so kindly held me here."

UNCLE.

" Yet thy dear mother needs thee much, I fear.
And pardon me, if I assume to know
What the distractions, which absorb you so.
To work for work's sake into break of day,
Exhaust your powers only to give them play,
Can this be wisdom—save for motive wise
With lamp still blinking to invade morn's skies?
Or is it pleasure, more thy powers to tax
And night divert instead, not soul relax,
Society frequent, with careless ease
Equally men delight and women please,
Like Ariel, ready for most varied part
With all the seeming of but ne'er a heart,
Brilliant as day is long, as night is broad,
Another Epicurus, little god,
Proudly to charioteer a reinless mind
Amused with state and study of mankind ?"

EDWARD.

" Steals over me a languor, worse than pain.
Women have I exhausted, used up men ?
To know society now bad at sight,
The glittering thing I have weighed, and find it light. ·
Even work no more has zest ; all days seem same,
Weary when eager now, and bore when tame."

UNCLE.

" Without one longing wish or earnest choice,
In all life's interests without a voice,
Save the one yearning cry, not unsublime,
For more and more to kill and pass the time,
You traverse vainly curious of shows
Aimless and joyless, life's one hope its close,
Into six feet of grave to drop and be,
Happy if nothing worse, nonentity."

EDWARD.

" Abhorrent that."

UNCLE.

      " So onward drawn and weak,
You more excitement still intenser seek ;
Range ocean, weary of it in the past
And in the present sick.   The time at last,
I looked for you, has come when you should know
In work no pleasure and in pleasure woe.
Earth and all in it God for you has cursed."

EDWARD.

" Why not at once then let the bubble burst ? "

UNCLE.

" Nature most strangely unto death allots
Her shadiest, loneliest, and loveliest spots,
Whose beauty lures to unsuspected graves
Man, who more open danger safely braves.
Civilization hath like hid offence,
Mind overstrains with thought, with feeling sense ;
Boasts of its splendours, and is cause occult
Of squalors, those contrast with and insult.
Dames aux Camelias reckless lives consume,
Which, full of pleasures, dare affront the tomb ;
While virtuous loves, inordinately strong,
Whose objects blighted perish old and young,
See earlier joys becoming later woes,
And shudder at prospective pains of close.
Being, to circumstance becoming strange,
Has to adapt itself and freely change.
I find that changed you, unadapted, slight
The world of good still left for your delight,
Ills to endure, and wrongs 'twere good to right."

EDWARD.

" In all the universe of space and time
Form is unstable, feeling pantomime.
I doubt all adaptation, deprecate
Physical, mental, moral, social state.

Can happiness prevail where discord rules ;
True goodness in a paradise of fools ;
Beauty, or knowledge in this rift of breath,
This tourbillon of time, and dance of death ?
By Magdalen channel from Magellan straits
   One issues between Westward granite hills
And Southward desolation on grim fates—
   Beyond the main isles countless scattered ills,
Rocks on which ocean rages without rest ;
And passes then 'twixt Furies East and West,
While breakers Northward all are ghastly gay,
And well by sailors named ' The Milky Way.
At sight of coast so dire, man holds his breath
And after dreams of peril, shipwreck, death.
The Milky Way in heaven as dread may be ;
Are we but surer of near misery ?
Are man and nature cursed ?   Can God be good ?
Is there a God indeed, or understood ?"

UNCLE.

" Doubt, if you will, that you can know
All heights of bliss, all depths of woe,
But never doubt there is a faith
Which triumphs over life and death.
Do right, and let it be well done,
And have no cause from God to run.
Believe that good is the intent,
 Purpose and outcome of event,
 Though in God's eyes the heavens are not clean
And conscience will no mortal screen,
But chides with hope to quicken good,
And pricks with goad to let bad blood.
Give penitential blush to night,
And glow of prayer to morning light,
So may thy lifelong journey be
Propitious, and closed graciously."

Mother had Christmastide with Uncle sped ;
   I also wont was with her to repair,

But London claimed me, Easter also stayed.
  Autumn now calls me home to give her care
  Much needed—more than I have been aware :
A chill unheeded to disease has tended.
  Gently her chamber entering I stand there
Myself unnoted and with breath suspended.
So shocked at what I see, now know has long impended.

Ah ! when we last had parted, there had been
  A sense of discord : for I had disdained
What I had heard her urge, and in her seen
  Of scorn for Lucy.   Though not unrestrained,
  I scorn as deep or deeper entertained,
And yet misliked to see it in another.
  I might have known, the shame and loss, which pained—
Affecting me, might also hurt this other,
Who loved me more than all ; and pardoned such a mother.

    And now she knows me come and near
      All smiling, not amiss,
    To stay an unavailing tear.
      I stoop, so weak she is,
    To lips, that kiss and whisper true,
      " I've loved thee with a love,
    Which never here a winter knew,
      And none shall know above."

    Three days of doubt, and in and out,
      And I am reading there,
    When falls a hush, an 'twere a rush
      Of death upon the air.
    " Mother, how art thou ?   Mother dear,
     Mother, own mother speak."
    A look of heaven's quiet cheer
      Lies loving on her cheek ;
    But dulled life's sun in eyes, that eath
      Open, and rayless show
    Clouded as mirror by a breath.
    Is it the dull damp chill of death
      Upon what once could glow ?

Deftly can death his darts disguise.
  Sudden or slowly sped,
They shock with agonized surprise
  The lovers of the dead.
" Mother ! " and silence.   Should she say,
  Or motion but a word,
I'll welcome it as break of day
  Doth carol of a bird.

My body shudders with a chill,
  And fear perturbs my soul,
While stayed mine eye above her, still
  As star above the pole—
The frozen pole.   Is it in awe,
  Or is it hoping so,
The little light, to warm and thaw
  The everlasting snow?

" Mother, thou art not in a dream ?
  Oh ! mother, mother mine ! "
Stiff icicles her fingers seem,
  And her wrist gives no sign.
My cheek is at her lips, but all
  My wishes find no breath.
Her arm I raise, and let it fall,
  And know that this is death.

And is she dead ?   And may I weep ?
  And have I now no fear,
That my distress may rive her sleep,
  And penetrate death's ear ;
The spirit fled recall and break
  The rapture of the blest,
Where angel harps high music make
  In palaces of rest ?

Ah ! on that brow and braided hair ·
  The parting soul hath left—
On cheek and lip, as life were there,
  A smile for the bereft,

And, save for mine unheeded cry,
  I might not deem her dead ;
But in her life the lightest sigh,
  Which left its wish unsaid,
Her ear interpreted, as Heaven
  Interpreteth desire,
Giving, forgiving seven times seven,
  Till angels might admire.

'Tis wild to think if e'er we wronged,
  With folly surely blind,
A spirit mild, that only longed
  To do us something kind ;
To know the life on earth is o'er,
  And, though renewed in heaven,
We can confession make no more,
  And plead to be forgiven.

Here Love's own Sprite appealed to me.

SPRITE OF LOVE.

" Oh, man ! and is it thus with thee ? "

EDWARD.

" Nay, I remember now,
When nearer to eternity
  Than love dared fancy, how
She kissed, and whispered—'twas adieu,
  " I've loved thee with a love,
Which never here a winter knew,
  And none shall know above."

SPRITE OF LOVE.

" It is grievous to be so forgiven;
  Yet exquisite the bliss
To know, you in the gain of heaven
  May count upon her kiss.
There also is a timely grace
  In the untimely pain ;

For, folding thee in their embrace,
   Her loving cares remain ;
Her warnings, echoing in thine ears,
   To heart an entrance crave ;
Shall all her counsels, prayers, and tears,
   Be buried in her grave ?
Wilt thou for Lucy grief-full moan,
   Languish, and perish for her lie ;
Or harden to a heart of stone,
   A cynic live, a doubter die ? "

I answered not ; for I remembered not
Or Lucy, or my wrongs ; had love forgot—
Even its misery ; now lived to teen
The memory of a mother, that had been.
Uncle soon comes to me, and both are brave
To lower her with tears, and look into her grave.

When rolls through solemn air deep toll of bell
   To hush the town, and fills the holden ear,
Is it of feast or fast, of heaven or hell,
   In passing time what is it that you hear ?
Being is wonderful, wonderful, wonderful,
   Anyhow, anytime, anywhere ;
But it is wonderful, wonderful, wonderful,
   Seven times wonderful so, then, there.

When life and love and death together meet,
   And you are burying what love holds dear ;
And, rising with your dead, your prayers beat
   Their wings at heaven's gate, while graves close here,
Being is wonderful, wonderful, wonderful,
   Wonderful, anywise, when, or where ;
Wonderful, wonderful, wonderful, wonderful,
   Nine times wonderful so, then, there.

When, leaving love and life behind, you fly
   To love and life beyond, and Christ is near,

And in His bosom now entranced you lie,
  And all heaven's wedding-bells ring in your ear,
Being is wonderful, wonderful, wonderful,
  Wonderful, wonderful, anywhere ;
Wonderful, wonderful, wonderful, wonderful,
  Past all say must be wonderful there.

So had I felt it once, and now recall,
  When lone in Paris of a Lord's Day morn,
Quitting the noisy throng of Rue Royale
  For deepest quiet, of a back-court born
  And chapel there, I heard the Gospel horn
Sounding the resurrection of the dead,
  And love for all the living, not forlorn
In God and Christ, His Son, their living head,
And of the Catholic Church, which He has loving wed.

And strangely now of all the Muses she
Most given to vanity and revelry,
The Muse of France, forgetting gallant days
And courteous nights, and seeking quiet ways,
Came to me with her various lyre, and clad
In sober gray, for she was something sad,
Sang me of Lamartine a sacred scroll,
Fitting and filling my receptive soul.

MUSE OF FRANCE.

HYMN OF LAMARTINE.

" Worn and lack-lustre eyed all through weeping and watch-
    ing for day,
Like one beaten and ready his arms down submissive
    to lay,
  ' Vainly,' Lamartine cried, ' morn beginneth to glow :
Nature only seems, miracle-working, betraying our sighs,
 Lately night, now vermilion in tint and with grayish blue
    eyes,
  Smiles only in mockery so.

" ' Nothing true and not anything false, all illusive and vain,
Lucubration of heart is, of hope but prolonging the strain;
   Sole realities here are our cark and our care.
What we designate life is of lightning a flash in the eyes,
A bright spark by which soul is scarce dazzled, before it now
      flies
   And is gone to enkindle elsewhere.

" ' More we open our eyes, more is night more exceeding
      profound.
God is nothing but only a dream-word the world to expound,
   An abysm more obscure on which launcheth the soul ;
And all floats, and all falls, just as lightly the dust in hot
   · days
Whirlabout is in clouds, from the puffy and pluffy high-
      ways
   Trodden up by splay foot of a fool.'

" Having said, he in consciously envious misplaced regard
Held low being, unfavoured by reasoning lofty and starred,
   But whose peace is too deep for a dream to impair :
On the ox, or the stone in the furrow his eyelashes root,
While appears this desire in his eyes—' Unto rock, unto
      brute,
   Ah ! would that I similar were.'

" Wide then errant, as eye of the pilot when lost he
      demands
Of the floating abyss a sure route to invisible lands,
   Stayed his eye all at once fix'dly set on a grave—
Grave dear, how dear ! reminder of bitter, how bitter !
      pains,
Where all hallowed and coverlet grass of a mother's remains
   In tears due of hamlet springs brave.

" There did he, when her angel, in likeness pure womanly
      veiled,
Had in light increate, had in God all its being exhaled,

As one blows out a lamp at the coming of morn,
In the shadow of altars, she loved through all time and all
 change,
Safe for her hollow out an abode low and narrow of range—
 A gate to the other sojourn.

" There in hope now, and slumbering lies she, whose smile,
 though unsought,
Found his eyes at the hour so supreme when time vanished
 in thought,
 Heart, fond source of his own, and dear form, that conceived,
Bosom warm, which had nursed him with milk and all
 tenderfulness,
Fondling arms, which a cradle were full of all darling
 caress,
 And lips whose each word he believed.

" There twelve lustres, dark, chastened repose after energies
 spent
In the life-long endeavour to act out with single intent
 A delight in all inward as outward morality,
Aspirations so high up to God ever mountingly streaming,
Faith so lively in death—in itself thus a virtue, and seeming
 An earnest of immortality ;

" Nights unwinkingly brave and to sufferers friendly in
 deed ;
Days of stint self-denying to succour some absolute need,
 With the tear ever ready to mingle with tear ;
Such most ardent consuming of sighs for a holier land,
Yet the burden of life long to carry a patience so grand,
 Whose crown was found nowhere here.

" All, alas ! to what end ? That a hole in the dust should
 belie
To absorb and for ever embosom humanity,
 Low and villainous furrows on it become fat ;
That the verdure of death, which now velvets her hillock,
 should e'en

Underneath his own feet there upsprouting more dense
   grow and green,
   Enough were some ashes for that.

" Never, never thus merely to brighten three steps of the
   earth
Would a God to such excellent glory have glad given
   birth,
   To so farseeing soul heroical breath.
Not misfallen his glance on memorial head-stone of
   doom ;
Oh, great virtue ! thine aspect more powerful is than the
   tomb,
   And more evident than death.

" And his soul, edified by such witness of wonder at hand,
Now delivered from Castle of Doubt in Debateable Land,
   Light his heart can the torch high of hope relume.
Happy he to whom God hath a mother so virtuous given ;
Life is hard then in vain, and in vain is death bitter : of
   heaven
   What son can doubt by her tomb ? "

The tender Muse then, to her lyre restrung,
Soft rhymes Berangeresque most sweetly sung.
" Virtues are ways of human love
   Taught by the Love Divine, and seem,
Connecting earth with heaven above,
   Steps in the ladder of Jacob's dream,
Or very feathers in love's wings—
Not love, but that which from it springs,
Bearing all healing song-fully
To the bosom of humanity :
And raising then to God, restoring all,
Recovering human nature from its fall.
Love in the heart, like unity in space,
Attests the Omnipresent God of Grace.
In loving touch with Him soul cannot perish :
   But living room can find for faith,

And virtues in God's Acre cherish
  Unvanquished by the sting of death.

" Though natural affection quails,
Love lives to worst the last of ails ;
And, raising virtues to the skies,
Gives promise to contending sighs.

" Who in yon cemetery dwells,
And more than sun the gloom dispels,
With step so light, so riant grace,
And goodness in bright eye and face?
Despairing, her detractors see
Such dimpled freshness ; Love is she,
Pride of her father too, the brave
Beautiful daughter of the Grave.

" Her window that, and we are ware
Of birds now warbling in cage there,
While flutter over tomb below
Two of a shining whitest show,
Like dove from heaven, in sight of men,
Hovering o'er Christ. To whom pertain
Those two white doves ? To Love, the brave,
Beautiful daughter of the Grave.

" You hear her laughter break with morn,
Where lilacs busk that bosky bourne.
See ! how the plants to beauty grow ;
What deathless vigour myrtles show ;
While amaranths bright blushing stand
Offering a garland to her hand,
Roses for Love all blowing brave
For the beautiful daughter of the Grave.

" Her roof-tree vined the wall o'ertops :
The falling night in wonder stops.
A voice divine, of love a song,
A voice of gladness holds you long

In joy, or trance.   Who, say you, can
Other than love so sing to man,
Pride of her father too, the brave,
Beautiful daughter of the Grave?

" Under her roof is fête to-day:
Her father giveth her away.
She weds: the wedding feast is spread :
She weds a minstrel.   Wish God-speed
To both—to Love and Song.   God raise
Children of song to be a praise
To Love, her father's pride, the brave,
Beautiful daughter of the Grave ;
Travail and joy to her although through loss—
To True-love, daughter of the Grave and Cross."

I sang consenting to her strain.

EDWARD.

" Who loving dies shall live again.
Yes, heavenward looking, earthly love
Can even sing, and death reprove,
Approving it as in accord
Joining with life to praise life's lord,
Till songs of love become a rouse
Befitting the very charnel house.
'Twas Christmas Eve in church and out:
   Mass celebrating stood the priest,
But in God's Acre, round about,
   Studded with crosses, where worms feast,
And Swithins mid the poor low lie
Still teaching lively charity,
Young men and maidens over graves
Catches of love sang, gleeful staves,
And the priest joined them : Who shall say,
That he from prayer passed to play?
Nigh fifteen centuries ago,
On idle walls of caverned woe

In tomb of Christian Antioch
Artist graved monogram of Christ in rock,
And Τοῦτο νικᾷ wrote—this conquers all,
   And everything : for Christ is love.
Immortal words ! While temples round them fall,
   Rock-hewn in tomb they lasting prove,
Love conquers death.   Immortal stone !
Making those words its very own."

I ceased.   She knew I would not quarrel,
And dropped upon my brows her laurel,
   " To True-love wedding me," she said ;
Then signed me with the rooked Cross,
Which disavaunces every loss,
   And further had her theme displayed,
But here she whimpered ; and the use
Of such frank tears proclaimed the Muse
Celtic, impassioned, knowing well
Our devil-angelled way to hell ;
The waxen wings, we spread to rise ;
Our efforts passionate and cries,
While phantom good we bad pursue,
False follow wide the only true,
And raise, that we to heaven may climb,
Ladders whose rounds are rising crime :
The pity of it all, I wist,
How at a Sepulchre wept Christ,
His God-forsaken cross, and all
That He had come by through our fall.
And though her eyes were quickly dried
By rapture, not to be denied—
Admiring rapture full of love,
Which seemed to see Him throned above,
She could not more the theme pursue,
But rose to have a nearer view,
Vanishing from me.   And my heart
   Went with her, where she seemed to go,
Upward and upward.   Nay, why start ?
   I found, and stayed with Him below,

← 2 E

In whom such comfort do we find,
    Whose love consoles us in such fashion,
We grow into His very mind,
In fellowship with Him are kind,
    All tender mercy, and compassion ;
Till Time's most imperious ocean,
    And its biggest billow, death,
Lose all aspect of commotion,
    Like becalmed Gennesareth.

No outward bravery, but inward treat
Of pure affections, their own happy sweet,
Outgoing only with their like to meet,
Or like excite, or better find in thee,
Great Heart of Love, Good God of them and me,
Controlled me now.   And, Lucy, unreturned,
It may have been a fancy to be spurned,
But, skirting her enclosure walls,
I saw her in her lighted halls ;
And each accompanying word
With purls of music from the harpsichord,
Which she in seeming played,
In seeming strayed
To my stedfast ear, and stole
Upon my powerless soul—
    A gentle captive to a welcome yoke.
So hears the wildered wight,
Listening in full starry night,
    Low matins of hid fairy folk,
And twice a hundred wimpling rills
On dusky, lone, and superstitious hills.
In Merlin magic-crystal ball
So Britomart saw Artegal :
Seemed I of power possessed sublimer
Than Soulis, Michael Scott, or Thomas, the Rhymer.
And as in shade of scaleless splendours hidden
The Peri, lost to heaven and thence forbidden,
Bursts of untasted joys most holy
Joins with sequacious note most melancholy,

My heart most sighful song achieved,
Which scantly through a moment lived.
Aspendius, the seer,
Harped gently, for his soul's own ear,
What none but he himself whole-souled could hear ;
My song, on air thus feeding, died
Unknown to Lucy, but not so denied.

EDWARD'S SONG.

" ' Goodbye,' and God be with thee : stay !
  ' Adieu,' and now to God is given
One for whom I, though cast away,
  Can wish that earth may still seem heaven.
I go, yet cannot ; like the sea,
  Receding with returning swell,
I go, whate'er my lot may be,
  Still wishing, ' Lucy, fare thee well.'

" O'er dead Patroclus when Achilles moaned,
His goddess Mother heard, and shrieked, and groaned.
Assembled all the Nereids of the deep,
And every ocean Nymph with her to weep ;
Thronged was the ocean cave ; each head was bowed ;
Each smote her breast, and swelled the lamentation loud ;
And when they all o'er sympathetic seas
Came to Achilles, she, her son to please,
Promised corruption should not taint, nor worm
Gnaw of Patroclus there the breathless form.
When too from God man fell, the Son was grieved ;
As of a brother, much beloved, bereaved.
Truth, justice, goodness, holiness, and power
Combined with wisdom in that fateful hour,
And every loyal virtue, pity, shame,
Mercy, humility with patience came,
Charity, magnanimity, fortitude,
Who still in heaven palaced now stand good,
Peace, righteous wrath ; and hand in hand all ran,
Summoned by God, with Christ to raise the man.

Life were a riddle else.   Doubt, spread thy wings;
Faith, courage take and penetrate all things.
I ware am of sore sorrow, weary care,
But overflowing pity everywhere,
And a dim sense of heaven still in air.

"Time flies, and stays for none,
Shall be, is now, then gone;
Yet evermore shall last
The future, present, past
Of the self-conscious 'I,'
Till self in it shall die.
Along the grooves of change,
With metamorphose strange
Transfiguring decays
Into still better days,
Becoming more and more,
   Felt Being shall be known
For all it was before
   In all it shall have grown,
And still shall hope to grow.
Past, present, future so :
Whence come we, whither go ?
Let time's clocks strike the hours they steal,
   ONE still all hours in heaven shall be ;
In being now we dream or feel
As we had timeless been, and still
Through all becoming look for weal
   In an untimed eternity."

Methought I now had vantage ground attained
Of steady light : but was it felt—not feigned?
In chambers sitting lone I late one night
Attacked was, in, I trust, last open fight
And forlorn hope, by Mephistopheles,
Changed somewhat, since I last had heard his hiss,
Some strong points of the New World in his face
To match its younger time and faster race,

Cute features shaded by a slouching hat,
In his whole body not one ounce of fat.
His first word " Gold," he, tossing overhead
A guinea—he had bitten, and looked, and said
That it was good—then catching it, now dresses
His thoughts in suits, he hard upon me presses.

MEPHISTOPHELES.

" Gold is a royal thing,
Glitters even upon wing."

EDWARD.

" Croesus lost it glittering.
It melts, as well as glitters,
And though it may never rust,
In flux is golden bitters,
In fix is gathering dust,
Since wealth breeds many cares
To increase what we acquire
Through pulseless declining years
For we know not whom, or heirs
Sowing their wild oats or tares,
And loving us for hire.
And hope after hope departs,
Which youth had cherished, till old,
When we look into heavy hearts,
Grown dull, and hard, and cold,
Still felt by fits and starts,
We there find nothing but gold."

MEPHISTOPHELES.

" Be thy pursuit then fame,
If gold is so hungry a slot.
It noble is, and no shame
To cherish the kindly thought,
And a so fair desire
To be in all men's mouths, and feel,
You are a taste, which they acquire
And portion of the common weal."

EDWARD.

"Ah ! fame is a sickly flower,
  Whose life is in the breath
Of a fickle, fretful power,
Hot and cold within the hour,
Blowing in a summer shower
  The chilling hail of death.
For, to win a world's heart,
  You must with it sympathize,
Never from its practise start,
  Nor above its maxims rise,
Be a worldly thing, and part
  Of the tinsel, you despise :
Only seem the world above,
  Be below it, and its slave,
Hunger, labour for its love,
  Though the passion may deprave,
Treachery and slander prove,
  Ruthless opposition brave ;
And some morning find the name
  You have won, and think to wear,
Turned into a blistering shame,
And in every mouth a name
  To be spit out anywhere."

MEPHISTOPHELES.

"Than fame a more splendid allure
Power can itself assure."

EDWARD.

" Have you been abroad perchance
Leading Jonathan a rare dance ;
Tammany Halls directed ; trusts,
Rings, rails, jails, fire-engines, lusts,
Towns and States controlled, and laid
Bets on every card you played ;
Handled all the reins of rule ;
Filled your pockets, been no fool ;

Name to conjure by become,
Yet yourself been seemly dumb,
Clever fellow ! well, you beat,
And are dangerous to meet.

" But I hold such labour vain,
　When with it alone we glow ;
Ay, or labour for the gain,
　We can make of it, or know
Only to be greater men,
　And not better, wise for show.
Yea, Babylon's great lord,
　From empire when estranged
To herd with brutes, and browse the sward,
　Was ne'er than I more changed.

" I know not now a man self-made,
But as God gifted him and lent him aid ;
I deem not now of aught as true,
That I have done it, or can do ;
I think not now to be profound,
Or rich, or powerful, or renowned.
Earth has not any motive power
To draw my worship for an hour ;
Cross are our purposes, I seek no more
To win a world, which I so wooed before ;
Nor care I anything to be,
If not in God, nor God in me."

MEPHISTOPHELES.

" Yet is brain a knowing power,
Wise to entertain the hour,
Till Ulysses find a way
Back to his Penelope."

EDWARD.

" Penelope ! With devilish craft of tongue,
　You other than Penelope intend.

But think not converse further to prolong.
  She, whom I loved and will love to the end,
Shall never suffer wrong from craft of mine.
Hence ! to the Hell, thou hast risen from, down ! thou
    swine."

Suns and worlds to no holiday owed
  A sense of beatification,
But to woman, who put a period
  To the six days of creation,
And afterwards bore a Son to God,
  And crowned the seventh's ovation.
A mother, whose regard I prize,
In heaven still loves me, and believes me wise.

CANTO I.

FORTUNE forsook my love, but not my toil
   Through passing years of unallayed distress
With all the gain rewarding midnight oil,
   That longer burns for me companionless.
   Lucy, still dear, has had her rich success ;
Although I shun her, while the season's show
   Centres around her reigning loveliness.
We meet to speak not, pass with distant bow,
Or sit like sphinxes paired in undiscoursive woe.

Notably gayest she amongst the gay,
   Too recklessly, too strenuously blest,
As sun, which high in heaven accustomed way
   Mid worlds admiring holds, while spots attest
   A fitful trouble in the glowing breast :
And to her husband iceberg can oppose
   More than sufficient rigour, as its crest
The Matterhorn erects with pride, and shows
Unyielding to embrace, and shakes off winter's snows.

Yet may the wiles of fashion full restore
   The utter woman in her frenzying wide
The courtly realm, she rules by smiling o'er.
   From fires, that kindle|round her glowing pride
   Letting the warmth into her chilled heart glide,
Ah, should she heat to more than seven times seven,
   Will she a home without the bliss abide ?
And never woman was by husband driven
To good on earth, though oft to hopes of it in heaven.

EDWARD.

" If of material things, beyond strict sense,
We theorise may with intelligence,
Predict events, and hesitate to trust
Our calculations even when found just,
Why may not speculation penetrate
Into the conscious immaterial state,
A God conceive, and evolution trace,
Like prayer answered by creative grace,
Progressive ever from and up to Him,
Whose is the Jacob-ladder, which we climb?
Though at the ghostly formulas, they raise,
Some trembling abdicate their reason, praise
Not God but creed—with oaths so mocking God—
I swear by Him, who is no passing mode."

PARTISAN.

" Do you, a mortal, such omniscience claim?
On wing of science soar to lower aim.
Lightnings and thunders Jovine we admire;
More fondly moved then, list Apollo's lyre,
Survey all Nature, feel its grace and power,
Most too when nakedest, at noontide hour,
Or starred by night; and with blind sense of bliss
Conceive the Universe, say what it is.
The mountains are the pillars of our home,
The prairies its floor, the heavens its dome
Wherein we dwell, The Unknowable beyond,
Which some call God—a fable old and fond.
In flood, and field, wood, wild, earth, sea, fire, air,
Below, above, abroad, oh! everywhere
Abundance garners plenty for all years,
And foresight careless slumbers void of fears.
And dreams salute us, dreams of regal port,
How, science aiding, we can earthquakes sport,
And mountains overthrow; or deltas raise,
And rivers scatter from long wonted ways;
As heaven, when swathed in fierce though noiseless fire,

Earth and the woods and plains in flames attire;
Strong haughty ocean rule, invade the skies;
Yea, snatch the lightnings for our own emprise,
About our wish instruct them forthwith hurled,
Our messengers of flame, around the world.
Man in his mansion stands, sublimely small,
Conscious and proud of being Lord of All."

The Canon having joined us, now our guide,
To utterance last of Partisan replied.

BISHOP DESIGNATE.

" Most minim Lord, yet great in that he knows
He is, and, while to matter and its shows
Sensibly bound, can still, in spirit more,
One God in each and over all adore
Winning him out of self to drink delight
From nature's double-handled cup of might.
Her chisel puts Canova's own to blush,
She too seems only Mistress of the brush,
And is so exquisite a poetess
That her Niagaras grow to loveliness;
While sun rays glory round it as it rolls,
Or standeth still a while above the poles,
Pouring a Benjamin portion of its glow
Forgetfully, or lovingly on all below.
And hast thou ne'er, thy spirit to inform,
From heights beyond the clouds o'er-looked a storm,
And, overwhelmed, as thy incurious gaze
Through rack has seen man dot the distant ways,
The curious problem, Pascal never solved,
' How mean, if great he is,' awhile revolved?
Though nobler far may be most tiny midge,
Than higher soaring crest of Alpine ridge,
When welcome calm hath passing storm subdued,
And fire, air, water, earth have peace renewed,
I too am drawn into the pact divine;
See all in God—their Maker also mine.

Sunned heights, in vision round me, giants, rise
Soothing mine awe with smiles sublimely wise.
Outstretched mine arms, I am not there alone ;
I shout out, 'Brothers !' and the claim all own ;
For not an echo but gives back the call,
And 'Brothers ! Brothers ! Brothers !' rings from all.
Still always finite, less than faith believes,
Is this rotund of space, which man perceives :
For law and love implicitly appear
    Making, sustaining all variety :
The Absolute and Infinite—God is here,
    Eternal Principal of Unity.
Thus man may lone on self retire, and find
Great God in reason speaking to his mind,
In conscience to his heart, yet equal know
Him as The One in all above, below,
In the dumb stone, and in the thundering sky. ·

PARTISAN.

" Ha, fear in man may father oft a lie,
And moveth him, when horror is abroad
In natural forms, to own in each a god.
Ocean, an-hungered, fleets and hosts discussed ;
Earth shook, and cities shuddered into dust ;
High heaven thundering the welkin cracked,
And wild with bolts and flames the world attacked ;
And man, of nature's stormy powers the sport,
Weak in defence, to worship had resort ;
Heaven he deified, air, earth, and sea,
And blindly reverenced whom he could not flee ;
Or cursed the powers his knees seemed to confess,
More likely foes than friends to feebleness.
In Forest Black, while deepening night advanced,
I lone astray once on an open chanced,
And saw an ancient crone, whose bending back
Under a sheaf of sticks seemed more a stack.
Over unsounding sward unseen I stept,
Till sudden on her ear strange English leapt

Inquiring of the way. Ah ! how she shook,
Crossed, blessed herself, cursed me, but dared no look.
She fancied me a fiend on fiendish work :
'Neath fairest seeming may all evil lurk,
And might in that lone place ; and in her breast
Fixed dread of it was its indent attest."

EDWARD.

" Still happy may be homes, most wildernessed.
Not the wild ass, than desert not less shy,
Not Pringle more the desert loved, than I
To shut the city out with all its sound.
Not far from London, yet lone silence round,
These lofty pines seem plumes upon the hearse
Of the last mortal in the Universe,
While sighs of winds are as a murmurous chime—
Upon eternity the wash of time.
Ah ! dearly here I feel with God alone,
    And printed see His laws in all the ways
And steps of Nature mounting to His throne ;
    Her beauty too, her grandeur, these are praise—
Praise, which in rising upward carries me,
As I were all an almost extasy."

BISHOP DESIGNATE.

" Deep reverence resides in solitudes,
As know the thoughtful, who invade the woods,
Which seem a God to meditate, or seek.
Hark ! did not now a loitering Zephyr speak,
As through the rustled leaves it breathed around,
And all things murmur no uncertain sound
Of something grand, if undefined, supreme,
The stutter of sublime though tongue-tied dream ? "

PARTISAN.

" With instruments and voices intertwined,
 In sense of harmony a heaven we find,
 Feel too in hushed, untroubled space profound
 And the still absence of particular sound :

2 F

For as all colours mingle in one white,
So in deep silence do all sounds unite.
But such lone, deaf, dead unity obscure,
Though mind may think, is heart-break long to endure ;
Therefore vague life some everywhere repeat,
Deem universal nature animate.
Wide o'er creation, as the wind sweeps stour,
Spirits are scattered broadcast by the boor."

BISHOP DESIGNATE.

" He conscious that intelligence with will
Is life and motion, can a bosom thrill,
And may a world, conceives, unreasoning,
A spiritual force in everything.
Now ignorance, now terror images
Its horrors thus, and thus its mysteries.
Where then man's lightning wielding thunder-hand,
When lost to soul is its own self-command ?
But it was heavenly thought, divine desire,
Sublimed the sad barbarian to aspire
On nature's powers with an untiring soar
Up to Jehovah—One for evermore.
The Chieftain Shepherd on Chaldæan plains,
Where through long night lone starlit silence reigns,
Commercing with the skies in great resolve
The riddle of the Universe to solve,
Yearning with prayer, saw the God, long sought,
High o'er the calming chaos of his thought
Sunlike arise on being, space, and time,
The Lord of heaven and earth to reign sublime."

PARTISAN.

" We dare not trust each simulance of sense,
Or hasty audit of intelligence ;
Phenomena and noumena alike
Are vaguely immanent, and feebly strike.
Feeling and thought are never in accord ;
There is no absolutely certain word ;

Proof is beyond attainment, and design
A purpose broken all along the line.
False to its worshippers was reason young,
Or rather sense to thought, which trusted long.
Mortals imagined outward seeming true,
Built on the dream tall towers of fancies new,
Unstable as the base from which they rose,
And with it shattered by Baconian blows.
Men now take nothing on the faith of show,
   Trust but what by experiment they test,
Doubt to believe, and first unlearn to know,
   Admit no theory till found the best,
No more roll suns around an earthly throne,
Dread a land's end, seek a philosopher's stone ; "

EDWARD.

" Nor elephants, nor tortoises adjust,
But safely hang in space a world of dust ;
Chaos describe, and thoughtfully resolve
How out of it a system could evolve ;
What every orb is in itself, its play,
If young, or old, and when to pass away ;
And how, and why through coruscating space
Systems their motions vary ; seek what place
The centre claims, and, since we know no end,
How link these orbs and systems, whither tend ;
For gravitation cannot self-depend.
We seek and, seeking still, from first to last
Find none but God, from whom are none out cast ;
By, from, in, to, for whom are all to be
Diversity in that All Unity,
Which we divine to be Divinity,
To which, the more we know, the more we grow,"

PARTISAN.

" Into an infinite, which we foreshow
By predicating Prothyle Nothingness,
Whence we presume the Universe to guess,

And prophesy, from what hath never been,
All that e'er was, is, or shall more be seen ;
From formless points to cliffs with clouds astride
Through shapes unnumbered seemly crystals guide ;
Grass, grain, flower, fruit, leaf, wood from earth compel,
Give law to—make a vegetable cell ;
Units chaotic into order plan ;
Mineral form, vegetable, monkey, man."

BISHOP DESIGNATE.

" In man material creation finds
Climax and close.   This truth is in all minds,
' How fearfully and wonderfully made,
How deep the foundations of his Being laid.'
Our embryonic cell, like that of worm,
Or plant, life's earliest material form,
Through all the stages of creation rose,
And unto Science all the manner shows.
Though now we hands have, nature must prevail,
And still appends a rudimental tail.
Though we have tongues, and speak from earliest years,
The dumb brute, in us still, may shape our ears.
For Child of Nature, Man, is sum of all,
Mineral, vegetable, animal.
To his long making, Stars have come and gone,
And planets froze, or frizzled in a sun ;
And living things beyond all count, or scan,
Dying, contributed to fashion man,
Consummated in mated man and wife.
With sage addition for each higher life,
Through fish, amphibian, reptile, mammal, mind,
We become spiritual, God to find,
And know, and learn to love, and mingle so
All things in earth and heaven, and bliss, and woe.
We learn with tool the hand to supersede,
With thought the tongue, which, in our struggling need,
With formal language meeteth growing thought.
Body, to veil us ceasing, is as not.

Soul readeth soul.   We photo the unseen;
Matter dissolves.   God shows in the terrene.
In all material space we nowhere find
A body great as man endowed with mind,
Who in a manner heads it to attest
God in the Flesh, to all men manifest,
Believed on in the world, received to Glory,
Still the old Gospel-climax of all story,
And proper issue of the large design.
Men comprehend, and crown it as divine;
Behold a purpose by their God proposed,
And gradual fulfilled, and part disclosed;
Feel in their constitution the whole plan,
And are evolving spiritual man,
Whom suns and systems boundless point the way
To an eternal and prevailing day."

PARTISAN.

"What Mystery is here!   Six thousand years
Has man to blood been striving and with tears,
Yet who shall penetrate the boundless past,
Inform the present of the first and last,
Where least is wondrous?   Take a crystal up,
A little one, and, lo! it is a cup
Of understanding bottomlessly deep,
In whose unfathomed shades close secrets sleep.
Who shall?   But end of questioning is none.
Oh! fools, that murmur, 'Man the round hath run;
Discovery is something out of date;
Fame's roll is ended; we were born too late.'
Not Mill, nor Darwin, not even Spencer-claims
Can more than postulate a few new names.
Science a babe is, dreaming in the grey
And very early morning of her day,
Evolving an illimitable plan,
Dissolving and revolving God.   But can
This sort of thing delight an honest man?
Though, like the bark which groweth on a tree,
The habit of a thing will grow on thee,

And he, who cheats another, safely may
Count upon cheating his own self some day."

EDWARD.

" Dost thou of Matter, or of Spirit doubt,
Or both ? "

PARTISAN.

          " I scarce know what you talk about.
If Spirit is with Matter, how allied?
If God is, is there anything beside ? "

BISHOP DESIGNATE.

" Self and not-self, in our first conscious thought,
Revealed as interactive, we are taught
That so related, though the while distinct,
Self only known as thus to not-self linked,
Some higher power these originates,
And holds in unity what He creates—
Soul, body, spirit, matter."

PARTISAN.

                    " Still we seem,
Of truth uncertain, walking in a dream ;"

EDWARD.

" But surely one of which a God is fount."

PARTISAN.

" While multitudes their fingers cannot count,
If science everywhere sees infinity,
Learned differ from unlearned but in degree ;
Five, or five millions—which is infinite?
One more surpasses either's little wit."

BISHOP DESIGNATE.

" Yet God at first by intuition known,
In all the many the Uniting One,
Essential Being is, and, making laws,
Is Principle of Unity and cause

By which we rise to an Eternal State
And nature becomes spiritual and great,
Whose method in its darkest episode,
  In quantitative qualitative ways,
Reveals to us and is revealed by God
  Unto His Own and everlasting praise."

PARTISAN.

" Particulars comparing to discern
General laws, we these compare and learn
The whole with them in broader few to find,
These few in broader still, so all to bind
In one, which man calls God, and feels a fool
Really knowing nothing, and at school
Scratching his pate for wit, and raising wool.
Like prospect widening ever as we rise,
Truth phantomlike pursued the further flies,
Till, wisdom growing down to blank distress
Beneath the lowest limit of her guess,
We ignorance avow, but rest postpone,
Knowing but as we see the more unknown ;
Then turn to evolution's wonders, while
Miracle darkens reason with a smile
As onward, upward, ever into higher
And still more implicate all things conspire,
And more involve the common-weal in vain
Progressing into ignorance again.
And one may deem it scarcely worth one's while
A cinerary spirit to beguile,
Consuming it with much so vain desire
Of compassing a Cosmos doomed entire,
While space and time are passing, phase on phase
Rising to set, developing disgrace ;
Yea, in the imminent wreck and rack of all
The Unknown God himself appears to fall."

BISHOP DESIGNATE.

" Exploiting the external, soon we grow
Dissatisfied with all mere outward show ;

Then inward upon self retire to find
Nothing but final vacancy of mind,
Till God appears, the Unity of all,
Present to universal Being and at call.
Forces, no longer combating, combine
Natural with human, human with Divine,
And love becomes the universal shrine—
Word, which with God in the Beginning was,
Was God, Divine Ideal, motive cause
And still intuitive to every thought.
If night, misreading, apprehended not,
It never overcame the Word of Light,
Which Flesh became, and ever shines more bright.
The Love of God in the now risen Son
After Him drawing all, in Him with God made one."

EDWARD.

" To call the Cosmos simply Organism,
Purely material, is an Idiotism ;
Atoms, though indivisible in thought,
  Yet coalesce and greater generate ;
All matter gravitates, yet œther not ;
  Negative elements diminish weight—
Such qualities each other contradict,
And matter so of a quick lie convict.
Let line have length, let surface breadth too boast ;
They fail to form even matter for a ghost.
Point, without parts or magnitude, define
But never deem it a material sign.
From such abstractions none can argue ought,
Save immateriality of thought.
Thence rise to spiritual Being, then
Know Spiritual God in order reign ;
And by the Greater all the less explain.
That protoplasm has senses, thinks, wills, moves,
Absorbs, excretes, grows, reproduces, proves—
From reason parted by incongruous chasm—
Only indifferentiate protoplasm.
The inorganic cannot life bestow,

Without addition to organic grow.
A living organism acts as none,
Nor all of the laws of physics, that roll a sun.
Man is material, yet self-willed, great,
Rational, active, insubordinate.
In the great Universe are beings, more
Than taled in folk or philosophic lore,
Great spiritual powers, which not blind
Place in the mighty Cosmic process find.
A continuity through all we seek,
A link, if hidden, lasting and not weak :
What then but Spiritual, God, The source
Of all material, mental, moral force ? "

PARTISAN.

" Why then unnatural should nature prove,
And storm disturb a world, whose God is love ?
You say of nature, providence attests
How God with it performs His High behests ;
With water irrigates broad waste and dearth,
Or oceans heaves upon an impious earth ;
Winter arrays a genial smiling host,
Or streams of warriors stiffens with His frost ;
Expireth hurricanes, or Zephyrs vague,
And from the land evaporates dews, or plague ;
Billets His frail man on a world so frail,
That falling man thinks primal Nature fell."

BISHOP DESIGNATE.

" Herein of doubt we find the secret core.
Dread we The God of Nature, or ignore,
Admitting doubt of such a God as He,
Soon we go further, say, ' No God can be.'
E'er so denying Him, we misconceive,
And life not worth the living misbelieve.
But, if content can make life good to live,
What right has man to more than God sees good to give?
All live in God.   What though we cannot prove,
We shall not cease to affirm Him, whom we love."

PARTISAN.

" Mercy and truth must kiss in a God of All."

BISHOP DESIGNATE.

" Is man so miserable in his fall ?
If God might have made better, might he not have made
    worse ?
Is man not bettered even by God's curse ?
From fall has not repentance higher risen ?
Earth, is it not more palace far than prison ?
Man, will he, nill he, subject to God's sway
Here, although humble in this palace, may
God's will oppose, but longer live to learn,
And cease to question it."

PARTISAN.

    " What if always stern,
Evil in seeming, or beyond our ken ? "

BISHOP DESIGNATE.

" Nay, but I know, and shall I doubt God then,
Not trust the love of which a Universe tells.
The worlds too many are for all to be hells.
The good in this alone would shame the Devil.
We may be weak, not one of us all evil.
Though but for grace of God not one were blest,
He is more gracious to the worst than best :
His prodigal sons are tenderly confessed,
While we distant feel Him, though
   Inexpressible by tongue.
Still attainable by woe
   In the extasy of song."

PARTISAN.

   " Lightning and thunder,
    Startling all heaven,
   Frightening all under,
    Down to hell even,

Roar ; and with dismal howl,
  Vagabond wind,
Join ; and old Ruin's owl
  Screech for mankind.
As bright sunblinks, some appear glad,
  But each has his care, you know ;
Over-anxious some seem, half mad :
Some, as willows, seem drooping sad ;
And some, who don't care to seem sad,
  Are, as thunder-clouds, heavy with woe.
Man, from one error blundering to another,
Unwitting murders father, marries mother,
And, jealous of God's favour, kills a brother ;
The false believes, or wilful entertains,
And, suffering a very mint of pains
In waste of power and search of novelty,
Evil as good to know, as his God to be,
Would, if he could, a Universe unmake
To find the centre, and Olympus shake :
Tortures a slave to see his parting breath,
Use reckoning not but knowledge, to the death ;
Nonentity then equally explores,
And, seeing only self, his hopeless self abhors.
Reckless of all, but eager after each,
He finds, or makes a hell within his reach."

BISHOP DESIGNATE.

" Mere matter has no mind, sense, will for ill ;
God is its intellect, its soul, its will :
Had He been pitiless, man had soon despaired,
And courted death, and hoped not to be heired.
God has in nature placed immortal man,
A comely tenant, portion of His plan,
Climateric of earth, to rule the sphere,
And educate himself, while dwelling here ;
Reclaim this world from low to higher uses,
Himself too from inherited abuses :
In man and nature all God's ways explore ;
With them harmonious growing, Him adore

Whose laws are universal—not for one
But for His Unity with ill-will to none,
Though present suffering doubts.   Good-will to all
Cannot be bad for individual."

PARTISAN.

" Life is too sad."

EDWARD.

　　　　　　" Sore sorrow I admit,
Believe for good and mourn the need of it.
The Universe is not a stagnant pool.
Its powers are subject to eternal rule
Of interaction, death, or nothingness.
And if to be is somehow to progress,
What finite creature could all things arrange,
In lasting exercise and constant change,
Better than now we know?   Then let us free
Accept with joy the things we know to be ;
Believe the course of nature wise, divine,
Such as One God alone could so combine :
How know we but that grief and pain may prove
Needful to exercise of truest love?
Of fresh experience fresh powers are born
Material, spiritual, and adorn
The growing man, who apprehends, translates,
Line upon line, what God Himself dictates,
Till faith with reverence faileth not to lead
Through all the gods up to the God indeed.
And hast thou ne'er been sapient of state
Entrancing hope and overawing hate ;
Not sentient been of purity, and bliss,
In all creation round, as with a kiss
Saluting thee ; nor ever once at heart
Felt of the whole to be unworthy part,
And wished thy soul to take and wash it clean
In godliness, which never knew a sin?"

PARTISAN.

"Such aspiration I may once have had :
Experience has taught me I was mad.
Evil seems natural to time and space."

BISHOP DESIGNATE.

"But these are given by God to purge for grace,
And shall eternally with evil cease,
And all be harmony and lasting peace."

PARTISAN.

"But may not progress cease ; man fail, and die?
May time not prove your God a braggart's lie?
And can a mortal speak for eternity?"

EDWARD.

"We interactive, limited, appear
With thought by time and space conditioned here—
Abstractions, these shall yet take higher mode,
And vanish into harmony with God
When, change unnoted, time with infinite grace
One Now shall be, and everywhere one place.
Yea, now even, parted but by parts of speech,
God is within the meanest mortal's reach.
There is no near and far, whose arbiter
Is only like and unlike character.
Nothing divides save ignorance, hate, fear,
Or joins but when we grow with knowledge near,
With liking like ; none e'er from God depart
While His will doing with a loving heart.
As seems the sun in motion round the earth,
Our bodies seem derived to us by birth,
But are God's force, in contact with our own,
Conducting our slow progress to His throne.
His ways to comprehend we search, and see
Little by little, more eternally,
'Never enough'—most mortal cry abroad,
Speech of the whole great Universe of God."

PARTISAN.

" To hear all that, man's ear had surely need
Be wider than the church can stretch its creed."

BISHOP DESIGNATE.

" Philosophy, imagination aid
Science to read the thought, while half unsaid.
Humanity in every passing phase
Contributes to complete the happy phrase—
God, who for devils forges now a chain,
While love and reverence, not fear, master men.
Troglodyte, Neolith, Monad, Savage man
As well as cultured show, since art began,
How nations in all lands consentient crave
Help in the present, hope beyond the grave.
First animate, then fetich featureless,
Then many multiform, then one to bless,
By general consent with growing grace
God has Himself commended to the race ;
By outward symbol first in stock and stone ;
Then by man's spirit ; later by His Own.
One after other dropped are veils of sense,
Till law appears, not chance malevolence ;
And, more and more, God comes to human thought,
The Universal Spirit One long sought.
Confucius, Menu, Zoroaster, Buddh
Touched on the spiritual land of good,
Which starry systems diadem and type,
That man may see in both one workmanship.
Socrates, Plato, Aristotle guess,
Descartes, Spinoza, Kant such God confess,
Kepler, and Newton : Darwin, Huxley even
The God of Nature own, and chance of heaven,
Something by which The Cosmos is designed,
And its procession first and last defined ;
The Inorganic and Organic Cause,
Force of all creeds, and histories, and laws."

PARTISAN.

" Force of all evil too."

BISHOP DESIGNATE.

           " Nay, sin began
Only with moral law, and late in man.
Then conscience waked and ever since has striven
To better man, and fit for rise to heaven.
The might of nature first the man oppressed
By splendour's sun, or horror's icy crest.
When conscience stirringly began to feel
A sense of moral from material ill,
He good and evil traced to One, and pause
To both gave in an Infinite Animate cause.
Heart soon opponents substituted twain
In constant combat and alternate reign,
And powers of nature individualized.
Greece the Panthéon later humanized,
And, finding constant pleasure in the New,
Worshipped The Beautiful, and sought The True,
Of God discovering much, till Athens spurned,
And, knowing good, to factious evil turned ;
Then all to Rome succumbed, whence civil law
And order grew, and added power to awe,
Both failing.   Last the Christ appeared at need
The Law Divine to act, and fully read
And educate the conscience to retain—
Oracular, obeying God, not men."

EDWARD.

" China, Chaldæa, Nineveh, Babylon—these,
Phenicia, Egypt, India, Persia, Greece,
Rome, and Judæa, all prepared the way
For latest truth in loftiest essay.
God in Idea, never fully grown,
Must yet in part to every self be known.

Brave reverence and scorn as stout
  Round That Idea meet,
Not that there is no God to doubt,
  But this must thought complete—
The God ; and now a separate God no more
Of blood, gens, tribe, or nation as before—
The God with all for all, who in Him dwell
Self satisfied, no longer to rebel ;
The end beyond all ends ; The only ' I '
Whose wise control can Spirit gratify—
Supreme desire of every knowing soul
Longing with Him to be again made whole."

PARTISAN.

"A God for very few.   Sad, thoughtful men
May sometimes wish, but look, feel, search for him in vain."

BISHOP DESIGNATE.

" The Logos has proclaimed His Kingdom come,
And all to it are freely welcome home.
Heart now sees use, and right, and worth in truth
Long to discover, Spiritual ruth ;
And recognizes God as truly love,
Righteous but merciful, judging to reprove :
With added stops can now harmonious raise
To touch of God organic diapase.
To man His perfect will becomes New Birth,
And as in Heaven done is taught on earth.
For neighbour ready self to sacrifice,
Man more and more a willing self denies ;
His individuality resigns,
More to promote it, as he more refines,
Godlike, developing in use for all,
And self recovering from Adam's fall.
A fair effect at one with its First Cause,
He bides the issue of Eternal Laws ;
And after sexton Death has dressed his sod,
Forgets himself in harmony with God."

PARTISAN.

"A God may be, but thine, I see too clear,
Consists not with the discord patent here."

EDWARD.

" God's meaning in Idea had remained,
But for our need, unknown and unattained.
Two forces wanted are to active strain ;
Neither may passive be ; one force is vain.
Demand, supply, while incompleteness reigns,
Are still enforcing all becoming pains,
With possible and opportunest flow
For every kind of force, the powers know.
Mineral to plant is alien, and yet
Plant upon it attains to high estate ;
Animal upon that ; and upon all
Spirit with God's help rising from all fall.
The higher on the lower so fruitioned,
The ego by non-ego so conditioned,
We to a self-revealing God aspire,
Who still transcending need attracts desire
Consummated and winged to mount still higher.
He draws us up by our believing prayer,
His will too: nothing can be casual there.
Evolving so the Cosmos never ends ;
To Supernatural natural ascends
And is Eternal.   What shall e'er destroy
A still aspiring Universal joy ?
Blue and not black the sky is ; you by night
Through shadow dark of earth behold the light
Still in an atmosphere of distant day ;
So in ourselves we see all black, or grey,
But pass through death of self to life in God,
Through night of earth to light in heaven abroad ;
Our pulses in a beatific heat
And unison with that of nature beat ;
Our steps, no longer following a hearse,
Move to the measure of the Universe ;

2 G

Faith in Eternal God becomes at length
Immortal courage and invincible strength.
I feel the God—in all my pulses feel,
Confess Him now in Nature's common weal.
Breathing into the elements our soul,
We everywhere rapture find from pole to pole,
Now to the extasy of nature rise,
Now in the sunshine revel and the skies,
The beauty and magnificence of earth
And the sweet air it has of heavenly birth.
And wandering far and wide a waste of wood,
When issuing on a chanceful open rood
Girdled majestic with columnar trees,
Like some sublimest fane of Ancient Greece,
A forest temple built of trees by God
High roofed with heaven, low carpeted with sod,
Its altar am I in the sun ablaze,
And from my spirit rises prayer with praise.
Afar from discords, and from ills afar,
Peace in the woods, and heaven where you are
Alone in stillness with the God, who made
That nature in whose bosom you are laid,
An extasy all holy lights the face,
And man is conscious of a God's embrace."

PARTISAN.

"Unknowable is God, beyond our soar,
Beneath our plumb, a fancy—nothing more."

BISHOP DESIGNATE.

" Ah, stale, though modern, miserable lie !
Now let me think no longer : let me die,
Utterly perish, be reduced to nothing,
Which cannot be.   And I am only frothing
Maddened by the conception, not indeed
Of nothing, but of nothing run to seed—
The Unknowable.   Who knows of that to say,
'It is,' denies it so.   Sad, foolish play !
Spencer of God, The Unknowable, tells more
Than most great thinkers dreamed of God before :

Not that our God is fully known, but so
We better love, and praise the more we know.
And what of Self?   Though some may deem it base,
And others false, worthless in any case,
Feeling and thought in it we conscious find—
Motions of Self, which, more than them combined,
Their sovereign is, and may with right control,
And rate, and rank phenomena of soul,
Above the Real the Ideal place,
All worthy praise, whose not imperfect grace
Attaints of unreality the real."

PARTISAN.

" A pretty dream, and truly most ideal."

EDWARD.

" Ideal true, and most consummate end
Which all the passing Real must portend
In progress still to realize, and be
The Ideal Real of Eternity,
Conceived by, and conceiving The Supreme
Alpha and Omega of the Cosmic scheme."

PARTISAN.

" Tis real strange, but my ideas course
More on the other pessimistic horse
So fearfully, that I would sooner be
Dissolving matter than worse mystery."

BISHOP DESIGNATE.

" The shifty winds with jibbing sails of dust
Unstable are, even earth's more solid crust
With its interior fires, exterior floods,
Storms, lavas, earthquakes, ashes, rivers, muds.
Of their combined appearances we know
That they dissolve, unconscious come, and go.
Is it such fortune you desire to share?
Nirvana, or Gautama?   I more dare,
While I can see brave glory in yon Sun,

And reason fresh developed in its run ;
A consummation, to which all things tend ;
A process growing to a purposed end ;
Beyond perception, and defying scaith,
Divinest reason feel, not reason's death,
But living faith, which holds the leading rein
And guides to God the souls of humble men.
When we from Space and Time demand to hear
  Cause of the various change, and ordered growth
In this phenomenal becoming sphere,
  Faith sole sure answers us, ' The God of both ;
The Author of world processes and laws,
The Unbecome and Non-phenomenal Cause,
Stooping our imperfection to embrace ;
The God of all because The God of Grace.' "

PARTISAN.

" Our times are out of joint.   Oh, wretched plight !
To feel the wrong the more we love the right,
When wishing most the good of others, grieve
That we can be deceived, and may deceive.
In all your talk I nothing find but chaff,
Yet care not now to scoff, and may not laugh,
While faint at heart men grow, and glad that they
So soon shall pass and utterly away.
For, capable of much, at last they see
All, that they may do, shall most little be,
And death still find them in a happy sort
To see it cut the threads of lives too long though short ! "

BISHOP DESIGNATE.

" Thinking that Spirit is the moment's chance
Of matter whirling in eternal dance ;
Their very conscious selves an idle show,
Force without flavour, matter all they know ;
The moral and divine a silly kind
Of twists of brain conceiving mists of mind
Unstable, lost in which they morbid craze,
Wisdom a folly, that demented strays,

Matter itself no matter ; all abroad
Infinite nothingness The only God,
Eternal Nothing ?"

PARTISAN.

    " No such mighty fraud,
But that the surest, and so best, of all
Is just the best within our ready call :
For guessing at sights with indifferent specks,
The swan with two nicks seems the swan with two necks.
And vain are words, whose sounds the sense reports,
But head interprets as the heart exhorts.
False prepossession wholly stops our ears,
Or misconjectures what it vaguely hears ;
Nine-tenths of law to land it is, and, spite
Of reason, to argument nine-tenths of right ;
And seldom has our faith in it been broken ;
How few convincing words have e'er been spoken.
St. John a city saw without a church ;
His New Jerusalem had no such smirch."

CANTO II.

WE argument not hastily renew,
But homeward way through wooded waste pursue.
From possible approach of grievous harm
Now squirrel darts, now rabbit in alarm,
And once a knot of vipers, ambushed near,
Unfolding rustles off in wriggling fear,
Unbroken silence else. The Partisan
Was first again to speak, and thus began.

PARTISAN.

" That grace through church to kings and subjects flowed,
Priest-craft proclaimed, and ruled the world—its feod.

State-craft the lesson learned, abused the grace,
To escheat church, enslave the populace.
Thus pleading, ' Grace of God,' ungracious popes
And graceless Kings controlled from upper slopes
The baser levels, and with lips profane,
Thanked God for giving what they took from men.
But when by naming Christ one could affright
And cock-crow devils out of hell-black night,
The laity began to see, such faith
Had little in it save a shibboleth—
An oath supporting Church, State, God, and King.
I can nor take, nor trust the wordy thing,
Small policy of our old stalking-horse
Deceitful as the Trojan.   Full of force
Inimical to liberties, parliament may,
While guaranteeing them, the more betray,
And block with words the current of event.
We must reform our crafty parliament."

EDWARD.

" Sad yield of chaff, with smallest liberal grain
Aborted into large conservative gain
By bribes to vested interests and classes,
Is parliamentary life.   Indignant masses,
Drowsed by resultant little, less or more,
Scorn the most liberal parliamentary score."

PARTISAN.

" Men apt are good to see in evil strong,
And, when high-placed, feel licenced to do wrong.
Walpole-Pitt ministers, kings might their ends
By money gain, of members making friends ;
Members their rotten boroughs also buy,
And cheat the country, pricing themselves high ;
Germanic princelings their own subjects sell,
Talleyrands their masters, and their fortunes tell.
Corruption has not passed with that near time
From this most Simon-pure old-worldly clime.
Kings, viceroys, ministers, peers, members will,
Generals, Governors, be human still,

Ambassadors themselves attemptable :
The very woolsack lacks not golden taint
Of chances opportune with comely feint
Of national good, and long invested right,
And place and honour due to leading light.
If we would rectify our public life,
We must not lance it with too spare a knife.
Law we should codify, and give our state
A constitution sound, not yet too late ;
Decentralize our effete parliament,
And bring it into touch with more event ;
In one Imperial Council round the throne
Unite our empire, so to hold its own ;
And friendly hand to willing grasp expose,
Till discords arbitrate, and wars repose.
We talk, and little do but waste our breath ;
Progress to stay, we talk ourselves to death,
The commons swearing by a God, in which
Some private faith deny, yet public preach—
A God so varying in different minds,
There seems not only one, but one of all kinds."

Bishop Designate.

" Men differ must, but One the God we preach,
In whom may many see a good for each."

Partisan.

" Who church and state control for selfish gain,
Public advantage take of private men.
But privilege is an accursed thing
Beyond what natural gifts and graces bring ;
So warps the judgment, that to privileged saints
Bowels of mercy seem sad moral taints.
Seeing in ill to others God's good will,
They look their good to find in others' ill,
And in the present make to their own mind,
What they in the hereafter think to find,
A miserable world beyond redress,
Damned e'er its time by privilege pitiless.

'Fear God, and honour king,' was Solomon's say,
The crown to save, and make divinity pay.
'Live, and let live,' in vain pretends to give
The life, it barely lets another live.
'Give, and forgive,' a precept is undone
By shrewd mistrust of self and every one.
Divided classes front to front oppose,
And if there is a God, God only knows."

BISHOP DESIGNATE.

" God's rule has ever been the world to win
By His endurance of man's mortal sin.
So evil claims to reign by ' Right Divine,'
And tricks the conscience making feeble sign.
God surely may be said to suffer thus,
And seems to wrong Himself, enduring us,
While training conscience to a sense of law
Divine, not human, love without a flaw.
Sword of Norse legends forged was underground
With hammer-blows, while mortals heard no sound :
So God shapes conscience seemingly uncared,
Growing to beauty.   And though long deferred,
If now considerate of the common-wealth,
We spoiled no neighbour, legalized no stealth,
Whether by cunning fore- or after-thought,
For selfish good to common vantage wrought,
Manhood, to man himself becoming dear,
Might out of love cast weak and evil fear.
But heroes of to-day, like those of old,
Still field to field lay, pile too gold on gold ;
With subtle brains advantage to secure,
Still sweat the souls and bodies of the poor.
Wrongs thus too common, crimes are common too :
God so would scourge from hearts He would renew,
The lusts of rule, greed, envy, selfishness,
And equal rights restore, and wrongs redress."

PARTISAN.

" We know the world is racked and torn with rage,
And privileged men seek still more privilege.

To every such I say, 'Thy God on earth
Died for the people : and thy sterling worth,
Or flimsier rank assumed and privileged state,
Not naturally born, wilt abdicate?'
Dying Lorenzo turned his face to the wall,
When Savonarola, 'Wilt thou render all
Their proper honest dues, and be—you can,
I never doubted it—an honest man ;
Or, chance the worst—with our first parents prize
A stolen apple more than Paradise?'"

BISHOP DESIGNATE.

"In our progressive, but most motley state,
Can one strict dues of others estimate
Save thus, 'To all we love owe, none should hate.'
That God might more than daily bread accord
To daily toil, no prayer was of our Lord.
But some put two days' labour into one ;
By some too work superior is done ;
What more than meets one's daily want and waste,
May not suffice another's rank-born taste.
Let us not judge our fellows, rather seek
To raise the fallen and support the weak,
And, while we honour God, none disallow.
God shall judge all ; all knees to Him shall bow.
Life may be hard ; but God is still supreme,
And what is best for man is clear to Him.
When wind blows snow o'er fields, as spray o'er seas,
And, as through bare-pole rigging, roars in trees,
By night through wood and field fox silent prowls ;
And shall a man, who hungers, live on howls,
Or commit suicide, and be a prey
To worms, that batten on pronounced decay?
While lakes are ice, and very dews are rime,
Bright eyes may see in heaven a summer time ;
The worst tick, we can harbour under skin,
Is a mood fractious, angry unto sin.
Suspect your God ! nay, for your doubts but flavour
  Your main suspicion, that He still is true ;

They are the condiments, which give it savour,
　And simply bite the tongue of faith in you.
Patient of suffering, taking what God gives,
Braced by the exigencies of our lives,
E'er we aspire to higher, let us less—
Reach the full stature of our littleness.
A dove may coo at the least household noise,
And not the biggest dog give better voice ;
Cackle of geese Rome's Capitol once saved ;
We know not what we can, till we have braved.
And great events in life occur
　Undated in their time,
Whatever makes the character
　Of any man sublime."

EDWARD.

" Caught through ice-floor of lake by four grown men,
· With five miles' walk there and five home again,
A day's sport, three small fishes parted were,
Which unto one of them left empty air :
Yet the ice-floor, though not with skaters gay,
Was no bad place to muse a winter's day ;
And morrow saw them seek with equal pluck
The fisherman's unfailing lack of luck.
So with most wintry lives of millions more,
Daily through drilled holes in the world's ice-floor,
Catching three pickerel to divide 'mongst four.
Such men do never out-door labour shirk,
But help their wives' or mothers' indoor work,
Blessed when they see suns rise and set serene,
Though revolutions vex the mortal scene :
And rendering to God the love they owe.
Man's is but inlet to God's love aglow
All nature through, and which they all have proved,
Who pay the price in letting themselves be loved.
When we are amiable, well we feel
At heart of nature still a God of weal ;
Not that we so project, but God receive
And revelation happily believe."

PARTISAN.

" Yet wealth in single hands is doubtful good,
Compelling labour to life-servitude :
Its very charities are sops of guile
To make wronged right lethargic first, then vile,
Strength, freedom, justice, and intelligence
Owe little unto spare munificence.
Reforming not our criminals, we curse ;
By penalties deterrent make them worse.
State doles themselves are meanly truculent,
In garb of charity guise punishment.
Poor-houses, casual wards, starvation wages,
Impossible tasks, prescriptions of state-sages,
Can cure no evil under heaven's blurred sun.
What has our militant church-Christianity done,
But drug the savage, and the masses cheat,
And tread the refuse underneath its feet ? "

EDWARD.

" Not the true church, which wars with evil solely,
Levels the lofty, elevates the lowly :
And self-help, grown by Self-denial wise,
In aid of all offering self-sacrifice,
Shall win, because there are more weak than strong,
More poor than rich, and more, who suffer wrong
Than by injustice gain.   So heights declined,
Lords may abased be, common men refined,
Rights equal safe evolved, wrongs disappear,
Heirs of the million and the millionaire."

BISHOP DESIGNATE.

" How wondrous is the winnowing of good
Now eminent among the multitude.
Rivalry, fashion, luxury abate
The flow of loving-kindness in the great ;
But charity, estranged from Upper Classes,
Finds permanent sweet home among the masses.
There wants to wants are steadfast friends, not foes,
And suffering seeks to cheer its fellow woes.

Good word accompanied by better deed,
Sympathy is developed wide as need ;
'Tis poverty's most healthful exercise,
The trait in it most patent to quick eyes,
Though strange, most real, simple to the wise.
Trades-unions thus for equal wage combine ;
Their common gains to them seem most divine.
In sadder strikes for better, sometimes worse,
They share in due proportion lightening purse.
And time may come when good so winnowed is,
Each in the common good shall find his bliss ;
Character broadened, boldened, and refined,
Classes and masses share one equal mind."

PARTISAN.

" I too in far-off day can dim descry,
But it may all be only in my eye,
When force of mind and body men of might
Shall use for public good, not private right :
Administrative and inventive powers,
Genius, and talent consecrate their hours,
And energies to break their daily fast,
And the remainder on the waters cast."

BISHOP DESIGNATE.

" Man now o'ercomes the world, who self commands,
And with his lot content keeps open hands.
God is directing all with infinite pains :
Who lose, once had ; may have by loss fresh gains.
Deny not good because of evil there,
Nor love because of hatred anywhere,
Nor God because of social wrong to right.
Society is but a giddy height,
That crumbles to the mass, its broadening base,
Reposing on and trusting God's free grace.
Society is class humanity,
But Universal is Christianity."

PARTISAN.

" When David to Botzaris thought to raise
A monument all-worthy of his praise,
He chiselled into life, as fondly laid
Upon a tomb, a young and fragile maid
Tracing the honoured name ; and in her form
Showed womanhood in marble budding warm,
Each limb and feature suffering the rage
Of freedom travailing out of tutelage :
Life dawning sought to drag from glory's bed
The liberty, which seemed the secret of the dead.
David the model frail in Paris found :
She sate for him, but not by guerdon bound ;
Far more she coveted his iron Christ,
And kept for it her long continued tryst ;
Then to her poor home bore it for good-will.
To her, alas ! was it of iron still ?
Evil environed, born was bred in her,
And destitution caused her early err.
Years later, meeting David promptly known,
She saved his life at peril of her own—
He had given her Christ, and, though an iron one,
That was one thing at least by him well done.
The travail on Botzaris' monument
Ne'er imaged any so sublime event,
As of this woman drawing, what she prized,
A little better life out of an iron Christ."

Silence again assumes a brief command.
Now is my welcome hermitage at hand.
The Partisan too is about to part,
To town and task returning, touched at heart.
Now he is going, but not gone before
Pleased in his ear The Canon news to pour,
How he New Bishop named, in leaf though sear,
May nobly housed soon bloom a youthful peer.
To whom the Partisan,

PARTISAN.

        " Dear honoured friend,
May you outlive a house, no man can mend."

BISHOP DESIGNATE.

" God bless you."

        I, when the Partisan has gone,
To the Canon thus,

EDWARD.

        " That shot was a random one."

BISHOP DESIGNATE.

" To him I blessing meant ; the man esteem,
God under other name may visit him.
So broad his sympathies, his soar so high,
So deep his search, he surely draweth nigh
To The Unknown, who known in Christ, is true—
Our God, his also, if he only knew."

EDWARD.

" God speaks with many tongues, in many ways,
By matter first, by Spirit in these days."

BISHOP DESIGNATE.

" Attractions and affinities mind reads
Into dead matter, spiritual needs.
When atoms join, and later life-cells die—
Rupture themselves, that they may multiply,
Spirit dependence mutual descries
Maturing into full self-sacrifice.
When sex appears to vary and to part,
It only joins the more with greater art,
Till life in round, and height, and depth of earth
O'er death prevaileth by exceeding birth,
While flower, fruit, wine, milk, honey pleasing prove
Prodigal nature one well-spring of love.

Not having wit their aged ones to nurse,
To mere brute beasts long life would be a curse ;
But they die young, are for each other game ;
Men shoot the wild too, breed for use the tame ;
The young increasing few to age attain ;
All happy actors on a stage of pain.
If soon the savage perish, final cease,
Yet herds, troops, packs, flocks, families increase,
Whose young so tended are by love, they know
To tender it in turn, and loving grow.
To women babes are dear : men toil for both.
Thus wisdom all acquire, and truth to troth ;
Till ordered families at length prevail,
Which foes unorganized in vain assail.
Families, tribes, nations, more and more combine
Old worlds and new, and hate begins to pine,
In ever widening environment
A varied issue life's supreme event,
Hereditary progress, natural plan,
God's laws evolving spiritual man.
Soon in life's struggle they shall winning prove,
Who love to live, that they may live to love ;
God put His Sceptre into man's own hands ;
Man reign by love, which God Himself commands."

EDWARD.

" Among the forces, in the Cosmic scheme,
Loosing and binding, is there one Supreme."

No angel flashes from an opening sky
And heights, where all things plain are, to reply ;
Only I know The Sprite of Love at hand,
Plying his mystic art and magic wand ;
And one, Great-heart, as to command, appears,
And one, proud Intellect, both of high careers,
Ready for light and leading to contest,
Which wisest is, most capable and best.
The vices all and virtues listen round :
Which shall on that side, which on this be found ?

Sharp looks proud Intellect ; but, by Great-heart won,
The seeming battle ends, e'er well begun.
It is an interlude of thought, not sense,
And still my question hangs as in suspense.
The Bishop yet no judgment has pronounced,
When, visiting him, straight is one announced,
Our noble soldier, not now country squire,
But Duke of all my town and half my shire,
Heir of the ancient uncle lately dead.
He still unmarried, never like to wed,
Loves Lucy ever, whom he once so frayed.
Our ducal neighbour's guest now, he had heard
Of mutual friend Bishop, and prepared
Had come, too late, to see The Partisan.
In the new groove the conversation ran.
Intellect I beheld, a sight most strange,
Pass into Duke, to Bishop Great-heart change,
While giving utterance free, like foes of note,
To the contention in my prior thought.

THE DUKE.

" Mechanical, physical, electrical
Forces unseen are mensurable all,
Quantities causal of effects exact,
Facts, which in nature act and interact."

BISHOP DESIGNATE.

" And so-called spiritual forces too,
Invisible, are calculably true :
Their powers can be demonstrated in man,
Valued as factors in the social plan.
The Universe rolls round ;
  Worlds sleep, but as they spin ;
Streams drown not, but exhaled are found
  Returning to begin :
Thought, restless too as ocean,
  Finds an apparent joy
In motion, but without emotion
  Which must the heart employ ;

And having tasted bliss
  Of a superior strain,
Once having known how sweet it is
  A heart to entertain,
A yearning sense of void,
  Which nothing else can fill,
Proves labour should, to be enjoyed,
  Have heart in it, and will
Intelligently moved
  To effort for a choice,
Which reason makes and can be loved,
  When Conscience has a voice."

THE DUKE.

" I never heard that speak, bah ! "

BISHOP DESIGNATE.

                        " I how long.
Making for righteousness against all wrong,
It louder grows, as we its love discern,
And, learning more to love, love more to learn,
And give our hearts to God with the respect
And active power of all pure intellect."

THE DUKE.

" Pure intellect, whose honour you assail !
But heart is a false quantity, bad spell ;
Spoiling the character of our best play,
It makes life's epic halt upon the way ;
True intellect alone has any chance
Against the foolish charms of ignorance."

BISHOP DESIGNATE.

" I sometimes feel, as though I was all shoddy ;
At other times, as if I had no body,
Yet was a somebody and had a mind,
Which makes me long distinguished place to find,
Act in the world some most conspicuous part.
I never feel so, when I think of heart ;

2 H

It humbles me.   The most obscure, least shrewd,
May have more heart than I, and do more good.
Why, pagan heart ambitious, proud,
Voluptuous was in touch with God.
Its heroes, sages, statesmen ran
  The course of glory, lived and died
For friends, for country, and for man ;
Nor know I ought more idle than
  The vanity of intellectual pride.
As night from nether air
  Shoots brilliant lights on high
To meet and whirl in colours rare
  Round an extatic sky,
So exercise of mind
  Is only seeming bright,
And nothing anywhere can find,
  But sense of its own night."

THE DUKE.

" Doubt philosophic is, for nothing is sure."

BISHOP DESIGNATE.

" If not the Moral Law."

THE DUKE.

              " So speaks the boor :
But I have never been of squeamish mood.
Evil to me is tragic, more than good,
A finer study, common, and to hand :
While there is something in my straight demand
For much and earnest work of powers, which can
No higher good discern for mortal man.
Through years of Tower and age, of youth and prime,
Raleigh sought nothing but to busy time :
Laws of morality to me are nonsense,
And I have never had a squirm of conscience."

BISHOP DESIGNATE.

" Bacon knowledge at each source
  Eager wooing won, and trod

In familiar intercourse
  Through the Universe with God ;
Walking on to noble ends,
Rose upon and ruined friends—
Raleigh, Essex, both belied,
Till they on a scaffold died ;
Knew the right, and in temptation
Soiled the ermine of a nation.
Intellect success enthrones ;
  And when heart is hard or base,
For all conscience-pricks atones
  Crowning evil with success.
To know is Being ; so is eating, drinking,
Wishing, and willing : larger, to my thinking,
The question raised, dividing you and me,
' What Being may become and ought to be ? '
To this I answer, maximum of being
Is more than living, thinking, moving, seeing,
Feeling, and acting ; lies in heart-swayed will
Knowing to choose the good, reject the ill ;
In good, not goods, increase, than their great, greater ;
And life desire, more always meaning better.
A modern Sir Walter lived to bruit,
Worth is not work, though work is Absolute."

THE DUKE.

" Yet long has mind been known, and crowned of men.
Sparta renowned the thief, who thieved again
Still undiscovered ; honoured mental art,
And supple strength of limb, nor thought of heart
Dimly conceived : nor hath the worship ceased,
Though passed away the rite, the prayer, the priest.
Around the footstool of successful wrong
Through all the ages worshippers still throng
Adoring mind, which can contrive, dare, do,
And be, however false, to vigour true.
In highest offices of law, church, state,
War, science, letters, art, trade, cheat is great.

Minerva had of mind her shield and sense,
Mercury too Caduceus and pence."

BISHOP DESIGNATE.

" Chaldee, Phenician, equal base and bold,
The New World Aztecs, Normen in the Old,
Arab, New Zealander, Feejean show
Vigour of mind with savage strength may grow.
Material progress may mind gauge, alas,
Yet ice the breast, or indurate to brass.
Subservient to every selfish mood,
And more abused for ill than used for good,
The civilization cannot long prevail,
On which we may the human heart impale."

THE DUKE.

"What say you?   Cannot mind at all excel ;
From evil that which you call good compel ;
Forces of nature all, both old and new,
Discover, regulate, and so subdue ;
Develop every latent power of man,
And artfully improve God's primal plan ? "

BISHOP DESIGNATE.

"To whitest heat heart stimulates the mind :
Motive for action you in heart should find."

THE DUKE.

" Motive indeed, and sometimes motive base,
Which recks not me, but damages your case.
Slave to the greatness of a pure desire
   To gratify itself and not restrain,
Strong passion shows to you as noble fire,
   Yet rebel is against mind's calmer reign.
The noblest heathen heart but little knew
To cultivate the virtues, or but few,
Which in their mastery took taint of vice.
Ambitious patriotism not too nice,

Voluptuously mighty warmth of heart,
  Stoic and arrogant stern fortitude,
Their moral vigour spent on one fine part,
  And over-doing did no other good.
Church-loving priests their flocks not only fleece,
But inquisition, to restrain increase ;
First Charles could to Family be true,
Betray his country and his Strafford too ;
Napoleon Prime might friends, relations, state,
And all who served him never once forget,
The Devil can be equal good and great ;
Our Second Charles and Fourth George, both base,
More than their Sires advanced The British Race ;
Regent and Fifteenth Louis, Voltaire sage
Helped France to heights beyond the gallant age ;
Despots have their little Naps,
And their fancy liberty Caps."

BISHOP DESIGNATE.

" They enticingly adorn,
  And amuse ; instruct, not save ;
Flower about a nation borne
  By corruption to the grave.
Letters, art, philosophy,
  By a decoration caught,
Wed the sensuous, breed vanity,
  Dissipating power on thought,
Commerce fondling slavish gains,
Social license hugging chains."

THE DUKE.

" Man may know, that he is dying,
  Even paint each fresh decay ;
Sing of it instead of sighing,
  And laugh out his little day."

BISHOP DESIGNATE.

" Yet moral fall is national decline :
Though sin most deadly makes no sign.

If seen upon inviolate soil
A foreign foe in quest of spoil,
Would frenzied populace unite
In summoning to va-ward fight
For gold, soon melted into shot ;
   Or books, to cartridge paper torn ;
Or bodies, cast into the lot?
Ha ! vengeance scarce would have a thought,
   And glory only move to scorn.
While silence held the hosts around,
To one known cry each trump would sound ;
Against the foe each eye, hand, foot
Advance, or to receive him root ;
Call, to which peaceful men reply,
In every age the battle-cry
Even of inhumanity,
'For faith and country, kith and kin—
   For sires, homes, altars, and the right
Incarnate, human and divine,
   Manhood, for moral nature fight !'"

THE DUKE.

" What, you would fight then ?"

BISHOP DESIGNATE.

       " Nay, but I could die
To give all immorality the lie."

EDWARD.

" In that New Land, where Roger Williams first
Freedom of conscience brought to light and nursed,
Founding a state whose motto was no scrawl,
But in attempted act, ' Love conquers all,'
Where too an empire over savage men
Without a weapon conquered was by Penn,
And never quaker suffered loss of life
From Indian tomahawk, or scalping-knife ;
The sword of tyrant George was crossed with one
By revolution forged for Washington :

God knows if struggling liberty abused it,
But never human being better used it,
Conscience the sole possessor of his ear."

THE DUKE.

" He might have doubted that, which few can hear
Or loudly h earing never may attend.
Whose heart this strange world breaks not, it must bend."

BISHOP DESIGNATE.

" He may have erred ; from England, then forsaken,
Columbia more than right have outraged taken,
And, hasting to be rich, so fouled the gain,
Which yet may canker, as once wasting Spain :
But Tolstoies now 'gainst despotisms war,
By moral methods healing moral scar.
And grand is moral power.   The man, how great,
Who having conquered self, defying fate,
Singly against a world with right can range !
Him earth and hell opposed may crush, not change.
Affronting power persuasively, unarmed,
Foe to all violence, and unalarmed,
With ultimate prevailing moral force
Attacking evil at its wilful source,
For power not cruel, and not false for fame,
No boor for knowledge, and not rich with shame,
Sovereign in his heart sit moral powers
Controlling mind and body, all his hours ;
To pleasure he no passing license lends,
But all his aims and means to moral ends."

THE DUKE.

" Yet no fair test of nature's larger plan
Is the brief life of individual man :
Rather from nations learn, that force and brain— "

BISHOP DESIGNATE.

" Are under law, and, as in single men,
God meets, and punishes at destined times
With national disasters national crimes.

In Greece, when lofty thought with art and song
And pleasure walked, while intellect was young,
Faction red-handed ruled each changeful hour,
Till license called a despot into power,
Which suicidal bled itself to death,
And earth beside, its fame no fleeting breath,
But trumpeting till now an evil praise.
And long years after, when in Christian days
Greece, though abased yet ardent, strangely bright
Amid the pitchy gloom of general night,
Suddenly wrecked was scattered through the dark
In many a glowing ember, living spark,
Set Italy aflame and Florence fired,
Intellect bursting forth, afresh inspired,
The same brief, bright, mad course of license ran,
Ending too where in darkness it began.
For gain corrupted, pleasure weakened, power
Factious enslaved the genius of the hour ;
Vice reigned, and fame, the creature of goodwill,
Was only won by doing more of ill,
Till tyranny with hydra-head and strong
Crushed in its all-pervading grasping wrong
The wish and power with every right of thought,
And left the body politic to rot."

The Duke.

" Bah ! Social order vilest still may be
Better than dynamite and anarchy.
Solomon was a man of lasting peace,
And built a temple out of his increase ;
Had also quite a large seraglio."

Bishop Designate.

" Where he his pleasure found, to be his woe—
Of wives and concubines one only good."

The Duke.

"His songs endure, deep books, and proverbs shrewd."

BISHOP DESIGNATE.

" Whose writing wearied him."

THE DUKE.

                " A page unfurled
To him was man, all nature, the whole world."

BISHOP DESIGNATE.

" And nothing new, all going, coming again,
Vain repetition, felt to be all vain."

THE DUKE.

" He made his nation glorious."

BISHOP DESIGNATE.

                " But vile,
Idolatrous, u nruly all the while,
And, when he died, dividing to its fall."

THE DUKE.

" More wicked he than most, yet pride of all."

BISHOP DESIGNATE.

" Fear God, " he said, but failed Him so to fear,
Until too old the voice of God to hear.
Mind may of heart a foul disease descry,
And know of cure, heart has no will to try.
Knowledge avails nought without change of heart :
That willingly must choose the better part—
The fear of God, His stamp and image, seal
Of the divine and human commonweal,
Impressed on passionate Being so to be
A constant thing, which one can feel and see
Fond likeness of The God, who wills that thus
His love may be fulfilled, and felt in us
A safe experience importing truth :
For what we love, or hate alone to us is sooth.

THE DUKE.

" Let me but know, I care not how, what, whom—
Exploring nature to the crack of doom."

BISHOP DESIGNATE.

"Such noble Spirit should be lord of sense,
Which ministers to its intelligence ;
Should heart inform that it may govern will
The proper end of Being to fulfil,
Its powers employing to develop man
Not on his own but God's much larger plan,
Powers lower bond to higher to attain
The highest good harmonious without strain ;
Conscience evolving more as man the more
    Himself and fellows learns to love, and know
In the Good God One worthy to adore,
    Whom not to love would be eternal woe."

THE DUKE.

" Methinks the devil may as long sustain
And fully employ the whole of heart and brain :
Through no man can all evil ever run."

BISHOP DESIGNATE.

" One form palls quickly, being over-done ;
And Satan fails his henchmen to unite,
The vices stand opposed in open fight."

EDWARD.

" Each for himself and few for other,
    They, hateful, hated each of each,
Meet but to fall on one another
    Devoured by others' over-reach ;
Or, suicidal in excess
Of their own deadly eagerness,
Consumed they, as on prairies fire
Itself encounters to expire.

Escaping over burned-up sin,
Men shuddering see the peril, they were in.
But virtues all in circle ring,
Hands join, and round man dance and sing,
Not Pilon graces, not one block
Of impertransible rude rock,
But individual, to attract
With every phase of love in act,
And joined, like colours in heaven's bow,
Swiftly revolving, till they show
Pure as the glow of an eternal bliss,
 Having for God an eye that can,
Lustered with glory, like to His,
 Clear in it hold a tear for man.
So as in arms of moral love,
Wisdom and power, which gods approve,
Holiness, justice, goodness, and truth,
Man with infinity of ruth
Embraces, never to asperse,
The order of the Universe,
Where ills have antidotes assigned,
And issue in the good of humankind."

BISHOP DESIGNATE.

" In home, camp, temple, senate, court,
Exchange, mart, forum, field, and sport
The Knightly virtues can dispense
The whole round table of munificence,
Whose Lord is Christ, the Son of God
Acknowledged with approving nod.
Christ ! Ah, great character ! I wis
 Nothing is weak, waste, wanting here ;
Perfect this God-head man-hood is
 To the womanliness of a tear ;
God's approbation all the while,
His Father's will, His Father's smile,
Love, the true force, which made Him strong
 For houseless nights and hungering days,

That companied with sinners, wrong
  Enduring blessed, and moved to praise ;
Cursed hypocrites, but to the close
Forgave with hope and prayed for foes ;
Words, miracles of mercy prove
His cross and passion were all love."

About to speak the Vices were, I wist,
But paling vanished at the Name of Christ :
The double contest, prior in my soul
And after 'twixt my friends, attained one goal—
The first, conclusive, summing up the whole.
Canon and Duke have gone ; and now, alone,
Love's Sprite is present with my Guardian Own,
The virtues also. And before they go,
Love recalls Intellect and Heart, and, lo,
They melt into each other, and are one,
One too in me : their victory is begun.
As Dawn weds Sun, so Intellect should Heart.
What God hath joined, let no man put apart.
. Dawn clouded and with paling stars bedewed,
Cold, cruel, gray, or blood-red and fire-hued,
Appears to be half-living and half-dead,
Till rises sun, and they are duly wed :
And deeds of darkness to the Demon hurled,
The heart of daylight warms and works the world.

I with the Canon now to town return,
Into the morning still my lamp to burn.

CANTO III.

I LOOKED, and saw into the heart of things,
Where stood an angel with enfolded wings.
I think it was of Love the noble Sprite,
Now glorified in sovranty of light,

Centring the Universe and shapely strong,
Whose riper argument was terser song,
While all the Caryatic Virtues round
Choiring harmoniously swelled the sound.

CENTRAL ANGEL.

" Who for nothing worketh, toiling, but in vain,
    For some earthly object, work on him will pall ;
Tasting not success, with unrewarded pain
    Sick and faint, he surely goeth to the wall ;
Hath not any heart in what he finds no gain ;
    Hath not any strength to recover from a fall.
Who for nothing worketh, save the joy he knows
    In the exercise of passions and of powers,
May ambitious prove of eminence in woes ;
    Cares not for the good, or evil of his hours ;
Slave of self or impulse, toss he, or repose
    On a bed of thorns, or gather, scatter flowers.
Who for nothing worketh, even while he feels
    In the joy of action no supreme delight ;
Works till spirit wavers ; works till body reels ;
    Works for God and duty, works with all his might ;
Where no moth corrupts, nor thief breaks through and steals,
    God for him is hoarding treasure day and night.
Better, if not stronger, is the man who loves
    Objects of earth's labour sought for with a will,
And the road towards them ; whom too duty moves ;
    Earth and heaven helping, he defeats all ill."

CENTRAL ANGEL AND VIRTUES.

" Doing what you ought is duty ;
    Doing it because you ought,
Excellence too cold, and beauty
    Recognised, but charming not ;
Barely is it virtue, pronely
    And for self, not others, done ;
Proud, yet cowardly, and only
    Just to all, but kind to none.

Bring to duty Love : pursuing
  What you should, because you would,
Add the loving of well-doing
  To the moral habitude.
Do thy duty gladly, kindly :
  Do it fully, for you can,
Heartily, though never blindly,
  And in league with God and man.
Such is goodness—love and duty :
  All the holiness of right
Robed in love's attractive beauty,
  Crowned with love's persuasive might."

CENTRAL ANGEL.

" 'Twas to keep man out of evil
  Life was wedded unto toil :
Him to bless, not please the devil,
  That God cursed the soil.
Idleness breeds wicked fancies ;
  Edens suit not Adam's race ;
Labour every joy enhances,
  And it is God's grace.
Fearless then the tempests cuff, and
  Winds and tides defy unawed,
Seeking harbour large enough, and
  Home at last in God."

CENTRAL ANGEL AND VIRTUES.

" All the world demands thy labour ;
  Earth is heavy with her woe,
Not transfigured on Mount Tabor,
  But mad-sick below.
Laws unequal, sloth, and ruin,
  Vice, each phase and form of ill
Hurry her, herself undoing,
  Ever down the hill.
Out then on the wild commotion,
  Not to wrecks of others blind,
Nor as ships, which crossing ocean
  Leave no track behind,

Map the currents, reefs, and shoals, to
    Warn such as may heedless stray ;
And help earnest simple souls, to
    Keep the narrow Way."

EDWARD.

' But runs through whistling grove and grassy glade
No stream my thirsty evening to invade ;
No table spreads with wine and goodly cheer ;
No darling love enchantress draweth near."

CENTRAL ANGEL.

" Yet art thou not alone while God is nigh—
The love of God : with it thou shouldst not sigh,
But loving live, and labour, till you die."

CENTRAL ANGEL AND VIRTUES.

" Thine to compass sea and land—
Soldier, sailor, to command ;
Seeming impotent to smite,
Yet transfixing with love-light
Brains, in which false heart believes,
Skulls of dragons and of deeves ;
And no holiday to know,
Whilst an evil reigns below.
Heart and hand to love engaged,
Upon hate thy war is waged :
Dreading neither scaith nor scorn,
Leading every hope forlorn,
Never shall thy soul be quit
Of this final fighting fytte."

All disappeared ; but consciousness remained
Of struggle, for a victory to be gained.
Up ! Up ! To Arms, Oh, heart ! and willing, free,
Make thou an utter conquest of all me ;
To life the zest restore, to work the joy ;
Be thou my passion now, and whole employ.

I see the rising rolling tide
Of mortal vanity and pride :
Before me real life expands,
    Smites filmless eyes with staggering pain,
And pricks my naked grasping hands ;
    Shall it all loss be, or some gain ?
God help me ! Who, that ever stood
Thus face to face with what he would,
Yet might not hope to fully do,
But shuddered at the daunting view ?
Pain must revisit, languor still oppress ;
Accept the pain, but, heart, my powers redress ;
Put me upon the way, and guide to where
Self itself loses to find all things there.
Mind trying failed, whilst thou wast on the rack ;
To thee I yield me now, a willing hack,
Not to frail passion, but that love more strong,
Which suns all worlds, and moves the heavens to song.
Maundering in desert, shall I call to mind,
And long for fleshpots left so far behind ;
To Canaan journeying at no Elim tent,
But bitter Marahs brine with fresh lament ?

So young, if old, are all true Cosmic ways,
    Spirits still come and go, or never have gone.
Material force in spiritual phase
    Has to the natural man been always known :
And ruling principles of action free,
Which some call motives, may they Spirits be ?
If, influenced to ill, men acting know,
That they from act may straight to judgment go,
Defying God, as though they said, " Who cares ? "
They entertain a Devil unawares :
Others an angel may, and all must God.
Living and active Principles abroad
Everywhere, although nowhere to our senses,
Personal as spiritual influences,
Prayed to, or trusted, are communicated,
Coming or going as they are loved or hated.

And now A Spirit of All Grace drew near
Glowing, to chase remaining shades of fear ;
Peitho nor voice persuasive had, nor face
Charming and winning as this Angel Grace.

SPIRIT OF ALL GRACE.
" Oh, foolish man, arise !
  Be no more a pitiful thing
Of purposeless tears and sighs,
Forgetful that the skies
  Would rather hear thee sing.
Earth needs thy helping hand,
  Would hail thy hopeful song.
Sorrow is over the land ;
  Strength has been failing long.
For this arduous suffering earth
  Thy heart is sore ; then go,
Go now, and give gladness birth,
Go, carry health and mirth
To places, where never hearth
  Has known the loving glow
Of a heart that pities woes,
And is moved by a God, who knows.
What though altogether gay
  You may never hope to become,
While sin with remaining sway
Can a finger upon you lay,
  Or look however dumb ;
What though a stroke you miss,
  Or unwary ship a wave,
If, struggling through to bliss,
  You row the wrecked to save ?
To know of the evil, and not
  To better it, is to prolong,
Is in indolence to rot
  Corrupted by the wrong.
And to feel it is only sorrow,
  But pleasure with it to fight :
For you cannot help but borrow
  In giving others delight."

2 I

Through many a scene of woe
  By pity I am led,
As oft too long ago,
But seldom now, and know
  Few living, many dead
Wont, living, there to dwell—
Chance better housed now in hell.
Rotten structures roomed with dens
Fouler far than cattle pens,
Vested interests, endure
Privileged to kill the poor :
Fuzzy, but still unemployed,
Laws, impeaching them, are void.
Indian, gipsy, brute, or slave
Hut, or wigwam, tent, or cave,
Maniac—ghoul—haunted tomb
Healthier were and choicer home.
God attires the mind of worm
In a wriggling grovelling form ;
In refined and functioned clay
Lodges soul and gives it play,
That by body, well preserved,
Spirit may be right well served ;
We, on reasonable plan,
Well should house the working man.
England palaces a throne,
Yet, if she would hold her own,
Her foundations must rebuild ;
More than send her poor afield,
Cleanse and house them ; spare not purse,
Lined now with a people's curse.

Ragged and rude from mud
In the streets seem children to bud,
Poor etiolated flowers ;
While more-grown folks loll their hours
Round gin-shops and rickety stalls
  Of shellfish, and fruits that want care,
And vegetables, with calls

That hunger.   How many falls
   Have some had to settle down there !
And courts of the evil whore
   Where the thief becomes belluine,
And lanes and rooms I explore,
Dens with litters on the floor,
   Styes all of human swine—
Pit, whose bottom hell only knows,
   Of foul folly and gross mistake,
Where all to fast ruin goes
   Like some broken-down breaking-up rake ;
While with angry curse, and worse
   Inhuman deed and blow
Men seem to wish to nurse
To enormity God's curse,
   Which lashes them with woe.
And behold ! the whole brigade
   Of diseases has quartered here,
And others breed, and parade
With fell purpose to invade
   The country far and near :
From some no physic saves—
   Not named they, nor understood ;
And some, like young Indian braves,
   Have just tasted their first blood.
Want too is clamorous blind,
   And famine laughs in its face,
And pokes its ribs to find
   Some secret fleshy place.
Though death here has treated been
   To his hundreds at a breath,
Lank still he looks and lean ;
For famine, uncommonly clean
Picking the bones, had mean
   Skeletons left to Death.

Finding such ancient miseries still new,
I ask of love, " Have we to thee been true ?

What have we been and done of any worth
To value life by, or to better earth ?
To God our Father have we glory given,
And done His will, as it is done in heaven,
Here messengers and ministers of grace
Helping to raise to Him the human race ;
Or power and passion upon woman wasted,
And altruism dilettanté tasted ;
Or charities dispensed, and never missed,
And never truly imitated Christ ?
Yet sad for the woes I have seen,
   And been glad to soothe, I say,
Sitting thoughtfully in the sheen
Of mine own firelight, " I have been
More happy, than I have been
   For many a too long day."
Life is a daily walk abroad.
Who takes it Enoch-like with God,
Happy he, happy foul or fair.
   Thou, who hast made the world, My Lord,
Bearing its burden, take my care.
   I hang it on Thy Living Word,
Love—Thine Own Word.   Below, above,
                    Dei Agnus,
                    Deus Magnus !
Thy name, Eternal God, is love,
Warm torrent pitiable forth
From Balder grave in icy north ;
As though the buried sun still shone,
A living geyzer thence yronne,
And flows my wearied manhood to sustain,
And reconcile to human-kind again,
And that means woman—once I thought her more,
Who could the Paradise, she lost, restore.

I miss the counsel sage and kind of mother,
   Whose death loose cast me upon self-command.
I since have lost too her much older brother—
   Uncle, bequeathing me his wealth and land :

For he was rich in both.   And now I stand
Not unrelated, nor without a friend,
   But natheless holding mine own self in hand,
Rents, dividends, and clients without end,
And time and thought employ, and energies expend.

Covering from Cupid's battles my retreat,
   Business, wealth, honour are but such to me.
Would they had been to lay at Lucy's feet,
   And pleasing her to me been jubilee;
   Toil only, duty mine; fame, vanity;
Lucy alike; though often meet we now.
   I cannot help: society is she,
The fashion still.   And we can more than bow,
Can even words exchange and passing smiles allow.
Yet lurks there not, beneath such passing smile,
Ambush of hate in me, in her of guile?

         Dark are ocean charts with dormant
            Burial places of the brave;
         Wide diseased with spots informant
            Of ships riding one last wave;
         Goodwin Sands, and Islands Sable,
            Or more open spaces, where
         Raging winds and seas disable
            Boston Cities, foundering there.
         And the chart of life has many
            Spots of danger sadder still:
         But of all there is not any
            Sad as heart without a will
         Borne on currents stronger, faster,
            Pride of race that breaks, not stoops,
         Idle title, gold disaster—
            Sailors trust not painted poops—
         Love, in mart of fashion thronging,
            That could sell itself for gain;
         Love, that would not follow longing;
            Love, that perished in its pain.

Earth uneasy too may city
  Into dust unconscious shake ;
Hurricanes, devoid of pity,
  Masterful blow wider wreck.
Sweeping Caribbees, they ravage
  Cultivated prairies West,
Though the slave is free, and savage
  By no settler now oppressed.
Alarics, Attilas, Generics fall may
  Upon earth with meteor host ;
Visigoths, Huns, Vandals all may
  In the rack, they make, be lost.
Neither storm, nor strife can rival
  Desolated heart's sore rage,
Echoed, but with faint revival,
  From Melpomenean stage :
Let not it prevailing rule us.
  Better all wild winds unchain
With o'er-heaving seas to cool us,
  Than such madness upon brain ;
Better be a world's wide wonder,
  And to smiters turn the cheek :
For heaven drops its angry thunder,
  When to judgment rise the meek.
Again the ardent Spirit of All Grace,
  With triumph although slender in its tone,
Enwrapped my soul in a prolonged embrace,
  And counselled, to help make it all its own.

SPIRIT OF ALL GRACE.

" Whose will good conscience may direct,
Shall never fail of self-respect.
But good resolve, in most a mood
Of passion, oft is passing good—
False to itself, a dream ill-starred
By night-mare conscience ridden hard,
Till that is thrown, and then free will
Is only good for doing ill.

Yet e'er such final fall's defection,
How good each partial resurrection ;
With after lapse however base
How good is good in saddest case ;
However changeable the mood,
However brief its hour, how good !
Nay, goodness is Divine, and never
So falls as from its source to sever,
But reascends in human sighs
To return rory from the skies,
And still on earth expands an ocean
Nothing can foul, and no commotion—
Not bursts of nether flame prevail
To shoal, or cause the tide to fail,
Whose fount unfailing flows above
From Christ's own full and reigning heart of Love."

Oft are familiar simple incidents
Unsought occasion of supreme events ;
De Morny and Walewski, quarrelling
About an opera-box, fore-crowned a king ;
Sent Maximilian to a piteous doom,
Shot like a traitor, and denied a tomb.
Issues, long gathering to sudden head,
Are not so caused, but so consummated,
Burst, by occasion pricked: for with no lack
The last straw always breaks the camel's back ;
And revolution in my changing heart
Now signalized was by most minor part.

A young commander, not unknown to fame,
A sailor nephew, visiting me came,
A favourite of mine who, if I died,
Should to my lands succeed and much beside.
A tale of hairbreadth-'scapes and ventures bold
To Desdemona as Othello told,
He modest filled my mind and stirred my breast
With unaccounted hardships well confessed.
A youth of culture, yet the ardent boy
And eke the man had known no idle joy.

Uninterrupted service in all climes,
Rough work and stern had his been, and hard times
Adrift, ashore now, on his beam-ends thrown,
No utterance heard I of dissembled moan :
He only longed to be at sea again ;
Whence this reflection grew upon my brain.
Is there on land a life so rude to brave,
As is a life upon the ocean wave ?
What showy differences then avail
To sailor close imprisoned, under sail,
Driven before, or whistling for a gale.
All lots, or rich, or poor, in this agree,
That one may happy as another be.
Conditions and possessions make not bliss :
God's gift of life can hardly come amiss.
When good the heart, and faith and reason sound,
Tramp limpest upon earth in wonted round
Need never envy monarch on his throne ;
Each is a traveller, though in different zone,
With equal risk to heaven ; arctic rude,
Torrid, or temperate, life with God is good.
I found the youth in love, and yet afraid
To wed her, whom he pleased to me pourtrayed.
She waiteth the promotion with employ,
Which he expects.   I antedate their joy,
Providing income, they nor hoped, nor sought ;
Had I not also loved—far-reaching thought.
He, parting, could not have so happy been,
Had he been cousin to salute a Queen.

Of Lucy then I think ; and now a tear
   Drops big, but single, from no stoic eye,
Unwiped by me, unkissed by her not here,
   To wash her life pure of its one great lie
   Forgiven, to be forgotten by-and-by.
Her truth to other is to me no pain.
   Though sighing oft for her, I even could die
If needed, deeming life no longer vain
With love and her begun, and ended for her gain.

I cannot yet with peace her halls parade ;
  Invited, am engaged, not self-possessed,
Not yet mine own, once hers—by her betrayed :
  Would women were true women, and man blessed.
  Would she had wed to be at home caressed,
Drawn from, not driven into stranger arms.
  Where look for hope, find faith? The heart oppressed
Drinks the intoxication of her charms,
In memories sweet dissolves, forgetting, its alarms.

Our old, old walks, unvisited since death,
  In taking her who bore me, snapped what bound—
Attaching still, I shall with bated breath
  Revisit soon ; nor would, but not unowned
  Must be the Duke of town and country round
Kindly inviting. Shall I bliss repeat,
  Not dulled by wild regret, and sorer stound?
There too her own lord's home is. We must meet
The self-same air to breathe, which love made once so
    sweet.

Had she but mated with a loving heart
  Less worldly than her own, and it had drawn
Her best of being forth with tuneful art
  And ardour heightening from early dawn,
  An ash she might have been upon a lawn,
A roof-tree cherub-laden there to prove.
  She would have been an Eve to gaze upon,
And paid one boundless largesse of such love
As issues from heaven's mint—the currency above.

CANTO IV.

ON grandly wooded spur and terminal hill
  Of grassy range, that finely flanks the sea,
Lonely the Ducal Castle, venerable,
  O'erlooks two vallies opening out to be

A princely park with wider marge of plain,
And ceding conjoined waters to the main.
Inland the Park is girt by heights of moor,
And slopes of grass and wood, and dells obscure—
Deer-forest all, whence may occasional stray
Down to the park the deer, our pastime's prey;
Though sport adventurous we follow too,
And wonted proper chase at large pursue.
Many the guests are, various my friends,
But to the Duke my intimacy tends.
We questions of morality avoid,
Whose fair discussion once an hour employed.
Knowledge is still his one approved pursuit,
Which to promote he taste would every fruit.
Chymic, magnetic, and electric powers
And photographic ply our active hours,
And all the sciences are called in play
To entertain the night till break of day.
Thought to much profit and of widest range
We in his laboratory famed exchange,
But not one word of Lucy.   Hence his charm
I recognize, and take of it no harm.
Curiously learned, he unassuming can
Act well, as host, the perfect gentleman,
Who once forgot himself, and may at heart,
Though now he shows it not, despise the part.
Lucy, some miles off, in less grandeur dwells,
   And more secluded wilderness enchants.
I often thither stray ; and holier spells
   Compel me further to our earlier haunts.
Ah ! I have now been here so brief a space :
Or long, how short it seems !   And, now her face?
Nay, but another sisterlike appears,
The face of Home, and I possess its ears.
Puck also nigh, with interposing wing,
Is giddy fluttering round me, as I sing.

EDWARD.

" Sweet home, where the School-boy ran holiday wild,
When the world took the man, it with you left the child :

You kept him, and still in your bosom retain,
And now I, beholding you, find him again.
Each object is storied with childhood's regrets,
And plays, like a hand on the harp which it frets,
With so lively a thrill on the chords of my soul,
That I feel as an Hebe from paradise stole
To lighten the eyes, which are washed with warm tears,
And lead me along, as she cancels my years,
To nut in the glen, or the spotted trout snare,
To startle the gull, paitrick, rabbit, or hare,
Shells gather and pebbles, that brighten the bree,
Fish or plunge from the rock, or now launch on the sea."

HOME SPIRIT.

" Life-renewing the thought is, like sunshine in May ;
But happier thou than the motes in its ray.
For the pleasures of childhood, like larks on the wing,
Are so innocent all, that their memories sing ;
And, while ruthless time sprinkles bleak snows on the head,
And ices the blood, till fond wishes are dead
To allures of a world, that yet clings like a vine,
Make the soul live again in the dear Auld Lang Syne,
And the dimming eye light, and the wasted cheek glow,
And age own the rapture young feelings bestow."

PUCK.

" Here gladly forget all that trust misbelieved,
Here light fancies that erred, here fond hopes that deceived,
And, phœnix-like soaring, replumed from a fire
No longer to scorch thee, mount higher and higher
Into the memory of the past.
The eagle, having cast
Its draggled plumage, in no search
Of cruel meaning quits its perch,
But downward smites retreating gales,
While upward, cleaving them, it sails
With wings outspread and lids undone
To meet the glances of the sun :

And thou, as risen from the dead,
Reborn of trust, which once betrayed,
Shouldst gently cast thy soul away,
    Far from a once intrusive devil,
Into dreamed innocence of play
With thoughts and wishes, such as May
Upon its first ideal day
    In extasy of revel,
If there be May-days in the sky,
Sets floating in a cherub's eye."

HOME SPIRIT.

" Yet other memories intrude :
    For upon time's weird waste of sand
The latent waters will exude,
    Even when you dance a Saraband.
What is an idle spot to most,
To some is peopled by loves lost ;
They fill the world with memories green,
And are wherever they have been.
And you remember, nor hath night
    A darkness deep enough to strow
Over the sorrow of the great delight,
    That blushes in the burning bush, we know."

EDWARD.

" I to oblivion's fount would never wend
To be chased, flying out of Glend."

PUCK.

" Still memory is not so strong
    As the forgivingness of love.
Forgiving and forgetting wrong,
    Revel in present bliss, and rove
These ancient and once hallowed ways
Bright in the light of other days,
And dream, as when a loving lad,
Most willing blind, most gladly mad.
To Lucy's mansion this the way ;
You know it, and have called before to-day."

EDWARD.

Oh, I have called, I cannot say last when :
For I am calling evermore again."

PUCK.

" Her lord is yachting out of sight and·mind :
The winds are fair to him, to thee the fates are kind."

Puck, changing into likeness of her dog,
Decoying me, I follow in a fog :
I follow as with far less tender needs
Claris and Laris tracked the skipping kids.

    If I look too fondly
      Into Lucy's eyes ;
    If my words in whispers
      Rise on wings of sighs ;
    If I go too often,
      Often stay too long,
    Heaven may not forgive me,
      Yet I mean no wrong :
    For her kindness charms me.
      But I now inquire,
    Why I fan the embers
      Of her smouldering fire,
    While my heart keeps aching,
      That she tears hath shed
    Knowing how I love her,
      And how she is wed.

" Lucy," on tree once graved, now mossed I find,
Yet lettered perfect in the tree's deep rind.
The mosses from the name I do not purge,
Though that the gentle Dryad seemed to urge.
Within my heart the name inflamed she saw,
Where once cut deep enough my blood to draw
And nothing now obscured by misery :
Assuming harsher style she speaks to me.

Her following bitter words have tears within,
Sounding as though they had of Kainéd been :
Or was it conscience spake
For Lucy's sake ?

DRYAD.

" Is it manly, coming, going,
   To be tender no one nigh ;
Manly, others present, showing
   What they see not in a sigh ;
Like a nightingale May-mooning
   In a covert out of sight,
Is it manly, importuning,
   To bring secret love to light ?
Manly ! seeing her heart-blighted
   Wedded to a golden chain ;
Manly ! feeling though she slighted
   Yet she loved you, loves again ;
Manly ! is it not inhuman,
   Thus to seem without a plan ?
Manly ! knowing her a woman,
   Is it manly in a man ?
Dost thou in unshapen malice
   Play her own once double part ;
Proffering love's tempting chalice,
   Only seek to wring her heart ? "

EDWARD.

" Nay ! I love, and cannot leave.
   Still she holds me ; still I cling ;
Cannot bear to see her grieve,
   And am but a waxen thing."

I from the Dryad turned with feeble will
Now by no dog led, yet to Lucy still.
Fever burning, anguish blinds,
   And temptation tosses me :
Their own places are our minds,
   But what conscience makes them be.

Chains and darkness ! I am bound,
  Cannot see to break the chains :
Is it hell I feel around ?
  Am I wicked in its pains ?
But night puts on a comely brow :
We are in Lucy's arbour now.
Diana reigns, and heaven high
Reads this clear language in her chaste cold eye.

DIANA.

" Kind hand, press not his
  With so tender a might
As sighs thou art soft,
  And as purity white.
But songs of an angel
  A syren may sing ;
Not the words, but the passions
  Breathed into them, cling.

" Encircle her not with
  That love-making arm.
About her it winds like
  The rounds of a charm ;
Its tenderness drawing
  Her nigh is profound ;
But what if a serpent
  About her hath wound ?

" Stay, stay those wild kisses.
  They know but their bliss ;
Yet fires of perdition
  Are hot in each kiss.
Fiends striving with angels
  Swell high the emotion ;
And fierce, fierce the joy
  Of unworldly devotion.

" As a tempest of sighs is
  Breathed wild on the air,

Ah ! over him drop not
    The night of that hair.
It is lit by her eyes ;
    They have flared to his soul.
His brains flame on his temples,
    And he is a fool."

While sinless stars shudder,
    And moonlit flowers blush,
And songs without sounds al
    The wilderness hush,
Sudden conscious I, flying,
    Self flying with fear,
Quit Lucy still stainless,
    And honoured as dear,
While beautiful as heaven
    To me deep down in hell
Crying up to be forgiven
    For loving her too well.

To London and its Surrey Hills I haste :
City and wilderness seem equal waste.
Withdrawn is Lucy from my world of sighs—
My heart's best blood, with bitter tears from eyes
Dropping to be regathered not again—
She was a portion of my heart in vain
Ah ! breaking still : 'tis such a worthless heart.
Has time no cure for its inveterate smart ?

Had I been revenge pursuing,
    Could I have more evil done
Than perplexing, dimly wooing,
    Only to recede, and run ?
Flight is better than dishonour.
    Farewell ! loved on earth in vain,
Time must ne'er cry shame upon her,
    Heaven may give back again.

Once I thought only Lucy to kiss,
    And without her no Eden I knew ;

Though of Adam, Eve, Eden, and bliss
  The story may be but too true.
Wan the world is with sorrows and cares,
  Land and sea too are full of dead men;
But no ghost of salt tears or chill stares
  Ever frighted, or troubled us then.

What though closed was the gate never wide,
  That led into the Eden of old,
And her home was to me oft denied,
  She could come to me out in the cold.
Though no hearth blazed with wood by the cord,
  Glows more grateful of heart fired the breast :
She was welcome, I know not the word,
  Could have told her, how much I was blest.

Now with a longing shudder I grow mad,
  Now toss, a shipwrecked thing from hope to fear
On fancies now of Lucy good, now bad,
  With a dull sense of some disaster near.
  Oh ! Lucy was, and still is, passing dear :
Position, honour, wealth, which overflow
  Around me, stagnate passionless and drear,
Whose waste expanse I arduously row,
Looking to God above from vanity below.

Can it be ? and yet it must,
  Leaping now from mouth to mouth.
Who shall hence in woman trust,
  Wrong his manhood, fool his youth
For your raven locks or flaxen,
  And your blue or hazel eye,
For a thing so weak and waxen,
  That may with a hundred sigh ?

Conscience, and no Dryad now,
  Undisguised and stern appeared,
Billowy ridges on his brow,
  And grim tempest in his beard ;

2 K

While the lightnings of his eye
  Showed the thunders on his lips :
And as he was drawing nigh
  All the world seemed in eclipse.

CONSCIENCE.

" For a lie you lived to languish
  All through slowest years and long,"

EDWARD.

" Crushed now into instant anguish,
  And one burning sense of wrong."

CONSCIENCE.

" Fool ! "

EDWARD.

" To be deceived so wholly."

CONSCIENCE.

" Fool ! "

EDWARD.

" To mourn for one so vain.
Curses on my tenfold folly :
  Tenfold curses on her rain."

CONSCIENCE.

" Ah, she has her husband fled,"

EDWARD.

" With that soldier, ducal now."

CONSCIENCE.

" And shall be divorced—— '

EDWARD.

" Re-wed ? "

CONSCIENCE.

" Not by him, who broke her vow."

EDWARD.

" Promised marriage——"

CONSCIENCE.

" From it flying,
Rushing wild into the snare,
Hopelessly deceived."

EDWARD.

" He lying ? "

CONSCIENCE.

" God ! be merciful to her :
Cloying more with more of leisure,
  Fighting on a vanquished field,
Fallen, and at another's pleasure,
  Proud, but wanting now a shield ! "

EDWARD.

" Did I rain upon her curses?
  Let my bitter tears appease."

CONSCIENCE.

" Ah ! for those she none the worse is,
  None the better now for these."

EDWARD.

" Conscience, wilt thou never sleep?
  Had I anything to do
With the fall of her, I weep?
  Have I not been ever true—
True to falsehood, true to faith ? "

CONSCIENCE.

" True ! who lured her virtuous ruth
Into fires of lust and death?
  Better falsehood, than such truth.

Did you in the light of love
　　All her misery display,
So beget the wish to rove,
　　Lead her on, and leave her stray
On the very verge of charms
　　Wild, and shuddering, and calling,
Dropping into any arms
　　Ready to receive her falling—
Falling, flying self-contempt
　　So forsaken, flying fate
Holding her from bliss exempt
　　And repenting now too late?
Still she loyal might have been."

EDWARD.

"Can I for the wrong atone?
To her ruin half-foreseen
　　Have I been a stepping-stone?"

Hardly thinking, sitting still,
　　With a shudder now and then,
Me, without a wish or will,
　　Barely sensible of pain,
Torpid depths of brine benumb,
　　Like the woman turned to salt
In a bitter desert come
　　To an everlasting fault,
Lost, since Lucy now is lost,
　　And I was in part her loss.
True I had in love been crossed,
　　But a man can bear a cross :
This is wrecking woe heart-breaching,
　　Yet I neither groan nor sigh,
Only into space forth-reaching
　　"Lucy," "Lucy," "Lucy," cry,
Empty air no more presenting
　　Than to Herod, when remorse
Brought not back, to him lamenting,
　　Mariamne then a corse.

Brief the earl's case ; and, not appearing, she
Is no more bond to him now than to me.
We of a favoured club the haven share :
One afternoon I find him early there
In minor smoking-room retired alone
Intent upon a journal widely known,
" Truth," which is much more often true than false.
What there he reads so rancorously galls,
It is of Lucy surely something good,
That moves his wrath to such abandoned mood,
As makes his blue thin lips of pride unpurse
With an untongued, but conscious bitter curse.
I turn away ; and when I look again,
Upon me fall his eyes so full of pain,
Malice, and jealous rage, and hate extreme,
That he more horrid is, than he can seem.

THE EARL.

" So, sir."

EDWARD.

" My Lord."

We both have risen rash,
Frowning like clouds opposed about to crash.
But pride restrains him to a formal bow ;
And he withdraws, and I am lonely now
Even as he, by Lucy so forsaken.
But why now wrath with me ?   Is he mistaken,
Thinking in me another paramour ?
Let him, if so his pride more hurt endure.
I do not hate him, but I scorn him quite :
Beneath my hate he is, as good as out of sight.

Public Opinion in his room appears,
Having just passed him ; now with flaunting jeers
Strict weighing finds him wanting, and a cad :
I had not known he was so current bad.

PUBLIC OPINION.

"That silly Earl has but one fine trait—
He dresses well, though how let tailors say.
So little good is his interior man,
His lady, God forgive him, from him ran :
Paris had not French polished him enough,
But left a stubborn cross of British rough.
Some hint that she an ancient lover had,
And that the proud Earl knew it, and grew mad,
And smote her once ; and then she fled with—well,
You know it all, but scarcely what a hell
Burns in that formal bosom, which, though proud,
Rigid not frigid, glows for quite a crowd,
' Just like a prince,' he says, though I would scorn
To couple so with him the gentleman first born."

Disquieted, my dull cigar I dropped.
Public Opinion was not so estopped,
But led my rising passions in their play :
Each had a forceful last wild word to say.
"Strike Lucy did he ? " Anger first informs,
Thrilling my heart and frowning as it storms,
"Strike Lucy did he ? And I may not strike,
With interest due returning his mislike,
Lest I to rumour so should substance lend,
Proclaim my love, but not her fame defend.
Strike Lucy did he, and escapeth scaith ? "
Pity and shame then follow with one breath,
"Strike did he ? And I was, and am the base
And living cause of that supreme disgrace,
Making her fall into the final shame,
Coupling with that disgrace a blighted name."
"Strike Lucy did he ? " Fear with trembling hand
Raves o'er the chords, it so would reprimand,
"Strike her, and he, with whom she now hath fled,
Is—? Ah, would God that she had been struck dead ! "
Remorse succeeds, and with a wailing cry,
"Strike Lucy did he ? " And I was not nigh,

Though I had often been too near before.
" Strike her ! "   With head low bowed and conscience sore,
I heard despair upon my breaking heart,
But not yet broken, hurling swift as dart
" Strike her ! " and with it strike me not in vain,
Shivering my shrilling heart-strings ; silence then.

Stirring I quit the club, and distant saw
And followed hard the Earl.   I nearer draw
With what intent was plain, if not to heaven,
To lower hell, though not to me so driven,
Or rather sped by a resistless hate,
Arrested soon by interposing fate.
A brougham drew up.   My Lord at once leapt in ;
   While hurrying forward I, with brows deep knit,
A lovely form of captivating sin
   Beside him saw, and he was kissing it,
Losing himself, and not the less undone,
That he looked proud as though the winning one.

There leave him, who disdains the common trot.
Public Opinion is to him as not.
He hath a god indeed, a god unfeigned,
By whom his ways considered, not arraigned,
Approved are ; he unto himself is God,
Conceives none higher than his own tall nod :
And when a sanctuary he invades,
For churches are to him religious maids,
He goes not of a judgment day in fear—
A judge would hardly dare condemn a peer,
And God has not ordained to damn him here—
There leave him : not the less shall heaven judge,
And hell receive, who so believe in fudge.

Now kings should take good counsel with their fears,
And heads diminished hide, and dock their tales of peers.
When thunder stormed a gladiatorial show,
Caligula with puny fist a blow,

Winged with pale curses, straight at heaven aimed—
" Empire intolerable is so maimed,
With Jove divided.   Either he or I
Must speedily succumb—" was his fool cry.
But brave Vespasian sighed his latest breath
More shrewdly jesting with the touch of death—
"A God I am becoming now, I think—"
And eyelids closed, but with a covert wink
On his Apotheosis' very brink.
When upon Lexington Percy's regiments
From Boston marched, a boy, who watched events,
Called, " You to Yankee-Doodle go apace,
But you will soon come back to Chevy Chase,"
By Goffe and Whalley ! overweening pride
Of Bubbledom on fashion's swelling tide
Is near the burst and ebb of all its joy :
Truth spake its doom by mouth of that strange boy.
My God !   Wouldst thou my term this instant speak,
That I might perish utterly, and quick
As Otis in his farm-house porch-door died
   Watching a sudden storm, when from above
Fire on that day once only lightning eyed,
   Flashing struck only him, and him for love ;
And yet I would survive a little while
The blooming peers to judge, and sentence with a smile.

CANTO V.

OUT on life's ocean still our moral Grevilles
Surrounded fight armada-hosts of devils.
But from the fight the righteous sometimes run,
While some end well, who may have ill begun.
For conscience comes in aid of little wit,
And none are blind when disallowing it ;

Yet we admire how any can do well,
Whose ways are one to heaven, many to hell.
Ah, painful is the narrow path to find
In waste of legal jungle broad, and blind,
And tricky, as some half-compounded pill,
A most ungodly tortuous jumble still.
When God on urban strife is felt to frown,
I seek, like Thoreau, Jefferies, Hamerton,
My homely hermitage in Surrey woods,
Not natal, but at hand for shady moods :
I fly to woods whose secrecy relieves
And answers every question, doubt conceives,
So tutorful are woods, so wise, so true ;
St. Bernard none more sage companions knew.
And Lucy, ah ! I find her also there,
As ever dear : for she is everywhere
Lucy the lost.   I to the woodlands hie :
   "Friends, pray for me who have no strength for prayer,"
So Newman wrote, such too was Gordon's cry ;
   I go into the woods, and find God there :
Even Satan in the Wilderness found Christ,
And was rebuked by Him, whom he enticed.
Upon Mount Horeb, not in whirlwind, flame,
   Thunder, or earthquake shock, but still and small
The voice of God unto Elijah came ;
   And erst in Eden, when The Lord of all
With Adam condescended to commune,
Nature must calm have been, in perfect tune
Music of silence making, not to stay
The still, small voice upon its ear-ward way.
Not to Elijah came, nor liker thought
More still, more small a voice to Adam, not
More sure than unto me in mine own wood
Voices, that thrilled me, and I understood.
Pure reason, happy Intuition too,
Imagination, Faith, all round me drew.
And long it were to tell, and hard to say
How each I knew, by what distinguished trait,
But Beautiful were all, and not one sad ;

And much in common each with other had,
While, gathered round to meet and help my soul,
Each aided all, and me to self-control
With songs, that worded thoughtful prove to me,
How God does all things well and righteously.

With my old friend, the Bishop, my glad guest,
Charmed was my time, too soon beyond arrest,
With terrible occasion to recall.
Last of our walks and talks, though charming all,
Is present with me ; thorough wood and field,
And from Leith Hill surveying Sussex Weald.
Heaven had come down to earth for one whole day,
And saint might praise in it, and sinner pray,
And we discoursing went upon our way.
Though barely named, yet Lucy was to each
The secret motive and purview of speech.

EDWARD.

"Lucy to you was dear.   She, to my cost,
Once dear to me, still dearer now, is lost.
E'er man appeared, and passed for want of breath,
Evil was in this Universe, and death ;
Angels had fallen, who shall say what strife
Parted the races then and ranks of life?
Now sage and boor alike are 'ware of wrong,
Whose moral source is in self-will too strong,
Opposing God and good, and man awakes
To know the venom of remorse's snakes,
A lost one in the universe of law,
Stolen his joys, and all his life one flaw.
Society would be a sorry jest,
Did we not gloze the errors of the best.
Evil is in us : we ourselves are such,
Opposed to God, but conscious of His touch—
Reforming contact, in the struggle felt
The only power, that can our hard hearts melt."

BISHOP.

"When first a law of God our parents broke,
Innocents, they to moral sense awoke,
Conscious of evil, knowing nought before,
Scarce knowing God, knowing Him never-more,
Or deeper knowing Him as merciful :
But may His wrath 'gainst willing evil cool ?
Some say, His joy was in earth's denizen,
And heaven scarce goodlier than Eden then.
True, through unnumbered ages lapsed in time,
While earth through phases passed, each phase sublime,
Manifold changes had her beauty wrecked,
And stripped her, that she might anew be decked,
And from the chaos, littering her o'er,
A Venus issue fairer than before.
But for our blissful Eve-and-Adam dawn
A scene was chosen from all harms withdrawn,
And summer calms prevailed while Adam stood,
A little while prevailed.   The seeming good
Was but the moral of God's righteous plan,
Fleeting in Eden, as it was in man,
To last but Eve's brief bliss, then join her tears,
And since, uncertain, fill our hopes with fears.
For if a spot of earth there still may be,
Where light can nothing false, foul, angry see,
And all bright qualities of every land
Burst into blossom in an Eden band,
We know it not.   Should Christ with mighty train
In pomp millennial descend to reign,
He Eden may disclose, and fix His throne,
Where sin and mortal entered once alone.
We know it not : for still the Seraph stays,
And still his flaming sword round Eden sways,
Since man's prime fall unpoised the staggering world,
And he o'er earthquake went from Eden hurled,
And by weird lightnings livid earth surveyed
Doomed by the Lord to overturn of spade."

EDWARD.

"What mortal ravage now when passions rise,
And, storming spirit, make it willing prize !
Each gentle, good, and gracious thought is laid
With all its prostrate hopes among the dead.
No whirl of wind and sea, no quake of earth,
Ravage tumultuous wrought at either birth ;
No agony of tempest hiding heaven,
Loosening a world before it roaring driven ;
No toppling thrones of Lucifers ; no hell,
For mind is its own place, can paint too well
The savage unimaginable ill
Of a disordered heart, and wrongful will.
Weakness is always miserable, worse
Is strength which, lent to ill, becomes a curse ;
In all sheer madness of demoniac might,
Restraint dissolves, and riots into night ;
Hills rending torrent-like, wrecks drowning vales,
And with fell furies laughing sups on wails ;
But when the lash of conscience hissing falls,
And vile the shivering wretch on heaven calls,
Or clasps an aching head with fevered palms,
And dares not look to mercy for spare alms,
But crouched together as in horrent lair
Abideth judgment ! who shall paint despair ? "

BISHOP.

"Nature in disarrangement to reform,
If not repair, is visited by storm.
Misery too may passion heavenward send,
Till in the saint the worn-out sinner end ;
Rout evil from the bosom sorely awed,
And thrash the wailing creature back to God.
Ambition and dissension, rising winds,
And hurricanes of spirit, breathed by fiends !
Earth ravaged, and humanity unblessed,
Intrigue in heaven, their evil powers attest.
Yet oft the monsters in their carrion flight
Dip death-tipped beaks in embryos of night,

Dart lightning-eyed to strike the prosperous crime,
And cleanse, although with blood, their page of time;
Disorder, doing thus God-service, shows
Nothing can truly heaven discompose.
And knowing love in such display of power,
Standing we gaze, and wonder, and adore :
Though oft humanity with tear prevails,
And adoration droops her wings, and quails."

EDWARD.

" As beauty o'er her mirror fond delays,
And doats on imaged grace, it fair displays,
Nature to God seemed good, and still appears
To wisdom ripened with unfolding years.
Science, more clear than ancient revelation,
Dictates anew the poem of Creation :
Now, with particular progress in each kind,
Greatest variety unified we find—
The attribute of God, not course of fate,
But His sublime phenomena of State.
Nor change, nor death proves ultimate decay.
Changed for the better, creatures of a day,
All things from lower pass to higher, end,
Begin, combined in seeming to contend,
The lower feeds the higher on the road
From atoms up to man, from man to God,
In whom all live still, and there is no death,
Nor idle if some seeming waste of breath,
But evolution evermore, supreme
Above the highest angel's feeble dream."

BISHOP.

" All dissolution is but new creation,
A ferment that evokes regeneration :
What comes in judgment may in mercy go,
And leave us fresher from the fiercer blow.
Ah, God is great ; and all His works perform
No oratorio grander than the storm,

Not even when a hush deep fills the ear,
And heaven cloudless is and Luna clear.
And orbs are dumb in space, and shoreless wave,
And ship, and sailor silent as the grave.
Evil mysterious with its wizard brood
As little disconcerts the grace of good,
While onward, upward, forming ever higher
Being more wonderful, space and time aspire,
Spirit and matter one in man combine,
Who with his forehead touches the Divine.
O'er His dear infant yearns the heart of God ;
In earth constructs for him a fit abode ;
All wants supplying lays him on his breast
In bosom of the Universe, to rest
And drink for ever of mixed woe and bliss,
Which make him know and grow like what God is.
Light springs from darkness, flames through smoke from coal,
Sweet rains wash fresh the air, salt tears the soul ;
And, though Pacific are the deepest seas,
Yet more find God in trouble, than in ease.
God means that man should heights Ideal gain,
Oft pricks the laggard, smites the erring swain ;
Condemns him, not for what he erst was born,
But what he fails to become, and chance may scorn :
So when the light of truth illumes his soul,
And shows him wandering from his distant goal,
He, retribution dreading, comes to know
The heaven above him has a hell below ;
And slow repenting feels, how deep that guilt, ,
Which to the cup of misery gave the tilt,
That o'er the world this endless deluge spilt
Of woe and weariness.   Then half to die
He wishes, as he scans the louring sky,
Sees sin in it too—nothing else but sin ;
Then through each form of nature, out and in,
Deems sin to be the breath of every blast,
Despair of every gloom, and death at last,
Believes of some fell sin each cloud is bred,
And each chill rain-drop by some sin is shed.

Then hating sin, he hateth passing well,
And shudders at the thought, and dreams of hell."

EDWARD.

" Man may be silly, never at the worst
A bubble, which God blows to see it burst.
He means His creatures should with aid from Him,
Though often stumbling, still to heaven climb ;
And deems His grace, which pharisees asperse,
Right in The Maker of The Universe,
Himself a Sufferer in Christ, The Just
Forgiving the repenting rising dust.
Say, who shall limit the repenting space ?
Not God.   May creatures then reject free grace ?
Had we the life-elixir, Reynard's ring,
Philosopher's stone ; desire at fullest swing,
Could we with wave of fairy wand command
For our material wants supplies to hand,
Who would to proper uses put these powers,
Or well employ their unlaborious hours ?
Yet human will enlightened may combine
In such full harmony with the Divine,
That time may come, when word of man shall be
Enough to cast this mountain in that sea.
Shall centuries of Jewish mother-hood,
Longing to infant superhuman good,
Have given us Jesus, and a later day
Fail evolution on its constant way ?
Having a will with God's in unison,
Man would, as Christ with God, with Christ and God be
    One."

BISHOP.

" In form and colour, Lucy perfect seen,
Should too in spirit have an angel been ;
But ways of matter and of spirit warp,
And plaintive is the Universal harp.
When portions of ourselves from life depart—
Friends we have watched, we go with them in part,

Part with each friend, till what of us remains,
After so many passing-mortal pains,
Belittled so, we unidentified
Had, strange to self and time, most willingly died.
God educates the Spirit, and restrains—
Reforms the rebel in material chains,
Transformed at last to spiritual wings,
On which the soul in heaven soars and sings.
The spiritual needs material growth ;
Well-being is joint property of both:
Material progress comes of and commands
An equal spiritual : they join hands.
As spirits more capacity betray
More intricate and complex organs play,
And liberate the growing conscious powers
For nobler exercise of grander hours.
And we shall pass, when found unsuited here,
To higher form in supernatural sphere—
Here Space and Time, but there Eternal Being ;
Here imperfection, there, both seen and seeing,
Perfection, when, the work of Space and Time
Concluded, all the bells of heaven chime.
Here God and man commune towards one goal,
His nature God revealing, man his soul
To whose adaptive ever-growing power
God more appears in Nature—more, and more :
Till, rent the natural veil, man God-like grown
Beholds The God unveiled, and knows as he is known."

EDWARD.

"Wisdom and power, upon whose ocean we
Wander and wonder everlastingly !
Wisdom and power, both measureless to man,
Which physical and moral worlds so plan,
That all along each physical shall range
With corresponding spiritual change,
Derangement impious of laws of soul
In those of matter equal storm control,

While, not in paradise and not in hell,
Men in a world that passes passing dwell !
Without a miracle, and in the course
Of nature, moving with resistless force
As God impelled it first, o'er sinners bold
And unrepenting is an ocean rolled,
And in the course of nature earth on fire
And the last mortals may in flames expire.
But God from cursedness alone, or hate,
His much loved image would not desecrate ;
Slur the bright, beautiful, which at command
Rose out of Chaos ordered to be land ;
Most tiny leaf from lowliest blossom rend,
Or one brief shadow over sunshine send.
Destruction coming, sent not to destroy,
Issues in higher good and greater joy ;
To free a butterfly bursts a chrysalis,
And wrecks a world, that man may know, God is,
And underneath His wings, widespread, secure
Trust, though in shadow, that His Love is sure."

BISHOP.

" The Word, the Will of God, both is and was
Of all the sensible sole ceaseless cause ;
Matter a chain-mail, closely wrought of things
Linking and interlinking, rings on rings,
Innumerous nature.   God the chain-mail made,
And in its panoply Himself arrayed
To be, appear, and speak in Man's affair,
Or higher, not forgetful how it wears.
Each linked ring burnishing, maintaining there
The lowest as the highest, all His care,
He all so qualifies, that each apart
Has The Whole Universe to take to heart,
And act, be acted on, receive, and send
A thrill of influence to Creation's end—
One as its God.   Thus all those seeming mights
He, Only Great, Almightily unites,

By Him continued, as by Him begun,
One as Himself, and proving He is One."

EDWARD.

" And thought of fire for earth need none dismay.
Yes, we may burn, but not to pass away :
That purest element may earth embrace,
And lick the spots and wrinkles from her face
To glorify her with a dying kiss ;
And its last smile may light us home to bliss—
A home unto repentant sinners given,
Their woes forgotten, sinful spirits shriven,
Still from sublime to rise to more sublime,
And follow up the loves begun in time.
Oh ! fair then as their heaven, methinks I see
In the bright feeling of Eternity,
And the sweet Sun-day of sabbatic calms,
Youngling immortals waving joyful palms ;
That, for which time was short, now easy, lo !
Beyond all stretch of thought the heavens grow.
And shall it not be happiness untold,
When men shall face to face their God behold ;
When, sensible in all to eye and ear,
Working out all in all, he shall appear
The Universal Cosmos as it were,
Almighty Spirit active everywhere,
The great deviser still by mind, by will
Great Providence, great operator still.
And though it may eternally be said,
True as when Judah's skies responses made
To eager trembling children of their sod,
' None to prefection ever can find God ; '
Yet even now, when ignorance will cry,
' Let not God speak, or I shall surely die,'
We can confess to Him in Christ revealed,
' All known is good,' and trust in all concealed.
God has in Christ to earth descending, sworn
To cancel all the sins, Himself hath suffering borne."

BISHOP.

" Pregnant of purpose, full of force and fact,
A mother's noiseless ways of quiet tact,
To simple nature true, profoundly move,
The heart of nature is so full of love.
Life's struggle is to love as well as live,
And helpful Nature waiteth more to give.
The deaf are mute, but we possess an ear
For what she has no speech, her silence hear,
Which looking forward, ever with good-will,
Full of an evolution-longing still,
Gives to prophetic thought a tongue in soul,
To faith a prospect of its longed-for goal.
Say ; what are hope and expectation ?   What,
But seasonable seed, not doomed to rot,
Whose autumn garner shall expected grain ;
An expedition out of heart and brain
Into the future, and an 'twere the pod,
That cherishes the purposes of God.
These gentle ushers of all higher things,
Bearing the present forward upon wings
Of outlook into prospect more sublime,
Are proper to advance and lead the time,
Wonderwise winging so, you may not hear
Their pinions glide though they be ever so near,
Yet having such expression and such aim
As cannot quite inaudibly proclaim,
They are on God's High Way.   This mocking bird
Has learned their note, and sings, what he has heard,
How fairest thoughts are truest things of heaven :
Accept nought less than by expectance given.
For that God given is, and nature's sign
Of upward growth into a fact divine
Too gradual to recover soon, if lost ;
But if firm grasped, then never to exhaust.
Do not Eternity for Time reject :
It is more glorious longer to expect

The whole grand truth by scientists denied,
By sages doubted, poets prophesied."

Home gained, my talk with kindly bishop ended.
With groom he, mounting, to the vale descended
For friendly call on downs of further side,
Whither I saw him soon slow uphill ride ;
Now see him carried to my door a corse.
Returning downward tripped the quiet horse ;
So was the Bishop thrown, and on his bed
Now in my Hermitage is lying dead.
Thus to the church the best, and thus to me
Dearest of men is lost, but not to Thee,
O God ! for Paradise at little cost
He by such fall regains, and is not lost.
Though England mourns him now beneath the sod,
He lives in all our hearts, and is at home with God.
The storm of doubt and passion of my grief
Have cleared of clouds and rains the heaven of my belief.
His voice has ceased, or heard, himself unseen,
　The words, nowise distinguishable, appear
Consentient with my thoughts, which now convene
　And give them voice and chorus in my ear :
So while the spheres their fiery courses run
With sounds of many thunders roared in one
Deafening the spatial to its utmost bound,
You hear your own thoughts, only think the sound.

And Lucy ?　Ah, she is not dead, but lost—
Ill worse than death—to save at any cost.
Now here in town I find, as late in wood,
Her always lost, lost, lost, and most to good.
Every heart some spot has tender ;
　Mine must soft for Lucy be :
God, to whom I homage render,
　When rejected by, loved me.
Am I, a man, to judge my Lucy then
By law, not God's ?　Ah, well I wot, that men,

Too little merciful, are prone to fetch
And carry for the pleasure of Judge Ketch,
Of whom 'tis pity he is mortal vain :
All judges are, who judge their fellow-men,
And clothing pride in worse humility,
  Of bad precedent in awe,
With a little brief authority
  Recognize it as good law.
I will not judge her. Hand, not heart, for pelf
She sold, and hurt me, but more wronged herself.
Acquainting me too with ill,
  And poverty and sorrow,
I look for Lucy still,
  Whom I may find to-morrow.

      They say, she is abroad
        With her paramour
      Reigning, a false god,
        In her fires secure,
      Cleopatrine state
        Girdling her, its queen
      Proud and passionate,
        Queen of men and sin.
      But I know her well,
        Wronged by him, enough
      To burn up his hell
        With more flaming stuff ;
      And I seem to know
        That it cannot last ;
      And I see a woe
        Coming-coming fast ;
      In her soul disdain,
        In his heart new lust,
      And in both the pain
        Of an old distrust.
      Will she quit it all ;
        Turn to God in doubt,
      Or but lower fall
        Burning out and out?

Shall I Lucy see
  In the streets some morrow?
Will she speak to me
  In her sin and sorrow?
Tempt me? I am mad
  So to think of it;
Yet have queens been bad—
Kentigern saved one, and sad
  Nuns e'en walked the street.

Knew I song of Indian passion
  Stirring earthquakes, rousing storms,
Sing I would not in such fashion
  As move elemental forms
Unto Lucy's swift undoing,
  But insinuate through air
Such to her melodious wooing
  As made heaven everywhere,
Till she conscious was of blessing—
  Kindly nature all abroad
Soothing her distress, caressing,
  Folding her to heart of God.

In that bosom she would, hearing,
  Learn another gladder song
Of more infinite a cheering,
  And a passion far more strong,
Of a love divinely gracious
  Making all her spirit His,
Till becomingly audacious
  She desired no other bliss;
Till earth's supervacuous wailing
  In itself no more believed,
Conscious of a joy unfailing
  In a love, that ne'er deceived,
And a trust beyond all shames
In a Name above all names.
Thus I fall into fair dreams
  Of Lucy and a vision

Illumined, till to sense it seems
The act of her contrition.

DREAM.

" Wooingly coloured, and winsomely shaped,
　Lovingly nurtured with mother for nurse,
Just such a blossom as should have escaped,
　Tended and guarded, the blight of the curse,
True as young Eden she promise fulfilled,
　Graces of culture enhancing her charms,
Also to fortune wed trusty, which willed
　Out of her future all times' alarms.

" Ah ! false as Eden ; than down-dropping star,
　Brilliant a moment 'twixt heaven and earth,
Changefuller, waywarder, giddier far
　She disappeared from the place of her birth.
Where is she wandering ?　Who shall say where ?
　All know the home of the angels that sinned :
Thinketh the weary one—' Let me go there,
　Anywhere out of this home of mankind.'

" Stop her for mercy's sake !　Even for such
　Christ on the cross died : let her not go.
She, much forgiven, may, loving so much,
　Enter the kingdom through penitent woe.
Meekly she enters, and humbly begins,
　Taught and then teaching, and casting her lot
In with the sisters that turn from their sins,
　Holily lovely now, changed, not forgot."

　　Can it be Lucy after all
　　　Shining as in a beam ?
　　So gazing into dream I fall
　　　To further dream.

VISION.

" 'Neath classic braids of silken hair
　A queenly forehead shows :

No flaunting ringlets ruffle there
   A deep repose.
And hers the clear, calm, steady eye,
   And fair, not rosy cheek,
Look which, though looking through the sky,
   Yet looking meek,
Looketh as though it gladly would
   Its native country gain,
Yet will, God seeing it for good,
   On earth remain.

" These cheeks no streams of lava foul ;
   No pent fires heave that breast ;
Upon her halcyon calm of soul
   A saint might rest.
For penitence is deepest peace,
   More blissful than great joy,
Depths of unfathomed sun in seas,
   No storms annoy.
Pleasingly bright, she is not gay,
   But happily serene,
Minding me of a holy day,
   And heavenly scene.
Heaven hath reminted the dear face,
   Which earth had troubled sore,
Sin only seen now in the grace,
   That passed it o'er.

" And is this Lucy ?   Yea, I seem
   Her living self to trace ;
Or do I only see in dream
   An angel face ?
Not brilliant is the glow of bliss
   Angelic, only bright ;
Of pure sweet dream an angel is
   The perfect light.
They say, that angels visit some,
   And for a time appear :
Lucy herself may have become
   An angel near."

And now of her to reckon only ill
Beyond my power is, as against God's will :
Good is so mixed with it in memory dear,
She holds my love, and claims my ready tear.
Lead, kindly light, and no less kindly cloud,
Lead Thou me on through shine, shower, shade, and shroud ;
For, sympathizing with my moan,
Thou hast a feeling of Thine Own
   Loving the lost.   And, if I should repine,
I a poor fellow am.   O Lord,
Bless Lucy, rest her in Thy Word,
   Make her consistent, make her Thine.

CANTO VI.

THOUGH to gnat-life some seconds give full play,
A thousand years to God are as one day.
Through vital changes in all nature ran
Palœo-neo-lith, rude, savage man
For many thousand years.   He struggled on ;
At length his way through bronze and iron won
To silver, and now golden, brighter times
And less material, hearing heavenly chimes
Changing them into hours of Grace, that then
Pure spirit far-descended true may reign.
The sword of Wallace, laid on granite block,
Impressed itself, a cross, upon the rock ;
Fit sword, by legend so with cross allied,
Its patriot-bearer for his country died.
With sword of spirit now and loving glance
We more illume and pierce dark circumstance ;
Time's deeps explore, and, should its storms assail,
Perish ourselves may, but good cause prevail.
My God and Father ! help me play my part
In my small interact with all my heart.

My latest visit proved my long " Good-bye "
To the bold partisan about to die.
Elect, eject, an infidel avowed,
Again elect, no longer disallowed,
He fair had taken and retained his seat ;
And now is dead, his victory complete.
Tasking his failing frame, a light of mark
He in The House had stood, and now is dark,
Through years of storm, strain, struggle well sustained,
By Christians done to death, not now disdained.
We with one heart like ends had various sought ;
And at our parting last he hid no thought.

THE PARTISAN.

" Much I admire to see our British race
Still willing suffer the prolonged disgrace
Of standing armies, wars, and peers, and thrones,
Land-laws, and privilege, no use atones,
And scorn, and servitude ; and, though combined,
 Divided show as of uncertain mind."

EDWARD.

" Thy party coat hast thou too long then worn ? "

PARTISAN.

" The masses only our slow methods scorn ;
Not ready we, though able, nothing less
Than once in New and far World wilderness,
To rout our drumming masters.   Ah ! how long
Suffering desires the right ; endures the wrong
Of ill enough to build a palace, but
Not enough good to raise and roof a hut.
Yet, fittest to survive and most profound,
Mere common-sense, though humble, holds its ground.
Thought must live longest, which has that within ;
A touch of nature makes the whole world kin.
The common peoples more and more prevail ;
Abnormal oligarchies all must fail.

Hardy, and long lived, and so commonest,
By law Darwinian common things are best."

Such his last words to me.   I could not find
How with things sacred to approach his mind.
A popular leader he : less worthy post,
Your Tory coachman thinks, than fashion's vet can boast,
Who "all the Royal Family attends,
And to the canine headship condescends : "
This other to the Canaille, and offends.
Embittered into controversial pride,
He had, in speech, our common God denied.
What good for all is, pride from some conceals ;
But God to simple folks Himself reveals.
All races too have sayings of mankind,
Touches of nature, thoughts in every mind
Fruiting in proverbs, which most sage condense
And give quintessence of experience ;
While popular myth in legendary mode,
Can justify to man the ways of God.
By intuition so, or better choice,
The voice of God is most the people's voice.
Danté and Milton, men beyond our soar,
Of great and daring heart and deeper lore,
Bunyan too, not less noble though unschooled,
Were men inspired, or we have all been fooled:
Writing, like Shakspeare they in vulgar tongue
For common-people dreamed immortal song,
Where good and evil are most living things,
And God Supreme the final issue wings.
Angels and devils, powers of heaven and hell,
Realities to soul, within us dwell—
Conceptions sage, if vulgar, and still play
A part most active in this latter day.
"Watchman, what of the night ? " Is this my human cry
"Is sun-day yet appearing in the sky ?
The hosts of darkness, are they full in flight ?
Watchman, what of the day ?   What of the night ? "

The Watchman thus, " Rejoice ! the sun is nigh,
The lingering powers of darkness turn to fly ;
The battle of the dawn is over-past ;
The victory is won by sun at last.
Behold he rises ; now a glow of love
Suffuses earth below, and heaven above.
He runs, and climbs to gain the zenith near ;
Without a shadow, all in light is clear.
Clean-sweeping rays have left in bluest space
A cloudless hazeless Universe of grace."

But, say you, unprofounded depths repose,
Whence never fish to fool, or fly arose ?
Ah ! whether is fish wanting, fly, or fool ?
In arm of Cader-Idris lies a pool
By story vouched unvisited by fish ;
Yet once rose one there to my ardent wish.
And now the more we matter probe, we find
Forces in it of spiritual kind.
Shall we discover more, and learn to use,
And as we more discover, less abuse ?
We orbs now analyze by spectroscope,
And even Hell flames by Eternal Hope.
Soon bright intelligence may, flashed afar,
Girdle the Universe, from star to star
The peoples signalling, both what they are,
And whither sailing on the mighty broad,
And all acknowledging a common God.

No one may over his own shadow leap,
Live out of his own time, the future reap,
Administer the present in the past ;
But, though his circumstances form his cast,
Both this and these he so may modify,
You will not know him, when he comes to die.
I dare to trust now, having slowly learned,
To take from God a victory unearned.
Evil I fight with God's own weapon—good,
Leaning on Christ now, and his Holy Rood.

I 'ware have been of spirits that opposed,
And spirits that for me with these have closed ;
Though vigorous the battle various fought,
Prevailing victory has wisdom taught ;
I can the mystery of evil face,
Believing now the mastery of grace ;
And now a Judge am, though My Guardian Sprite
Anxious maintains his ancient oversight.

GUARDIAN SPRITE.

" You deemed ambition dead—
    Halt only, vaulting late
When you a judge were made."

EDWARD.

" A judge of lustres eight."

GUARDIAN SPRITE.

" A Judge ! and still so young.
    Shall we a pæan raise,
Exalted into song,
    And triumph in your praise ? "

EDWARD.

" Nay : I have quit the race
    For riches, honours, fame,
And in a quiet place
    Would nurse an honest name."

GUARDIAN SPRITE.

" 'Tis good to be approved
    Your own profession's pride,
A judge by all men loved,
    And God upon your side.
But your ambition once,
    The law to codify,
Now think you to renounce ? "

EDWARD.

' " Nay : for I live to try.
Yet, labour as I may,
　It is too huge a curse
For one to lift ; and, while I pray
　Never to make it worse,
I hope to leave it some fine day
　To my executors :
Else, in far other haunts
　Than legal ones, I seek
To succour woes, and wants,
　Which make our neighbours weak ;
No more in Lucy's orbit move,
Nothing hear of her I love."

GUARDIAN SPRITE.

" Arms of prayer yearning fling
　Round the knees of God, and there,
Lucy still expecting, cling :
　God can reach her anywhere."

No longer than two hours agone
　Unto a duty blind,
For that a brother had fallen ill,
　I sudden was assigned ;
Now read the list of cases,
　I shall to-morrow try.
Full of a special wonder
　The first there holds mine eye—
A woman's name !　I know it,
　My Lucy !　Can it be ?
And to be tried for murder
　To-morrow, and by me ?
The murder of——　My God ! and still
　I horror-stricken gaze ;
Now rigid sit ; now shudder ; and
　Now kneel, as one who prays,
Hour after hour, till dawn appears,
　Or prostrate on the floor.

Ne'er may I pass again such night,
   As man never passed before.

It is a bright May morning,
   And the birds from bush and bower
Pour out their grateful throats in song
   To please the gracious hour.
Heart-sick, I am at once to try—
   The moment is at hand—
A woman, who has done to death
   A noble of the land.

When to Rome's Coliseum
   For gladiatorial game,
Or himself to fight the lion,
   The mighty Emperor came,
The proud patricians crowded
   To grace the royal sport ;
And the great world of fashion now
   Fills all the brightened court.

A tall and stately lady
   Rises quiet in the Dock,
And sudden, not unlooked for
   But terrible, the shock.
I, on the instant know, and,
   Sinking back into my chair,
Nor noble now, nor semple see,
   But only Lucy there.

As when in icy region,
   Benumbed by dreaded fate,
Sinks in some pathless snow-storm
   A lost one wandering late,
Found, warmed, what pangs shoot through him,
   As life, that ebbed, reflows ;
Such paralysis of being, such
   Benumbingness of woes,

Conscious of only Lucy, hold
   Me pale and rigid there,

Till she towards me looking
  Is of her judge aware.
Never shall I the horror
  Of her look forget, or shame :
Upon her pallid fainting lips
  I seem to see my name,

And fret to cast my robes away,
  And feel to laugh or weep,
And think through all that staring crew
  To Lucy's side to leap ;
But feelings now disguise must,
  That no one there may see
How love, remorse, dread, anguish
  Haunt, and are stabbing me.

For I am now to judge her, and,
  Great God ! Thou knowest all.
Her eyes to light re-opening
  Full conscious on me fall,
Love humbly dumbly showing, but
  Not craving any grace.
Then, by memory rushed, she drooping
  Before me hides her face.

"Not Guilty," is her answer
  With voice, that makes me glad.
And the opening I note, and
  The witness good and bad ;
Till, through my fitful anguish,
  Hope growing, gathering gives
Me faith she has not done it,
  And still in her believes.

Then is her own sad story read
  In silence dumb and pained—
" I never thought in any court
  To be for crime arraigned,

But for murder by my woman's hand—
  'Tis too horrible ! Oh, why
Did I unwilling live, and he,
  Who wished not death, so die.

" It was upon that fated morn,
  Wild words between us passed :
Oft had he vowed to leave me, seemed
  To purpose it at last :
And knowing I had ceased to please,
  And he might other wed,
I, maddened by my misery,
  Sore wished that I was dead.

" Forget not what high station
  I quitted years before
For marriage promised then by him,
  Who is alas no more.
Deceived, yet true, though true I now
  A surfeit had of shame,
And rather thought to die than lose
  The soil of a great name.

" A brace of ready pistols
  There always loaded lay ;
I seized and turned one on myself,
  Nor turned it so in play ;
But, hotly sensible of hurt,
  To shame and sting him, cried,
' How thus I killed myself, the world
  Shall tell your future bride.'

" My hand he caught, the weapon turned,
  But how it cracked and sped,
I know not, all is vacancy,
  Save that I saw him dead.
For by the heights above us,
  And by the depths beneath,
I swear, I sought not, thought not his,
  But only mine own death."

What saith the Judge unto the twelve,
　　As he looks from face to face,
And only thinks of Lucy lone,
　　Her danger, and disgrace?
Saith, " Whether did she seek for flight,
　　Or help in that sad hour,
When, staggering from her struggling arms,
　　Down fell her paramour?

" Her sudden shriek through all the house
　　Rang wild to rend the skies;
Though, if his death she meant, heed not
　　Her story, nor her cries.
But if she prized a living dog
　　More than a lion dead,
And if his act against her wish
　　The fatal bullet sped,

" You will not visit on the head
　　Of this unhappy one,
Nor will you brand as murderous,
　　What chance, or God hath done."
The twelve withdraw, and then a hum
　　Swells from the crowded rows,
And some, once envious of her joys,
　　Rejoice now in her woes.

And wearily we wait, and
　　Hot falls the sultry air,
And dark the court, and darker grows
　　In the forked lightning's glare.
Ah! wherefore now on Lucy
　　Should man and nature frown?
And the thunders crack and bellow,
　　And the rains come lashing down.

And still the jury linger;
　　Such their unwilling way,
When thoughts of doom they ponder.
　　A man might bear delay;

But a woman, and my Lucy ?
　O God ! they come.　Alas !
" Manslaughter " their small mercy ;
　Mine, sentence now to pass,

Long years of prison and disgrace,
　Whose pains on me begin,
The horror and the anguish,
　The consequence of sin—
Mine somewhat, if more Lucy's.
　I dare not look on her,
But in the fashionable crowd
　Am conscious of a stir,

And see a lady sinking back,
　Enhancing the brave sport—
Her miserable mother
　In a fit borne out of court.
As she quits the dock, she also sees ;
　Our eyes one moment meet,
And shuddering I leave the bench
　And in my chamber sit—

Not long.　Her cell I seek.　Head bent,
　Without a thought to please,
She at my feet falls, clasping hard
　My trembling yielding knees,
And weeping, weeping, weeping, while
　I dare not soothe her pain,
Nor stoop to raise her, or I sure
　Had knelt beside her then.

" Rise, Lucy, dearest Lucy, I
　No bruised reed would break ;
Thine innocence believing, now
　Would serve thee ; freely speak."
At this she sudden moved again,
　In a riot falls of sobs,
As the fountains of her being all
　Were welling up in throbs,

And gasps, and, broken at the heart,
  Were running off in tears,
Until I shake with sympathy,
  And pallid grow with fears :
For now the ravages I note,
  Which passion there has made,
Disease and woe, and last this shame,
  God's burden on her laid.

Hast ever seen in pastoral vale
  Fat hills on either side,
Swept by a sudden thunderstorm,
  In new-born cataracts slide
Down a thousand separate fresh ravines
  To the river at the base?
So sudden storms of passion wreck
  The beauty of a grace.
But what shall years of evil, woe,
  Disease, shame, leave behind?
We may an infant paradise,
  But no old Eden find.

She of her mother questions me,
  But I can nothing tell ;
Though by that mother sold, she yet
  Still loves that mother well,
Whose pride may now, from swoon restored,
  Unbroken, although marred
By the disgrace of Lucy, show
  Her hardened heart more hard :
Nought has she done, nought tempted even
  In her own daughter's aid,
Not visited her prison cell,
  No sympathy conveyed ;
She never has her daughter sought
  All through these years of sin.
Now whose shall be the Lucy,
  Who never can be mine?

Let men, who are content to live
  A little while on earth,
And in it take their foolish fill
  Of sorrow-mingled mirth,
Eat dirt, and wish not heavenly food ;
  Let men, who can alone
The future face in present peace,
  And their own past atone,
Deride the judge, who now can sink
  His ermine in the priest,
Deride me : for I Lucy love,
  And point her to the Christ.

She listens, and so listening calms ;
  Peace swathes her like a stole ;
The grave fresh dawn of heaven, I see,
  Is winning on her soul.
God grant, that she may live ; but death
  Is illumining her face :
God give her time to know, and feel
  Assurance of His grace.
She is weary of a life of sin ;
  And I want to help her so.
Then, leaving her to heart within
  And God above, I go.

Some more straight-lined are than was music Lully ;
He, frighted by a hell-fire priest and bully,
Gave his last opera to feed the flame,
But kept a copy of it all the same.
Demurely pacing, lovely penitent
Once to St. Paul's Cross doing penance went,
And drew all ravished eyes too fond to blame :
Lucy in other wise repents her shame
Which, never prize, to me is lasting dole
Less amorous of her form, than curious of her soul.

Soon was I 'ware of the hard mother's fate :
Mercy on her had closed its long wide gate,

Borne out of court insensible, she had
   Not only fainted then, but, well-a-way !
The proud and recreant woman was gone mad—
   Worse than suspended on that cruel day.
Let us dismiss her with her pride to doom ;
   She came not back to court, to prison not :
For, when to life restored, she had become
   A mumbling paralytic idiot.
But a much valued, honoured, trusted friend,
Who consecrated life the sick to tend,
A Lady nurse I knew, to whom all told,
I stirred her heart, beyond the touch of gold.
A visitor to Lucy she repaired ;
No distance overtasked, nor trouble scared,
All seemed such pleasure, done in mercy's name,
So much she pitied Lucy in her shame.
And since my e'erwhile visits sometimes grieved,
I, rarely going, thus good news received.

Too long for Lucy vainly without cease
Have I on throne urged pardon and release ;
And doubtless well had won within the year,
But the accident was to the accident—a peer.
Yet our Victorias are no turbaned Czars,
Nor our home secretaries scimitars.
To some my urgency a scoff became—
To men with faith in nothing but ill fame,
Not to that Lady nurse : she could not blame,
But, honouring pertinence not more than just,
She much approved my love, and thus discussed.

LADY NURSE.

" Folly is topped by scientists, who flout
Anthropomorphic thought, yet think truth out,
Though with less reason, in as human fashion
As I, who of God's love speak and Christ's passion,
And say, God suffers in enduring sin,
And Christ did to the death our love to win ;

And His own people also with Him must
Suffer all others' sin, their own in dust,
Die to themselves, and rise no more to fall :
And all for self prove willing self for all—
A mystery profound, but feeling blest,
Which sole can lay the tumult in man's breast."

EDWARD.

" Man welfare seeks in individual bliss :
'Tis human nature, so is sacrifice ;
And neither should the other once impeach,
But, offering each for all, prove all for each.
On self-devotion both at last depend ;
Self-interest of self-sacrifice is friend,
Because God wills, we so should perfect right,
And with humanity in Him unite,
Self-centred none, but interactive all
In and with God, beyond attaint of fall ;
Man in humanity, and, still more broad,
Humanity in Christ, and Christ in God,
Whose law is love ; whose will, on earth when done,
God, Christ, man shall be, and in heaven begun,
Not a self conscious but Eternal one."

LADY NURSE.

" Yet most deem love of self to be
Sole motive of all energy ;
And, noting spare assuasive grace,
Or show of goodness in a face,
Fancy it feebleness of mind,
Or some foul cozening fiend to lurk behind."

EDWARD.

" Each his own appetence to please,
And soothe a conscience ill at ease,
Keeps some shrewd Knave like that to grin,
And cap his evil with another's sin.
But Hades in profoundest hell
Holds none more impious infidel ;

And if he be of prophet ken,
It is in judgment upon men,
That God permits a Hobbes to mouth
Tonguing so damned and black untruth.
For me I will in love believe,
Which, though deceived, will ne'er deceive ;
Which, kindling not heart's ruddy core
With sickening introspect of sore,
But wishing better mind to wrong,
And pitiful of evil, long
Forgiving till forgetting ill,
Hopeth, endureth, trusteth still ;
Love, which may lose, but ought to win ;
Love, which pure God may revel in,
Light of the world, of heaven a ray :
    For God, regarding to approve
The creature, He had made of clay,
    Smiled on, and warmed it into love ;
And often since, the soul of man,
    Which may itself and God forget,
Clings to, and lives for, whom it can,
    Or, thrust aside, remembers yet."

LADY NURSE.

" But many Easter eggs he must have eaten,
    And chestnut glands of festive Jupiter,
Marrowing him, to be at last not beaten
    Daring some latest fall with Lucifer."

EDWARD.

" When Count Soldanha was set free,
    But dead, upon his steed ;
And Bernando, greeting, knew him dead,
    And who had done the deed ;
And later came and dared them all—
    King, Condé, and Grandee—
I would, had I been there alive,
    Have joined him 'gainst all three,
So hate I black ingratitude,

So hate I base bad faith ;
I, rather than approve them, would
  Have chucked the chin of death.
And, not because true love is blind,
  Or justice fooled, doth heaven
Make sacrifice, give counsel kind,
  Rejoice to hear it given ;
But true love slakes all evil will,
  As balsams, 'neath which vipers nest.
Feed and unvenom them—to kill
  No more in Araby, the blest."

LADY NURSE.

" Good fruits may upon sun attend,
  And flowers feed on light ;
But even wrong becomes a friend
To love, which ministers amend
  By tendering always right."

EDWARD.

" Knowing the pity of it all,
The aimless steps from fall to fall,
How wistfully I pine to pour
Sunshine of heart the wide world o'er,
Tears rainbow, fading smiles re-bloom,
And each dark torch of hope relume.
While honouring, since my first known hour,
Every fair element of power,
What though the secrets of the world
  Of matter and of spirit lay
Unto my mental eye unfurled,
  And all to me were day,
Where highest angels cannot see—
Day unto God alone, and me :
What though the stores were mine that lie
  Within the cumbered wombs of stars
Blazing a hot or frosty sky,
  And I had fineless jars

Ruby, and Malachite, and gold,
The countless wealth of stars to hold ;
What though my word were a command
Throughout the universe of land,
Sea, fire, and air, where'er an ear,
Or aught in any way can hear :
What though I reigned a God intact,
But heartless, and a loveless fact,
That could not love, nor be beloved ;
Oh, misery ! to rest unmoved
By any woe, by any weal !
   I'd give the knowledge, wealth, and power
Even of a God, that could not feel,
    To purchase heart but for an hour ;
To know it all my soul coerce
    With a violence sweet to brook ;
Would abdicate the Universe
    For the power to feel a look,
Be wealful author of some piteous deed,
To raise a fallen brother Christlike bleed.
Red Montluc scorned your man of grit,
Holiday soldier, hypocrite,
Who, if he might for heaven trim,
Would carry all his blood with him."

The Sprite of Love still further self expressed :
To whose appearing I myself confessed.

SPRITE OF LOVE.

" Love is the antidote of woe,
   The sole efficient in creation.
Let sleepless all-eyed angels go,
Wherever God may have a foe
   Or any ill a station,
And they shall find or soon, or late
There is no ill save only hate ;
And if they love exhibit, ne'er
Shall ill once look on ought so fair,

But it shall change at once to well,
Or shrieking shudder back to hell."

EDWARD.

" Not purer, more joyaunt
  Sunned blue seemed to me ;
Not deeper, more buoyant,
  More trusty the sea ;
Not to ships fair winds fonder
  Or truer could show,
Not night's stars, though they wander,
  Than the Lucy, I know.
As Hercules killed Hart of Grease,
And Hart of Grease killed Hercules,
Poor hound and deer, so, I, her hound,
Still follow on to mortal bound,
And not in hate, but Guardian chase,
Her faithful hound, if but to gaze
On her no longer glitterand eye,
Attend her grave, and hope beside her there to lie."

SPRITE OF LOVE.

" Lucy shall change before that last.
Your lives though parted, hers recast
In mould of love, that can adore,
Nor ask return, or ask no more,
Your souls be, day by day affined,
Abodes of love by love designed,
No Cupid winging cruel darts,
But Kama gardening fond hearts,
Each shoot of his a planted rose,
Which in the grateful bosom blows
With no more air, than what may thence
Convoy its odours to Christ's sense ;
While summer round unchequered blooms
Unvisited by chills or glooms,
Until Eternal Spring 'neath brighter skies,
Addeth two primroses to paradise."

Ah ! Love, Himself, is by my side and sings,
To soothe the sorrow of his spreading wings.

SONG OF LOVE.

" Why should'st thou go love lost bemoaning ?
    Love's labour never can be lost,
While still thou lovest : not disowning,
    Thou hast a love worth all the cost ;
    A love within thee is not lost.

" As the sun colours all with light,
    And holds the planets, while they rove,
Love, leavening the spirit quite,
    Makes every thought, act, feeling move,
    And every life-pulse beat to love."

To me his whispers, sweet and low,
The song seem of a God : hark ! now—

SONG OF LOVE.

" I am not lost to thee while dear,
    And thou art never lost to me ;
Surely thou feelest me so near,
    That I am as the soul in thee,
    And thou and I are one, say we."

Such vision failed the Lady nurse to daunt,
Not strange to spiritual visitant ;
And while in ravished air love, gone, still glowed,
She commented.

LADY NURSE.

    " Such counsel to love owed
A comfort is, and an assurance sweet—
    A comfort needed now.   For Lucy fain
Has spreading wings already on her feet.
They will bring heaven down e'er you and she can meet—
    Here not to meet again,"

Twice had seven moons their waning horns declined,
And prison walls my Lucy still confined.
An uncomplaining peace at last possessed
With quiet joy her late unquiet breast ;
More than her tongue could tell, her look would show ;
But while her heart fell calm, her strength sank low.
She to consumption drooped, a ready prey,
And in the prison hospital now lay.
Meek, loving, penitent, and hopeful too,
Death seemed to brighten to her nearer view ;
When in a letter, I from far had penned,
Pardon came, freedom, by mine efforts gained,
And intimation of an open home—
Too late, alas ! for now her time was come
Smiling to point her the celestial way.

    How grateful she, and now to thank me fain,
Her gracious nurse informed an after-day :
    Happy the tears by hope made bright in vain,
But " Hence to move were death," the doctors said,
And with a change of room resigned she stayed,
Next morn confessing to our friend.

LUCY.

" A child
Trained for the world, I on a poor man smiled.
To me his troth he pledged, but not to bind,
And faithful wooed, until I proved unkind.
Quitting him, I became a lady grand,
And dowered an earl with beauty, and a hand.
Ah ! proud in fancy only, all my heart
Remained with him, from whom I chose to part.
Sad choice ! My lord had wedded me, and yet
A form alone, and I a coronet.
Though love I might have learned, if he had taught,
Else to society I fled from thought,
Ah ! there again to meet my best beloved.
He as a stranger passed me, so reproved.
Cold grew my heart amid the shows of bliss
Empty of joy, and killing with each kiss,

When he, once more my lover, on me smiled.
To passion soon my longing was beguiled.
Still was I loved, and only that it proves,
How selflessly and well a good man loves,
I would not now with shame suffuse thy face :
For he the peril fled of love's too strict embrace.
Hate of my wedded life, pride too, and pain,
That shunned the eye of him so loved in vain,
Urged, and another wooed, with whom I fled,
Remarriage promised ; was divorced, not wed.
The anguish of that life I cannot speak :
Some troublous sweets it had, but wild, and weak.
Disgraced, unhappy, then how oft I sued
To be re-wed, and wished that I was good.
Weary his Grace became, and looked at last
With one not fallen to mate : but that is past ;
The end you know.   I murdered him, they thought :
Yet one, who pled for me, believed it not—
My lover once, then judge, ah ! still how dear.
Ah me ! when from the dock I saw him near,
The shame, regret, remorse ; an instant light,
Illumining the wrong, enhanced the right,
The honour that with him I might have had,
The good rejected, wrecked the chosen bad.
Self ruined, felt I, in that instant vain,
Eternities of woe, extremities of pain."

Heart-breakers may themselves have hearts to break.
The traitor oft undone is by his make.
But ne'er in Lucy did my faith quite fail,
Still warbled in its nights the nightingale,
And birds awake were in its foggiest morn
Presaging sunny day, not quite forlorn.
Now Lucy looked so broken, low and sad,
Her gracious nurse all further speech forbad :
Till calmed by sleep, she, to divine command
Awaking, and aware of heaven at hand,
Whispered—

LUCY.

" My judge, but lover ever true,
Approached me in my cell, and taught like you ;
And by his actions, as his words, subdued,
I first saw mercy in a God all good.
That he should for my pardon just have striven,
Registered late on earth, though long in heaven,
I thank him, say ; and, if a humble sigh
And penitent can bless him e'er I die,
' I bless him, ay, ten thousand times,' she sighed,
' God bless him!'" and so blessing me, she died.

From black slum fertile of dead river springs
White water lily, purest of all things ;
So my regenerate Lucy.   May I die,
Lifting to heaven and her my latest sigh.
An Indian Brave, his home not quite within
    But on the borders of The Great Lone Land,
Where the Kisaskatchewan rolls with din,
    At duty's call, obedient to command,
Left : and his beautiful young squaw, who low
Sick unto death lay, grieved to see him go.
Fast by the shores of the far Fishing Lakes
His paddle flashed, when softly from the brakes,
Or leaves, that rustled o'er the splashing waves,
Came fond his name.   " Who calls ? " he asked the Caves.
Was it his well-beloved, who had in vain
So called him, hark ! is calling him again ?
Landing he idly searched, and, till he went
Back to his tribe, knew nothing how she spent
Her parting breath thus : so still Indians tell,
And settlers long have named the place, " Qu'appelle."
She, crossing to the Great Lone Land, had called :
" Who calls ? " he cried, but, ah ! she came not, though
    recalled.

On circuit then I could at distance mourn :
But our friend followed to the traveller's bourne
Her, whom my agents had been charged to move,
And lay, where she was born, my first, last, only love.

Oft in one grave united love reposes,
And lives again in briar roses ;
So may my truth her fond contrition meet,
And I lie buried at her feet.
Nay, shocked not once when met the biers
Of good Juana, young in years,
And Isabel, her mother, prime
In added lustres, and more crime.
The longing grows to see, where she is laid :
I now am standing by her narrow bed.

Years have my forehead deeply ploughed,
  Cheeks blanched, and grizzled hair ;
Yet still above the sward am I,
  And Lucy under there,

Oh, never mine, and now no more !
  And yet this thing is best.
Though all my being yearns for her,
  Thank God ! she is at rest,

At rest amid the scenes, which once
  She loved with me to roam ;
And, since it knew her presence well,
  More kind will be the loam.

And, " Lucy," they have carved me—
  Simply " Lucy " on the stone,
As it is graven on a heart,
  Which was, and is her own.

Here too at last shall I repose ;
  Here oft till then return,
And, wandering hence into the woods,
  Think, listening to the burn,

That singing to the ocean runs,
  " The life has one sure bliss,
Which ends in no great troubled sea,
  But resting place like this."

Yes, here she buried is, and I
  Am weeping by her grave ;
But I know she in the faith died
  Of Him, who came to save.

And I her fate no more bewail ;
  Calm, trustfully depart,
The anguish, that so racked a life,
  No longer at my heart ;
But in its stead a wonder full of awe
Conceiving God, life, love, and righteous law,
Like solemn bell-notes clear tolled one by one
In forest depths recluse of Amazon,
When the Campanero is at mid-day stirred,
And nothing but its silvery sounds are heard.

CANTO VII.

THERE are who deem God hard and stern
  Expecting us quick good to grow,
While evil slow is to unlearn,
  And reaping where he doth not sow.
But Christ, The Word of God to men,
  And True Incarnate Love,
Thought not His smiters to arraign ;
On Him the Spirit not in vain
  Descended like a Dove.
Of woman born, yet God with us,
  Son of God's Love hung bleeding :
To Christen with blood generous,
And win all hearts most mutinous,
  Son of God's Love hung bleeding.
From thorn-crowned head, spear-opened side,
Nailed hands and feet, a crimson tide—

2 N

Rivers of red compassion ran,
All for the Love of God and man.
For " God with us " was man at heart,
And, grieved we should from God depart,
To Father cried, " Not mine, but thine—
Thy will be done : for thine is mine ; "
Kissing for us a Father's rod,
Is now our Advocate with God.
Shrouded in gloom, while earth all shaken
Seemed, like Himself, quite God-forsaken ;
Nailed to the Cross above the grave,
He was to fill, and us to save ;
He, by humanity out cast,
Heart-broken, loving, to the last
   Believing, dying for us, prayed,
" Father, forgive : they do not know
The evil of the thing they do ;
   Love yet shall conquer, though betrayed,
Not strife but peace, not wrath but grace."
And heaven received Him to His place,
The glory, which He covets still,
   That with which angels hailed His birth,
" Honour to God ; to man good-will ;
   Joy, love, and peace on earth."
So can I ne'er but deem God just ;
And should He slay me, I would trust
Him weaving what seems ill design
Into a surplice all divine,
Not only in the end, but wove
Throughout, from the beginning, Love.

And in the name of Christ I from the past
Summoned the first man to affirm this last.
In God the first still lives, and surely there
Has known and watched his children everywhere.
Was it upon my brain fair fancy drew,
   That now an opening in heaven was seen
As by Saints Paul and Stephen, and I knew,
   Unconscious of the distance still between,

The father of all men at sight,
Adam extatically bright,
And not so far, as real near,
Whispering in my very ear,
And ringing in harmonious chime
His pondered digest of all time ;
While in my thoughts to answer I appeared,
Revolving what I reverently heard.

ADAM.

" My son, behold, I know what you would ask,
To answer be my not ungrateful task.
Good will to all was the efficient cause
Of all creation, and of all God's laws ;
Though we are free to turn His good to ill,
In still returning good God glories still.

" The infant born, wrapped, reared in love—
Child, boy, no dread of chance can prove,
But feels, so happy all things fit,
Its ruler, or his favourite ;
Paternal power to wish exalts,
And thinks to run where manhood halts.
Untempted still, and unannealed,
No purging fire has dross revealed ;
No task has daunted, or o'erthrown
Him, standing not to fall alone.
Nor may a mother make the bliss,
Her loved one tastes, else than it is ;
By saying, that it will not last,
The future dull, while bright the past.
Hope, in Delilah lap unshorn,
Not yet its Fancy false can scorn ;
Fears in the future no offence,
Fooled by fair young experience."

EDWARD.

" Yes, a vale of tears that opens out
    On that other valley—The Shadow of Death,
Youth hopeful faces with little doubt.

Thank God too, men with lingering faith,
Till the wicked cease to trouble
 And the weary are at rest,
Keep blowing still hope's bursting bubble,
 With strange expectance to be blest ;
And thus more readily and strong
Encounter and support life long,
In which success most brilliant knows
But nobler pangs, superior woes ;
Though disappointed seven times seven,
Still winged with hope chase joy to heaven,
Perhaps in anguish and disgrace
Thrust from the portals of that too blest place."

ADAM.

" Both grief and pain to all unsought
Come running through the common lot.
Then, why the one so fly and fear,
So court a smile, shun, dread a tear ?
High heaven knows, and glad am I
For the honour of humanity,
There are who, neither fancy fed,
 Nor hope deceived, can open-eyed
Erect, against a world make head,
 And seas of trouble swim with pride ;
Who, scorning pleasure, wedding toil,
Live patient years of far off spoil,
Peace and life peril, nobly wise,
Or, wisely good, self sacrifice ;
Men of all nations and all times,
Whose virtues, now their praise, were once their crimes."

EDWARD.

" And yet how any can confront,
Wonders me pondering, the brunt
Of a wide world's huge woe and sorrow."

ADAM.

" Ah, did we see in the to-morrow,
But to-day, and yesterday again ;
Earth's round of toil pursued in vain ;

The world but as it is, and life
As this life only, trouble and strife,
Wishes with wants, and woes with wails,
Where riots hell, and seeming chance prevails—"

EDWARD.

" Some curse might God ; a thing unwise,
Safe nor to curse Him, nor despise."

ADAM.

" Each breath of air was once divine,
And water cheered unmixed with wine.
Land and the yeasty deep were dear ;
The changeful heavens, the varied year,
All sights and sounds of night and day,
Country, and town—all life was gay.
This wondrous world to thee seemed bright,
Beauteous with freedom, love, delight.
Chaste still the moon, still warm the sun,
The streams still songful as they run ;
Warble the birds still, still the trees,
Bend whispering to the amorous breeze ;
Still violets grace the wood, the wild
By tints of broom still, heath beguiled ;
And gardens, open to the bee,
To God still breathe, regaling thee :
Still laugh the vallies, echo still
Laughing again from hill to hill,
While noisy music on the shore
Billows make, breaking into roar.
But if earth only meets the eyes,
Which once saw fancied paradise ;
If pain and sorrow, sin and death
Have chilled with disenchanting breath,
And shed in tears, however tender,
Delightful, but unreal, splendour
From a now dreamless universe ;
If mists from nature's face disperse

Revealing, as they melting fade,
Life in the light of daily bread ;
That surely, though a sober thing,
And in a minor key, may sing,
Not sorrow for a tranceful past,
But pleased awake to truth of life at last."

EDWARD

" A simple air, a soulless toy,
Mere innocence itself will cloy."

ADAM.

" And not in pleasure, not in joy,
  Rests happiness, nor yet in sorrow,
Which weeps the eyes out of the world,
Is that despair, whose wild waves, curled
  Above us to-day, may whelm us to-morrow.
Life is no pasturage of sweets,
Where good hope feeding never bleats ;
And yet its wants are unborn blisses,
Its very sighs are prayed for kisses,
Its wails in darkness seem to grope,
But are at worst bewildered hope.
Man feeleth not his trouble less,
But the more longs for blessedness,
Whose peacefulness can ills beguile ;
Pleasure itself has no such smile.
While breath of God's own inspiration,
More trusty than imagination,
Faith whispers of eternal spring,
Till death appears a welcome thing—
Faith, which in griefs and labours rude
Rough stepping stones beholds to good,
Life discipline ; immortal gains
To spirit in supported pains ;
Deep inward happiness aglow,
Exalted by fierce outward woe ;
Sees breaking waves Armadas break
To sink with all their wealth of wreck

In harmless ruin, thence to rise
In profitable memories.
Ah ! better for such evil day
Is England now, and Spain shall be, some say."

EDWARD.

" We lose not, if by loss we gain
And mastery of ourselves retain."

ADAM.

" Inoperative goodness taints.
Virtue is active, never faints ;
And trial quickens even saints,
Keeps their arms bright and free from rust,
Stained not but glorified with dint and dust.
Great heart o'er-masters worst conditions,
And firms himself mid oppositions,
Raising, and with the best of wills,
Trophies upon surmounted ills.
Reflection draws with trembling bliss
Its present good from past amiss ;
Even the rock once grazed may be,
A light-house in our memory.
And since from throne of God adored,
On heights of Paradise Restored,
Emotion yet may dangers passed
Review and thank, forget at last,
Who will not screw his courage up
To drink life's sweet and bitter cup,
And kiss the rod, not kick the goad,
That drives him on a Godward road."

EDWARD.

" Trial is God's fine art of Love ;
He tries the Christian but to prove.
Joy mates with grief ; the hand of pain
Let pleasure kiss ; heaven drops in rain.
So let me live the truth of life ;
Stand upon solid ground, though rife

With thistle and the prickly pear,
Rather than cloud-land rosier.
Let pain revive, do all but kill ;
Grief triumph over all but will ;
That, to God stedfast and the right,
Is overbalancing delight.
Firm as a rock, and firmer—strong
As Prometheus to his chained so long,
Or He, more utterly accursed,
Who suffered sinless for the worst,
Assimilating poisons we,
Content beneath the Upas tree,
    Can at command, though stern yet sweet,
Drink with a certain holy thrill
The bitterest cup, God weeps to fill ;
    With aching heart and bleeding feet
Climb to the summit of distress,
And call and count it blessedness."

ADAM.

" If for God's honour : since His own
He too in action seeks alone—
A conscience, of whose spur the sense
Touchingly moves Omnipotence.
That honour is the general good,
And justice wisely understood—
Love's light divine, which white we see
All good attaining righteously ;
God's own fair nature breaking through
Man's tearful soul in various hue
Of virtues naturally blending
    To minister unearthly grace ;
And as it were a rainbow bending,
    In pity o'er a fallen race.
Yet nothing can more cruel prove,
Than the kindness of excess of love ;
Who fondles him a fool may tell,
Only a wise man knows, who loves him well."

EDWARD.

" The devil good with evil would requite
    The world good with good, and ill with ill ;
God says, that Good for Evil is the right."

ADAM.

" Choose you : but be the choice whiche'er you will
'Twixt God and Devil, earth's poor go-between
Is a most double end, despairing mean,
A fall betwixt two stools, a moonlight wail,
And owl in concert with a nightingale."

EDWARD.

" For others living as God would,
    And none for self save as for all,
And best for self in general good,
    Our energies at full and call
To gain approval of The God,
Imaged by Christ, and whose the rod,
But more the smile, which welcomes, when
That image He beholds in men,
It naturally comes, like dawn,
God brightens what He smiles upon,
And, as sun-flowers opening on well sunned lawn,
We more resemble, as our powers expand,
The Word of God's love, grow to Christ's command."

ADAM.

" With no propriety intense
    Insulting all the fair delight,
God taxes not with Peter's pence,
    True Christians are rare men of might.
Pharisees may with grounded nose
Earthly advantage follow close
Along a crooked running line,
    Lids orbless raised to heaven, alas !
God not to see, and with a whine
    Fallen and dying brothers pass.

But Christ's eleven, seeing love
In the broad face of heaven above ;
Arts, sciences, professions, trades
Using as charity's wise aides ;
Able, learned, rich in means and thought,
Working what miracle once wrought ;
By holy lives, quiet loving ways,
Wise tender words, free honest days,
Hearten a fallen world to lift.
And hail the Cross, and its great gift
Of liberty to love, and go
Straight to the heart of every foe,
With mercy salve the utmost scaith,
And draw the bitter sting of death.
Though dying Watteau might a cross despise,
Too meanly sculptured, raise to it thine eyes !
Haste, Soldier ! go, its mystery unfurled,
Exalt to heaven the Cross, and light the world—
No symbol fierce, as seen by Constantine,
Of Salamandrine conquest battle-sign ;
No form in dust by red Pizarro traced,
As falling he expired on it effaced ;
No clansman signal, which horrific sped,
Like flame through heath, and tears from heaven shed
All vain to stay, though pity poured its flood,
The fire of hell that burned with thirst for blood ;
But lustre crossing universal night,
Peacefully flooding depth, surmounting height,
Unscaling eyes of moody passion blind,
Christ, Word of God, Good Genius of Mankind,
Whom, honours far exceeding old renown
Of myrt and laurel, berried thorns should crown,
Before whom now thy mother casts her own green down."

EDWARD.

" Lest fire should blinkingly miscarry
Founding his bronze, the statuary
With movables, child-bearing bed,
Rafters, and boards the furnace fed,

Sooner with all and life to part,
Than not so save his dearer art—
The art by which he served his Time.
Like service may ennoble rhyme.
Humbly to serve the world with skill
Is nobler than to rule it ill."

ADAM.

" Nor ever vain is sacrifice
    Of man, or woman for the race.
A Joanne, or a Roland dies,
Whose mantle on another's rise
    Drops, and though soon the fated place
Licks sacrificial blood again,
    Another fills it as before,
And now a Wallace, now a Vane ;
And still shall each grand death remain
    A monument for more and more."

EDWARD.

" For God, or man in loving faith
    To die is comely ; though to fall
Dupe of ambition, fooled by death,
    Is saddest death of all,
Scaffolds at times show higher worth,
And goodlier than ought else on earth."

ADAM.

" Sacrifice is a trait divine,
    A spirit that no more can perish,
Than light can cease from suns to shine,
    Or misery good hope to cherish.
Our standard-bearers drop for ever,
    But, passed from dying hand to hand
And borne aloft, the standard never
    Is lowered in the rising land.
Uplift the Cross, and pass it on :
Lo ! after it the world has gone.

Not robed priests, not church officers,
But non-commissioned humble sirs,
In Christ's army now, the masses leaven
And are filling up the ranks for heaven :
Earth thrilled to heart attempts the skies,
And goodness lives, whatever dies."

EDWARD.

" Of the redemption of our kind,
We vaguely know what is behind,
And cannot see what is before."

ADAM.

" Once, making music on its shore,
A lake lay out with dreamy eyes
Drinking the beauty of bright skies ;
An hour passed, and each star in space
Was shuddering o'er the ice-bound place.
Long cooling, gradual was the change,
    But not less real though unnoted,
Till suddenly the liquid strange
    Solid became, where nothing floated :
And God mayhap, with unobserved
Perpetual working, hath reserved
For sudden unexpected burst
The glory of the last, the first,
Since Eden wrought us bitter woe,
The only Paradise below,
When wisdom of experience bought
Hath universal yearning wrought,
And virtue phœnixlike shall rise,
Young from the ashes of old vice,
And goodness then at one grand birth
Produce a renovated earth,
Crowns, rags, dungeons, palaces hurled
Anywhere everywhere out of the world,
Without a prison, church, or throne,
Christ only monarch of his own."

EDWARD.

" So, ushered by no beat of drum,
May man's final insurrection come.
Experience, knowledge, light-like spreading,
    Under an influence from above,
Warmth ever with their radiance shedding,
    And prophesying truth and love,
May silent make the wide world grow
To purely love, and truly know.
Then love shall reign o'er heart and head,
When knowledge has been perfected ;
And smitten without hand shall pass
The burdens from the rising mass,
Till powers of error and of wrong
Live only in undying song."

ADAM.

" Let all then the sword of the spirit wield,
    Strike ignorance, vice, and folly down,
And tyranny without her shield,
Exposed, and flying from the field,
    Smite swift upon the crown :
By knowledge in each growing phase
    Of light and love mankind control,
And let that patriot have praise,
Who will no other standard raise,
    But moral standard of the soul :
Teach men to know, and love the right :
    Then shall they shame all sin and wrong
Retiring, as from day flies night,
    When sun awaketh rising strong ;
And then the great wide world shall be
Free, knowing, willing, loving to be free."

EDWARD.

" Blest liberty of love, sans wish or thought
To wrong or God, or man in ought,

Seeking but good to do with right
And all our powers, and their whole might !
Most holy weakness ! strength divine !
Such liberty my Lord makes mine,
And is that freedom, blessed thing,
Which in a hovel housed can sing ;
Imprisoned may to heaven soar,
Though earthquakes shake not wide the door ;
Enslaved, will still in spirit be,
Its own unfettered master, free
Informing, plenishing the soul
Expanded to receive life whole
In tenderest, holiest embrace,
Until the rapture on the face
Seems rather that of God than man.
Blest liberty of love ! that can
To kiss the sinner stoop, and rise
To meet the lustre of God's eyes,
And feel that His approval brings
Joy, and possession of all things :
What He permits must now be best,
And faith can trust Him for the rest."

ADAM.

" Moses, Buddh, Zoroaster, Christ, life, death
The past instructing should confirm our faith.
Goodness has never died, is never dimmed,
And, though its Lord expires, its lamps are trimmed.
Vanish its lights may here and there
To flame up brighter otherwhere,
Or wane to mellow wider gloom,
Fiends knowing not their nearer doom
As the church, paganizing, wins
And rules the world, and Constantines.
Mohammeds may have vaguely drawn
Night to the verge of ruddy dawn,
And fiends beheld, with least of terror,
What mingled truth with most of error,

And chuckled over hell's fierce glow
With somewhat mitigated woe :
But savagely shall sting the pain
   Which, opening blind baleful eyes,
Discloses all long efforts vain
   Against the tides of truth, that rise,
Have ever slowly rising, been
Only unnoted, not unseen.
As ocean to a careless glance
   Seems bounding forward to retire,
Yet swells with steady grand advance
   As the tide rises higher, higher ;
So good has ill, all unaware,
   Up time's waste sands advancing driven,
And soon may opposition scare,
   And whelm in unexpected heaven.

EDWARD.

" God showed to Moses not His face ;
To Tishbite voice, not lips, of Grace ;
In Jesus full embodied shone
   Beyond the time, He was before.
Though then rejected, Christ has never gone,
   But was and is forevermore ;
In each new age more full appears,
   And with a readier welcome now,
To opening eyes and widening ears.
   If still we slow are love to vow,
And long the consummation lags,
Yet under all our warring flags,
Since the first rouse of an offence
Seemed to disorder providence,
   Has love been growing more and more,
Man deepening in its sacred lore,
Life rising to what is above
Full apprehension, measureless Love—
That Life Eternal, which is one
With knowing God, and Christ, His Son,

Each generation's sphere of time
  Is adding thus a higher round
To the Human Epic, rhyme on rhyme,
Round over round, by which we climb
  To heights of Love still far beyond :
Though now on Steppe, when tempest raves,
Towns, long submerged and swept by waves,
With rubbish strew, and bone, and skull
Shores desolate of lonely Issik-Kull."

Thus to Adam when, the cloud about to close,
Eve suddenly was by his side, who knows
From what high station come ; and then I knew,
That they had never been but one, these two.
And as they vanished into God, behold,
I thought of Eden, and young time grown old ;
And feeling in my inmost soul,
As heaves the sea from pole to pole,
From the first sigh of fallen Eve
The world's long earnest yearning heave ;
And realizing heights supreme,
Beyond an angel's wing or dream,
Which Eve and Adam have attained,
For that they true to love remained,
I knew romance if pure, and only lost,
  May sacred memory right well employ ;
Blind Angelo, intaglios of cost
  With finger tracing, still could weep for joy ;
Hearts do not always break, or bronze ;
Cliffs, that were soft to ocean once,
Now grottoes green round sandy bays,
Dear haunts are of l'Allegro fays ;
Foam left by tide, if stranded might,
  When tossed by breeze seems Iris riven ;
And of true love the wreck as light,
Relict of passion heat as white,
By memory swept is still as bright,
 · And full of flashing hints of heaven.

Thou past, my past, whose opportunities
  Now nothing are, but I am evermore
As I have used them well, or used amiss,
  Or never used what nothing can restore,
  Into thy night my heart's strong chords explore
Cable-wise fastened there to no decay :
  For spider-like that heart from its strong core,
As time extendeth gives the cable play,
And oft-times loves to rest, and anchored so to sway,

And feel the strain on some particular strand,
  And down that pour its own warm life, until
The past, to which 'tis anchored, lives to hand
  Electric reinstated so to fill
  An orb of light with seeming, now though still
Yet most attractive : for the heart with stress,
  Like New-Church knight, its chord belays with skill
More near and nearer drawing to caress,
If so it may, the front of that mild blessedness.

Blessedness mild, and mostly melancholy
  As what the happy spirit leaves behind
On the charmed face of death ; so very holy
  Those scenes, and forms, and loves time out of mind,
  Which now God's hands irrevocably bind :
Nor can a move be changed, that's in the past—
  Gone, and forever, when we lift the blind,
We see it gone, and never look our last
On the calm star, that lights the cloud rift in the vast.

Ah ! may through shrouding smoke no wrecks afire
  Flaming out blaze on anguished eye and soul,
Nor fragments of an injured world—the dire
  Sphere of your action, where you played the fool,
  And burning deeds, which never seem to cool.
You may in spirit have been born anew,
  Yet, as through limb, once wounded and now whole,
Old aches dart, so when you the past review,
What has forgiven been you may repent anew.

CANTO VIII.

OH ! man, or woman, mind you not,
　　The love of life's young day ?
And has time's round of changes brought
　　One matching with its May ?
How soon the fountain sullies, soon
　　The brightest day-light ebbs in night
With clouds investing oft full moon,
　　And summer suffers blight ;
How soon warm thoughts of friendship chill,
　　Of love to lust decoy,
And vanity usurps the will,
　　And years pollute the boy.
Yet some may long the boy retain,
　　Some from pure boy-hood never fell :
It will with sweet true love remain,
Which, too, can bring it back again
To the seared conscience of a Cain ;
　　Greek Hebe knew none other spell.
She ever standing held love up
　　To immortality's fond lip,
A cup of love, her only cup,
　　A cup for gods to sit and sip.
Manhood drinks drooping on life's road,
　　And love to youth restores it,
Cleanses, enlivens, soul, heart, blood :
For truth to love is truth to God,
　　Who, being love, adores it,
And longs to see from pole to pole,
His image worshipped in each soul—
That deathless love, which from the grave
Shall rescue whom it fails to save,

Faithful as deathless, yet to be
To mortals immortality.

Like two gold finches on cross-top of larch,
Singing as having sipped, and not of starch,
Two loves I saw.   One winged Cupid seemed,
The other wingless Eros, or I dreamed—
Each on a branch of Cross.   Atop the Christ
Had glorified stood.   They the spot had kissed ;
Now under sate, and leaned against The Tree,
With each an arm around it clingingly.
Which tenor was, which bass ?   Who knows ? perchance
As one they sang ; and this was their romance.

CUPID.

" Truth, or tradition equal true,
To artful Love all arts are due.
How came the once white rose so red ?
    Love frisking, light as folly's spectre,
Where worried Gods had made him bed,
On fragrant bud, which candid spread,
    Toppled a bowl of purple nectar.
When he, creative, Chaos thrilled,
    The harping worlds sang all aglow ;
Seemed song and minstrelsy born skilled
    In that prime oratorio.
Again when earth decaying thistled,
On reeds of Syrinx Pan first whistled.
Festive at marriage, love to plays
In Argos first gave birth and bays ;
The parting warrior to recall,
First traced his shade on Sicyon wall ;
Nor less than passion-heat could render
In cold, hard marble beauty tender.
With arts, conceits, plays, pomps, delights,
And solaces of days as nights,
Love relishes unsavoury life,
Dull labour, and perennial strife ;
And more than gain invents all grace,
And beautifies plain nature's face.

The monster Polypheme, one-eyed,
Who men devoured and heaven defied,
For gentle Galatea sighed;
Iphigenia smoothed from rough,
Though Cyprian, Cymon loutish slough.
Harsh, dwarfish, cursed, though kingly, gnomes
Have maidens haled to happiest homes.
Thurlow himself, more usual brute,
Could mollify to amorous lute.
To love as death are Marlboroughs loyal,
Crowned heads and clowns; astronomers royal—
An Airey found life-long attraction
In eyes dowered doubly by refraction.
   All friendly greetings, warm hand-shakings—
And who so chill, or all alone,
As none such ever to have known—
   All merry meetings, merry-makings,
May-days to love are chaste advances
Rustic, or courtly games, and dances,
Masks, revels, gay and frolic hours
Fore-running strew love's way with flowers.
And what so blithe or brilliant here,
But algate comes of something dear,
And would indulge for it a tear?"

EROS.

" And never shall be man advised,
Till true-love hath his tears surprised;
So tearful is its kindly more,
And all its less so tender sore.
A blissful purgatory of pain,
Schooling men for their greater gain,
Its partings many as its meetings,
   Upon its songs still sighs attend,
Its truest, purest full of bleatings
   In search of an Eternal Friend
To be its everlasting good,
When lesser fails its constant mood.

.

Saul, asses seeking, found a crown ;
Loves earthly lost bring heaven down.
The pure-souled maid, whose adverse fates
Delay her lover while she waits
By well of Bethlehem true to tryst,
Sees down in it the Star of Christ—
Most deeply sees ; and in her sorrow
  Low in that well that star appears,
A light of hope for her to-morrow,
  A quenchless flame of love that cheers.
And men in mortal love, astray,
With hands that supplicate their way,
Hungry, athirst, to heaven appealing,
Meet with their God His love revealing.
Touched into spiritual life,
By true-love taught, on stage of strife
Acting their passion-play of heart,
They from the school of Time depart ;
For heaven pluming here in shell
  Of earthly feeling, soar above
Out of it ; rise with God to dwell,
  Here having learned, that God is Love."

CUPID AND EROS.

" From age to age the story runs,
Repeated with the circling suns,
Since when Jove's messenger conveyed
Psyche to heaven, long delayed,
There to wed Cupid lost, and found.
  Assiduous hours with rosy twine,
And gathered gods, rejoicing round,
  Made highest heaven more divine.
Vulcan contrived ambrosial fare ;
Ganymede lavished nectar rare ;
Apollo harped, while Muses sang,
And Venus danced ; and if bells rang,
Knelling on earth for Psyche dead,
Love raised her to heaven's bridal bed—

Love, born before all gods, the nod
Creative, very God of God,
Whose will is Love, whose will is law,
By love fulfilled without a flaw,
Forming, informing to inshrine
And raise love human to divine,
Sati to Siva, Psyche then
To Cupid, till Orphean men
From Hades their first loves demand,
   In lost Euridyces see heaven,
And Songs of Solomon grow grand,
   Holy, and rapturous, swelling, even
Rising in Dante's hymn from hell
Through Purgatory up to dwell
With Beatrice in Paradise ;
Heard too in Petrarch's humbler sighs
For Laura, grace divine, true beauty,
All virtue, which to Love is duty ;
Called ' Charity,' by name to come,
   No further using ancient blindness,
When vice, hate, discord shall fall dumb,
   Canonized into loving-kindness ;
None envy aid to need, decry
Fair countenance of Charity,
Or live by gain of other loss,
Than that which sole-sustained earth's cross—
Romance of tragedy and ruth,
Whose Hero is Eternal Truth,
Whose touching ray Ithurielly transforms
Into winged hosts of heaven prostrated worms."
Ceased they to sing, and I to see,
But all my past grew clear to me ;
My Guardian Sprite too spake now all aglow,
Lovely as is the blush of morn on snow.

GUARDIAN SPRITE.

" Beautiful love, which still the more it knows
Sees only more to love, and tempers woes,

And makes us just as wise, and good as just,
Filled with a rational implicit trust
In God, whom all the sciences confess,
And whom, the more we know, we doubt the less !
Its eyes by knowledge washed in truth, and sure
Of seeing God in all, they are so pure,
Exploring but to learn with reverent awe,
That He throughout the Universe is law,
And love is its fulfilment, love to God ;
That His creative Word, and life abroad,
Common to all His creatures too, is love—
Christ, God below, and greater God above.
This human love, perceiving thus with eyes
Become to love in God insanely wise,
And teaching man to be no less content
Than with unlimited environment ;
This love has proper home in heaven ; earth whole
Is worlds too little for so large a soul.
Not that eternal Love dilates a breast
To break a rib receiving it as guest,
Though Philip Neri felt as if it had,
But it is holy rapturously glad,
Suspends on crosses holly wreath,
With Amarynthine crowneth death ;
Roses without, lilies within,
Beginning to grow out of sin
And suffering, a soil to prove
The winnowed purity of Love."

Soon passed what vision was : but deepening awe
There in my home-woods filled me, sense of law,
And spiritual truth, and issue clear
Of God in interact with manhood here,
And of myself with all.   I wondered too,
I still in part foresaw what still came true.
Might I the Ravens twin of Ancient Days
   Summon from Bodethal, or Arvakar stride,
Abysmal secrets I of time and space
   Might then explore—the yet unprophesied,

Though not unaided now in my essay
To read the lessons for life's little day.
Fear, anger, sorrow, shame, remorse, despair,
    Pity, frivolity, misanthropy,
And happy issues safe from broods of care,
    And good and evil fame, and memory,
Intellect, Great-heart, Sophist, Puck unwise,
Visions, dreams, voices, intuitions rise,
Imagination, reason, nature, faith,
Over and under, round me heaven, hell, death,
Angels, and cherubs, gracious Spirits, Fiends,
And legal ghosts, and essences of winds,
Fays, Dryads, Nymphs, and Muses, gods appear,
Dian, Apollo, Mercury are here,
Minerva, Cupids, and conflicting states,
Loves, desires, passions, virtues, vices, hates,
Ancient and modern Choruses, and trite,
Public opinion, and My Guardian Sprite,
And other personal forms of vital traits,
And more than all I name : for in strange ways
Spirits do come and go in these our days ;
I feel the wonder of it in these woods
Tempering my bad, nursing my better moods.
Such shades to me have ever sacred been,
More than Olympian heights, where Gods convene ;
And first this Surrey Hermitage and Home,
Which with my nephew I, a lymniad, roam.
A Captain he, appointed to command,
Has come to part ; our parting is at hand.
Abroad on duty young he perish may,
Or death here make of me more natural prey,
And we be destined not to meet again ;
Therefore, accorded to my wish not vain,
His wife and children shall with me abide
The strokes of time, and what may hap beside.
Should he survive, I to his care commend
My manuscripts, none living to offend,
But order well and print ought worthy found,
Likely to dure when I am under-ground.

EDWARD.

"The woodlands harbour song-birds. Hark, that strain
So full of melting tenderness! I fain
Would in such song survive the poor to cheer,
Guide, and enlighten, as they, full of fear,
Through darkness peering, longing for slow day,
Smarting with bitter want, are kneeling to pray,
That revolution in the womb of morn,
Not hateful, may of holy love be born,
And wealthy England gradual become
To an enlightened poor a grateful happy home.
So sing I not an Epic of Kings,
   A man may live a nobler one—
A life of loving all living things
   And magnifying God in His Son.
To do it worthily were fame,
Or but attempt to celebrate the same.
Things soulless try. The tree, once cursed, forgiven
Is eloquent of Christ now high in heaven.
Minsters these groves are : birds choir in the trees.
Taught by such wood-notes wild my song may please,
And be, as Albion's white cliffs are, pure ;
As its once wooden walls were, brave and sure."

NEPHEW.

" Woods are grove-minsters. Grave but not uncouth,
With branches interlaced, and leaves more smooth
Than ought save woman's cheek, of various hue
To pleasure eye, of every shape to woo
To quick delight soul's most fastidious sense,
They swell in ceilings gradually dense,
While through their veil with thousands of blue eyes
Omniscience now seems smiling from the skies."

EDWARD.

" Not blindly peoples all and Britons paid
Divinest honours unto wizard shade.

Trees light, clothe, feed, warm, physic man, and build,
Furnish, adorn, and paint the home, they shield ;
Axe and plough handle, towns too raise and pave;
And sailing make him master of the wave,
The world ; support him tottering to their bed,
And not forget, but coffin him when dead.
And whether lotus, mulberry, or date,
Oak, ash, or boabab, in solemn state,
Banian, or bread-fruit shared the mind of Jove,
Each nation had its consecrated grove,
As struggling up to God from first to last
The Universe was rising from the past,
To higher function called, and higher still,
By the solicitude of God's good will."

NEPHEW.

" Yet savage burn, and civilized undress,
Clearing the forest, bare the wilderness."

EDWARD.

" Still wilds are witness to God's splendid cares :
The woodland ravage oft Himself repairs,
Who traced with palms the equatorial line,
And raised for frost a standard in the pine.
Streams countless, floods and oceans, waters great
Lend unto seeds their chariots of state.
Birds wander wilful, or from winter's rime,
Seeds so from pole to pole bear, clime to clime.
Now north, now south, in prairies now, now floods,
Beasts catching in their hides drop seeds of woods ;
Nay, oft in excrement may bird on wing
Or brute cast out the leaf-producing thing,
Or shot, or sickly falling there may die,
And the seed flourish from it bye and bye.
With all her might and multitude of powers,
Nature co-operating aids the bowers."

NEPHEW.

" Few trees of old stood lone as border towers."

EDWARD.

" Upon a burned or frozen, rabid waste
Yon haughty oak, in lonely grandeur placed,
Scourged fiercely, sore beset, might soon begrime,
With wreck and ruin the surrounding clime.
But with its brothers massed, uniting here,
Strong in their countless strength, to each one dear,
Let all wild winds of angry heaven assail,
Hurricanes whirl aloft their giant flail,
Oceans of storm, rolled after them, behold
His head still lofty, and his bearing bold—
Each so depends on, and supports the other.
All wise Almighty! who can be thy brother,
Thy father, or thy friend? Or who can give
Counsel to Thee, or look on Thee, and live?
Nought wastest Thou, no tittle of Thy power,
Since Thy far back and first creative hour.
To Thee alone Thy first creation clung ;
Thy next to that ; on it Thy third one hung.
Each Thou on each still makest to depend
Throughout creation, not begun to end ;
World upon world, and these upon a sun ;
Systems upon each other, and on one,
Or sun, or system, mightier than they :
Universe upon universe away
To utmost bound, if such there be, of space,
And these, and all upon that nobler place—
The centre of creation, throne of God,
Whence He beholds and rules the bright abroad,
Around Him wheels it orderly and great,
And where He weaves, or cuts the threads of fate."

NEPHEW.

" Unity is a faculty divine."

EDWARD.

" Divine the spirit in which men combine,
Not self up-hold and others down ; not rise,
Exploit their fellows and disorganize ;

But family, tribe, nation, race connate
In one humanity, assimilate ;
Increase so, more in touch with God than gain,
Or rule, or science, simple common men.
Thus The Christ rules : and God has thus a host,
Who, pleased with little, need and trust Him most.
He evermore controls material force
To better human nature, not to worse.
That we our force may use, as He intends,
For highest general universal ends,
He organizes us for good of all,
And still in matter's mortar brays us small
Chastising sore the rebel human sprite,
Till common good is law, and true love might,
And life worth living Christlike for the right.
Then God shall show unveiled a smiling face,
When man reflects the smile of His free grace,
And inhumanity dies in the embrace.
Then rich and poor shall share in God's own peace ;
Then ancient rivalry forever cease ;
But rivalry in good, fond emulation,
Maintain society in one ovation,
Surviving in a progress constant, joint,
Up to the highest and selectest point."

NEPHEW.

" Yet night oft drops on a declining race,
And bricks and mortar barely point its place.
Earth's giants may have dwarfed in Afric shades
And polar lands icebound, unturned by spades.
Moors, glittering erst on Darro-Xenil bank,
May now gold-fish be in Alhambra tank.
Far in the New World's central solitude,
When Stephens by a buried city stood,
And overhead in long procession fast
From tree to tree man-making monkeys passed,
Seemed they reversions from old Toltec wombs
Infesting their once temples, homes and tombs."

EDWARD.

"Still stepping stones of progress, God, to Thee
All vanities of vanity must be.
One after other, falling in their prime,
May come and go the masters of the time ;
Deep down in heart of change this still is sure,
Earth for the meek is, God too for the pure.
He from each earlier draws each later age
Better, more humble, sager, and more sage ;
The ages prunes, and, lopping off decay,
With it manureth to improve to-day ;
The future teacheth by to-day's abuse,
The past all halloweth to present use ;
And so while nations fall shall others rise,
And progress never fail, alas ! nor sighs.
For out of Eden ever Westward, ho !
Has progress journeyed with its sin and woe,
Since with the wheat it still the tares must grow,
Until encompassing both land and main,
Rounding the world, it meets itself again ;
Instant in Nipon, quelling feudal lords,
Nationalizes both their lands and swords.
Thus ruined evil holy shows, as whence
By God educed still better things commence—
Sad, holy as the dust, which here we tread,
The heaped brown dust of years of leaves long shed.
From earth so dressed and fructified the dust
Shall rise again in grass, and that robust
To richer still and higher life in grain,
Nor storms have shaken leaves to earth in vain.
Yes, ye eternal forests, shadowy woods,
Grave sublime temples of all solitudes !
Flames all consuming may through forests march,
Cornfields are shooting from the stumps of larch ;
A resurrection more than vanished smokes,
Fruits, fruit trees blossoming from roots of oaks :
Storms the air rectify, and ruin too
On men and nations falls to make all old things new

Till, faith confirmed, triumphant joy begins,
That God is with us and that goodness wins.
Beyond the eye of full discovery,
God holds the infinite in Unity,
And is in nature's good, while all its ill
Is rectifiable by His Good Will.
Ay, were man dust again, and thought withdrawn
From all the circuit of the Sons of Dawn,
But present still, conceived in God's intent,
In possibility still immanent,
Praise would not fail ; for great with one accord.
Phenomenal of God, His speechless Word,
Evolving orderly in all its ways
Nature in calm and storm would be becoming praise."

NEPHEW.

" Rare grace seems latent in the multitude,
So sudden Rome became for a time so good
While Rienzi quelled the Nobles and their brood,
Ah, soon to rise, and, with the Prince of Air,
Trouble again the moral atmosphere."

EDWARD.

" When, older than the hills, trees first appeared
On swampy isles in vapourous darkness reared,
They mists and noxious airs from heaven withdrew,
And sun unveiled ; then stored its sunbeams new,
Died, and, now buried, still those treasures hoard,
Which to discover we have earth explored.
Upright no more, nor green, nor leafy now,
Black as a frown upon the thunder's brow,
Prime lords of earth, first peoplers of the soils,
Night from their resurrection-breath aghast recoils,
Breaking and bursting on the raptured sight
Into a myriad founts of heat and light.
Would we our moral atmosphere might redd,
Clear mists and vapours from truth's sunbright head ;
Its rays receive and give, die, fuel be
For glow of heart in chill of misery ;

A portion of God's glory now display,
Proclaim His purpose, point to it the way ;
His willing agents honoured to promote
The consummation, which sure signs denote,
Evil consume in its own burning shame,
And gather all up in His higher Name.
All are called, and lowest may list
Part to play in The Passion of Christ.
Oh ! let us wake, arouse ourselves to see
The wide profundity of misery,
That heaves and roars upon around the world,
While man from billow is to billow hurled,
I charge thee by thy hopes of life to come,
When they shall beat for thee the muffled drum,
And roll through air the melancholy wave
On wave of sound, that bears thee to the grave ;
Ay, by thy hope of bliss, and dread of woe,
For there is such a thing as judgment, Oh !
I charge thee to be charitable here :
So may the gates of death be passed, nor fear
To shudders move thee then, as face to face
Thou meet'st thy Maker in His Holy Place.
There love is throned, and Charity shall be
Welcome to all of His Eternity."

With counsel thus the Captain I detain.
We long have parted.   Shall we meet again ?
His wife and children long to me have come,
And, once more fond, mine is a happy home.
Gracious to rich, to poor beneficent,
My niece waits his return, her one event :
And in his children I again am young,
While waxing old and waning, warbling song.
Having three lustres on the bench consumed,
I in the fourth, by fatal warning doomed,
With medical advice now wise concur,
And cease from wonted wig and gown, and fur.
Time comes when death alone is left to choice :
'Twas Hobson's own.   He had in it no voice,

But died of doing nothing : breathed his last,
The only thing to do, and then was past.
And now I rather live the end to see :
I neither dread it, nor futurity.

When life's battle and scaith
Earn the knighthood of death,
War shall spirits still wage,
    As they now do on earth ;
Fears, which foster our rage,
Hates, their wild heritage,
    Still to wilder give birth ;
In the heart make its home
    An unquenchable hate,
And no love ever come
    The fierce fire to abate ?
Ah, this thing I am bold
Both to sing and to hold,
That the Christ in the heart
    Is love, life evermore
When this state we depart,
    And the other explore ;
That all forms of true love
    Are but portions of Him,
Help us here and above
    To more—more, till we brim,
Then expand a fresh marge :
    For so magic love's cup,
It shall ever enlarge,
    And still ever fill up.

Child of heredity, or seeming chance,
The tossing drift of shifty circumstance,
Diseased in body and with little brain,
Feeble in will, may moral power attain
To take in God's esteem a higher place,
Than the most gifted insolent of grace.
Despairing drunkard, miserable bawd,
Lust combating and blinded, seeking God,

May value more to Him, than unco good
Folks, who have always done just what they should.
Few talents, many, like are in God's eyes ;
Best fullest use of each has equal prize ;
And, little men and women, in respect
Of high endeavour, shall be God's select.

However dark the moral heavens now seem,
Good hope of brighter is not all a dream ;
Stars twinkle in their firmament of night,
And streaks of dawn proclaim approaching light.
Man undevout, unmindful of his God,
May know no agent but himself abroad,
Nor view the glad, though haply distant, end
To which diversely all the actions tend
Working unwittingly the will divine,
Evil still falling to its last decline ;
Yet shall Heaven's Kingdom come, hell's pillars nod,
Earth hail the reign of Charity, and God.

Assist me, God, the veil of time to raise,
And ever shall I sing, and only praise.
The coming hour appears, and half unfurled
Unwarlike standard of the coming world,
A red-cross banner in no army van,
And under it the parliament of man.
O'er land and sea careering quick as sound,
Men too the globe with lightning gird, and, round
In vessels curious navigating air,
Here now are now not strangers anywhere.
Duties and ranks may part, but not divide ;
No famine there, oppression none, no pride ;
And ignorance would, meeting, fear and fly
The soul and education in man's eye.
America, Africa, Europe, Asia now
Around one altar in one family bow ;
Lions with lambs sport ; demons only flee
Christ in the bosom of humanity.

Seraphic hosts, and powers that never fell,
Yet pitying regard, and wish us well!
And all ye spirits, that in bliss repose,
God-and-man lovers, who have known our woes!
If trusty winged to you my notes may rise,
Hear, and with jubilation rend the skies,
Descend, while hills to valleys shout again,
Creation no more travaileth in pain,
Reborn earth joins, assist her to rehearse,
The pristine music of the Universe,
Come from your happy glorious abode,
Inaugurate with her The Reign of God.

God for a moment raised time's curtain so,
Dropped now, all mirk again with sin and woe.
Would I for men might sculpture Christ to the life!
With heavy woe oppressed, and racked by strife,
Men gat most lightsome joy, and heart-whole truce
Beholding suddenly Olympian Zeus.
What terrible had been to life's regard
No longer feared was, and no longer hard,
So nobly Phidias had there conceived,
And carved a god to be at once believed.
Yet if they scorned my Christ, who humble is,
I would commend Him then as Nemesis.

Through space The Lord is glorified:
  In stately march all spheres sublime,
Journeying to Eternity, bright-eyed,
  Glow with a rapture yet unchilled by time.
No end I know, beginning none,
  No height, breadth, depth, and, vocal all,
Their peoples sing, and heaven hath undone
  Her gates, rebounding on a vacant hall
Whose hosts with harps, 'twixt Suns and Bears,
  Space thronging, order march and song;
Grand Hallelujah through the vast careers,
  And echo finds no moment for her tongue.

Earth tuneful moves, as move she may,
  With banner bright as any there,
Looks beautiful, and beautifies the way
  Of Nature's all and most augustly fair,
The choicest planet on Sun staid ;
  Yet years in thousands grouped are dark,
And now another since man seeming made
  On Harp of Universe a discord, Hark !
Immortal man, forgetful more
  Than mindless dust, which loyal proves,
Like a dog barking into temple door,
  Or shriek in moonshine quiet, all good commoves.
Man, list ! Earth hurries thee to doom :
  Could'st now the issue, fearless face ?
Would'st enter now Jehovah's Presence room ?
  Art here so just as there be sure of grace ?
Hark, bells are ringing, " Come to Judgment." Who
Have dared to call it ? You : and what are you ?
Proud scornful men, who law and grace report
To your own vantage, others hale to court
And forward thrust the scythe-armed hand of Time
To strike " Eleven " down, that " Twelve " may chime ;
Most mighty men of leading and of light,
Dreading too much the peoples' growing might,
Which, once despised, now moves you in a scare
To call on God to judge, and not to spare ;
The rag-tag and the bob-tail of your order,
Judges and jingoes too, who preach disorder,
Attack fair unions to allay false fears,
And set the frenzied peoples by the ears ;
High priests of privilege, peers, commoner men,
Who power by talent, force, or fraud attain,
And to the plebs deny each little climb,
Deeming them base, the very dregs of time,
Incapable of thought, and born to serve,
And then go get, well, what they may deserve !
Now would mine eyes were fountains, and that I
Ten thousand had, all streams, none running dry,
Then should I ever pour prophetic tears

In pity for proud power, as judgment nears.
For in all streets and highways of that morn
Shall lamentation first be screaming born,
And wailing in all vineyards.   Who are ye,
So bold to call The Judgment Day ?   Ah me !
Summon all skilled in mourning to prepare
To mar their faces, garments rend, and air :
For when The Lord, of whom ye have enquired,
Shall so appear, He may not be desired.

Self-worshipper, who wouldest others spoil,
All to thy service turn, thy loves even soil,
And sour thy sweetest pleasures by abuse,
Friends, brethren, family good but for ill use ;
Wouldest have all love thee, thyself love none,
But condescend to be a worshipped one ;
Ah ! only worthy seen in any grade,
Surely for thee alone the world was made,
Its weakness thine advantage, and its strength,
Thine envy, plundered and laid prone at length ;
I care not what thy faith may faithless be.
To know it one has better to know thee ;
Cunning, malicious, wise as Reynard live,
    Tricky as any Howleglass, still you,
Like Faustus, must surrender to, and give
    The much more cunning devil his worthless due.

Thy sacred feasts God hates ; thy solemn rites,
Thy churches, offerings and oblations slights ;
Thy viols, and thy songs are weary noise ;
Belial and Moloch have thy secret voice
Adoring golden calves, and fiery strife,
Blood, and damnation, lust, and pride of life ;
And thou hast patterned God as like to thee,
To such a God indulged a suppliant knee.
Now make an end ; thy creeds and altars heap,
Mosaic tables, breads, and wines, and weep ;
Forms penitential cast on lighted pyre,
And pass thyself to glory thorough fire

Consuming what would fain with-hold thy love
Meeting embrace of Christ, on whom The Dove,
Overt from heaven, forewete the gracious Nod,
And merciable con-descent of God.
Repent : God yearns for thee, and in co-emption,
Who would to Christ deny even thy redemption ?

Learning how to live, we ever
  Live to learn, and death is sweet,
Finishing yet coming never
  Till it knows life's task complete.
Reaper stern ! thou hast no terror
  For the faithful soul : though death
Sore is, sorer chance of error
  Passes with the lapse of breath.
Here we, oft our good mis-making,
  Learn from error wisdom's way,
From the lion's carcase taking
  Honey for the after day.
Over error more and more we
  Triumph with a willing mind ;
We on error mount to glory,
  And the error leave behind.
Death ! and no more chance of folly :
  Death ! and what we lived to learn
All made good, and death made holy,
  Heaven kissing ; is death stern !

Faces parting are for ever
  Separated as the poles ;
Distance only cannot sever
  Bonds of thought uniting souls.
Thus may body leave a body
  Quietly, as tide doth stream,
Each to each in soul, not shoddy,
  Crossing ocean, fused in dream.
Death from Lucy parts not : lonely
  Planets still may cycles roll ;

Griefs, years shake the body only ;
  Not death moves her from my soul.

Love in body is an ardour
  Never felt beneath the pall ;
Love in spirit dies much harder,
  And not often, if at all.

Eros entering the porch, which
  We are wont to call the tomb,
Lifts again his lowered torch, which
  Afterglows the dying gloom :
Companied by hope and faith,
Soul with Eros passes death.

And of lovers one, fore-running,
  Leaving here a mourning mate,
Having entered bliss may, sunning,
  Sometimes sun at heaven's gate,
  And stand, and wait.

Oh, Lucy ! Lucy ! Lucy !
  I stay from thee too long ;
Yet, as I pass to mine own grave,
  By thine sing one more song.
Oh, Lucy ! Lucy ! Lucy !
  Thy name, which mosses fill,
Is time-worn there ; but in my heart
  Love writes it deeper still.
Oh, Lucy ! Lucy ! Lucy !
  Thou dust art to thy kind ;
But not one memory of thee
  Has faded from my mind.

Oh, Lucy ! Lucy ! Lucy !
  Oh, Lucy tell me where
I now shall find thee, Lucy !
  Art thou for ever fair ?
Oh, Lucy ! Lucy ! Lucy !
  Art thou a blessed saint ?

Art waiting for me now, or now
  Hast come in swift descent.
Oh, Lucy! Lucy! Lucy!
  To fill my soul with bliss,
The rapture of the old young love,
  Which dost thou ever miss?

Oh, Lucy! Lucy! Lucy!
  The world is waxing dim;
The shadows thicken into night;
  I sing my evening hymn.
Oh, Lucy! Lucy! Lucy!
  Be waiting for me soon;
Be waiting for me at heaven's gate;
  I ask it as a boon.
Be waiting for me soon, Lucy!
  But if thou art not there,
Then shall I need the whole of heaven
  To keep me from despair:
For there was that in thee, Lucy!
  This only do I know,
Which I shall love for ever, be
  Thy portion bliss, or woe.

Greek pride a Delphic stone once thought
Earth's central most attractive spot:
But The Word, Love, more humble rules,
  Neither to conjure, nor coerce,
In hearts of saints, on tongues of fools,
  Right reason of the Universe.
And we shall nothing owe above
To man, or God, save only love,
When we, recalled, shall rise and run
To do His gracious bidding like the sun.
Suns and systems seem to perish,
  Individual forms, and ways;
But the love of God shall cherish
  All, and all be love and praise.

Time is a bitter draught, unless
  Its sweetness love impart ;
Eternity will fail to bless,
  The breast without a heart.
No other bliss can earth bestow,
  Or paradise above,
Save ever more of God to know :
  For God Himself is Love.
Notburga once from Jungfernhöhle sighed,
"Otto ! thou beckonest : I come :" and died.
My song expires, and with enfeebled breath,
But loving hope, I face approaching death.
Mine is that Lady nurse to Lucy true :
  Abroad my nephew, still in his command,
With me his wife, his boys and maidens too,
  I almost feel the grasp of his strong hand.
Other relations lack not, other friends ;
But few need tend him, whom God's love attends.
With God communing is no loneliness ;
Silence is full of His serene address,
"Whether you live, or die, you are the Lord's—"
Inspired, and ever re-inspiring words.

Doubts and demons ! would ye now
  Keep me from my Lord's embrace?
By the halo round that brow,
  Which your thorns no more deface ;
By His Cross to which I cling,
  Rescued from your grasp for aye ;
By my Saviour and your King,
  Demons, from my soul away !
Are ye mindless of the fight
  Lost upon the plains above ?
Fear ye nothing, Jesu's might
  Only equalled by His love?
See ye not earth from me roll ?
  Hear ye not All angels nigh ?
Hence! around my parting soul
  Heaven gathers ; demons ! fly.

The whole dread harmony of heaven descends,
Ten thousand thunders red with levin spends
Way-lighting, scorching, crashing into dust
Irreverence, self will, and haggard lust :
Then magical, with diapason all
Louder than Irised oceans in one fall,
Wide-harping upon beams of boundless grace,
With lyric sunshine glorifying space,
Louder than when Apollo chanted strong
Of Zeus and Here hymeneal song,
Sounds jubilee, that draweth out its year—
Jubilee love, that casteth out all fear,
Jubilee joy, which comes to none,
Save those at one
With God, themselves, and all around
Without a bound
    Or below, or above,
      And who immerse
    In depths of love
      The Universe.

    I will sing of Jesus ; Death,
      Listen to my song,
Stay thy dart a little,
      I will not be long.
I will sing of Jesus ;
      Thou wilt gladly hear,
What I have to sing of
      One to both so dear.
He is high in heaven, death !
      And I cannot see
Through the hosts of angels
      Hiding him from me ;
But he is descending,
      He is coming, lo !
Coming now to take me !
      I will gladly go.
God hath hither sent thee, death !
      Whom I did not like,

With thy dart uplifted
  Ready poised to strike ;
But the Saviour's sign is
  Stamped upon my brow ;
Wait for him a little ;
  He is coming now.
Coming now, I see Him, death !
  Hear Him, feel Him, feel
Arms of love around me,
  Heaven o'er me steal.
Angel, loving angel !
  Strike : for He is come
To receive my spirit
  Happy going home.

EPILOGUE.

ROUND Surrey Hermitage, to Edward dear,
Now mine, each waste I know, and wood revere.
And having followed him to welcomed death
Through the much sorrow of a broken faith—
Love lost and found, forgiven wrong confessed,
Restored to better mind, and final blessed—
I, roaming devious as shifty breeze,
Still hear his living voice among the trees.
My heart aglow, can he be shining nigh?
Not fear, but love dims, wets, wipes, dries mine eye.
Like birds and flowers outstanding white
   On faience of cerulean ground,
Pale face of death shows Lunar bright,
   By heaven backed and haloed round.
Grave Pauline raptures, tender organ strains,
Fond hymns of earth, that soothe our mortal pains,
And soar to wed in open ears of heaven
The spiritual song of the forgiven!
'Tis love, you breathe o'er wreaths of flowers, which shrine
The coffin on its catafalque supine.
The dead shall suffer change, a mystery;
Corrupt take incorruptibility;
The spirits joining, mansions rise of glory,
In which to rehabilitate Love's story;
Drop in eternity time's passing mode,
And, one in Jesus, become one with God.
Ah, Holy Love! when hope in thee is bright,
To all immortals giving second sight;
When faith, by thee at anchor, has achieved
The deepest joys, that prophecy conceived;

When time and space surpassed are, death is dead,
And change unnoted to expectance wed;
When pulses equal throb, and hearts combine,
And beat in lasting unison with thine;
Then, not till then, shall nature cease to moan,
Then, and then only, God be truly known.

But what shall I of Edward further say
On this reviction of his dying day?
In knowledge growing and discernment, he,
Approving good, sought better, still to be
Emptied of self, yet larger beneficed
With more and more of the true mind of Christ,
To love a servant in each varied sphere
Of active exercise, and influence here.
Thus lived he; so he wrote; and to this end
His song and story I to man commend,
Reporting feebly, now that he is dead,
The purpose to which all his soul was wed.
Should my report to critics worthless seem,
Some despise Edward, some my proper theme,
I still shall hold a good life never dies,
But must to act in its admirers rise:
And fittest to survive, concluding strife,
Love yet as law shall unify all life.
Puck, were he here, might with contention base
Thus inauspicious put my confident case.

PUCK.

" To preach a sentiment, you never act,
Easy as lying is, but too abstract.
You look too little like the humble love
Taught by your Christ, commissioned from above.
Worship of Beauty, Common-sense of Use
With leisure you to luxury abuse;
Squander your time, and sacrifice your pelf
Not in Christ's service, but to please yourself.
Taste, knowledge, gain, contend to win your heart,
Gold, book-lined shelves, and walls well hung with art.

Civilization is your proper mind,
Self to exalt and state, not human kind,
To whom great capital, or town, or purse,
A cruel cheat, is a most prosperous curse.
Modernmost feeling, under fashion's sway,
When fully acted is a godless play ;
Your Christianity but blatant folly.
Return to savagery, and be jolly."

EDITOR.

" Is life a blessing at its very worst :
Then can no betterment be gain accursed.
Man, to himself a law, God sentences
As he has used his opportunities.
No man was born at once to right all time ;
Body and soul together slowly climb.
You cannot worse think, think you what you will,
Than of himself the Christian stumbling, still
Groping through darkness to the further side
Of the Slough of Despond, uncertain of his stride.
Evil and good are so commingled here,
Who acts with judgment, yet may judgment fear,
Should he the right for wrong in it deny,
Which might be borne with—bettered by and by.
The best of roads to good at present may
Straight, narrow, hilly, be a miry way.
Cleansing and levelling, firming all the path,
One may his fingers soil, incur God's wrath,
Yet faith retain in grandest of old fables—
Herculean labours and Augean stables.
The nature, which God gave, He elevates ;
Our ignorance He, knowing, educates ;
Dissipates cloudy ills obscuring heaven ;
Imputes not sin, which man repents, forgiven ;
If we have fallen, helps us rise to stand
And do the loyal right of His command.
Hence to the Devil, Puck, and let him know,
We pity both thy folly and our foe."

PUCK.

" Keep for thyself thy pity : worse than devil,
Thou can'st not gloze thy manifested evil."

EDITOR.

" I, fool, confess it.   Conscience slow from seed
Flowers in show to fruit in slower deed,
Yet certain is a conscience all the while,
And universal now—the latest style.
I Jokai-ly from Zrinyi would quote,
Though with new reading, an old anecdote—
' To hell the devil seems to carry you,
Who now would have me, with hell full in view,
Let him upon my back spring, and then straight
Spur me too thither carrying double weight.'
To savagery ne'er can we return :
Although its lost simplicity we mourn,
And want that back, we wish it well-advised,
Under the rule and regimen of Christ,
Not a mere temporal but Eternal State,
Kingdom of God within us consecrate.
Don't, silly, smile ; we now contend to win it.
Be serious, and we may all be in it."

Mayhap you have the thoughtful dreamer met ;
  Not one in Comus crew with grovelling snout
Insensible to spiritual fret,
  And the long windings of the immortal bought,
  But with a wonder in him, ever stout,
And keen delight in stirring of deep thought :
  For though in it may be a sense of doubt
Teaching that he is human, he is not
To riot upon earth, but rise to God knows what,

Or may to lowest hell of Hades drop—
  A plumbless depth, though he was meant to soar.
His soul is breath divine ; and what may stop

Its upward wing, or down-drop under-shore?
Is there a fine he would not venture o'er?
Yet much a guide is needed.   Shall he say
  Christ, or the Devil, where Christ has gone before
And Christ for nothing, or the Devil to pay;
Or chance alone, and meet Mischance upon the way?

Than threads of fancy else were webs, he weaves
  In darkling closets of his littered brain,
Then might he raise his head, who inly grieves
  O'er hope despairing, and o'er vision vain,
  That, when the worm is fed, the soul again
In the Great Soul essential, which abroad
  Pervades all nature, is absorbed to reign
Immixed with Deity.   Presumptuous clod?
Nay, but a man, who seeks close union with his God,

And sometimes trembles like an abject slave;
  Yet, though most human, he can feel divine,
Like Plato thoughtful in his darkling cave,
  Inward retiring, freedom can incline
  To ponder loftily.   Though storms combine
To check the falcon, nobly will it rise
  With loosened silk, till heaven its prey resign;
His soul so soars, not body to despise,
But passion to exalt, and at soul-quarries flies.

Shall any ask, how Edward loving could
  So much of wrong behold in legal right?
We think, in life the needed hardihood
For love to stand, and make its footing good,
  Had wronged for him the long repute of might;
Yet much forgave he, having lived to learn
That specious virtue may be overstern.
Upon it when conceit and pride attend,
They introduce masked hate, an evil friend,
And censure shows of utter blessedness,
Which might to smiles seduce its iced excess.

From a seed " Proso " Kirghese monads make
" Buza " a beer, and boose, and self abuse,
And, drunk to-day, to-morrow water take,
    Made drunk again by such tee-total ruse :
Teetotalers can be intemperate.
We should our spirits always regulate,
And judge not others, but rejoice to see,
    Mingled in many a happy sober lot,
Snows innocent of cider-apple tree,
    Pink blushes of ambrosial apricot,
And sing of woman, sing and learn.

    Hence ! all vulgar tongues profane.
Greedy of lusts, and curious to decern
    Lawful from lawless by exiguous plane,
An altogether perfect beast
Once throne of England filled at least,
Gross monster, Harry Bluff, so hight ;
Hades, rejecting, fled in fright
But to whelm him under refluent wave ;
Or, if the Lord his soul might save,
Ne'er may his shade on earth appear
To linger round his horrid bier.
Vile hypocrite ! if soft, inhuman
And trebly cursed in name of woman,
Though purged through hell the shade would still
Want heaven round it not to kill.
So may all woman spoilers feel,
Upon their necks, time's lasting heel.

On scaffold once stood Mediæval saint
To soothe her husband writhing, bound, and faint.
He feared that dawn, discovering, should propose
By wrongs to her fresh vengeance to his foes :
She cared not, that true Gertrude von der Wart
Declining upon wheel, which broke her heart,
Along her husband's racking limbs her own
His visage marred to smooth with kisses sown,
And hair wind-tossed all through that long long night,
Which prayerful ascended heaven's lone height.

Day dawned : unheedful she of gathering crowd.
Noon came, knights, ribald queen.   They, mocking loud,
Had borne her thence ; but Landenberg brave spake,
" Great is her love ; " and shame, for pity's sake,
Revenge even gave her back to cling, or break.
Fearful the crowd retired with wrathful Queen ;
But the priest parting blessed her, God unseen
Tears wiping, dews of anguish, death-damps chill
Through one more night and morning dying, still
These two alone.   He feared her risk in vain,
For broken thanks still bound her to remain,
Till smiling faint he sighed with parting breath,
" Thine, Gertrude, is fidelity to death."
Such love to Lucy Edward's.   To her cost,
Ah ! Lucy played the double part, she lost,
Learning from tutors in The House of Peers,
That honours are too dearly bought with tears.
Wedding an Earl, who took her to his bed,
She thought with Duke to rise, but fell instead.
Then railed the Earl, and scorned her deadly fall,
And still the memory can with curse recall :
For still he loves himself ; the Duke, now past,
Loved knowledge, rank, and pleasure to the last.
Hamlet of such says, " Should a Lord of beasts
Himself a beast be, still with Kings he feasts ;
There shall his crib be standing.   'Tis a chough
Spacious in dirt possession "—come by, how ?
Oil may the waves of good St. Kilda stay,
Yet whales attract endangering the way ;
Soft words of leaders calm the plebs, and please
With opportunity their enemies.
By truce your oligarch, or despot gains ;
Nations one instant slumbering wake in chains.
Dally no longer with an effete time ;
Delay is likely doom, and certain crime.
Round the stone table Barbarossa's beard
   Has grown already twice ;
The end of all things shall have then appeared,
   When it has full grown thrice.

                                    2 Q

From naval duties having long retired,
The bold Berserker in me has expired.
What most in self your man of war desires,
Force, in his devil too he most admires,
And fitly in his Lord of Host adores—
In cathedrals marble and bronze warriors.
While armies, officered by upper classes,
Impoverish and overawe the masses,
We sow the wind and reap the hurricane
Of foreign wars to ease domestic strain,
Letting its blood, as dying Henry Fourth
Counselled his son, who proved of kingly worth.
And God this cruel craft of power permits,
But circuits earth, and all so fits,
That dogs of hell in sin's own womb
Its proper issue are and doom.
Reckless of heaven's frowning brow,
Earth is with bayonets bristling now.
Gaul, Teuton, Goth, Sclave, Ind, and Turk
Trumpet the air to horrid work ;
With fife and drum, and flags unfurled
Quick marching shake the crazy world.
Host upon host in armies grand,
Confronted peoples ready stand :
So clouds the face of heaven obscure,
For thunderous tempest gathering sure.
If dreading not, nor meaning harm,
Say, would Society so arm ?
Times dangerous are and places where
Weapons are found in peaceful wear.
For sure as needle turns to pole,
    Each bullet will a billet seek,
Each bayonet a breast, and roll
    Dread thunders where forked lightnings streak.
Defence conspicuous is to some
Defiance, and offence will come ;
Derisive shout from host to host   .
End soon in making good some boast ;
Felt power to do it will but spur

Lion as pard on barking cur.
Parry, or thrust—what's in a name?
Either is war ; their swords the same.
Weapons were forged for instant use,
And idle only mean brief truce.

I the prophetic past unseal,
The future see—as present feel.
Earth reels beneath the rush ; the yell
Stirs to its leaping heart deep hell.
The peoples close ; the battle thickens ;
At every pore earth bleeds ; Mars sickens.
A desert lie the death-strewed lands ;
   Hither all desert birds obscene,
Innumerous as your native sands,
   On kings and captains gorge your spleen.
Too few the birds of prey to scare,
Survivors lonely sigh on air—
"Alas ! is this our boasted strength
With foes in dust now matched at length ?
What fought we for, if to be free
And to be great is thus to be ?
Our foes could hardly wish us worse—
   Our own worst foes in being theirs.
Oh, monstrous War ; our heaviest curse
   Light on the head of him, who dares
In mere defence a world to arm,
And say that it can mean no harm."
So shuddering the nations grand
   Behold in each a bleeding friend,
And weep a desolated land ;
And raising now a rebel hand
   'Gainst rulers, who enraged contend,
The weapons, forged by Kings and given
   To stab the mutual hearts of men,
Are turned by wise decree of heaven
   On their own bosoms back again ;
And while their minions round them fall,
And they themselves perish, say, shall ruin then close all ?

Shall we not rather thought take, e'er too late,
Recall the prophecy, revoke the fate ?
Shall Barbarossas not suspend their arms,
Forces disband, and disconcert alarms ;
Statesmen not modify aims selfish, seek
Rather to better all, than worst the weak ;
Nations not peace in combination find,
And happy way to civilize mankind?
But there are minor wars, less bloody fight,
More cruel still than guns and dynamite.
Both Lear and Gloucester learned and Shakespeare told
How Kings, peers, all might wish they had been bold
To feel as wretches feel, and timely shake
To such their superflux for conscience' sake.
Though humblest life is worth a fellow's living
In trust that God means blessing by the giving,
There is no good for any, but must fall
Into the harmony of just to all.
The poor demand of us not bread, so much
As justice large, and not by way of crutch,
But opportunity to hold their own,
Or get what we can, keeping, ne'er atone.
Let us then moderate our gross desires
And light our torch of hope at heavenly fires,
And for heaven's sake no longer let our kind,
Anarchic, or more oligarchic, blind,
Stagger through laws of God and ills of man,
Vagabonds from Beersheba to Dan,
Like meteor stones, chaotic from their birth,
Whose millions threaten heaven and fall on earth.

Who has of Cid, and not of Leper read,
With whom he shared his saddle and his bed ?
But chivalry must now be commonplace ;
The gold of liberal principle rings base.
Humanity o'erleaping caste and sect
Is deemed a vicious want of self-respect
Hatching a brood of equal liberties
Too rude to priests and aristocracies.

Large minds, broad sympathies are reckoned signs
Of infidelity in our divines ;
Unworthy sheep we seem, who flock with goats,
And put our lives in question by our votes.
And yet if all sought profit so to share
As honesty and wisdom deemed most fair,
Or merciful distributed excess,
Heaven would more just appear in our much less,
All quite enough have over nature's least,
And man at cheapest dearer be than beast.
But fortunes, growing still, cold-hearted, seem
   To pinch the masses ; air is zeroey,
And, earth unmelted by a chilly beam,
Glaciers are filling up loch, frith, and stream,
   And calving dismal icebergs in the sea.
"The Amoeba, once immortal," science saith,
" Commiserating life, invented death ; "
And there is heard abroad a general sigh,
" Is real goodness dead, or going to die ?
With weary woefulness good melts in tears,
And in the ill, it rose from, disappears.
All being is to utter ruin run ;
Earth now and heaven are alike undone.
Loki has villain Hoder taught to throw,
And strike Good Balder dead with misseltoe.
For him doth nature universal mourn ;
He gone is thither, whence is no return ;
Or, hating bloody sports of Gods and men,
Hopeless of better things, he will not come again.
Faiths are all ancient now and ever-more :
There is no God on earth left to adore."

Nay, upon floods and fleets of wreck and ruin
Dove-like God's Spirit broods the whole renewing ;
Despair can never quench the hope, whose flame
Pentecost-fires to light descending came.
Flowers of enchantment, like the Lily, white
On wall of ruined Lauenburg invite

With look, whose whisper in the gazer's thought,
" Pluck me " to hope, to fear is " Pluck me not."
On hand advanced a serpent darts unkind :
But whoso dareth then to pluck will find
That lily changed into a lovely maid
Dispensing golden good, unknown to fade.
Religion flowers upon like ruin bare :
Fiends dart at such as think to pluck and wear.
The flower is love.   Let us to pluck it dare.
Christ did, and on the Cross displayed, you can,
The love of man for God, and God for man ;
Rent Temple-veil, broke down partition wall ;
To love, The Holy of Holies, welcomed all.

We best know God's elect by growing spread
Of quiet influence rising from the dead.
With Phidias Alcamenes strove,
Whose should the choice Athene prove,
First low on earth, then lofty raised,
To be by public voice appraised.
Scorned was the Phidias at first sight,
Proportioned to a heavenly height ;
But, carved as low on earth to please,
The Alcamenes charmed with ease,
Which yet in lofty station seen
A scoff became, it looked so mean :
And Phidias won, had else been stoned —
A hazard, which the gain atoned.
So Christ, now lifted up appears
To draw all eyes of future years.
To His own time an outrage, He,
To more now what He died to be,
Shall to a farther distant day
Be Lord of all with righteous sway.
Say you, I prophesy in vain,
And Christ shall never come again ?
Nay, now I see Him known as then.;
Though from that far off day, I trow,
Men shall yet better see and know,

Say you, the darkness deepens down
Upon the age, as on the town ;
Slums are too lost for hopes of grace ?
Ah ! now I little human trace,
But look beyond the present time,
  Judging it by and of the past
A holier growth—a lesser crime,
And see the future read my Edward's rhyme,
  And know it to be truth at last.

San Bernadino tablet bore
  With " Jesu " graved and ringed in gold ;
And preached so, soon the multitude like wore,
  For traffic made and profit sold.
No more on playing cards were gravers plied :
Artists and shopmen prophesied
The richer trade to push—acclaim
For the sham-sake of Jesu's name.
Richer the world is for its share
  In Christ's Kingdom come below ;
Peace and goodwill make gold to spare.
Would Britain so much better were,
  As it is greater wealthier now,
Hoards molten not to grist for creeds,
But golden deeds for Jesu's needs.
No liberality dispensed from purse
Filled mammon-wise, and lined with many a curse ;
No tithe of anise, cummin, mint, and rue,
Can equity appease, or stint its due.
In Goslar city and cathedral fane
Fulda and Hildesheim, two holy men,
Bishop and Abbot for precedence vied,
And round God's altar with unhallowed pride,
Offering up their flocks in war's fierce rite,
Incensed the Devil with blood to win the fight.
But Himmelreich is further to be found
Far from their Hartz, and upon Neckar ground.
There dwelt on holy hill a hermit old,
On roots and berries fed and nothing sold,

But freely gave to travellers storm-stayed,
Sick, famished, wandered, weary, or way-laid.
One night a pilgrim worn, numbed, dripping, late
Knocked at his door and had not long to wait.
The ancient lit a fire, warmed, fed his guest,
And couch of moss appointed Him for rest;
To altar then repaired, as prayer should,
And knew not that The Guest behind him stood,
Till, glancing round, he saw, and looked amaze.
The Stranger's brows all ringed with glory-rays
Dazzled the old man's eyes. "Thy prayer is heard,"
Whispered the angel, or the Lord, "prepared
Come to thy rest:" and said not in the moss—
The hermit's bed and to his gainful loss
To Christ resigned—but stooped the saint to kiss,
And rapt his soul at once to Paradise.

The skylark, flickering upward wings
    Until it gains celestial air,
Then happily and sweetly sings
    As though it were in heaven there.
Boors often may the notes despise,
And net the songsters of the skies;
Such scurvy taste for larks prevails,
    And songsters have so many foes;
Gamekeepers shoot the nightingales,
    That pheasants may at night repose.
But to my mast-head nail I Edward's flag;
No skull and cross-bones white upon black rag,
With general piracy of private pelf,
And wrong to others for offence to self;
But the red cross upon a pure white ground,
Which, to commend unto the world around,
I would manœuvre not on narrow lines,
Collide not with or laymen, or divines,
But save my ship, and wish none other worse,
To all love, law, and life without a curse—
Judgment, which may lost paradise restore,
"Neither do I condemn thee: go, and sin no more."

Where is the music of thine angels, say,
Oh, Fra Angelico?   Thy brush can pray
And harmonize its colours into song.
The expression of thine angels wants not tongue,
But is as when that moved at Jesu's birth,
And Bethlehem Shepherds heard it, " Peace on earth ;
Glory to God on high ; good-will to man."
I see it dumb on lips, whence tongued it ran :
And Erceldoune and Gounod will agree,
" That tongue is still the chief of minstrelsy."

Joys feigned by wish to youth appear
Sure, as to age woes limned by fear ;
Their very heavenliness in sooth
Their strongest reason is to youth.
And if it adventure not quite to fly,
  It will mount some other way—
On the arch of a rainbow to the sky,
  Or the ladder of a ray.
Oh ! seeming fresh from God's own fingers,
Around the soul such glory lingers,
  Such perfume and such song,
And a beatitude so rare,
It will deem all things must be fair,
Good, true, and noble, as they never were—
  Deceived, and, not till long
After the first fond young hope dies,
Awaking out of paradise
To higher prospect, fuller grace
Than graduates in time and space ;
To passion, not as Cupid blind,
But, seeing after God's own mind,
A sacred love, the light of law,
The life of life, and full of awe.

Rother, whose twelve on voyage hie
  To woo him Oda, sang a song,
Which should at need betray him nigh,
  That they in after-duresse long,

Hearing again, knew Rother near :
So falls upon my mindful ear,
"Time is a bitter draught, unless
　　Its sweetness love impart :
Eternity will fail to bless
　　The breast without a heart.
No other bliss can earth bestow,
　　Or paradise above,
Save ever more of God to know :
　　For God Himself is Love."

THE END.

PRINTED BY WILLIAM CLOWES AND SONS, LIMITED,
LONDON AND BECCLES.

59.
354.
150.

Ingram Content Group UK Ltd.
Milton Keynes UK
UKHW050629190623
423681UK00009B/482

9 781145 525146